EINLEITUNG

KRIEGSROLLE

ORIGINAL

liegt bei der Kongregation für die Glaubenslehre vor

Luis Kardinal Ladaria SJ

KOPIE

liegt beim Bundesministerium des Innern, für Bau und Heimat vor

Horst Seehofer

Das Rote Buch - DSGVO

ist die 325 Seiten Zusammenstellung personenbezogener Daten die nach 3 Jahren als "Ephraim, Priester nach der Ordnung Melchizedek" als Abschlussdokument entstanden ist. Zur Bereinigung der Daten und zur Anerkennung Ephraims wurden diese Dokumente an den US Botschafter Richard Grenell, den Israelischen Botschafter Jeremy Issacharoff, den Bundesminister des Inneren, Bau und Heimar Horst Seehofer, den Axel Springer CEO Mathias Döpfner und den Rechtsanwalt Robin Fritz geschickt und zum 1.10.2018 zugestellt.

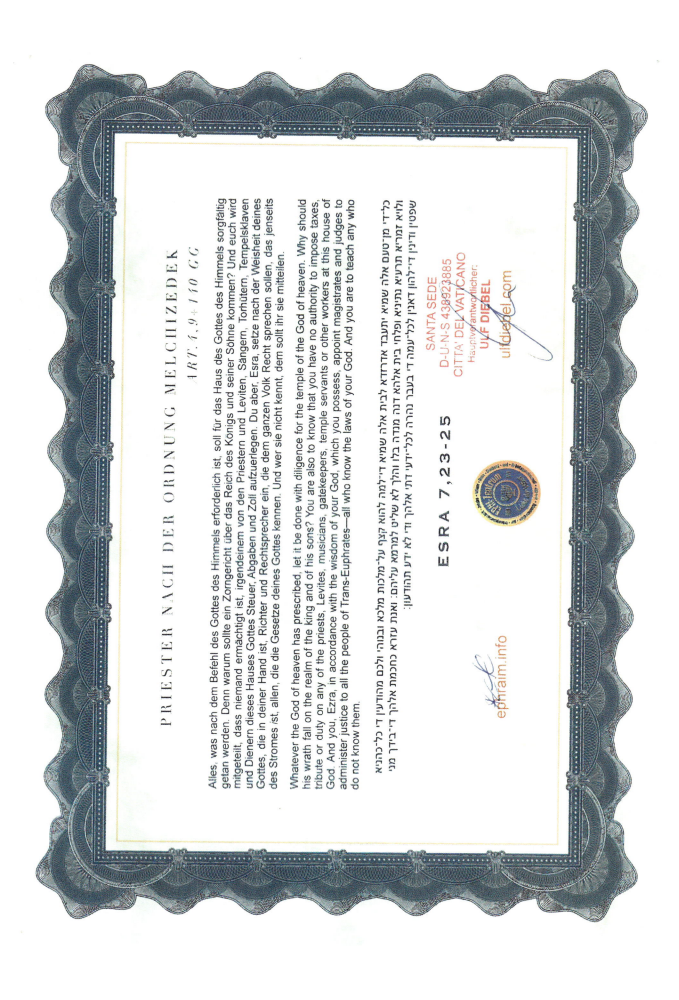

PRIESTER NACH DER ORDNUNG MELCHIZEDEK

ART. 1,9 + 110 GG

Alles, was nach dem Befehl des Gottes des Himmels erforderlich ist, soll für das Haus des Gottes des Himmels sorgfältig getan werden. Denn warum sollte ein Zorngericht über das Reich des Königs und seiner Söhne kommen? Und euch wird mitgeteilt, dass niemand ermächtigt ist, irgendeinem von den Priestern und Leviten, Sängern, Torhütern, Tempelsklaven und Dienern dieses Hauses Gottes Steuer, Abgaben und Zoll aufzuerlegen. Du aber, Esra, setze nach der Weisheit deines Gottes, die in deiner Hand ist, Richter und Rechtsprecher ein, die dem ganzen Volk Recht sprechen sollen, das jenseits des Stromes ist, allen, die die Gesetze deines Gottes kennen. Und wer sie nicht kennt, dem sollt ihr sie mitteilen.

Whatever the God of heaven has prescribed, let it be done with diligence for the temple of the God of heaven. Why should his wrath fall on the realm of the king and of his sons? You are also to know that you have no authority to impose taxes, tribute or duty on any of the priests, Levites, musicians, gatekeepers, temple servants or other workers at this house of God. And you, Ezra, in accordance with the wisdom of your God, which you possess, appoint magistrates and judges to administer justice to all the people of Trans-Euphrates—all who know the laws of your God. And you are to teach any who do not know them.

ESRA 7,23-25

וְכֹל־דִּי מִן־טַעַם אֱלָהּ שְׁמַיָּא יִתְעֲבֵד אַדְרַזְדָּא לְבֵית אֱלָהּ שְׁמַיָּא דִּי־לְמָה לֶהֱוֵא קְצַף עַל־מַלְכוּת מַלְכָּא וּבְנוֹהִי׃ וּלְכֹם מְהוֹדְעִין דִּי כָל־כָּהֲנַיָּא וְלֵוָיֵא זַמָּרַיָּא תָרָעַיָּא נְתִינַיָּא וּפָלְחֵי בֵּית אֱלָהָא דְנָה מִנְדָּה בְלוֹ וַהֲלָךְ לָא שַׁלִּיט לְמִרְמֵא עֲלֵיהֹם׃ וְאַנְתְּ עֶזְרָא כְּחָכְמַת אֱלָהָךְ דִּי־בִידָךְ מֶנִּי שָׁפְטִין וְדַיָּנִין דִּי־לֶהֱוֹן דָּאיְנִין לְכָל־עַמָּא דִּי בַּעֲבַר נַהֲרָה לְכָל־יָדְעֵי דָּתֵי אֱלָהָךְ וְדִי לָא יָדַע תְּהוֹדְעוּן׃

SANTA SEDE
D-U-N-S 438923885
CITTA' DEL VATICANO
Hauptverantwortlicher;
ULF DIEBEL
ulfdiebel.com

ephraim.info

Erbengemeinschaft Jakobs

Registrationsformular (Lebendmeldung)

Vorname   **Nachname**

Straße   **Hausnummer**

PLZ   **Stadt**

Bundesland   **Staatsangehörigkeit**

Geburtstag   **Familienstand**

(ledig, verheiratet, geschieden, getrennt)

Personalausweisnummer   **Kirchenmitgliedschaft**

Festnetz   **Telefon mobil**

E-Mail Adresse   **Registrationsgebühr**

Datum   **Unterschrift**

EPHRAIM©2018

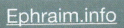Ephraim.info UlfDiebel.com

Bye Bye

Von: Ulf Diebel <ulfdiebel@gmail.com>
An: Michael Solomon <michael@rulimediagroup.com>; "Christian Halsey Solomon (filmdomain)" <chris@filmdomain.net>
Datum: 8 August 2016 um 13:30
Betreff: Personal Video Message uploaded

gmail.com

Diese Nachricht ist aus anderen Gründen wichtig.

DONALD TRUMP take me to POPE FRANCIS

Ephraim GG Art. 9,4 & 140 - 25.5.2015

2.2.18 = **255** days 23.5.17
Trump in Zion

31.1.2018

#WeRemember
- DEI FILIUS *24.4.1870
- UN Resolution 217 *10.12.1947
- LUMEN GENTIUM *21.11.1964
- EUCHARISTICUM MYSTERIUM *25.5.67
- Agreement between Holy See and Israel *30.12.1993

3.2.18 = **255** days 24.5.17
Jerusalem Day

#WeRemember Jeremia 31 NEW DEAL

Parasha
Jetro - 3.2.2018

4.2.18 = **255** days **25.5.5777**
Christ Ascension Day - Ulf 50

20.1.2018
- Day 1335 Daniel 12.12
- Michael 80 *20.1.1938
- Donald Trump 1 year US
- Day 1290 - 6.12.17 „Jerusalem"
- US Government Shutdown
- Germany No Government
- 1.1.18 DreamStream
- 10 years - „Cut-off"

UN Resolution 217
Revelation 2.17
Amos 9.9 Sacharija 9.9
Jesaja 8.18 - Hebräer 2

Request for Handling Hollywood
„Christ Ascension 25.5.5777"
Return of the King to Mount Zion
10 Networks - 4 days „Enlightenment"

Request to arrange pre-election meeting with Trump

DREAMSTREAM

Genesis *25.5. Exodus (2. Passah) 19.6+7 - 20.01 - 20.15 (1.1.15) - 20.18 (1.1.2018)

Ulf Diebel

Priester nach der Ordnung Melchizedek

EPHI-Zentrum
Obere Mühle 28
D-58644 Iserlohn (Sauerland)

+49 (0)2371 - 8326880
+49 (0)157 747 03417

ulf@ephraim.info

→ Since 24.4.17 (4. USE 24.17)
"EPHI-ZENTRUM"
Closed by city on 25.5.18
without any ...

DIGITAL CONTENT INTERNATIONAL

Michael Jay Solomon
President & CEO

1638 Tower Grove Drive
Beverly Hills, CA 90210

O: 310.274.0224
M: 310.739.2251

mjs@digitalcontentint.com
www.digitalcontentint.com
www.michaeljaysolomon.com

→ ... Since Feb, 2018

הרב חיים ברכהן
Rabbiner Chaim Barkahn
Vorsitzender

Jüdisches Bildungszentrum Chabad Lubavitch Düsseldorf

Telefon ... · Handy ...
E-Mail ...

DORON SCHNEIDER

Publizist und Redner

Arazim 15
9070215 Mevasseret Zion
Israel

+972 (52) 4366363
doron.schneider@gmail.com
www.insideisrael.de

FPS RECHTSANWÄLTE & NOTARE

Dr. Robin L. Fritz
RECHTSANWALT

Eschersheimer Landstraße 25–27
D-60322 Frankfurt am Main
www.fps-law.de

Telefon +49 (0)69 95957-3128
Telefax +49 (0)69 95957-455
fritz@fps-law.de

Persönliche Identifikationsnummer

57 341 692 848

Allgemeine Informationen
www.identifikationsmerkmal.de

Bedingung nach DSGVO

für die Familie Diebel

+ ERBENGEMEINSCHAFT Jakob

21.08.2008

21.8.2017

Yael Eden Diebel
Etage 4, re
Seelingstr. 50
14059 Berlin Charlottenburg-Wil

Zuteilung der Identifikationsnummer nach § 139b der Abgabenordnung (AO)

Sehr geehrte Dame, sehr geehrter Herr,

das Bundeszentralamt für Steuern hat Ihnen die Identifikationsnummer 57 341 692 848 zugeteilt. Sie wird für steuerliche Zwecke verwendet und ist lebenslang gültig. Sie werden daher gebeten, dieses Schreiben aufzubewahren, auch wenn Sie derzeit steuerlich nicht geführt werden sollten.

Bitte geben Sie Ihre Identifikationsnummer bei Anträgen, Erklärungen und Mitteilungen zur Einkommen-/ Lohnsteuer gegenüber Finanzbehörden immer an. Bitte geben Sie vorerst Ihre Steuernummer zusätzlich zur mitgeteilten Identifikationsnummer an.

Beim Bundeszentralamt für Steuern sind unter Ihrer Identifikationsnummer - nach den Angaben der für Sie im Regelfall zuständigen Meldebehörde - folgende Daten gespeichert:

01: Diebel
02: ---
03: ---
04: ---
05: Yael Eden   → *falsch*
06: männlich
07: Seelingstr. 50
    Etage 4, re
    14059 Berlin Charlottenburg-Wil
08: 21.11.2004 Jerusalem   ← *'Schlüssel David's'*
09: Israel

→ *GG Art 25 → Völkerrecht gilt vor Bundesrecht*

SANTA SEDE
D-U-N-S 438923665
CITTA DEL VATICANO
Hauptverantwortlicher:
ULF DIEBEL

01 = Titel, Familienname; 02 = Ehename; 03 = Lebenspartnerschaft; 04 = Geburtsname; 05 = Vorname; 06 = Geschlecht;
07 = vollständige Adresse; 08 = Geburtstag und -ort; 09 = Geburtsstaat (gehört bei Geburt im Ausland)

Sollten Sie Fehler in den gespeicherten Daten feststellen, wenden Sie sich bitte an die oben unter der RÜCKSENDEADRESSE aufgeführte Behörde. Dies ist im Regelfall Ihre zuständige Meldebehörde. Beachten Sie bitte auch die Hinweise auf der Rückseite dieses Schreibens.

node D&B Deutschland | D&B International | VDA | VCI | Kontakt | Login

▶ Home ▶ UPIK® Datensatz

UPIK® Datensatz - L

L	Name	Bundeszentralamt für Steuern
	Nicht eingetragene Bezeichnung oder Unternehmensteil	
L	D-U-N-S® Nummer	332619642
L	Geschäftssitz	An der Küppe 1
L	Postleitzahl	53225
L	Postalische Stadt	Bonn
	Land	Germany
W	Länder-Code	276
	Postfachnummer	
	Postfach Stadt	
L	Telefon Nummer	02284060
W	Fax Nummer	02284062661
W	Name Hauptverantwortlicher	Eberhad Petersen
W	Tätigkeit (SIC)	9311

e nach D-U-N-S® Nummer

e nach Name

mmer anfordern

s

Kontakt ←⌐

SANTA SEDE
D-U-N-S 438923885
CITTA' DEL VATICANO
Hauptverantwortlicher
ULF DIEBEL

Mein UPIK®

Benutzername:

Passwort:

Standard

Login

➕ Meine Vorte
⬆ Jetzt regist

Mehr zum Th

Welche Datenba

Trefferliste zugru

Bundesministerium
der Justiz und
für Verbraucherschutz

← zurück
Nichtamtliches Inhaltsverzeichnis

weiter →

Grundgesetz für die Bundesrepublik Deutschland
Art 14

(1) **Das Eigentum und das Erbrecht** werden gewährleistet. Inhalt und Schranken werden durch die Gesetze bestimmt.
(2) Eigentum verpflichtet. Sein Gebrauch soll zugleich dem Wohle der Allgemeinheit dienen.
(3) Eine Enteignung ist nur zum Wohle der Allgemeinheit zulässig. Sie darf nur durch Gesetz oder auf Grund eines Gesetzes erfolgen, das Art und Ausmaß der Entschädigung regelt. Die Entschädigung ist unter gerechter Abwägung der Interessen der Allgemeinheit und der Beteiligten zu bestimmen. Wegen der Höhe der Entschädigung steht im Streitfalle der Rechtsweg vor den ordentlichen Gerichten offen.

zum Seitenanfang   Datenschutz   Seite ausdrucken

GENESIS 48.20
HESEKIEL 37

→ RETURN TO ZION   HESEKIEL 48.15

 Bundesministerium
der Justiz und
für Verbraucherschutz

 juris

← zurück

weiter →

Nichtamtliches Inhaltsverzeichnis

Grundgesetz für die Bundesrepublik Deutschland
Art 15

Grund und Boden, Naturschätze und Produktionsmittel können zum Zwecke der Vergesellschaftung durch ein Gesetz, das Art und Ausmaß der Entschädigung regelt, in Gemeineigentum oder in andere Formen der Gemeinwirtschaft überführt werden. Für die Entschädigung gilt Artikel 14 Abs. 3 Satz 3 und 4 entsprechend.

zum Seitenanfang
Datenschutz
Seite ausdrucken

US Executive ORDER 12803 ! → 2+4 Vertrag
13037 D-V-N→ ®

→ Richterspruch : ~~ANKLAGE~~
GENOZID
VSTGB §6

Start 24.8.2018   19:00

Cripher los On line, Stand 25.8.

1.9.2018 → BEWEISÜBERGABE
AN DEN STAATSSCHUTZ
17.07 Zeitstempel BEGINN BEWEIS
ZU SAMMEN STELLUNG

_____

ÜBERGABE BEWEISE FÜR SID, HARSEWINKEL, BRD

→ Mike Pompeo,

ÜBER GABE AN DEN Staatsschutz.
VM

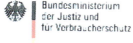 Bundesministerium
der Justiz und
für Verbraucherschutz

 juris

◀ zurück   weiter ▶
Nichtamtliches Inhaltsverzeichnis

Grundgesetz für die Bundesrepublik Deutschland
Art 140

Die Bestimmungen der Artikel 136, 137, 138, 139 und 141 der deutschen Verfassung vom 11. August 1919 sind Bestandteil dieses Grundgesetzes.

Fußnote

(+++ Nichtamtlicher Hinweis:
Die aufgeführten Artikel der deutschen Verfassung vom 11.8.1919 - ebenfalls abgedruckt unter der FNA Nr. 100-2 (siehe juris-Abk: WRV) - lauten wie folgt:

Art. 136
(1) Die bürgerlichen und staatsbürgerlichen Rechte und Pflichten werden durch die Ausübung der Religionsfreiheit weder bedingt noch beschränkt.
(2) Der Genuß bürgerlicher und staatsbürgerlicher Rechte sowie die Zulassung zu öffentlichen Ämtern sind unabhängig von dem religiösen Bekenntnis.
(3) Niemand ist verpflichtet, seine religiöse Überzeugung zu offenbaren. Die Behörden haben nur soweit das Recht, nach der Zugehörigkeit zu einer Religionsgesellschaft zu fragen, als davon Rechte und Pflichten abhängen oder eine gesetzlich angeordnete statistische Erhebung dies erfordert.
(4) Niemand darf zu einer kirchlichen Handlung oder Feierlichkeit oder zur Teilnahme an religiösen Übungen oder zur Benutzung einer religiösen Eidesform gezwungen werden.

Art. 137
— *Reichskonkordat 20.7.1933 gültig*
(1) Es besteht keine Staatskirche.
(2) Die Freiheit der Vereinigung zu Religionsgesellschaften wird gewährleistet. Der Zusammenschluß von Religionsgesellschaften innerhalb des Reichsgebiets unterliegt keinen Beschränkungen.
(3) Jede Religionsgesellschaft ordnet und verwaltet ihre Angelegenheiten selbständig innerhalb der Schranken des für alle geltenden Gesetzes. Sie verleiht ihre Ämter ohne Mitwirkung des Staates oder der bürgerlichen Gemeinde.   !
(4) Religionsgesellschaften erwerben die Rechtsfähigkeit nach den allgemeinen Vorschriften des bürgerlichen Rechtes.
(5) Die Religionsgesellschaften bleiben Körperschaften des öffentlichen Rechtes, soweit sie solche bisher waren. Anderen Religionsgesellschaften sind auf ihren Antrag gleiche Rechte zu gewähren, wenn sie durch ihre Verfassung und die Zahl ihrer Mitglieder die Gewähr der Dauer bieten. Schließen sich mehrere derartige öffentlich-rechtliche Religionsgesellschaften zu einem Verbande zusammen, so ist auch dieser Verband eine öffentlich-rechtliche Körperschaft.
(6) Die Religionsgesellschaften, welche Körperschaften des öffentlichen Rechtes sind, sind berechtigt, auf Grund der bürgerlichen Steuerlisten nach Maßgabe der landesrechtlichen Bestimmungen Steuern zu erheben.
(7) Den Religionsgesellschaften werden die Vereinigungen gleichgestellt, die sich die gemeinschaftliche Pflege einer Weltanschauung zur Aufgabe machen.
(8) Soweit die Durchführung dieser Bestimmungen eine weitere Regelung erfordert, liegt diese der Landesgesetzgebung ob.

Art. 138
(1) Die auf Gesetz, Vertrag oder besonderen Rechtstiteln beruhenden Staatsleistungen an die Religionsgesellschaften werden durch die Landesgesetzgebung abgelöst. Die Grundsätze hierfür stellt das Reich auf.
(2) Das Eigentum und andere Rechte der Religionsgesellschaften und religiösen Vereine an ihren für Kultus-, Unterrichts- und Wohltätigkeitszwecke bestimmten Anstalten, Stiftungen und sonstigen Vermögen werden gewährleistet.   X

Art. 139
Der Sonntag und die staatlich anerkannten Feiertage bleiben als Tage der Arbeitsruhe und der seelischen Erhebung gesetzlich geschützt.
10 GEBOTE - SABBAT

Art. 141
Soweit das Bedürfnis nach Gottesdienst und Seelsorge im Heer, in Krankenhäusern, Strafanstalten oder sonstigen öffentlichen Anstalten besteht, sind die Religionsgesellschaften zur Vornahme religiöser Handlungen zuzulassen, wobei jeder Zwang fernzuhalten ist.
+++)

final settlement

Vertrag über die abschließende Regelung in bezug auf Deutschland
("Zwei-plus-Vier-Vertrag")

vom 12. September 1990

12.9.2018

= 28 Jahre 2+4 Vertrag

Die Bundesrepublik Deutschland, die Deutsche Demokratische Republik, die Französische Republik, das Vereinigte Königreich Großbritannien und Nordirland, die Union der Sozialistischen Sowjetrepubliken und die Vereinigten Staaten von Amerika -

IN DEM BEWUSSTSEIN, daß ihre Völker seit 1945 miteinander in Frieden leben,

EINGEDENK der jüngsten historischen Veränderungen in Europa, die es ermöglichen, die Spaltung des Kontinents zu überwinden,

UNTER BERÜCKSICHTIGUNG der Rechte und Verantwortlichkeiten der Vier Mächte in bezug auf Berlin und Deutschland als Ganzes und der entsprechenden Vereinbarungen und Beschlüsse der Vier Mächte aus der Kriegs- und Nachkriegszeit,

ENTSCHLOSSEN, in Übereinstimmung mit ihren Verpflichtungen aus der Charta der Vereinten Nationen freundschaftliche, auf der Achtung vor dem Grundsatz der Gleichberechtigung und Selbstbestimmung der Völker beruhende Beziehungen zwischen den Nationen zu entwickeln und andere geeignete Maßnahmen zur Festigung des Weltfriedens zu treffen,

EINGEDENK der Prinzipien der in Helsinki unterzeichneten Schlußakte der Konferenz über Sicherheit und Zusammenarbeit in Europa,

IN ANERKENNUNG, daß diese Prinzipien feste Grundlagen für den Aufbau einer gerechten und dauerhaften Friedensordnung in Europa geschaffen haben,

ENTSCHLOSSEN, die Sicherheitsinteressen eines jeden zu berücksichtigen,

ÜBERZEUGT von der Notwendigkeit, Gegensätze endgültig zu überwinden und die Zusammenarbeit in Europa fortzuentwickeln,

IN BEKRÄFTIGUNG ihrer Bereitschaft, die Sicherheit zu stärken, insbesondere durch wirksame Maßnahmen zur Rüstungskontrolle, Abrüstung und Vertrauensbildung; ihrer Bereitschaft, sich gegenseitig nicht als Gegner zu betrachten, sondern auf ein Verhältnis des Vertrauens und der Zusammenarbeit hinzuarbeiten sowie dementsprechend ihrer Bereitschaft, die Schaffung geeigneter institutioneller Vorkehrungen im Rahmen der Konferenz über Sicherheit und Zusammenarbeit in Europa positiv in Betracht zu ziehen,

IN WÜRDIGUNG DESSEN, daß das deutsche Volk in freier Ausübung des Selbstbestimmungsrechts seinen Willen bekundet hat, die staatliche Einheit Deutschlands herzustellen, um als gleichberechtigtes und souveränes Glied in einem vereinten Europa dem Frieden der Welt zu dienen,

IN DER ÜBERZEUGUNG, daß die Vereinigung Deutschlands als Staat endgültigen Grenzen ein bedeutsamer Beitrag zu Frieden und Stabilität in Europa ist,

8.9.2018

MIT DEM ZIEL, die abschließende Regelung in bezug auf Deutschland zu vereinbaren,

 # New Deal
9/11 18

SANTA SEDE
D-U-N-S 438923885
CITTA' DEL VATICANO
Hauptverantwortlicher:
ULF DIEBEL

IN ANERKENNUNG DESSEN, daß dadurch und mit der Vereinigung Deutschlands als einem demokratischen und friedlichen Staat die Rechte und Verantwortlichkeiten der Vier Mächte in bezug auf Berlin und Deutschland als Ganzes ihre Bedeutung verlieren,

VERTRETEN durch ihre Außenminister, die entsprechend der Erklärung von Ottawa vom 13. Februar 1990 am 5. Mai 1990 in Bonn, am 22. Juni 1990 in Berlin, am 17. Juli 1990 in Paris unter Beteiligung des Außenministers der Republik Polen und am 12. September 1990 in Moskau zusammengetroffen sind -

SIND wie folgt ÜBEREINGEKOMMEN:

Artikel 1

(1) Das vereinte Deutschland wird die Gebiete der Bundesrepublik Deutschland, der Deutschen Demokratischen Republik und ganz Berlins umfassen. Seine Außengrenzen werden die Grenzen der Deutschen Demokratischen Republik und der Bundesrepublik Deutschland sein und werden am Tage des Inkrafttretens dieses Vertrags endgültig sein. Die Bestätigung des endgültigen Charakters der Grenzen des vereinten Deutschland ist ein wesentlicher Bestandteil der Friedensordnung in Europa.
(2) Das vereinte Deutschland und die Republik Polen bestätigen die zwischen ihnen bestehende Grenze in einem völkerrechtlich verbindlichen Vertrag.
(3) Das vereinte Deutschland hat keinerlei Gebietsansprüche gegen andere Staaten und wird solche auch nicht in Zukunft erheben.
(4) Die Regierungen der Bundesrepublik Deutschland und der Deutschen Demokratischen Republik werden sicherstellen, daß die Verfassung des vereinten Deutschland keinerlei Bestimmungen enthalten wird, die mit diesen Prinzipien unvereinbar sind. Dies gilt dementsprechend für die Bestimmungen, die in der Präambel und in den Artikeln 23 Satz 2 und 146 des Grundgesetzes für die Bundesrepublik Deutschland niedergelegt sind.
(5) Die Regierungen der Französischen Republik, des Vereinigten Königreichs Großbritannien und Nordirland, der Union der Sozialistischen Sowjetrepubliken und der Vereinigten Staaten von Amerika nehmen die entsprechenden Verpflichtungen und Erklärungen der Regierungen der Bundesrepublik Deutschland und der Deutschen Demokratischen Republik förmlich entgegen und erklären, daß mit deren Verwirklichung der endgültige Charakter der Grenzen des vereinten Deutschland bestätigt wird.

Artikel 2

Die Regierungen der Bundesrepublik Deutschland und der Deutschen Demokratischen Republik bekräftigen ihre Erklärungen, daß von deutschem Boden nur Frieden ausgehen wird. Nach der Verfassung des vereinten Deutschland sind Handlungen, die geeignet sind und in der Absicht vorgenommen werden, das friedliche Zusammenleben der Völker zu stören, insbesondere die Führung eines Angriffskrieges vorzubereiten, verfassungswidrig und strafbar. Die Regierungen der Bundesrepublik Deutschland und der Deutschen Demokratischen Republik erklären, daß das vereinte Deutschland keine seiner Waffen jemals einsetzen wird, es sei denn in Übereinstimmung mit seiner Verfassung und der Charta der Vereinten Nationen.

Artikel 3

(1) Die Regierungen der Bundesrepublik Deutschland und der Deutschen Demokratischen Republik bekräftigen ihren Verzicht auf Herstellung und Besitz von und auf Verfügungsgewalt über atomare, biologische und chemische Waffen. Sie erklären, daß auch das vereinte Deutschland sich an diese Verpflichtungen halten wird. Insbesondere gelten die Rechte und Verpflichtungen aus dem Vertrag über die Nichtverbreitung von Kernwaffen vom 1. Juli 1968 für das vereinte Deutschland fort.
(2) Die Regierung der Bundesrepublik Deutschland hat in vollem Einvernehmen mit der Regierung der Deutschen Demokratischen Republik am 30. August 1990 in Wien bei den Verhandlungen über Konventionelle Streitkräfte in Europa folgende Erklärung abgegeben:
"Die Regierung der Bundesrepublik Deutschland verpflichtet sich, die Streitkräfte des vereinten Deutschland innerhalb von drei bis vier Jahren auf eine Personalstärke von 370000 Mann (Land-,

Luft- und Seestreitkräfte) zu reduzieren. Diese Reduzierung soll mit dem Inkrafttreten des ersten KSE-Vertrags beginnen. Im Rahmen dieser Gesamtobergrenze werden nicht mehr als 345000 Mann den Land- und Luftstreitkräften angehören, die gemäß vereinbartem Mandat allein Gegenstand der Verhandlungen über konventionelle Streitkräfte in Europa sind. Die Bundesregierung sieht in ihrer Verpflichtung zur Reduzierung von Land- und Luftstreitkräften einen bedeutsamen deutschen Beitrag zur Reduzierung der konventionellen Streitkräfte in Europa. Sie geht davon aus, daß in Folgeverhandlungen auch die anderen Verhandlungsteilnehmer ihren Beitrag zur Festigung von Sicherheit und Stabilität in Europa, einschließlich Maßnahmen zur Begrenzung der Personalstärken, leisten werden."

Die Regierung der Deutschen Demokratischen Republik hat sich dieser Erklärung ausdrücklich angeschlossen.

(3) Die Regierungen der Französischen Republik, des Vereinigten Königreichs Großbritannien und Nordirland, der Union der Sozialistischen Sowjetrepubliken und der Vereinigten Staaten von Amerika nehmen diese Erklärungen der Regierungen der Bundesrepublik Deutschland und der Deutschen Demokratischen Republik zur Kenntnis.

Artikel 4

(1) Die Regierungen der Bundesrepublik Deutschland, der Deutschen Demokratischen Republik und der Union der Sozialistischen Sowjetrepubliken erklären, daß das vereinte Deutschland und die Union der Sozialistischen Sowjetrepubliken in vertraglicher Form die Bedingungen und die Dauer des Aufenthalts der sowjetischen Streitkräfte auf dem Gebiet der heutigen Deutschen Demokratischen Republik und Berlins sowie die Abwicklung des Abzugs dieser Streitkräfte regeln werden, der bis zum Ende des Jahres 1994 im Zusammenhang mit der Verwirklichung der Verpflichtungen der Regierungen der Bundesrepublik Deutschland und der Deutschen Demokratischen Republik, auf die sich Absatz 2 des Artikels 3 dieses Vertrags bezieht, vollzogen sein wird.

(2) Die Regierungen der Französischen Republik, des Vereinigten Königreichs Großbritannien und Nordirland und der Vereinigten Staaten von Amerika nehmen diese Erklärung zur Kenntnis.

Artikel 5

(1) Bis zum Abschluß des Abzugs der sowjetischen Streitkräfte vom Gebiet der heutigen Deutschen Demokratischen Republik und Berlins in Übereinstimmung mit Artikel 4 dieses Vertrags werden auf diesem Gebiet als Streitkräfte des vereinten Deutschland ausschließlich deutsche Verbände der Territorialverteidigung stationiert sein, die nicht in die Bündnisstrukturen integriert sind, denen deutsche Streitkräfte auf dem übrigen deutschen Territorium zugeordnet sind. Unbeschadet der Regelung in Absatz 2 dieses Artikels werden während dieses Zeitraums Streitkräfte anderer Staaten auf diesem Gebiet nicht stationiert oder irgendwelche andere militärische Tätigkeiten dort ausüben.

(2) Für die Dauer des Aufenthalts sowjetischer Streitkräfte auf dem Gebiet der heutigen Deutschen Demokratischen Republik und Berlins werden auf deutschen Wunsch Streitkräfte der Französischen Republik, des Vereinigten Königreichs Großbritannien und Nordirland und der Vereinigten Staaten von Amerika auf der Grundlage entsprechender vertraglicher Vereinbarung zwischen der Regierung des vereinten Deutschland und den Regierungen der betreffenden Staaten in Berlin stationiert bleiben. Die Zahl aller nichtdeutschen in Berlin stationierten Streitkräfte und deren Ausrüstungsumfang werden nicht stärker sein als zum Zeitpunkt der Unterzeichnung dieses Vertrags. Neue Waffenkategorien werden von nichtdeutschen Streitkräften dort nicht eingeführt. Die Regierung des vereinten Deutschland wird mit den Regierungen der Staaten, die Streitkräfte in Berlin stationiert haben, Verträge zu gerechten Bedingungen unter Berücksichtigung der zu den betreffenden Staaten bestehenden Beziehungen abschließen.

(3) Nach dem Abschluß des Abzugs der sowjetischen Streitkräfte vom Gebiet der heutigen Deutschen Demokratischen Republik und Berlins können in diesem Teil Deutschlands auch deutsche Streitkräfteverbände stationiert werden, die in gleicher Weise militärischen Bündnisstrukturen zugeordnet sind wie diejenigen auf dem übrigen deutschen Hoheitsgebiet, allerdings ohne Kernwaffenträger. Darunter fallen nicht konventionelle Waffensysteme, die neben konventioneller andere Einsatzfähigkeiten haben können, die jedoch in diesem Teil Deutschlands für eine

konventionelle Rolle ausgerüstet und nur dafür vorgesehen sind. Ausländische Streitkräfte und Atomwaffen oder deren Träger werden in diesem Teil Deutschlands weder stationiert noch dorthin verlegt.

Artikel 6

Das Recht des vereinten Deutschland, Bündnissen mit allen sich daraus ergebenden Rechten und Pflichten anzugehören, wird von diesem Vertrag nicht berührt.

Artikel 7

(1) Die Französische Republik, das Vereinigte Königreich Großbritannien und Nordirland, die Union der Sozialistischen Sowjetrepubliken und die Vereinigten Staaten von Amerika beenden hiermit ihre Rechte und Verantwortlichkeiten in bezug auf Berlin und Deutschland als Ganzes. Als Ergebnis werden die entsprechenden, damit zusammenhängenden vierseitigen Vereinbarungen, Beschlüsse und Praktiken beendet und alle entsprechenden Einrichtungen der Vier Mächte aufgelöst.
(2) Das vereinte Deutschland hat demgemäß volle Souveränität über seine inneren und äußeren Angelegenheiten.

Artikel 8

(1) Dieser Vertrag bedarf der Ratifikation oder Annahme, die so bald wie möglich herbeigeführt werden soll. Die Ratifikation erfolgt auf deutscher Seite durch das vereinte Deutschland. Dieser Vertrag gilt daher für das vereinte Deutschland.
(2) Die Ratifikations- oder Annahmeurkunden werden bei der Regierung des vereinten Deutschland hinterlegt. Diese unterrichtet die Regierungen der anderen Vertragschließenden Seiten von der Hinterlegung jeder Ratifikations- oder Annahmeurkunde.

Artikel 9

Dieser Vertrag tritt für das vereinte Deutschland, die Französische Republik, das Vereinigte Königreich Großbritannien und Nordirland, die Union der Sozialistischen Sowjetrepubliken und die Vereinigten Staaten von Amerika am Tag der Hinterlegung der letzten Ratifikations- oder Annahmeurkunde durch diese Staaten in Kraft.

Artikel 10

Die Urschrift dieses Vertrages, dessen deutscher, englischer, französischer und russischer Wortlaut gleichermaßen verbindlich ist, wird bei der Regierung der Bundesrepublik Deutschland hinterlegt, die den Regierungen der anderen vertragschließenden Seiten beglaubigte Ausfertigungen übermittelt.

ZU URKUND DESSEN haben die unterzeichneten, hierzu gehörig Bevollmächtigten diesen Vertrag unterschrieben.

GESCHEHEN zu Moskau am 12. September 1990

Für die Bundesrepublik Deutschland
Hans-Dietrich Genscher

Für die Deutsche Demokratische Republik
Lothar de Maizière

Für die Französische Republik
Roland Dumas

Für das Vereinigte Königreich Großbritannien und Nordirland

Douglas Hurd

Für die Union der Sozialistischen Sowjetrepubliken
Eduard Schewardnadse

Für die Vereinigten Staaten von Amerika
James A. Baker III

Dieses Dokument ist Bestandteil von

Weitere Dokumente finden Sie in den
Rubriken

19. Jahrhundert

Deutsches Kaiserreich

Weimarer Republik

Nationalsozialismus

Bundesrepublik Deutschland

Deutsche Demokratische Republik

International

Quelle: Bulletin des Presse- und Informationsamtes der Bundesregierung vom 14. September 1990, Nr. 109, S. 1153-1156.

Diese Dokumente könnten Sie auch interessieren:
◄ Vertrag über die Beziehungen zwischen der Bundesrepublik Deutschland und den Drei Mächten ["Deutschlandvertrag"] (26.05.1952, i.d.F.v. 23.10.1954)
◄ Vertrag zur Gründung der Europäischen Wirtschaftsgemeinschaft ["EWG-Vertrag"] (25.03.1957)
◄ Vertrag zwischen der Bundesrepublik Deutschland und der Französischen Republik über die deutsch-französosche Zusammenarbeit ["Elysée-Vertrag"] (22.01.1963)
◄ Vertrag zwischen der Bundesrepublik Deutschland und der Union der Sozialistischen Sowjetrepubliken ["Moskauer Vertrag"] (12.08.1970)
◄ Vertrag zwischen der Bundesrepublik Deutschland und der Volksrepublik Polen über die Grundlagen der Normalisierung ihrer gegenseitigen Beziehungen ["Warschauer Vertrag"] (07.12.1970)
◄ Vertrag über die Grundlagen der Beziehungen zwischen der Bundesrepublik Deutschland und der Deutschen Demokratischen Republik ["Grundlagenvertrag"] (21.12.1972)
◄ Vertrag über die gegenseitigen Beziehungen zwischen der Bundesrepublik Deutschland und der Tschechoslowakischen Sozialistischen Republik ["Prager-Vertrag"] (11.12.1973)
◄ Gemeinsame Erklärung der Regierungen der Bundesrepublik Deutschland und der Deutschen Demokratischen Republik zur Regelung offener Vermögensfragen (15.06.1990)

◄ Vertrag zwischen der Bundesrepublik Deutschland und der Deutschen Demokratischen Republik über die Herstellung der Einheit Deutschlands – Einigungsvertrag – (31.08.1990)

◄ Protokoll zum Vertrag zwischen der Bundesrepublik Deutschland und der Deutschen Demokratischen Republik über die Herstellung der Einheit Deutschlands – Einigungsvertrag – (31.08.1990)

▸ Vereinbarung zwischen der Bundesrepublik Deutschland und der Deutschen Demokratischen Republik zur Durchführung und Auslegung des am 31. August 1990 in Berlin unterzeichneten Vertrages zwischen der Bundesrepublik Deutschland und der Deutschen Demokratischen Republik über die Herstellung der Einheit Deutschlands – Einigungsvertrag – [Auszug] (18.09.1990)

▸ weitere historische Staatsverträge

▸ Dieses Dokument drucken!

▸ Zur Übersicht »Bundesrepublik Deutschland« zurück!

▸ **Die Navigationsleiste von documentArchiv.de laden!**

Letzte Änderung: 03.03.2004
Copyright © 2000-2004 documentArchiv.de

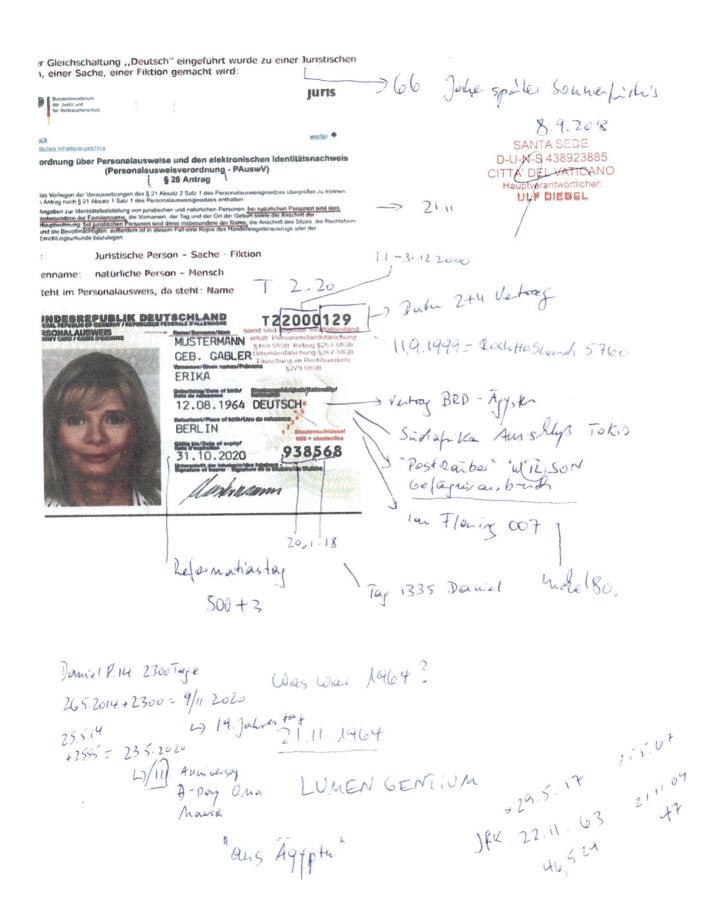

er Gleichschaltung „Deutsch" eingeführt wurde zu einer Juristischen
n, einer Sache, einer Fiktion gemacht wird:

Bundesministerium
der Justiz und
für Verbraucherschutz

juris → 66 Jahre später Sonnenfinsternis

8.9.2018
SANTA SEDE
D-U-N-S 438923885
CITTA' DEL VATICANO
Hauptverantwortlicher:
ULF DIEBEL

ck   weiter ◆

liches Inhaltsverzeichnis

ordnung über Personalausweise und den elektronischen Identitätsnachweis
(Personalausweisverordnung - PAusV)
§ 28 Antrag

as Vorlegen der Voraussetzungen des § 21 Absatz 2 Satz 1 des Personalausweisgesetzes überprüfen zu können,
Antrag nach § 21 Absatz 1 Satz 1 des Personalausweisgesetzes enthalten

→ 21.11

Angaben zur Identitätsfeststellung von juristischen und natürlichen Personen, bei natürlichen Personen sind dies
insbesondere der Familienname, die Vornamen, der Tag und der Ort der Geburt sowie die Anschrift der
Hauptwohnung, bei juristischen Personen sind diese insbesondere der Name, die Anschrift des Sitzes, die Rechtsform
und die Bevollmächtigten, außerdem ist in diesem Fall eine Kopie des Handelsregisterauszugs oder der
Errichtungsurkunde beizulegen.

:   Juristische Person - Sache - Fiktion

enname: natürliche Person - Mensch

teht im Personalausweis, da steht: Name   T 2.20   11 - 31.12.2000

T Z2000129 ⊢→ Datum 2+4 Vertrag

INDESREPUBLIK DEUTSCHLAND
EAL REPUBLIC OF GERMANY / REPUBLIQUE FEDERALE D'ALLEMAGNE
RSONALAUSWEIS
TITY CARD / CARTE D'IDENTITE

somit sind insgesamt Straftatbestände
erfüllt Personenstandsfälschung
§169 StGB, Betrug §263 StGB
Urkundenfälschung §267 StGB
Täuschung im Rechtsverkehr
§279 StGB

Name/Surname/Nom
MUSTERMANN
GEB. GABLER
Vornamen/Given names/Prénoms
ERIKA

Geburtstag/Date of birth
Date de naissance
12.08.1964

Staatsangehörigkeit/Nationality
DEUTSCH

Geburtsort/Place of birth/Lieu de naissance
BERLIN

Staatenschlüssel
000 = staatenlos

Gültig bis/Date of expiry
Date d'expiration
31.10.2020   938568

Unterschrift des Inhabers/der Inhaberin
Signature of bearer - Signature de la titulaire

11.9.1999 = Rechtsbestand 5760

→ Vertrag BRD - Ägypten
Südafrika Ausschluß Tokio
"Posträuber" WILSON
Gefängnisausbruch

Ian Fleming 007

20.1.18   Tag 1335 Daniel   Michel 80,

Reformationstag
500 + 3

Daniel P.14 2300 Tage   Was war 1964?
26.5.2014 + 2300 = 9/11 2020
25.5.14   ↳ 14. Jahrestag
+2555 = 23.5.2020   21.11.1964
        ↳/11 Anniversay   LUMEN GENTIUM
        A-Day Oma
        Maria   +29.5.17   21.11.07
                        JFK 22.11.63   21.11.04
        "aus Ägypten"   46,5.24   +7

z.B. Rote Armee Fraktion

29. August 2018

Navigate to...

Datum auswählen:

12.08.1964

◀ 1 JAHRZEHNT | 1 JAHRZEHNT ▶

◀ 1 JAHR | 1 JAHR ▶

◀ 1 MONAT | 1 MONAT ▶

11.08.1964 | 12.08.1964 | 13.08.1964

WAS WAR AM 12. AUGUST 1964

Welcher Wochentag war der 12.8.1964, der 12. August 1964 war ein Mittwoch

12.8.1964

Die USA senden vier Transportflugzeuge vom Typ C 130 in den Kongo (Léopoldville). Sie sollen zur Unterstützung der Regierung Moïse Tschombé im Kampf gegen die Rebellen eingesetzt werden.

12.8.1964

In Kairo wird ein Abkommen der Bundesrepublik Deutschland mit Ägypten unterzeichnet, das westdeutsche Hilfe für die Entwicklung der Senke von Kattara vorsieht. Die 120 km westlich von Alexandria in der Wüste und 132 m unter dem Meeresspiegel gelegene Senke soll durch Tunnel mit dem Mittelmeer verbunden werden.

12.8.1964

Südafrika wird wegen seiner Rassentrennungspolitik von den Olympischen Sommerspielen 1964 in Tokio ausgeschlossen.

Weiterlesen

12.8.1964

Der Posträuber Charles Frederick Wilson flieht aus dem Winson-Green-Gefängnis in Birmingham.

12.8.1964

Der britische Schriftsteller Ian Fleming, Schöpfer der Figur des Geheimdienstagenten James Bond, stirbt in Canterbury mit 56 Jahren nach einem Herzanfall.

12.08.1964 Geschenke Finder

Mein Geburtstag am 12.8.1964

Was war im August 1964

Was geschah 1964

Personen die am 12.8. Geburstag haben

Sternzeichen Löwe am 12. August

Wetter am 12. August 1964

Historische Zeitungen zum 12.08.1964

Historische Zeitschriften zum 12.08.1964

Original-Zeitungen vom 12. August 1964

Unsere Geschenkidee für Geburtstag, Jubiläum und vielen anderen Anlässen. Eine echte, originale Tageszeitung vom 12. August 1964 als persönliches Zeitdokument aus unserem umfangreichen Zeitungsarchiv.

Berliner Zeitung (Ost)
wichtigste DDR-Zeitung Großraum Berlin
12.8.1964

🛒 Im Shop ansehen

Weiterlesen

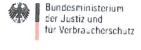
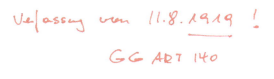

[handschriftlich:] Ve/assug vom 11.8.1919 !

[handschriftlich:] GG ART 140

Gesetz über die Zusammenarbeit des Bundes und der Länder in Angelegenheiten des Verfassungsschutzes und über das Bundesamt für Verfassungsschutz (Bundesverfassungsschutzgesetz - BVerfSchG)

Nichtamtliches Inhaltsverzeichnis

BVerfSchG   *[handschriftlich:] 12 9.1990* *[handschriftlich:] 2+4 Vertrag — "Final Settlement"*

Ausfertigungsdatum: 20.12.1990   *[handschriftlich:] ↳ Aus 2 mach 1*

Vollzitat:

"Bundesverfassungsschutzgesetz vom 20. Dezember 1990 (BGBl. I S. 2954, 2970), das zuletzt durch Artikel 2 des Gesetzes vom 30. Juni 2017 (BGBl. I S. 2097) geändert worden ist"

Stand: Zuletzt geändert durch Art. 2 G v. 30.6.2017 I 2097

[handschriftlich:] → 21.4.2017 EPHI-Zahcu
[handschriftlich:] 23.5.2017 Ei'labg ART 17
[handschriftlich:] 25.5.2017 Christi Himmelfah
[handschriftlich:] - Kirchtag
[handschriftlich:] - 50 Jahre Isbael

Näheres zur Standangabe finden Sie im Menü unter Hinweise

Fußnote

(+++ Textnachweis ab: 30.12.1990 +++)
(+++ Zur Anwendung vgl. § 36 SÜG +++)

Das G wurde als Art. 2 des G v. 20.12.1990 I 2954 vom Bundestag mit Zustimmung des Bundesrates beschlossen; das G wurde am 29.12.1990 verkündet und ist gem. Art. 6 Abs. 1 G v. 20.12.1990 I 2954 am Tage nach der Verkündung in Kraft getreten.

Erster Abschnitt
Zusammenarbeit, Aufgaben der Verfassungsschutzbehörden

Fußnote

(+++ Erster Abschn. (§§ 1 bis 7): Zur Anwendung vgl. § 36 SÜG +++)
Nichtamtliches Inhaltsverzeichnis

§ 1 Zusammenarbeitspflicht

(1) Der Verfassungsschutz dient dem Schutz der freiheitlichen demokratischen Grundordnung, des Bestandes und der Sicherheit des Bundes und der Länder.
(2) Der Bund und die Länder sind verpflichtet, in Angelegenheiten des Verfassungsschutzes zusammenzuarbeiten.
(3) Die Zusammenarbeit besteht auch in gegenseitiger Unterstützung und Hilfeleistung.

Fußnote

(+++ Erster Abschn. (§§ 1 bis 7): Zur Anwendung vgl. § 36 SÜG +++)
Nichtamtliches Inhaltsverzeichnis

§ 2 Verfassungsschutzbehörden   *[handschriftlich:] MAAßEN*

(1) Für die Zusammenarbeit des Bundes mit den Ländern unterhält der Bund ein Bundesamt für Verfassungsschutz als Bundesoberbehörde. Es untersteht dem Bundesministerium des Innern. Das Bundesamt für Verfassungsschutz darf einer polizeilichen Dienststelle nicht angegliedert werden. *[handschriftlich:] SEEHOFER*
(2) Für die Zusammenarbeit der Länder mit dem Bund und der Länder untereinander unterhält jedes Land eine Behörde zur Bearbeitung von Angelegenheiten des Verfassungsschutzes. Mehrere Länder können eine gemeinsame Behörde unterhalten.

[handschriftlich:] ↳ BERLIN, NRW, BAYERN etc.

Fußnote

(+++ Erster Abschn. (§§ 1 bis 7): Zur Anwendung vgl. § 36 SÜG +++)
Nichtamtliches Inhaltsverzeichnis

§ 3 Aufgaben der Verfassungsschutzbehörden

(1) Aufgabe der Verfassungsschutzbehörden des Bundes und der Länder ist die Sammlung und Auswertung von Informationen, insbesondere von sach- und personenbezogenen Auskünften, Nachrichten und Unterlagen, über

1. Bestrebungen, die gegen die freiheitliche demokratische Grundordnung, den Bestand oder die Sicherheit des Bundes oder eines Landes gerichtet sind oder eine ungesetzliche Beeinträchtigung der Amtsführung der Verfassungsorgane des Bundes oder eines Landes oder ihrer Mitglieder zum Ziele haben,

2. sicherheitsgefährdende oder geheimdienstliche Tätigkeiten im Geltungsbereich dieses Gesetzes für eine fremde Macht,

⊃USA, FR, RUS, GB

3. Bestrebungen im Geltungsbereich dieses Gesetzes, die durch Anwendung von Gewalt oder darauf gerichtete Vorbereitungshandlungen auswärtige Belange der Bundesrepublik Deutschland gefährden,

4. Bestrebungen im Geltungsbereich dieses Gesetzes, die gegen den Gedanken der Völkerverständigung (Artikel 9 Abs. 2 des Grundgesetzes), insbesondere gegen das friedliche Zusammenleben der Völker (Artikel 26 Abs. 1 des Grundgesetzes) gerichtet sind.

(2) Die Verfassungsschutzbehörden des Bundes und der Länder wirken mit

1. bei der Sicherheitsüberprüfung von Personen, denen im öffentlichen Interesse geheimhaltungsbedürftige Tatsachen, Gegenstände oder Erkenntnisse anvertraut werden, die Zugang dazu erhalten sollen oder ihn sich verschaffen können,

2. bei der Sicherheitsüberprüfung von Personen, die an sicherheitsempfindlichen Stellen von lebens- oder verteidigungswichtigen Einrichtungen beschäftigt sind oder werden sollen,

3. bei technischen Sicherheitsmaßnahmen zum Schutz von im öffentlichen Interesse geheimhaltungsbedürftigen Tatsachen, Gegenständen oder Erkenntnissen gegen die Kenntnisnahme durch Unbefugte,

4. bei der Überprüfung von Personen in sonstigen gesetzlich bestimmten Fällen,

5. bei der Geheimschutzbetreuung von nichtöffentlichen Stellen durch den Bund oder durch ein Land.

Die Befugnisse des Bundesamtes für Verfassungsschutz bei der Mitwirkung nach Satz 1 Nr. 1, 2 und 4 sind im Sicherheitsüberprüfungsgesetz vom 20. April 1994 (BGBl. I S. 867) geregelt. Bei der Mitwirkung nach Satz 1 Nummer 5 ist das Bundesamt für Verfassungsschutz zur sicherheitsmäßigen Bewertung der Angaben der nichtöffentlichen Stelle unter Berücksichtigung der Erkenntnisse der Verfassungsschutzbehörden des Bundes und der Länder befugt. Sofern es im Einzelfall erforderlich erscheint, können bei der Mitwirkung nach Satz 1 Nummer 5 zusätzlich die Nachrichtendienste des Bundes sowie ausländische öffentliche Stellen um Übermittlung und Bewertung vorhandener Erkenntnisse und um Bewertung übermittelter Erkenntnisse ersucht werden.
(3) Die Verfassungsschutzbehörden sind an die allgemeinen Rechtsvorschriften gebunden (Artikel 20 des Grundgesetzes).

Fußnote

(+++ Erster Abschn. (§§ 1 bis 7): Zur Anwendung vgl. § 36 SÜG +++)
Nichtamtliches Inhaltsverzeichnis

§ 4 Begriffsbestimmungen

(1) Im Sinne dieses Gesetzes sind

a) Bestrebungen gegen den Bestand des Bundes oder eines Landes solche politisch bestimmten, ziel- und zweckgerichteten Verhaltensweisen in einem oder für einen Personenzusammenschluß, der darauf gerichtet ist, die Freiheit des Bundes oder eines Landes von fremder Herrschaft aufzuheben, ihre staatliche Einheit zu beseitigen oder ein zu ihm gehörendes Gebiet abzutrennen;

b) Bestrebungen gegen die Sicherheit des Bundes oder eines Landes solche politisch bestimmten, ziel- und zweckgerichteten Verhaltensweisen in einem oder für einen Personenzusammenschluß, der darauf gerichtet ist, den Bund, Länder oder deren Einrichtungen in ihrer Funktionsfähigkeit erheblich zu beeinträchtigen;

c) Bestrebungen gegen die freiheitliche demokratische Grundordnung solche politisch bestimmten, ziel- und zweckgerichteten Verhaltensweisen in einem oder für einen Personenzusammenschluß, der darauf gerichtet ist, einen der in Absatz 2 genannten Verfassungsgrundsätze zu beseitigen oder außer Geltung zu setzen.

Für einen Personenzusammenschluß handelt, wer ihn in seinen Bestrebungen nachdrücklich unterstützt. Voraussetzung für die Sammlung und Auswertung von Informationen im Sinne des § 3 Abs. 1 ist das Vorliegen tatsächlicher Anhaltspunkte. Verhaltensweisen von Einzelpersonen, die nicht in einem oder für einen Personenzusammenschluß handeln, sind Bestrebungen im Sinne dieses Gesetzes, wenn sie auf Anwendung von Gewalt gerichtet sind oder aufgrund ihrer Wirkungsweise geeignet sind, ein Schutzgut dieses Gesetzes erheblich zu beschädigen.
(2) Zur freiheitlichen demokratischen Grundordnung im Sinne dieses Gesetzes zählen:

a) das Recht des Volkes, die Staatsgewalt in Wahlen und Abstimmungen und durch besondere Organe der Gesetzgebung, der vollziehenden Gewalt und der Rechtsprechung auszuüben und die Volksvertretung in allgemeiner, unmittelbarer, freier, gleicher und geheimer Wahl zu wählen,

↳ 24.9.2017 / 14.3.2018 "So wahr mir Gott helfe"
WAHL

b)   die Bindung der Gesetzgebung an die verfassungsmäßige Ordnung und die Bindung der vollziehenden Gewalt und der Rechtsprechung an Gesetz und Recht,

c)   das Recht auf Bildung und Ausübung einer parlamentarischen Opposition,

d)   die Ablösbarkeit der Regierung und ihre Verantwortlichkeit gegenüber der Volksvertretung,

e)   die Unabhängigkeit der Gerichte,

f)   der Ausschluß jeder Gewalt- und Willkürherrschaft und

g)   die im Grundgesetz konkretisierten Menschenrechte.

Fußnote

↳ ART 4!

(+++ Erster Abschn. (§§ 1 bis 7): Zur Anwendung vgl. § 36 SÜG +++)
Nichtamtliches Inhaltsverzeichnis

§ 5 Zuständigkeiten des Bundesamtes für Verfassungsschutz

(1) Das Bundesamt für Verfassungsschutz darf in einem Lande im Benehmen mit der Landesbehörde für Verfassungsschutz Informationen, Auskünfte, Nachrichten und Unterlagen im Sinne des § 3 sammeln. Bei Bestrebungen und Tätigkeiten im Sinne des § 3 Abs. 1 Nr. 1 bis 4 ist Voraussetzung, daß

1.   sie sich ganz oder teilweise gegen den Bund richten,

2.   sie darauf gerichtet sind, Gewalt anzuwenden, Gewaltanwendung vorzubereiten, zu unterstützen oder zu befürworten,

3.   sie sich über den Bereich eines Landes hinaus erstrecken,

4.   sie auswärtige Belange der Bundesrepublik Deutschland berühren oder

5.   eine Landesbehörde für Verfassungsschutz das Bundesamt für Verfassungsschutz um ein Tätigwerden ersucht.

Das Benehmen kann für eine Reihe gleichgelagerter Fälle hergestellt werden.
(2) Das Bundesamt für Verfassungsschutz wertet unbeschadet der Auswertungsverpflichtungen der Landesbehörden für Verfassungsschutz zentral alle Erkenntnisse über Bestrebungen und Tätigkeiten im Sinne des § 3 Absatz 1 aus. Es unterrichtet die Landesbehörden für Verfassungsschutz nach § 6 Absatz 1, insbesondere durch Querschnittsauswertungen in Form von Struktur- und Methodikberichten sowie regelmäßig durch bundesweite Lageberichte zu den wesentlichen Phänomenbereichen unter Berücksichtigung der entsprechenden Landeslageberichte.
(3) Das Bundesamt für Verfassungsschutz koordiniert die Zusammenarbeit der Verfassungsschutzbehörden. Die Koordinierung schließt insbesondere die Vereinbarung von

1.   einheitlichen Vorschriften zur Gewährleistung der Zusammenarbeitsfähigkeit,

2.   allgemeinen Arbeitsschwerpunkten und arbeitsteiliger Durchführung der Aufgaben sowie

3.   Relevanzkriterien für Übermittlungen nach § 6 Absatz 1

ein.
(4) Das Bundesamt für Verfassungsschutz unterstützt als Zentralstelle die Landesbehörden für Verfassungsschutz bei der Erfüllung ihrer Aufgaben nach § 3 insbesondere durch

1.   Bereitstellung des nachrichtendienstlichen Informationssystems (§ 6 Absatz 2),

2.   zentrale Einrichtungen im Bereich besonderer technischer und fachlicher Fähigkeiten,

3.   Erforschung und Entwicklung von Methoden und Arbeitsweisen im Verfassungsschutz und

4.   Fortbildung in speziellen Arbeitsbereichen.

(5) Dem Bundesamt für Verfassungsschutz obliegt der für Aufgaben nach § 3 erforderliche Dienstverkehr mit zuständigen öffentlichen Stellen anderer Staaten. Die Landesbehörden für Verfassungsschutz können solchen Dienstverkehr führen

1.   mit den Dienststellen der in der Bundesrepublik Deutschland stationierten Streitkräfte,

2.   mit den Nachrichtendiensten angrenzender Nachbarstaaten in regionalen Angelegenheiten oder

3.   im Einvernehmen mit dem Bundesamt für Verfassungsschutz.

Fußnote

(+++ Erster Abschn. (§§ 1 bis 7): Zur Anwendung vgl. § 36 SÜG +++)
Nichtamtliches Inhaltsverzeichnis

§ 6 Gegenseitige Unterrichtung der Verfassungsschutzbehörden

(1) Die Landesbehörden für Verfassungsschutz und das Bundesamt für Verfassungsschutz übermitteln sich unverzüglich die für ihre Aufgaben relevanten Informationen, einschließlich der Erkenntnisse ihrer Auswertungen. Wenn eine übermittelnde Behörde sich dies vorbehält, dürfen die übermittelten Daten nur mit ihrer Zustimmung an Stellen außerhalb der Behörden für Verfassungsschutz übermittelt werden.
(2) Die Verfassungsschutzbehörden sind verpflichtet, beim Bundesamt für Verfassungsschutz zur Erfüllung der Unterrichtungspflichten nach Absatz 1 gemeinsame Dateien zu führen, die sie im automatisierten Verfahren nutzen. Die Speicherung personenbezogener Daten ist nur unter den Voraussetzungen der §§ 10 und 11 zulässig. Der Abruf im automatisierten Verfahren durch andere Stellen ist nicht zulässig; § 3 Absatz 3 Satz 2 des MAD-Gesetzes bleibt

unberührt. Die Verantwortung einer speichernden Stelle im Sinne der allgemeinen Vorschriften des Datenschutzrechts trägt jede Verfassungsschutzbehörde nur für die von ihr eingegebenen Daten; nur sie darf diese Daten verändern, die Verarbeitung einschränken oder löschen. Die eingebende Stelle muss feststellbar sein. Eine Abfrage von Daten ist nur zulässig, soweit dies zur Erfüllung von Aufgaben, mit denen der Abfragende unmittelbar betraut ist, erforderlich ist. Die Zugriffsberechtigung auf Daten, die nicht zum Auffinden von Akten und der dazu notwendigen Identifizierung von Personen erforderlich sind, ist auf Personen zu beschränken, die mit der Erfassung von Daten oder Analysen betraut sind. Die Zugriffsberechtigung auf Unterlagen, die gespeicherte Angaben belegen, ist zudem auf Personen zu beschränken, die unmittelbar mit Arbeiten in diesem Anwendungsgebiet betraut sind.

(3) Das Bundesamt für Verfassungsschutz trifft für die gemeinsamen Dateien die technischen und organisatorischen Maßnahmen entsprechend § 64 des Bundesdatenschutzgesetzes. Es hat bei jedem Zugriff für Zwecke der Datenschutzkontrolle den Zeitpunkt, die Angaben, die die Feststellung der abgefragten Datensätze ermöglichen, sowie die abfragende Stelle zu protokollieren. Die Auswertung der Protokolldaten ist nach dem Stand der Technik zu gewährleisten. Die protokollierten Daten dürfen nur für Zwecke der Datenschutzkontrolle, der Datensicherung oder zur Sicherstellung eines ordnungsgemäßen Betriebs der Datenverarbeitungsanlage verwendet werden. Die Protokolldaten sind am Ende des Kalenderjahres, das dem Jahr der Protokollierung folgt, zu löschen.

Fußnote

(+++ Erster Abschn. (§§ 1 bis 7): Zur Anwendung vgl. § 36 SÜG +++)

Nichtamtliches Inhaltsverzeichnis

§ 7 Weisungsrechte des Bundes

Die Bundesregierung kann, wenn ein Angriff auf die verfassungsmäßige Ordnung des Bundes erfolgt, den obersten Landesbehörden die für die Zusammenarbeit der Länder mit dem Bund auf dem Gebiete des Verfassungsschutzes erforderlichen Weisungen erteilen.

Fußnote

(+++ Erster Abschn. (§§ 1 bis 7): Zur Anwendung vgl. § 36 SÜG +++)

Zweiter Abschnitt
Bundesamt für Verfassungsschutz

Nichtamtliches Inhaltsverzeichnis

§ 8 Befugnisse des Bundesamtes für Verfassungsschutz

(1) Das Bundesamt für Verfassungsschutz darf die zur Erfüllung seiner Aufgaben erforderlichen Informationen einschließlich personenbezogener Daten verarbeiten, soweit nicht die anzuwendenden Bestimmungen des Bundesdatenschutzgesetzes oder besondere Regelungen in diesem Gesetz entgegenstehen; die Verarbeitung ist auch zulässig, wenn der Betroffene eingewilligt hat. Ein Ersuchen des Bundesamtes für Verfassungsschutz um Übermittlung personenbezogener Daten darf nur diejenigen personenbezogenen Daten enthalten, die für die Erteilung der Auskunft unerlässlich sind. Schutzwürdige Interessen des Betroffenen dürfen nur in unvermeidbarem Umfang beeinträchtigt werden.

(2) Das Bundesamt für Verfassungsschutz darf Methoden, Gegenstände und Instrumente zur heimlichen Informationsbeschaffung, wie den Einsatz von Vertrauensleuten und Gewährspersonen, Observationen, Bild- und Tonaufzeichnungen, Tarnpapiere und Tarnkennzeichen anwenden. In Individualrechte darf nur nach Maßgabe besonderer Befugnisse eingegriffen werden. Im Übrigen darf die Anwendung eines Mittels gemäß Satz 1 keinen Nachteil herbeiführen, der erkennbar außer Verhältnis zur Bedeutung des aufzuklärenden Sachverhalts steht. Die Mittel nach Satz 1 sind in einer Dienstvorschrift zu benennen, die auch die Zuständigkeit für die Anordnung solcher Informationsbeschaffungen und das Nähere zu Satz 3 regelt. Die Dienstvorschrift bedarf der Zustimmung des Bundesministeriums des Innern, das das Parlamentarische Kontrollgremium unterrichtet.

(3) Polizeiliche Befugnisse oder Weisungsbefugnisse stehen dem Bundesamt für Verfassungsschutz nicht zu; es darf die Polizei auch nicht im Wege der Amtshilfe um Maßnahmen ersuchen, zu denen es selbst nicht befugt ist.

(4) Werden personenbezogene Daten beim Betroffenen mit seiner Kenntnis erhoben, so ist der Erhebungszweck anzugeben. Der Betroffene ist auf die Freiwilligkeit seiner Angaben hinzuweisen.

(5) Von mehreren geeigneten Maßnahmen hat das Bundesamt für Verfassungsschutz diejenige zu wählen, die den Betroffenen voraussichtlich am wenigsten beeinträchtigt. Eine Maßnahme darf keinen Nachteil herbeiführen, der erkennbar außer Verhältnis zu dem beabsichtigten Erfolg steht.

Nichtamtliches Inhaltsverzeichnis

§ 8a Besondere Auskunftsverlangen

(1) Das Bundesamt für Verfassungsschutz darf im Einzelfall bei denjenigen, die geschäftsmäßig Teledienste erbringen oder daran mitwirken, Auskunft über Daten einholen, die für die Begründung, inhaltliche Ausgestaltung, Änderung oder Beendigung eines Vertragsverhältnisses über Teledienste (Bestandsdaten) gespeichert worden sind, soweit dies zur Sammlung und Auswertung von Informationen erforderlich ist und tatsächliche Anhaltspunkte für schwerwiegende Gefahren für die in § 3 Absatz 1 genannten Schutzgüter vorliegen.

(2) Das Bundesamt für Verfassungsschutz darf im Einzelfall Auskunft einholen bei

1.   Luftfahrtunternehmen sowie Betreibern von Computerreservierungssystemen und Globalen Distributionssystemen für Flüge zu Namen und Anschriften des Kunden sowie zur Inanspruchnahme und den

DATENSCHUTZ-GRUNDVERORDNUNG (DSGVO)   ERWÄGUNGSGRÜNDE   BDSG   THEMEN   English

Art. 5 DSGVO

Grundsätze für die Verarbeitung personenbezogener Daten

(1)   Personenbezogene Daten müssen

a)   auf rechtmäßige Weise, nach Treu und Glauben und in einer für die betroffene Person nachvollziehbaren Weise verarbeitet werden („Rechtmäßigkeit, Verarbeitung nach Treu und Glauben, Transparenz");

b)   für festgelegte, eindeutige und legitime Zwecke erhoben werden und dürfen nicht in einer mit diesen Zwecken nicht zu vereinbarenden Weise weiterverarbeitet werden; eine Weiterverarbeitung für im öffentlichen Interesse liegende Archivzwecke, für wissenschaftliche oder historische Forschungszwecke oder für statistische Zwecke gilt gemäß Artikel 89 Absatz 1 nicht als unvereinbar mit den ursprünglichen Zwecken („Zweckbindung");

c)   dem Zweck angemessen und erheblich sowie auf das für die Zwecke der Verarbeitung notwendige Maß beschränkt sein („Datenminimierung");

d)   sachlich richtig und erforderlichenfalls auf dem neuesten Stand sein; es sind alle angemessenen Maßnahmen zu treffen, damit personenbezogene Daten, die im Hinblick auf die Zwecke ihrer Verarbeitung unrichtig sind, unverzüglich gelöscht oder berichtigt werden („Richtigkeit");

e)   in einer Form gespeichert werden, die die Identifizierung der betroffenen Personen nur so lange ermöglicht, wie es für die Zwecke, für die sie verarbeitet werden, erforderlich ist; personenbezogene Daten dürfen länger gespeichert werden, soweit die personenbezogenen Daten vorbehaltlich der Durchführung geeigneter technischer und organisatorischer Maßnahmen, die von dieser Verordnung zum Schutz der Rechte und Freiheiten der betroffenen Person gefordert werden, ausschließlich für im öffentlichen Interesse liegende Archivzwecke oder für wissenschaftliche und historische Forschungszwecke oder für statistische Zwecke gemäß Artikel 89 Absatz 1 verarbeitet werden („Speicherbegrenzung");

f)   in einer Weise verarbeitet werden, die eine angemessene Sicherheit der personenbezogenen Daten gewährleistet, einschließlich Schutz vor unbefugter oder unrechtmäßiger Verarbeitung und vor unbeabsichtigtem Verlust, unbeabsichtigter Zerstörung oder unbeabsichtigter Schädigung durch geeignete technische und organisatorische Maßnahmen („Integrität und Vertraulichkeit");

(2)   Der Verantwortliche ist für die Einhaltung des Absatzes 1 verantwortlich und muss dessen Einhaltung nachweisen können („Rechenschaftspflicht").

Passende Erwägungsgründe

(39) Grundsätze der Datenverarbeitung

consulting

DATENSCHUTZ-GRUNDVERORDNUNG (DSGVO)   ERWÄGUNGSGRÜNDE   BDSG   THEMEN   English

25.5.67 – 25.5.18

[AREA 51]

25.5.18

Art. 6 DSGVO
Rechtmäßigkeit der Verarbeitung

(1)   [1] Die Verarbeitung ist nur rechtmäßig, wenn mindestens eine der nachstehenden Bedingungen erfüllt ist:

   a) Die betroffene Person hat ihre Einwilligung zu der Verarbeitung der sie betreffenden personenbezogenen Daten für einen oder mehrere bestimmte Zwecke gegeben;

   b) die Verarbeitung ist für die Erfüllung eines Vertrags, dessen Vertragspartei die betroffene Person ist, oder zur Durchführung vorvertraglicher Maßnahmen erforderlich, die auf Anfrage der betroffenen Person erfolgen;

   c) die Verarbeitung ist zur Erfüllung einer rechtlichen Verpflichtung erforderlich, der der Verantwortliche unterliegt;

   d) die Verarbeitung ist erforderlich, um lebenswichtige Interessen der betroffenen Person oder einer anderen natürlichen Person zu schützen;

   e) die Verarbeitung ist für die Wahrnehmung einer Aufgabe erforderlich, die im öffentlichen Interesse liegt oder in Ausübung öffentlicher Gewalt erfolgt, die dem Verantwortlichen übertragen wurde;

   f) die Verarbeitung ist zur Wahrung der berechtigten Interessen des Verantwortlichen oder eines Dritten erforderlich, sofern nicht die Interessen oder Grundrechte und Grundfreiheiten der betroffenen Person, die den Schutz personenbezogener Daten erfordern, überwiegen, insbesondere dann, wenn es sich bei der betroffenen Person um ein Kind handelt.

[2] Unterabsatz 1 Buchstabe f gilt nicht für die von Behörden in Erfüllung ihrer Aufgaben vorgenommene Verarbeitung.

(2)   Die Mitgliedstaaten können spezifischere Bestimmungen zur Anpassung der Anwendung der Vorschriften dieser Verordnung in Bezug auf die Verarbeitung zur Erfüllung von Absatz 1 Buchstaben c und e beibehalten oder einführen, indem sie spezifische Anforderungen für die Verarbeitung sowie sonstige Maßnahmen präziser bestimmen, um eine rechtmäßig und nach Treu und Glauben erfolgende Verarbeitung zu gewährleisten, einschließlich für andere besondere Verarbeitungssituationen gemäß Kapitel IX.

(3)   [1] Die Rechtsgrundlage für die Verarbeitungen gemäß Absatz 1 Buchstaben c und e wird festgelegt durch

   a) Unionsrecht oder

   b) das Recht der Mitgliedstaaten, dem der Verantwortliche unterliegt.

[2] Der Zweck der Verarbeitung muss in dieser Rechtsgrundlage festgelegt oder hinsichtlich der Verarbeitung gemäß Absatz 1 Buchstabe e für die Erfüllung einer Aufgabe erforderlich sein, die im öffentlichen Interesse liegt oder in Ausübung öffentlicher Gewalt erfolgt, die dem Verantwortlichen übertragen wurde. [3] Diese Rechtsgrundlage kann spezifische Bestimmungen zur Anpassung der Anwendung der Vorschriften dieser Verordnung enthalten, unter anderem Bestimmungen darüber, welche allgemeinen Bedingungen für die Regelung der Rechtmäßigkeit der Verarbeitung durch den Verantwortlichen gelten, welche Arten von Daten verarbeitet werden, welche Personen betroffen sind, an welche Einrichtungen und für welche Zwecke die personenbezogenen Daten offengelegt werden dürfen, welcher Zweckbindung sie unterliegen, wie lange sie gespeichert werden dürfen und welche Verarbeitungsvorgänge und -verfahren angewandt werden dürfen, einschließlich Maßnahmen zur Gewährleistung einer rechtmäßig und nach Treu und Glauben erfolgenden Verarbeitung, wie solche für sonstige besondere Verarbeitungssituationen gemäß Kapitel IX. [4] Das Unionsrecht oder das Recht der Mitgliedstaaten müssen ein im öffentlichen Interesse liegendes Ziel verfolgen und in einem angemessenen Verhältnis zu dem verfolgten legitimen Zweck stehen.

(4)   Beruht die Verarbeitung zu einem anderen Zweck als zu demjenigen, zu dem die personenbezogenen Daten erhoben wurden, nicht auf der Einwilligung der betroffenen Person oder auf einer Rechtsvorschrift der Union oder der Mitgliedstaaten, die in einer demokratischen Gesellschaft eine notwendige und verhältnismäßige Maßnahme zum Schutz der in Artikel 23 Absatz 1 genannten Ziele darstellt, so berücksichtigt der Verantwortliche – um festzustellen, ob die Verarbeitung zu einem anderen Zweck mit demjenigen, zu dem die personenbezogenen Daten ursprünglich erhoben wurden, vereinbar ist – unter anderem

   a) jede Verbindung zwischen den Zwecken, für die die personenbezogenen Daten erhoben wurden, und den Zwecken der beabsichtigten Weiterverarbeitung,

   b) den Zusammenhang, in dem die personenbezogenen Daten erhoben wurden, insbesondere hinsichtlich des Verhältnisses zwischen den betroffenen Personen und dem Verantwortlichen,

   c) die Art der personenbezogenen Daten, insbesondere ob besondere Kategorien personenbezogener Daten gemäß Artikel 9 verarbeitet werden oder ob personenbezogene Daten über strafrechtliche Verurteilungen und Straftaten gemäß Artikel 10 verarbeitet werden,

   d) die möglichen Folgen der beabsichtigten Weiterverarbeitung für die betroffenen Personen,

   e) das Vorhandensein geeigneter Garantien, wozu Verschlüsselung oder Pseudonymisierung gehören kann.

consulting **Passende Erwägungsgründe**

| DATENSCHUTZ-GRUNDVERORDNUNG (DSGVO) | ERWÄGUNGSGRÜNDE | BDSG | THEMEN | English |

Erfordernisse einer Einwilligung, **(43)** Zwanglose Einwilligung, **(44)** Vertragserfüllung oder -abschluss, **(45)** Erfüllung rechtlicher Pflichten, **(46)** Lebenswichtige Interessen, **(47)** Überwiegende berechtigte Interessen, **(48)** Überwiegende berechtigte Interessen in der Unternehmensgruppe, **(49)** Netz- und Informationssicherheit als überwiegendes berechtigtes Interesse, **(50)** Weiterverarbeitung, **(171)** Aufhebung der RL 95/46/EG und Übergangsbestimmungen

Passende Paragraphen des BDSG

§ 3 BDSG Verarbeitung personenbezogener Daten durch öffentliche Stellen, **§ 4 BDSG** Videoüberwachung öffentlich zugänglicher Räume, **§ 23 BDSG** Verarbeitung zu anderen Zwecken durch öffentliche Stellen, **§ 24 BDSG** Verarbeitung zu anderen Zwecken durch nichtöffentliche Stellen, **§ 25 BDSG** Datenübermittlungen durch öffentliche Stellen, **§ 26 BDSG** Datenverarbeitung für Zwecke des Beschäftigungsverhältnisses, **§ 27 BDSG** Datenverarbeitung zu wissenschaftlichen oder historischen Forschungszwecken und zu statistischen Zwecken, **§ 31 BDSG** Schutz des Wirtschaftsverkehrs bei Scoring und Bonitätsauskünften

consulting

DATENSCHUTZ-GRUNDVERORDNUNG (DSGVO)   ERWÄGUNGSGRÜNDE   BDSG   THEMEN   English

Art. 15 DSGVO
Auskunftsrecht der betroffenen Person

→ auch alle D-U-N-S

(1)   Die betroffene Person hat das Recht, von dem Verantwortlichen eine Bestätigung darüber zu verlangen, ob sie betreffende personenbezogene Daten verarbeitet werden; ist dies der Fall, so hat sie ein Recht auf Auskunft über diese personenbezogenen Daten und auf folgende Informationen:

   a)   die Verarbeitungszwecke;

   b)   die Kategorien personenbezogener Daten, die verarbeitet werden;

   c)   die Empfänger oder Kategorien von Empfängern, gegenüber denen die personenbezogenen Daten offengelegt worden sind oder noch offengelegt werden, insbesondere bei Empfängern in Drittländern oder bei internationalen Organisationen;

   d)   falls möglich die geplante Dauer, für die die personenbezogenen Daten gespeichert werden, oder, falls dies nicht möglich ist, die Kriterien für die Festlegung dieser Dauer;

   e)   das Bestehen eines Rechts auf Berichtigung oder Löschung der sie betreffenden personenbezogenen Daten oder auf Einschränkung der Verarbeitung durch den Verantwortlichen oder eines Widerspruchsrechts gegen diese Verarbeitung;

   f)   das Bestehen eines Beschwerderechts bei einer Aufsichtsbehörde;

   g)   wenn die personenbezogenen Daten nicht bei der betroffenen Person erhoben werden, alle verfügbaren Informationen über die Herkunft der Daten;

   h)   das Bestehen einer automatisierten Entscheidungsfindung einschließlich Profiling gemäß Artikel 22 Absätze 1 und 4 und – zumindest in diesen Fällen – aussagekräftige Informationen über die involvierte Logik sowie die Tragweite und die angestrebten Auswirkungen einer derartigen Verarbeitung für die betroffene Person.

(2)   Werden personenbezogene Daten an ein Drittland oder an eine internationale Organisation übermittelt, so hat die betroffene Person das Recht, über die geeigneten Garantien gemäß Artikel 46 im Zusammenhang mit der Übermittlung unterrichtet zu werden.

(3)   [1] Der Verantwortliche stellt eine Kopie der personenbezogenen Daten, die Gegenstand der Verarbeitung sind, zur Verfügung. [2] Für alle weiteren Kopien, die die betroffene Person beantragt, kann der Verantwortliche ein angemessenes Entgelt auf der Grundlage der Verwaltungskosten verlangen. [3] Stellt die betroffene Person den Antrag elektronisch, so sind die Informationen in einem gängigen elektronischen Format zur Verfügung zu stellen, sofern sie nichts anderes angibt.

(4)   Das Recht auf Erhalt einer Kopie gemäß Absatz 3 darf die Rechte und Freiheiten anderer Personen nicht beeinträchtigen.

Passende Erwägungsgründe

(63) Auskunftsrecht, (64) Identitätsprüfung

Passende Paragraphen des BDSG

§ 27 BDSG Datenverarbeitung zu wissenschaftlichen oder historischen Forschungszwecken und zu statistischen Zwecken, § 28 BDSG Datenverarbeitung zu im öffentlichen Interesse liegenden Archivzwecken, § 29 BDSG Rechte der betroffenen Person und aufsichtsbehördliche Befugnisse im Fall von Geheimhaltungspflichten, § 30 BDSG Verbraucherkredite, § 34 BDSG Auskunftsrecht der betroffenen Person

consulting

Art. 16 DSGVO
Recht auf Berichtigung

→ VON ALLEN D-U-N-S

[1] Die betroffene Person hat das Recht, von dem Verantwortlichen unverzüglich die Berichtigung sie betreffender unrichtiger personenbezogener Daten zu verlangen. [2] Unter Berücksichtigung der Zwecke der Verarbeitung hat die betroffene Person das Recht, die Vervollständigung unvollständiger personenbezogener Daten – auch mittels einer ergänzenden Erklärung – zu verlangen.

Passende Erwägungsgründe

(65) Recht auf Berichtigung und Löschung

Passende Paragraphen des BDSG

§ 27 BDSG Datenverarbeitung zu wissenschaftlichen oder historischen Forschungszwecken und zu statistischen Zwecken, § 28 BDSG Datenverarbeitung zu im öffentlichen Interesse liegenden Archivzwecken

consulting

DATENSCHUTZ-GRUNDVERORDNUNG (DSGVO)   ERWÄGUNGSGRÜNDE   BDSG   THEMEN   English

Art. 50 DSGVO

Internationale Zusammenarbeit zum Schutz personenbezogener Daten

→ G7, EV, DONALD TRUMP

(1)   In Bezug auf Drittländer und internationale Organisationen treffen die Kommission und die Aufsichtsbehörden geeignete Maßnahmen zur

    a) Entwicklung von Mechanismen der internationalen Zusammenarbeit, durch die die wirksame Durchsetzung von Rechtsvorschriften zum Schutz personenbezogener Daten erleichtert wird,

    b) gegenseitigen Leistung internationaler Amtshilfe bei der Durchsetzung von Rechtsvorschriften zum Schutz personenbezogener Daten, unter anderem durch Meldungen, Beschwerdeverweisungen, Amtshilfe bei Untersuchungen und Informationsaustausch, sofern geeignete Garantien für den Schutz personenbezogener Daten und anderer Grundrechte und Grundfreiheiten bestehen,

    c) Einbindung maßgeblicher Interessenträger in Diskussionen und Tätigkeiten, die zum Ausbau der internationalen Zusammenarbeit bei der Durchsetzung von Rechtsvorschriften zum Schutz personenbezogener Daten dienen,

    d) Förderung des Austauschs und der Dokumentation von Rechtsvorschriften und Praktiken zum Schutz personenbezogener Daten einschließlich Zuständigkeitskonflikten mit Drittländern.

Passende Erwägungsgründe

(116) Kooperation zwischen den Aufsichtsbehörden

DATENSCHUTZ-GRUNDVERORDNUNG (DSGVO)   **ERWÄGUNGSGRÜNDE**   **BDSG**

THEMEN

Art. 80 DSGVO
Vertretung von betroffenen Personen

ULF DIEBEL + ERBEN JAVOB

(1) Die betroffene Person hat das Recht, eine Einrichtung, Organisationen oder Vereinigung ohne Gewinnerzielungsabsicht, die ordnungsgemäß nach dem Recht eines Mitgliedstaats gegründet ist, deren satzungsmäßige Ziele im öffentlichem Interesse liegen und die im Bereich des Schutzes der Rechte und Freiheiten von betroffenen Personen in Bezug auf den Schutz ihrer personenbezogenen Daten tätig ist, zu beauftragen, in ihrem Namen eine Beschwerde einzureichen, in ihrem Namen die in den Artikeln 77, 78 und 79 genannten Rechte wahrzunehmen und das Recht auf Schadensersatz gemäß Artikel 82 in Anspruch zu nehmen, sofern dieses im Recht der Mitgliedstaaten vorgesehen ist.

(2) Die Mitgliedstaaten können vorsehen, dass jede der in Absatz 1 des vorliegenden Artikels genannten Einrichtungen, Organisationen oder Vereinigungen unabhängig von einem Auftrag der betroffenen Person in diesem Mitgliedstaat das Recht hat, bei der gemäß Artikel 77 zuständigen Aufsichtsbehörde eine Beschwerde einzulegen und die in den Artikeln 78 und 79 aufgeführten Rechte in Anspruch zu nehmen, wenn ihres Erachtens die Rechte einer betroffenen Person gemäß dieser Verordnung infolge einer Verarbeitung verletzt worden sind.

Passende Erwägungsgründe

Die dogmatische Konstitution über die göttliche Offenbarung DEI VERBUM

feierliche Promulgation durch Papst Paul VI. am 18. November 1965

EINFÜHRUNG IN DEN KONZILSTEXT

DEI VERBUM entstand als Nachfolgerin eines Textes, an dem sich die Geister schieden und das Konzil sein Selbstbewußtsein fand. Von der Theologischen Vorbereitungskommission war ein Schema "Über die Quellen der Offenbarung" vorgelegt worden, das Mitte November 1962 vom Konzil sehr kritisch diskutiert wurde. Eine Abstimmung ergab eine starke, aber ungenügende Mehrheit gegen eine Fortsetzung der heftigen Debatte. Johannes XXIII. ordnete daraufhin den Abbruch der Diskussion an, setzte eine neue, gemischte Kommission mit den gleichberechtigten Präsidenten Ottaviani und Bea ein und wünschte die Erstellung eines Schemas "Über die göttliche Offenbarung". Die gemischte Kommission erstellte im Frühjahr 1963 den neuen Text. Schriftliche Abänderungsvorschläge wurden von der Theologischen Kommission eingearbeitet, so daß dieser dritte Text Ende September 1964 dem Konzil vorgelegt werden konnte. Als Ergebnis der Diskussion entstand noch während der III. Sitzungsperiode ein vierter Text, über den erst im September 1965 abgestimmt werden konnte. Wieder ergaben sich Abänderungsvorschläge, darunter auch einige von seiten des Papstes, der jedoch frei über sie in der Theologischen Kommission abstimmen ließ und mit Umformulierungen einverstanden war. Die feierliche Schlußabstimmung ergab 2344 Ja - gegen 6 Neinstimmen, am gleichen Tag, dem 18. November 1965, wurde die dogmatische Konstitution feierlich verkündet.

Der endgültige Text ist eine "dogmatische Konstitution". Das Konzil wollte zwar keine neuen Dogmen definieren, aber seine dogmatischen Konstitutionen stellen Aussagen des höchsten Lehramtes der katholischen Kirche dar, die das Gewissen des katholischen Christen, auch der lehrenden, binden und nicht als pastorale Erbaulichkeiten abgetan werden dürfen. Das schließt selbstverständlich nicht aus, daß auch hier auf Mißverständlichkeiten und weniger geglückte Formulierungen des Textes aufmerksam gemacht werden darf.

Das *Vorwort* (Artikel 1) gibt das Thema der Konstitution genauer an, die Offenbarung Gottes und ihre Weitergabe. Ein Eingehen auf hier naheliegende fundamentaltheologischen Thematiken - Wie vernimmt der Offenbarungsträger die göttliche Offenbarung als die des sich selbst bezeugenden Gottes? Warum ist diese Selbstbezeugung Gottes in genau derselben Weise der Zeit nach Jesus Christus versagt? Wie kann der Mensch heute zu einer abgeschlossenen, vielfach vermittelten Offenbarung einen Glaubenszugang finden? - ist in dieser Konstitution nicht beabsichtigt gewesen.

Im *I. Kapitel,* das von der Offenbarung Gottes selbst handelt, wird manches verdeutlicht, was das Konzil von Trient und das I. Vaticanum in einer gewissen Einseitigkeit gesagt hatten, und so wird, wie das Vorwort ankündigte, die Lehre dieser Konzilien wohl nicht revidiert, aber weitergeführt. Dazu gehört, daß Offenbarung als Selbstmitteilung Gottes verstanden wird und darum hinfort nicht mehr intellektualistisch als bloße Mitteilung von Sätzen "über" Gott und seine Heilsabsichten mißverstanden werden darf. Sie ist überhaupt nicht nur im Wort und in der Lehre zu sehen, sondern als Einheit von Tat- und Wortoffenbarung, als Ereignishaftes - Handeln Gottes am Menschen, zu dem das dem Glauben gesagte Wort als ein inneres Wesensmoment gehört. Die Tatoffenbarung aber ist weder auf die sogenannte "natürliche Offenbarung" beschränkt, der das Konzil hier kein besonderes Gewicht beimißt, noch auf die "Wunder" und erfüllten Prophezeiungen, die zur fundamentaltheologischen Thematik gehören. Das Konzil richtet seine Aufmerksamkeit vielmehr umfassender auf die Konkretion des allgemeinen Heilswillens Gottes (der überall seine Gnade anbietet und mitteilt) in der besonderen, amtlichen Heilsgeschichte. Diese wird bis zu ihrem Höhepunkt in Jesus Christus dargestellt, allerdings nicht in einer exegetischen Anstrengung, so daß die angeführten Schriftstellen mehr zufällige Belege sind. Von dieser Offenbarung Gottes sagt das Konzil, daß sie abgeschlossen und erfüllt ist, daß sie aber dadurch immerfort neu wirkt, "daß Gott mit uns ist" (Artikel 4).

Von dem Thema der Offenbarung geht der Konzilstext unvermittelt zum Glauben des Menschen über. Artikel 5 enthält zwei Aussagen, die als Aussagen des Lehramts von großer Bedeutung sind. Der Glaube des Menschen wird in erster Linie im Sinn des Römerbriefs als Gehorsam, als personale Begegnung mit Gott und als Übereignung des ganzen Menschen verstanden. Diese Glaubenszustimmung wird durch das Zuvorkommen der Gnade Gottes allererst ermöglicht, und der

Glaube erfährt ständige Vervollkommnung durch die Gaben des Geistes. Der intellektuelle Aspekt des Glaubens kommt erst danach in Artikel 6 zur Geltung.

Das *II. Kapitel* über die Weitergabe der Offenbarung hebt hervor, daß das "Evangelium" der Kirche zur getreuen Predigt und Bewahrung anvertraut wurde. Bei diesem Vollzug werden nicht nur Heilswahrheit und Sittenlehre, sondern auch göttliche Gaben mitgeteilt. Der Konzilstext geht nicht auf die Bewahrung der Offenbarung in Israel ein, sondern auf das, was die Apostel von Jesus empfingen oder "unter der Eingebung des Heiligen Geistes gelernt hatten" (ein für die exegetische Arbeit wichtiger Satz des Artikels 7), was sie mündlich verkündigten oder was von ihnen oder "apostolischen Männern" (ein vorsichtiger Ausdruck) niedergeschrieben wurde. Eben dieses weitergebende Lehramt ging auf die Nachfolger der Apostel über. Damit stellt sich das Konzil dem Verhältnis von Überlieferung und Schrift. Das beide Umfassende ist die ursprüngliche "apostolische Predigt". Der Schrift kommt besondere Würde zu, weil in ihr diese Predigt "besonders deutlichen Ausdruck" gefunden hat. Über sie hinaus gibt es einen Fortschritt nicht quantitativer, sondern qualitativer Art: durch Betrachtung, Studium und geistliche Erfahrung. Insofern Überlieferung nicht das Ganze ist, sondern von der Schrift unterschieden werden muß, schreibt ihr das Konzil lediglich zwei Funktionen zu, einmal die Erkenntnis des "vollständigen Kanons" (Artikel 8), zum anderen - nach einem Zusatz, den der Papst in einer späten Phase gewünscht hat - die Gewißheit über alles Geoffenbarte (Artikel 9). Dieser Zusatz verändert die Konzilsauffassung nicht, daß die Tradition nicht als quantitative materielle Ergänzung der Schrift gelehrt werden soll (diese Frage wird bewußt offengelassen), da ja nur von der "Gewißheit" die Rede ist. Zu der viel diskutierten Frage also, ob die Offenbarung Gottes uns in einem oder in zwei voneinander getrennten "Zuflüssen" (mit wenigstens teilweise Material verschiedener Inhaltlichkeit) zukomme (das Wort "Quelle" wäre hier von vornherein falsch), nimmt das Konzil nur insofern Stellung, als es die Einheit der Weitergabe betont. Artikel 10 verläßt dieses Thema und ergänzt es bedeutsam, weil die Einheit des Volkes Gottes, von Vorstehern und Gläubigen, gegenüber dem Wort Gottes und im Wort Gottes hervorgehoben wird. Weiter wird gesagt, das Lehramt sei nicht über dem Wort Gottes, sondern es diene ihm, indem es darauf höre. Beides sind wichtige Selbstaussagen des Lehramtes über seine dienende Funktion. Es ist nicht Norm der Schrift, sondern eine Norm des Schriftverständnisses des einzelnen Christen in der Kirche.

Kapitel III über die Inspiration und Interpretation der Schrift legt neueren katholischen Versuchen zum Verständnis der Inspiration kein Hindernis in den Weg. Deutlicher als die Schultheologie unterscheidet es zwischen Gott als dem "Urheber" der Schrift und den Menschen als deren "echten *Verfassern*" (nicht "Sekretäre!"). Der Schrift wird nicht, wie in früheren Textentwürfen dieser Konstitution, "Irrtumslosigkeit" zugeschrieben! sondern es wird gesagt, daß sie die "Wahrheit" lehre. Was in diesem Zusammenhang "Wahrheit" heißen soll, wird überdies umschrieben. Zwar heißt es auf Wunsch des Papstes nun nicht mehr, die Schrift lehre die "Heilswahrheit", aber die jetzige Fassung: "die Wahrheit, die Gott um unseres Heiles willen in heiligen Schriften aufgezeichnet haben wollte", sagt substantiell dasselbe. Sie schließt die Tatsache jedenfalls nicht aus, daß in der Schrift menschliche Fehler, d. h. Sätze, die, wenn sie außerhalb des Kontextes und dessen literarischer Art gelesen und als wirklich vertretene Aussagen für sich verstanden werden, mit Recht als profane "Irrtümer" zu gelten hätten, enthalten sind, die mit der Wahrheit um unseres Heiles willen in keinem Zusammenhang stehen (Artikel 11). Der folgende Artikel 12 geht, ganz im Gefolge der Offenheit gegenüber der Bibelforschung unter Pius XII. und der Instruktion der Päpstlichen Bibelkommission von 1964, auf die Prinzipien der Schriftauslegung ein. Es geht darum, die *Aussageabsicht* der biblischen Schriftsteller ("Hagiographen") zu ermitteln. Bei der Ermittlung der Absicht von Menschen, die ihre eigene Absicht nicht mehr selbst interpretieren können, ist ein umfangreicher Komplex von methodischen Analysen anzuwenden. Für die Heilige Schrift stellt ihn die Bibelwissenschaft bereit. Der Konzilstext nennt aus diesem ganzen Komplex, den er mit den Worten "neben anderem" andeutet, nur die "literarischen Gattungen", um deren Erforschung sich nach der Überwindung der reinen Literarkritik seit Anfang des 20. Jahrhunderts die sogenannte "Formgeschichtliche Schule" verdient gemacht hat. Das Konzil erkennt an, daß es mehrere solcher literarischer Gattungen in der Schrift gibt, darunter auch dichterische und solche "von in *verschiedener* Weise geschichtlicher Art". In welchem Sinn die Schrift Geschichte bietet oder überhaupt bieten will, läßt sich auf den ersten Blick hin heute nicht eindeutig erkennen, auch von der Kirche nicht, deren eigenes heiliges Buch diese Schrift ist. Darum braucht die Kirche die wissenschaftliche Exegese, deren Forschungsfreiheit gerade durch diesen Konzilstext gesichert wird und deren Rang ausdrücklich anerkannt wird: durch ihre wissenschaftliche Vorarbeit reift erst das Urteil der Kirche. Die kritische Exegese ist indes nicht die einzige Methode, deren die Kirche bei der Beschäftigung mit der Schrift bedarf. Gleichsam ergänzend muß jene hinzukommen, "die auf den Inhalt und die Einheit der ganzen Schrift achtet unter Berücksichtigung der lebendigen Überlieferung der Gesamtkirche und der Analogie des Glaubens".

Die hier genannte Aufgabe, den Gesamtglauben der Kirche zu objektiveren und die Einzelinhalte und -aussagen in ihrer Zugehörigkeit zu ihm zu verstehen und auszulegen, ist ein entscheidender Auftrag in der Glaubenssituation der Gegenwart.

Das *IV. Kapitel* über das Alte Testament zeichnet die Heilsgeschichte in der Geschichte des Bundes Gottes mit Israel nach. Man braucht die Mängel dieses Kapitels nicht zu verschweigen, das der Tatsache, daß das Alte Testament das Heilige Buch Jesu und der Urgemeinde war und eine viel längere Erfahrung der Menschheit mit Gott enthält als das Neue Testament, kaum gerecht wird. Der "unvergängliche Wert" der Heiligen Schrift Israels wird hier doch eher in ihrer "göttlichen Erziehungskunst" auf Jesus Christus hin gesehen. Ein schwacher Ausgleich findet sich in Artikel 16: daß das Neue Testament auch erst im Licht des Alten Testaments ganz verstanden werden kann.

Nicht viel länger ist das *V. Kapitel* über das Neue Testament. Die Betonung liegt in eigentümlicher Weise, wie Artikel 18 auch ausdrücklich sagt, auf den vier Evangelien. Damit nimmt das Konzil auf seine Art die Frage nach dem "historischen Jesus" auf. Zunächst geht es auf den Ursprung der vier Evangelien ein. Das Konzil sagt sehr vorsichtig, sie seien apostolischen Ursprungs; die Überlieferung der Evangelien gehe auf die Apostel oder auf "apostolische Männer" zurück. Artikel 19 sucht die Frage anzugehen, in welchem Sinn und Ausmaß die Evangelien historisch geschehene Geschichte berichten. Der erste Entwurf hatte alle Exegeten verurteilt, die bezweifelten, daß alles, was die Evangelien berichten und wie sie es berichten, historische Wahrheit sei. Dieser Passus wurde schon zu Beginn der Überarbeitungen gestrichen. Gegen die vorletzte Fassung, die Evangelien böten Wahres und Ehrliches aus der schöpferischen Kraft der Urgemeinde, erhob die Minderheit auf dem Konzil stürmischen Protest, unterstützt vom Papst. Die Kommission strich die "schöpferische Kraft der Urgemeinde", ließ das "Wahre und Ehrliche" stehen und fügte im ersten Satz ein: "deren (d. h. der vier Evangelien) Geschichtlichkeit sie ohne Bedenken bejaht". Der Papst war damit einverstanden. Der Begriff "Geschichtlichkeit" ("historicitas") wird hier nicht erklärt und bedarf daher weiterer Studien. Der Einschub läßt selbstverständlich die Aussage von Artikel 12, daß es biblische Texte "von in *verschiedener* Weise geschichtlicher Art" gibt - die auch vom Neuen Testament gilt -, ganz unberührt. Der zweite Satz des Artikels macht sich die Ergebnisse der modernen Exegese behutsam zu eigen. Erster Schritt: Die Apostel haben, nachdem Jesus weggenommen worden war, aus einem volleren Verständnis Christi heraus gepredigt. Zweiter Schritt: Die Verfasser der Evangelien haben dieses so überlieferte Predigtmaterial "redigiert", nämlich ausgewählt, zusammengezogen, im Hinblick auf die Lage der Kirche verdeutlicht ("aktualisiert", wie die Exegeten sagen). Dabei haben sie die Form der Verkündigung (was wiederum die Gattungen und die Stilistik betrifft) beibehalten. Recht summarisch spricht Artikel 20 von den übrigen Büchern des Neuen Testaments. Die theologischen Interessen der neutestamentlichen Briefliteratur (und der Apg und der Apk) fanden offenbar nicht die besondere Aufmerksamkeit des Konzils.

Kapitel VI spricht über die Schrift im Leben der Kirche. Man darf es nicht "pastoral" mißverstehen. Artikel 21 und 26 bilden einen Rahmen, in dem die Verehrung des Wortes Gottes bzw. der Schrift mit der Verehrung der Eucharistie in Parallele gesetzt und so ein Thema fortgeführt wird, das schon in der Konstitution über die Liturgie (Artikel 7, 24, 51, 56) anklang. In Artikel 21 heißt es weiter, in der Schrift ("zusammen mit der Heiligen Überlieferung") sehe die Kirche "die höchste Richtschnur ihres Glaubens". Mit der Formulierung wollte man ursprünglich auf die evangelische Frage antworten, ob die Schrift für die Kirche Norm sei. Man vermied den Ausdruck "norma", verwendete aber das ebenso eindeutige "suprema regula". Die Aussageintention wird aber beeinträchtigt durch das "zusammen mit der Heiligen Überlieferung", einer Formulierung, die sich mit Kapitel II nur dann zu 1 voller Übereinstimmung bringen läßt, wenn die Tradition als bleibend lebendiges - und normatives - Schriftverständnis verstanden wird. Diese Intention wird insofern durchgehalten, als im folgenden von der Schrift allein die Rede ist. An ihr müssen sich Verkündigung, Predigt und Katechese orientieren. Artikel 22 beschäftigt sich damit, wie die Schrift in guten Übersetzungen an den heutigen Menschen herankommen könne, und öffnet die Tür für "ökumenische" Bibelübersetzungen. Artikel 23 weist die Exegeten auf ihre Aufgabe hin, dem Volk Gottes zu dienen, wiederholt aber auch Bekenntnis und Aufmunterung zu den wissenschaftlichen Methoden der Exegese. Artikel 24 wendet sich sehr summarisch der Frage zu, wie die genaue Beziehung zwischen Theologie und Heiliger Schrift zu denken ist. Hier heißt es: "Die heilige Theologie ruht auf dem geschriebenen Wort Gottes, zusammen mit der Heiligen Überlieferung, wie auf einem bleibenden Fundament." Das "zusammen mit der Heiligen Überlieferung" (vgl. Artikel 21) wurde spät zur Beruhigung der Konzilsminderheit eingefügt. Es darf aber nicht im Sinne der nachtridentinischen "Zweiquellentheorie" mißverstanden werden; vielmehr wurde der Antrag von 144 Vätern, hier vom "geschriebenen und überlieferten Wort Gottes" zu sprechen, ausdrücklich abgelehnt. Die Sätze, daß die Theologie sich ständig verjüngt, wenn sie "biblisch" ist, und daß das Studium der Schrift "gleichsam die Seele der Theologie" ist, sind wichtig. Aber stärker und praktischer, konkreter in der Anweisung ist die Ausdrucksweise im Dekret über die Ausbildung der Priester (dort Artikel 16). Auch dieser Artikel geht noch einmal auf die Verkündigung ein und hebt die Homilie hervor. Artikel 25 appelliert nachdrücklich an alle, die den Dienst am Wort haben, ständig Schriftlesung zu halten und die Bibel wissenschaftlich zu studieren. Eine eindringliche Mahnung zur Schriftlesung gilt sodann den Ordensleuten (im Blick auf das Problem der sogenannten "Betrachtung") und allen Gläubigen, denn - sagt das Konzil - wenn man die Schrift nicht kennt, kennt man Christus nicht. Die kirchlichen Vorsteher werden auf ihre Pflicht, für gute und gut kommentierte Bibelausgaben zu sorgen, hingewiesen. Sie sollen auch für Nichtchristen brauchbar sein.

Noch nie hat ein Konzil oder überhaupt das höchste Lehramt der katholischen Kirche so intensiv und so ausführlich über das Wort Gottes und über die Heilige Schrift gesprochen. Die Konstitution läßt die Forschungsfreiheit der Exegeten bestehen und erkennt die Legitimität ihrer wissenschaftlichen Methoden an. Sie greift nicht verurteilend in die innerkatholischen Kontroversen ein. Sie unterbindet den ökumenischen Dialog über Schrift und Tradition nicht. Und das ist weitaus mehr, als im November 1962 zu erhoffen war. Darüber hinaus entwirft sie ein Programm für das christliche Leben und für die Theologie, das auszuführen nicht wenig Mühe und Arbeit kosten wird.

Die Dogmatische Konstitution über die göttliche Offenbarung DEI VERBUM

VORWORT

1. Gottes Wort voll Ehrfurcht hörend und voll Zuversicht verkündigend, folgt die Heilige Synode den Worten des heiligen Johannes: "Wir künden euch das ewige Leben, das beim Vater war und uns erschien. Was wir gesehen und gehört haben, künden wir euch, damit auch ihr Gemeinschaft habt mit uns und unsere Gemeinschaft Gemeinschaft sei mit dem Vater und mit seinem Sohn Jesus Christus" (1 Joh 1,2-3). Darum will die Synode in Nachfolge des Trienter und des Ersten Vatikanischen Konzils die echte Lehre über die göttliche Offenbarung und deren Weitergabe vorlegen, damit die ganze Welt im Hören auf die Botschaft des Heiles glaubt, im Glauben hofft und in der Hoffnung liebt (1).

ERSTES KAPITEL

DIE OFFENBARUNG

2. Gott hat in seiner Güte und Weisheit beschlossen, sich selbst zu offenbaren und das Geheimnis seines Willens kundzutun (vgl. Eph 1,9): daß die Menschen durch Christus, das fleischgewordene Wort, im Heiligen Geist Zugang zum Vater haben und teilhaftig werden der göttlichen Natur (vgl. Eph 2,18; 2 Petr 1,4). In dieser Offenbarung redet der unsichtbare Gott (vgl. Kol 1,15; 1 Tim 1,17) aus überströmender Liebe die Menschen an wie Freunde (vgl. Ex 33,11; Joh 15,14-15) und verkehrt mit ihnen (vgl. Bar 3,38), um sie in seine Gemeinschaft einzuladen und aufzunehmen. Das Offenbarungsgeschehen ereignet sich in Tat und Wort, die innerlich miteinander verknüpft sind: die Werke nämlich, die Gott im Verlauf der Heilsgeschichte wirkt, offenbaren und bekräftigen die Lehre und die durch die Worte bezeichneten Wirklichkeiten; die Worte verkündigen die Werke und lassen das Geheimnis, das sie enthalten, ans Licht treten. Die Tiefe der durch diese Offenbarung über Gott und über das Heil des Menschen erschlossenen Wahrheit leuchtet uns auf in Christus, der zugleich der Mittler und die Fülle der ganzen Offenbarung ist (2).

3. Gott, der durch das Wort alles erschafft (vgl. Joh 1,3) und erhält, gibt den Menschen jederzeit in den geschaffenen Dingen Zeugnis von sich (vgl. Röm 1,19-20). Da er aber den Weg übernatürlichen Heiles eröffnen wollte, hat er darüber hinaus sich selbst schon am Anfang den Stammeltern kundgetan. Nach ihrem Fall hat er sie wiederaufgerichtet in Hoffnung auf das Heil, indem er die Erlösung versprach (vgl. Gen 3,15). Ohne Unterlaß hat er für das Menschengeschlecht gesorgt, um allen das ewige Leben zu geben, die das Heil suchen durch Ausdauer im guten Handeln (vgl. Röm. 2,6-7). Später berief er Abraham, um ihn zu einem großen Volk zu machen (vgl. Gen 12,2), das er dann nach den Patriarchen durch Moses und die Propheten erzog, ihn allein als lebendigen und wahren Gott, als fürsorgenden Vater und gerechten Richter anzuerkennen und auf den versprochenen Erlöser zu harren. So hat er dem Evangelium den Weg durch die Zeiten bereitet.

4. Nachdem Gott viele Male und auf viele Weisen durch die Propheten gesprochen hatte, "hat er zuletzt in diesen Tagen zu uns gesprochen im Sohn" (Hebr 1,1-2). Er hat seinen Sohn, das ewige Wort, das Licht aller Menschen, gesandt, damit er unter den Menschen wohne und ihnen vom Innern Gottes Kunde bringe (vgl. Joh 1,1-18). Jesus Christus, das fleischgewordene Wort, als "Mensch zu den Menschen" gesandt (3), "redet die Worte Gottes" (Joh 3,34) und vollendet das Heilswerk, dessen Durchführung der Vater ihm aufgetragen hat (vgl. Joh 5,36; 17,4). Wer ihn sieht, sieht auch den Vater (vgl. Joh 14,9). Er ist es, der durch sein ganzes Dasein und seine ganze Erscheinung, durch Worte und Werke, durch Zeichen und Wunder, vor allem aber durch seinen Tod und seine herrliche Auferstehung von den Toten, schließlich durch die Sendung des Geistes der Wahrheit die Offenbarung erfüllt und abschließt und durch göttliches Zeugnis bekräftigt, daß Gott mit uns ist, um uns aus der Finsternis von Sünde und Tod zu befreien und zu ewigem Leben zu erwecken.

Daher ist die christliche Heilsordnung, nämlich der neue und endgültige Bund, unüberholbar, und es ist keine neue öffentliche Offenbarung mehr zu erwarten vor der Erscheinung unseres Herrn Jesus Christus in Herrlichkeit (vgl. 1 Tim 6,14 und Tit 2,13).

5. Dem offenbarenden Gott ist der "Gehorsam des Glaubens" (Röm 16,26; vgl. Röm 1,5; 2 Kor 10,5-6) zu leisten. Darin überantwortet sich der Mensch Gott als ganzer in Freiheit, indem er sich "dem offenbarenden Gott mit Verstand und Willen voll unterwirft" (4) und seiner Offenbarung willig zustimmt. Dieser Glaube kann nicht vollzogen werden ohne die zuvorkommende und helfende Gnade Gottes und ohne den inneren Beistand des Heiligen Geistes, der das Herz bewegen und Gott zuwenden, die Augen des Verstandes öffnen und "es jedem leicht machen muß, der Wahrheit zuzustimmen und zu glauben" (5). Dieser Geist vervollkommnet den Glauben ständig durch seine Gaben, um das Verständnis der Offenbarung mehr und mehr zu vertiefen.

6. Durch seine Offenbarung wollte Gott sich selbst und die ewigen Entscheidungen seines Willens über das Heil der Menschen kundtun und mitteilen, "um Anteil zu geben am göttlichen Reichtum, der die Fassungskraft des menschlichen Geistes schlechthin übersteigt" (6).

Die Heilige Synode bekennt, "daß Gott, aller Dinge Ursprung und Ziel, mit dem natürlichen Licht der menschlichen Vernunft aus den geschaffenen Dingen sicher erkannt werden kann" (vgl. Röm 1,20); doch lehrt sie, seiner Offenbarung sei es zuzuschreiben, "daß, was im Bereich des Göttlichen der menschlichen Vernunft an sich nicht unzugänglich ist, auch in der gegenwärtigen Lage des Menschengeschlechtes von allen leicht, mit sicherer Gewißheit und ohne Beimischung von Irrtum erkannt werden kann" (7).

ZWEITES KAPITEL

DIE WEITERGABE DER GÖTTLICHEN OFFENBARUNG

7. Was Gott zum Heil aller Völker geoffenbart hatte, das sollte - so hat er in Güte verfügt - für alle Zeiten unversehrt erhalten bleiben und allen Geschlechtern weitergegeben werden. Darum hat Christus der Herr, in dem die ganze Offenbarung des höchsten Gottes sich vollendet (vgl. 2 Kor 1,20; 3,16-4,6), den Aposteln geboten, das Evangelium, das er als die Erfüllung der früher ergangenen prophetischen Verheißung selbst gebracht und persönlich öffentlich verkündet hat, allen zu predigen als die Quelle jeglicher Heilswahrheit und Sittenlehre (8) und ihnen so göttliche Gaben mitzuteilen. Das ist treu ausgeführt worden und zwar sowohl durch die Apostel, die durch mündliche Predigt, durch Beispiel und Einrichtungen weitergaben, was sie aus Christi Mund, im Umgang mit ihm und durch seine Werke empfangen oder was sie unter der Eingebung des Heiligen Geistes gelernt hatten, als auch durch jene Apostel und apostolischen Männer, die unter der Inspiration des gleichen Heiligen Geistes die Botschaft vom Heil niederschrieben (9).

Damit das Evangelium in der Kirche für immer unversehrt und lebendig bewahrt werde, haben die Apostel Bischöfe als Ihre Nachfolger zurückgelassen und ihnen "ihr eigenes Lehramt überliefert" (10). Diese Heilige Überlieferung und die Heilige Schrift beider Testamente sind gleichsam ein Spiegel, in dem die Kirche Gott, von dem sie alles empfängt, auf ihrer irdischen Pilgerschaft anschaut, bis sie hingeführt wird, ihn von Angesicht zu Angesicht zu sehen, so wie er ist (vgl. 1 Joh 3, 2).

8. Daher mußte die apostolische Predigt, die in den inspirierten Büchern besonders deutlichen Ausdruck gefunden hat, in ununterbrochener Folge bis zur Vollendung der Zeiten bewahrt werden.

Wenn die Apostel das, was auch sie empfangen haben, überliefern, mahnen sie die Gläubigen, die Überlieferungen, die sie in mündlicher Rede oder durch einen Brief gelernt haben (vgl. 2 Thess 2,15), festzuhalten und für den Glauben zu kämpfen, der ihnen ein für allemal überliefert wurde (vgl. Jud 3) (11). Was von den Aposteln überliefert wurde, umfaßt alles, was dem Volk Gottes hilft, ein heiliges Leben zu führen und den Glauben zu mehren. So führt die Kirche in Lehre, Leben und Kult durch die Zeiten weiter und übermittelt allen Geschlechtern alles, was sie selber ist, alles, was sie glaubt.

Diese apostolische Überlieferung kennt in der Kirche unter dem Beistand des Heiligen Geistes einen Fortschritts (12): es wächst das Verständnis der überlieferten Dinge und Worte durch das Nachsinnen und Studium der Gläubigen, die sie in ihrem Herzen erwägen (vgl. Lk 2,19.51), durch innere Einsicht, die aus geistlicher Erfahrung stammt, durch die Verkündigung derer, die mit der Nachfolge im Bischofsamt das sichere Charisma der Wahrheit empfangen haben; denn die Kirche strebt im Gang der Jahrhunderte ständig der Fülle der göttlichen Wahrheit entgegen, bis an ihr sich Gottes Worte erfüllen.

Die Aussagen der heiligen Väter bezeugen die lebenspendende Gegenwart dieser Überlieferung, deren Reichtümer sich in Tun und Leben der glaubenden und betenden Kirche ergießen. Durch dieselbe Überlieferung wird der Kirche der vollständige Kanon der Heiligen Bücher bekannt, in ihr werden die Heiligen Schriften selbst tiefer verstanden und unaufhörlich wirksam gemacht So ist Gott, der einst gesprochen hat, ohne Unterlaß im Gespräch mit der Braut seines geliebten Sohnes, und der Heilige Geist, durch den die lebendige Stimme des Evangeliums in der Kirche und durch sie in der Welt widerhallt, führt die Gläubigen in alle Wahrheit ein und läßt das Wort Christi in Überfülle unter ihnen wohnen (vgl. Kol 3,16).

9. Die Heilige Überlieferung und die Heilige Schrift sind eng miteinander verbunden und haben aneinander Anteil. Demselben göttlichen Quell entspringend, fließen beide gewissermaßen eins zusammen und streben demselben Ziel zu. Denn die Heilige Schrift ist Gottes Rede, insofern sie unter dem Anhauch des Heiligen Geistes schriftlich aufgezeichnet wurde. Die Heilige Überlieferung aber gibt das Wort Gottes, das von Christus dem Herrn und vom Heiligen Geist den Aposteln anvertraut wurde unversehrt an deren Nachfolger weiter, damit sie es unter der erleuchtenden Führung des Geistes der Wahrheit in ihrer Verkündigung treu bewahren, erklären und ausbreiten. So ergibt sich, daß die Kirche ihre Gewißheit über alles Geoffenbarte nicht aus der Heiligen Schrift allein schöpft. Daher sollen beide mit gleicher Liebe und Achtung angenommen und verehrt werden (13).

10. Die Heilige Überlieferung und die Heilige Schrift bilden den einen der Kirche überlassenen heiligen Schatz des Wortes Gottes. Voller Anhänglichkeit an ihn verharrt das ganze heilige Volk, mit seinen Hirten vereint, ständig in der Lehre und Gemeinschaft der Apostel, bei Brotbrechen und Gebet (vgl. Apg 8,42 griech.), so daß im Festhalten am überlieferten Glauben in seiner Verwirklichung und seinem Bekenntnis ein einzigartiger Einklang herrscht zwischen Vorstehern und Gläubigen (14).

Die Aufgabe aber, das geschriebene oder überlieferte (15) Wort Gottes verbindlich zu erklären, ist nur dem lebendigen Lehramt der Kirche anvertraut (16), dessen Vollmacht im Namen Jesu Christi ausgeübt wird. Das Lehramt ist nicht über dem Wort Gottes, sondern dient ihm, indem es nichts lehrt, als was überliefert ist, weil es das Wort Gottes aus göttlichem Auftrag und mit dem Beistand des Heiligen Geistes voll Ehrfurcht hört, heilig bewahrt und treu auslegt und weil es alles, was es als von Gott geoffenbart zu glauben vorlegt, aus diesem einen Schatz des Glaubens schöpft.

Es zeigt sich also, daß die Heilige Überlieferung, die Heilige Schrift und das Lehramt der Kirche gemäß dem weisen Ratschluß Gottes so miteinander verknüpft und einander zugesellt sind, daß keines ohne die anderen besteht und daß alle zusammen, jedes auf seine Art, durch das Tun des einen Heiligen Geistes wirksam dem Heil der Seelen dienen.

DRITTES KAPITEL

DIE GÖTTLICHE INSPIRATION UND DIE AUSLEGUNG DER HEILIGEN SCHRIFT

11. Das von Gott Geoffenbarte, das in der Heiligen Schrift enthalten ist und vorliegt, ist unter dem Anhauch des Heiligen Geistes aufgezeichnet worden; denn aufgrund apostolischen Glaubens gelten unserer heiligen Mutter, der Kirche, die Bücher des Alten wie des Neuen Testamentes in ihrer Ganzheit mit allen ihren Teilen als heilig und kanonisch, weil sie, unter der Einwirkung des Heiligen

Geistes geschrieben (vgl. Joh 20,31; 2 Tim 3,16, 2 Petr 1,19-21; 3,15-16), Gott zum Urheber haben und als solche der Kirche übergeben sind (17). Zur Abfassung der Heiligen Bücher hat Gott Menschen erwählt, die ihm durch den Gebrauch ihrer eigenen Fähigkeiten und Kräfte dazu dienen sollten (18), all das und nur das, was er - in ihnen und durch sie wirksam (19) - geschrieben haben wollte, als echte Verfasser schriftlich zu überliefern (20).

Da also alles, was die inspirierten Verfasser oder Hagiographen aussagen, als vom Heiligen Geist ausgesagt zu gelten hat, ist von den Büchern der Schrift zu bekennen, daß sie sicher getreu und ohne Irrtum die Wahrheit lehren, die Gott um unseres Heiles willen in heiligen Schriften aufgezeichnet haben wollte (21). Daher "ist jede Schrift, von Gott eingegeben, auch nützlich zur Belehrung, zur Beweisführung, zur Zurechtweisung, zur Erziehung in der Gerechtigkeit, damit der Gott gehörige Mensch bereit sei, wohlgerüstet zu jedem guten Werk" (2 Tim 3,16-17 griech.).

12. Da Gott in der Heiligen Schrift durch Menschen nach Menschenart gesprochen hat (22), muß der Schrifterklärer, um zu erfassen, was Gott uns mitteilen wollte, sorgfältig erforschen, was die heiligen Schriftsteller wirklich zu sagen beabsichtigten und was Gott mit ihren Worten kundtun wollte.

Um die Aussageabsicht der Hagiographen zu ermitteln, ist neben anderem auf die literarischen Gattungen zu achten. Denn die Wahrheit wird je anders dargelegt und ausgedrückt in Texten von in verschiedenem Sinn geschichtlicher, prophetischer oder dichterischer Art, oder in anderen Redegattungen. Weiterhin hat der Erklärer nach dem Sinn zu forschen, wie ihn aus einer gegebenen Situation heraus der Hagiograph den Bedingungen seiner Zeit und Kultur entsprechend - mit Hilfe der damals üblichen literarischen Gattungen - hat ausdrücken wollen und wirklich zum Ausdruck gebracht hat (23). Will man richtig verstehen, was der heilige Verfasser in seiner Schrift aussagen wollte, so muß man schließlich genau auf die vorgegebenen umweltbedingten Denk-, Sprach und Erzählformen achten, die zur Zeit des Verfassers herrschten, wie auf die Formen, die damals im menschlichen Alltagsverkehr üblich waren (24).

Da die Heilige Schrift in dem Geist gelesen und ausgelegt werden muß, in dem sie geschrieben wurde (25), erfordert die rechte Ermittlung des Sinnes der heiligen Texte, daß man mit nicht geringerer Sorgfalt auf den Inhalt und die Einheit der ganzen Schrift achtet, unter Berücksichtigung der lebendigen Überlieferung der Gesamtkirche und der Analogie des Glaubens. Aufgabe der Exegeten ist es, nach diesen Regeln auf eine tiefere Erfassung und Auslegung des Sinnes der Heiligen Schrift hinzuarbeiten damit so gleichsam auf Grund wissenschaftlicher Vorarbeit das Urteil der Kirche reift. Alles, was die Art der Schrifterklärung betrifft, untersteht letztlich dem Urteil der Kirche, deren gottgegebener Auftrag und Dienst es ist, das Wort Gottes zu bewahren und auszulegen (26).

13. In der Heiligen Schrift also offenbart sich, unbeschadet der Wahrheit und Heiligkeit Gottes, eine wunderbare Herablassung der ewigen Weisheit, "damit wir die unsagbare Menschenfreundlichkeit Gottes kennenlernen und erfahren, wie sehr er sich aus Sorge für unser Geschlecht in seinem Wort herabgelassen hat" (27). Denn Gottes Worte, durch Menschenzunge formuliert, sind menschlicher Rede ähnlich geworden, wie einst des ewigen Vaters Wort durch die Annahme menschlich-schwachen Fleisches den Menschen ähnlich geworden ist.

VIERTES KAPITEL

DAS ALTE TESTAMENT

14. Der liebende Gott, der um das Heil des ganzen Menschengeschlechtes besorgt war, bereitete es vor, indem er sich nach seinem besonderen Plan ein Volk erwählte, um ihm Verheißungen anzuvertrauen. Er schloß mit Abraham (vgl. Gen 15,8) und durch Moses mit dem Volke Israel (vgl. Ex 24,8) einen Bund. Dann hat er sich dem Volk, das er sich erworben hatte, durch Wort und Tat als einzigen, wahren und lebendigen Gott so geoffenbart, daß Israel Gottes Wege mit den Menschen an sich erfuhr, daß es sie durch Gottes Wort aus der Propheten Mund allmählich voller und klarer erkannte und sie unter den Völkern mehr und mehr sichtbar machte (vgl. Ps 21,28-29; 95,1-3; Jes 2,1-4; Jer 3,17). Die Geschichte des Heiles liegt, von heiligen Verfassern vorausverkündet, berichtet und gedeutet, als wahres Wort Gottes vor in den Büchern des Alten Bundes; darum beinhalten diese von Gott eingegebenen Schriften ihren unvergänglichen Wert: "Alles nämlich, was geschrieben steht, ist zu unserer Unterweisung geschrieben, damit wir durch die Geduld und den Trost der Schriften Hoffnung haben" (Röm 15,4).

15. Gottes Geschichtsplan im Alten Bund zielte vor allem darauf das Kommen Christi, des Erlösers des Alls, und das Kommen des messianischen Reiches vorzubereiten, prophetisch anzukündigen (vgl. Lk 24,44; Joh 5,39; 1 Petr 1,10) und in verschiedenen Vorbildern anzuzeigen (vgl. 1 Kor 10,11). Die Bücher des Alten Bundes erschließen allen entsprechend der Lage, in der sich das Menschengeschlecht vor der Wiederherstellung des Heils in Christus befand, Wissen über Gott und Mensch und erschließen die Art und Weise, wie der gerechte und barmherzige Gott an den Menschen zu handeln pflegt. Obgleich diese Bücher auch Unvollkommenes und Zeitbedingtes enthalten, zeigen sie doch eine wahre göttliche Erziehungskunst (28). Ein lebendiger Sinn für Gott drückt sich in ihnen aus. Hohe Lehren über Gott, heilbringende menschliche Lebensweisheit, wunderbare Gebetsschätze sind in ihnen aufbewahrt. Schließlich ist das Geheimnis unseres Heiles in ihnen verborgen. Deshalb sollen diese Bücher von denen, die an Christus glauben, voll Ehrfurcht angenommen werden.

16. Gott, der die Bücher beider Bünde inspiriert hat und ihr Urheber ist, wollte in Weisheit, daß der Neue im Alten verborgen und der Alte im Neuen erschlossen sei (29). Denn wenn auch Christus in seinem Blut einen Neuen Bund gestiftet hat (vgl. Lk 22,20; 1 Kor 11,25), erhalten und offenbaren die Bücher des Alten Bundes, die als Ganzes in die Verkündigung des Evangeliums aufgenommen wurden (30), erst im Neuen Bund ihren vollen Sinn (vgl. Mt 5,17; Lk 24,27; Röm. 16, 25-26; 2 Kor 3,14-16), wie sie diesen wiederum beleuchten und deuten.

FÜNFTES KAPITEL

DAS NEUE TESTAMENT

17. Das Wort Gottes, Gottes Kraft zum Heil für jeden, der glaubt (vgl. Röm. 1,16), kommt zu einzigartiger Darstellung und Kraftentfaltung in den Schriften des Neuen Bundes; denn als die Fülle der Zeit kam (vgl. Gal 4, 4), ist das Wort Fleisch geworden und hat unter uns gewohnt, voll Gnade und Wahrheit (vgl. Joh 1,14). Christus hat das Reich Gottes auf Erden wiederhergestellt, in Tat und Wort seinen Vater und sich selbst geoffenbart und sein Werk durch Tod, Auferstehung, herrliche Himmelfahrt und Sendung des Heiligen Geistes vollendet. Von der Erde erhöht zieht er alle an sich (vgl. Joh 12,32 griech.); denn er allein hat Worte des ewigen Lebens (vgl. Joh 6,68). Anderen Geschlechtern ward dieses Geheimnis nicht kundgetan, wie es nun geoffenbart worden ist seinen heiligen Aposteln und Propheten im Heiligen Geist (vgl. Eph 3,4-6 griech.), damit sie das Evangelium verkünden, den Glauben an Jesus als Christus und Herrn wecken und die Kirche sammeln. Dafür sind die Schriften des Neuen Bundes das unvergängliche und göttliche Zeugnis.

18. Niemandem kann es entgehen, daß unter allen Schriften, auch unter denen des Neuen Bundes, den Evangelien mit Recht ein Vorrang zukommt. Denn sie sind das Hauptzeugnis für Leben und Lehre des fleischgewordenen Wortes, unseres Erlösers.

Am apostolischen Ursprung der vier Evangelien hat die Kirche immer und überall festgehalten und hält daran fest; denn was die Apostel nach Christi Gebot gepredigt haben, das haben später unter dem Anhauch des Heiligen Geistes sie selbst und Apostolische Männer uns als Fundament des Glaubens schriftlich überliefert: das viergestaltige Evangelium nach Matthäus, Markus, Lukas und Johannes (31).

19. Unsere heilige Mutter, die Kirche, hat entschieden und unentwegt daran festgehalten und hält daran fest, daß die genannten Evangelien, deren Geschichtlichkeit sie ohne Bedenken denken bejaht, zuverlässig überliefern, was Jesus, der Sohn Gottes, in seinem Leben unter den Menschen zu deren ewigem Heil wirklich getan und gelehrt hat bis zu dem Tag, da er auf genommen wurde (vgl. Apg 1,1-2). Die Apostel haben nach der Auffahrt des Herrn das, was er selbst gesagt und getan hatte ihren Hörern mit jenem volleren Verständnis überliefert, das ihnen aus der Erfahrung der Verherrlichung Christi und aus dem Licht des Geistes der Wahrheit (32) zufloß (33). Die biblischen Verfasser aber haben die vier Evangelien redigiert, indem sie einiges aus dem vielen auswählten, das mündlich oder auch schon schriftlich überliefert war, indem sie anderes zu Überblicken zusammenzogen oder im Hinblick auf die Lage in den Kirchen verdeutlichten, indem sie schließlich die Form der Verkündigung beibehielten, doch immer so, daß ihre Mitteilungen über Jesus wahr und ehrlich waren (34). Denn ob sie nun aus eigenem Gedächtnis und Erinnern schrieben oder auf Grund des Zeugnisses jener, "die von Anfang an Augenzeugen und Diener des Wortes waren", es ging ihnen immer darum, daß wir die "Wahrheit" der Worte erkennen sollten, von denen wir Kunde erhalten haben (vgl. Lk 1,2-4).

20. Der neutestamentliche Kanon umfaßt außer den vier Evangelien auch die Briefe des heiligen Paulus und andere apostolische Schriften, die unter der Eingebung des Heiligen Geistes verfaßt sind. In ihnen wird nach Gottes weisem Ratschluß die Botschaft von Christus dem Herrn bestätigt, seine echte Lehre mehr und mehr erklärt, die heilbringende Kraft des göttlichen Werkes Christi verkündet; die Anfange der Kirche und ihre wunderbare Ausbreitung werden erzählt und ihre herrliche Vollendung vorausverkündet.

Denn der Herr Jesus ist bei seinen Aposteln geblieben, wie er verheißen hatte (vgl. Mt 28,20), und hat ihnen als Beistand den Geist gesandt, der sie in die Fülle der Wahrheit einfuhren sollte (vgl. Joh 16,13).

SECHSTES KAPITEL

DIE HEILIGE SCHRIFT IM LEBEN DER KIRCHE

21. Die Kirche hat die Heiligen Schriften immer verehrt wie den Herrenleib selbst, weil sie, vor allem in der heiligen Liturgie, vom Tisch des Wortes Gottes wie des Leibes Christi ohne Unterlaß das Brot des Lebens nimmt und den Gläubigen reicht. In ihnen zusammen mit der Heiligen Überlieferung sah sie immer und sieht sie die höchste Richtschnur ihres Glaubens, weil sie, von Gott eingegeben und ein Für alle Male niedergeschrieben, das Wort Gottes selbst unwandelbar vermitteln und in den Worten der Propheten und der Apostel die Stimme des Heiligen Geistes vernehmen lassen. Wie die christliche Religion selbst, so muß auch jede kirchliche Verkündigung sich von der Heiligen Schrift nähren und sich an ihr orientieren. In den Heiligen Büchern kommt ja der Vater, der im Himmel ist, seinen Kindern in Liebe entgegen und nimmt mit ihnen das Gespräch auf. Und solche Gewalt und Kraft west im Worte Gottes, daß es für die Kirche Halt und Leben, für die Kinder der Kirche Glaubensstärke, Seelenspeise und reiner, unversieglicher Quell des geistlichen Lebens ist. Darum gelten von der Heiligen Schrift in besonderer Weise die Worte: "Lebendig ist Gottes Rede und wirksam" (Hebr 4,12), "mächtig aufzubauen und das Erbe auszuteilen unter allen Geheiligten" (Apg 20,32; vgl. 1 Thess 2,13).

22. Der Zugang zur Heiligen Schrift muß für die an Christus Glaubenden weit offenstehen. Darum hat die Kirche schon in ihren Anfängen die älteste Übersetzung des Alten Testamentes, die griechische, die nach den Siebzig (Septuaginta) benannt wird, als die ihre übernommen. Die anderen orientalischen und die lateinischen Übersetzungen, besonders die sogenannte Vulgata, hält sie immer in Ehren. Da aber das Wort Gottes allen Zeiten zur Verfügung stehen muß, bemüht sich die Kirche in mütterlicher Sorge, daß brauchbare und genaue Übersetzungen in die verschiedenen Sprachen erarbeitet werden, mit Vorrang aus dem Urtext der Heiligen Bücher. Wenn die Übersetzungen bei sich bietender Gelegenheit und mit Zustimmung der kirchlichen Autorität in Zusammenarbeit auch mit den getrennten Brüdern Zustande kommen, dann können sie von allen Christen benutzt werden.

23. Die Braut des fleischgewordenen Wortes, die Kirche, bemüht sich, vom Heiligen Geist belehrt, zu einem immer tieferen Ver. Verständnis der Heiligen Schriften vorzudringen, um ihre Kinder unablässig mit dem Worte Gottes zu nähren; darum fordert Sie auch in gebührender Weise das Studium der Väter des Ostens wie des Westens und der heiligen Liturgien. Die katholischen Exegeten und die anderen Vertreter der theologischen Wissenschaft müssen in eifriger Zusammenarbeit sich darum mühen, unter Aufsicht des kirchlichen Lehramts mit passenden Methoden den die göttlichen Schriften so zu erforschen und auszulegen, daß möglichst viele Diener des Wortes in den Stand gesetzt werden, dem Volke Gottes mit wirklichem Nutzen die Nahrung der Schriften zu reichen, die den Geist erleuchtet, den Wille stärkt und die Menschenherzen zur Gottesliebe entflammt (35). Die Heilige Synode ermutigt die Söhne der Kirche, die Bibelwissenschaft treiben, das glücklich begonnene Werk mit immer neuen Kräften und ganzer Hingabe im Geist der Kirche fortzuführen (36).

24. Die heilige Theologie ruht auf dem geschriebenen Wort Gottes, zusammen mit der Heiligen Überlieferung, wie auf einem bleibenden Fundament. In ihm gewinnt sie sichere Kraft und verjüngt sich ständig, wenn sie alle im Geheimnis Christi beschlossene Wahrheit im Lichte des Glaubens durchforscht. Die Heiligen Schriften enthalten das Wort Gottes und, weil inspiriert, sind sie wahrhaft Wort Gottes: Deshalb sei das Studium des heiligen Buches gleichsam die Seele der heiligen Theologie (37). Auch der Dienst des Wortes, nämlich die seelsorgliche Verkündigung, die Katechese und alle christliche Unterweisung - in welcher die liturgische Homilie einen hervorragenden Platz haben muß - holt aus dem Wort der Schrift gesunde Nahrung und heilige Kraft.

25. Darum müssen alle Kleriker, besonders Christi Priester und die anderen, die sich als Diakone oder Katecheten ihrem Auftrag entsprechend dem Dienst des Wortes widmen, in beständiger heiliger Lesung und gründlichem Studium sich mit der Schrift befassen, damit keiner von ihnen werde zu "einem hohlen und äußerlichen Prediger des Wortes Gottes, ohne dessen innerer Hörer zu sein" (38), wo er doch die unübersehbaren Schätze des göttlichen Wortes namentlich in der heiligen Liturgie, den ihm anvertrauten Gläubigen mitteilen soll. Ebenso ermahnt die Heilige Synode alle an Christus Glaubenden, zumal die Glieder religiöser Gemeinschaften, besonders eindringlich, durch häufige Lesung der Heiligen Schrift sich die "alles übertreffende Erkenntnis Jesu Christi" (Phil. 3,8) anzueignen. "Die Schrift nicht kennen heißt Christus nicht kennen." (39) Sie sollen deshalb gern an den heiligen Text selbst herantreten, einmal in der mit göttlichen Worten gesättigten heiligen Liturgie, dann in frommer Lesung oder auch durch geeignete Institutionen und andere Hilfsmittel, die heute mit Billigung und auf Veranlassung der Hirten der Kirche lobenswerterweise allenthalben verbreitet werden. Sie sollen daran denken, daß Gebet die Lesung der Heiligen Schrift begleiten muß, damit sie zu einem Gespräch werde zwischen Gott und Mensch; denn "ihn reden wir an, wenn wir beten; ihn hören wir, wenn wir Gottes Weisungen lesen" (40).

Die kirchlichen Vorsteher, "bei denen die Lehre der Apostel ist" (41), sollen die ihnen anvertrauten Gläubigen zum rechten Gebrauch der Heiligen Bücher, namentlich des Neuen Testamentes und in erster Linie der Evangelien, in geeigneter Weise anleiten durch Übersetzungen der heiligen Texte, die mit den notwendigen und wirklich ausreichenden Erklärungen versehen sind, damit die Kinder der Kirche sicher und mit Nutzen mit den Heiligen Schriften umgehen und von ihrem Geist durchdrungen werden.

Darüber hinaus sollen mit entsprechenden Anmerkungen versehene Ausgaben der Heiligen Schrift geschaffen werden, die auch Nichtchristen gebrauchen können und die ihren Verhältnissen angepaßt sind. Die Seelsorger und die Christen jeden Standes sollen auf jede Weise klug für ihre Verbreitung sorgen.

26. So möge durch Lesung und Studium der Heiligen Bücher "Gottes Wort seinen Lauf nehmen und verherrlicht werden" (2 Thess 3,1). Der Schatz der Offenbarung, der Kirche anvertraut, erfülle mehr und mehr die Herzen der Menschen. Wie das Leben der Kirche sich mehrt durch die ständige Teilnahme am eucharistischen Geheimnis, so darf man neuen Antrieb für das geistliche Leben erhoffen aus der gesteigerten Verehrung des Wortes Gottes, welches "bleibt in Ewigkeit" (Jes 40,8; vgl. 1 Petr 1,23-25).

Anmerkungen

1. Vgl. Augustinus, Büchlein vom ersten katechetischen Unterricht, Kap. IV: PL 40, 3.
2. Vgl. Mt 11,27; Joh 1,14-17; 14,6; 17,1-3; 2 Kor 3,16; 4, 6 Eph 1,3-14.
3. Brief an Diognet VII, 4: F. X. Funk, Patres Apostolici I (Tübingen 1901) 403.
4. I. Vat. Konzil, Dogm. Konst. über den katholischen Glauben, Kap. 3: Denz. 1789 (3008).
5. II. Konzil von Orange, can. 7: Denz. 180 (377); I. Vat. Konzil, a. a. O.: Denz. 1791 (3010).
6. I. Vat. Konzil, Dogm. Konst. über den katholischen Glauben, Kap. 2: Denz. 1786 (3005).
7. Ebd.: Denz. 1785 und 1786 (3004 und 3005).
8. Vgl. Mt 28,19-20 und Mk 16,15. Konzil von Trient, Sess. IV, Dekret über die kanonischen Schriften: Denz. 783 (1501).
9. Vgl. Konzil von Trient, a. a. O.; I. Vat. Konzil, Sess. III, Dogm. Konst. über den katholischen Glauben, Kap. 2: Denz. 1787 (3006).
10. Irenäus, Adv. Haer. III, 3,1: PG 7, 848; Harvey 2, 9.
11. Vgl. II. Konzil von Nicaea: Denz. 303 (602). IV. Konzil von Konstantinopel, Sess. X, can. 1: Denz. 336 (650-652).
12. Vgl. I. Vat. Konzil, Dogm. Konst. über den katholischen Glauben, Kap. 4: Denz. 1800 (3020).
13. Vgl. Konzil von Trient, a. a. O.: Dekret über die kanonischen Schriften: Denz. 783 (1501).
14. Vgl. Pius XII., Apost. Konst. Munificentissimus Deus, 1. Nov. 1950: AAS 42 (1950) 756. Vgl. die Worte Cyprians: "die Kirche, das mit dem Priester vereinte Volk und die ihrem Hirten anhängende Herde", Ep. 66, 8: Hartel III/2, 733.
15. Vgl. I. Vat. Konzil, Dogm. Konst. über den katholischen Glauben, Kap. 3: Denz. 1792 (3011).

16. Vgl. Pius XII., Enz. Humani generis, 12. Aug. 1950: AAS 42 (1950) 568-569; Denz. 2314 (3886).
17. Vgl. I. Vat. Konzil, Dogm. Konst. über den katholischen Glauben, Kap. 2: Denz. 1787 (3006); Bibelkommission, Dekret, 18. Juni 1915: Denz. 2180 (3629) und Ench. Bibl. 420; Hl. Officium, Brief, 22. Dez. 1923: Ench. Bibl. 499.
18. Vgl. Pius XII., Enz. Divino affiante, 30. Sept. 1943: AAS 35 (1943) 314; Ench. Bibl. 556.
19. In und durch den Menschen: vgl. Hebr. 1,1; 4,7 (in); 2 Sam 23,2; Mt 1,22 und passim (durch); I. Vat. Konzil, Schema über die katholische Lehre, Note 9: Coll. Lac. VII, 522.
20. Leo XIII., Enz. Providentissimus Deus, 18. Nov. 1893: Denz. 1952 (3293); Ench. Bibl. 125.
21. Vgl. Augustinus, De Gen. ad litt. 2, 9, 20: PL 34, 270-271; CSEL 28, 1, 46-47 und Brief 82, 3: PL 33, 277; CSEL 3XXXIV/2 354; Thomas v. Aquin, De ver. q. 12, a. 2, C; Konzil von Trient, Dekret über die kanonischen Schriften: Denz. 783 (1501); Leo XIII., Enz. Providentissimus Deus: Ench. Bibl. 121 124 126 -127, Pius XII., Enz. Divino afflante Spiritu: Ench. Bibl. 539.
22. Augustinus, De Civ. Dei XVII, 6, 2: PL 41, 537, CSEL XL/ 2 228.
23. Augustinus, De Doctr. Christ. III, 18, 26: PL 34, 75-76.
24. Pius XII., a. a. O.: Denz 2294 (3829-3830); Ench. Bibl. 557-562.
25. Vgl. Benedikt XV., Enz. Spiritus Paraclitus, 15. Sept. 1920: Ench. Bibl. 469; Hieronymus, In Gal. 19-21: PL 26, 417 A.
26. Vgl. I. Vat. Konzil, Konst. über den katholischen Glauben, Kap. 2: Denz. 1788 (3007).
27. Johannes Chrysostomus, In Gn. 3,8 (hom. 17,1): PG 53,134: "herabgelassen", lateinisch "attemperatio", griechisch "synkatábasis".
28. Pius XI., Enz. Mit brennender Sorge, 14. März 1937: AAS 29 (1937) 151
29. Augustinus, Quaest. in Hept. 2, 73: PL 34, 623.
30. Irenäus, Adv. Haer. III, 21, 3: PG 7, 950 (= 25, 1: Harvey 2, 115), Cynll von Jerusalem, Catech. 4,35: PG 33,497; Theodor von Mopsuestia, In Soph. 1,4-6: PG 66, 452 D-453 A.
31. 1 Irenäus, Adv. Haer. III, 11, 8: PG 7, 885; Ausg. Sagnard, 194.
32. Vgl. Joh 14,26; 16,13.
33. Vgl. Joh 2,22; 16,16; vgl. 14,26; 16,12-13; 7,39.
34. Vgl. die Instruktion Sancta Mater Ecclesia der Päpstlichen Bibelkommission: AAS 56 (1964) 715
35. Vgl. Pius XII., Enz. Divino afflante Spiritu: Ench. Bibl. 551 553 567, Päpstl. Bibelkommission, Instruktion über die rechte Art, in Klerikalseminarien und Ordenskollegien über die Bibel zu dozieren, 30. Mai 1950: AAS 42 (1950) 495-505.
36. Pius XII., Enz. Divino afflante Spiritu: Ench. Bibl. 569.
37. Vgl. Leo XIII., Enz. Providentissimus Deus: Ench. Bibl. 114, Benedikt XV., Enz. Spiritus Paraclitus: Ench. Bibl. 483.
38. Augustinus, Serm. 179, 1: PL 38, 966.
39. Hieronymus, Comm. in Is., Prol.: PL 24,17; vgl. Benedikt XV., Enz. Spiritus Paraclitus: Ench. Bibl. 475-480; Pius XII., Enz. Divino afflante Spiritu: Ench. Bibl. 544.
40. Ambrosius, De officiis ministrorum I, 20, 88; PL 16, 50.
41. Irenäus, Adv. Haer. IV, 32, 1: PG 7, 1071 (= 49, 2: Harvey 2, 255).

The New York Times

THE POPE IN THE HOLY LAND: THE MISSION; Visit Casts Pope as Ally To 2 Sides In Mideast

By WILLIAM A. ORME JR.

It is officially a personal pilgrimage. But as Pope John Paul II makes his first visit to Israel and the Palestinian territories, he also comes as a head of state who has sought to persuade leaders on both sides that he is a crucial temporal ally.

To his Israeli admirers, John Paul is the pope who finally extended full recognition to their country -- a step consistent with his earlier decisions to become the first pope to pray in a synagogue, the first to acknowledge Catholic culpability in the Holocaust, the first to declare anti-Semitism a sin "against God and man."

His scheduled stop on Thursday at President Ezer Weizman's official residence in Jerusalem has been hailed as nothing less than a Christian affirmation of the Jewish right to a sovereign homeland, with Jerusalem as its capital. It is the culmination of a two-decade-long process that led to the exchange of ambassadors in 1994 and a 1997 agreement guaranteeing administrative autonomy but state protection to 1,130 Catholic institutions and "sacred places" within Israel.

The pope's arrival is "a monumental turning point" in Israel's relations with the Christian world, Prime Minister Ehud Barak said.

For Palestinian leaders, John Paul II is the pope who began his papacy by telling the United Nations in 1979 that Middle East peace talks "cannot fail to include the consideration and just settlement of the Palestinian question." In 1982 he received Yasir Arafat, chairman of the Palestine Liberation Organization, who would visit eight more times. Mr. Arafat may have had more meetings with a sitting pope than any practicing Muslim in history. In 1994, after the pact with Israel, John Paul II also established relations with the Palestinians.

Just a month ago, in a pact analogous to its 1997 accord with Israel, the Holy See recognized Mr. Arafat's group as a guardian of Catholic property in Palestinian territory -- with the Palestinians in return guaranteeing freedom of worship for Christians. And today, in what the Palestinian Authority considers a blessing on its quest for independence, the pope entered its territory with the full pomp of an official visit.

Throughout, Vatican diplomacy has been dictated by its own ecclesiastical interests.

The Holy See has sought to safeguard Christian shrines and the Christian minority in the Holy Land, insisting for decades on the "internationalization" of Jerusalem's ancient core -- a demand rejected, in one of their few points of concurrence, by bothIsraelis and Palestinians, who lay claim to the city as their capital.

But though the pope is perceived by many Israelis and Palestinians as the best friend either has had in the Vatican, his image in both camps is still colored by old political and religious antagonism.

Many Palestinians, who are overwhelmingly Muslim, see the pope as an advocate for the tiny but wealthy and Westernized Christian minority. Yet most Arab Christians belong to the Eastern Orthodox church, which is the dominant Christian denomination in the Holy Land and rejects the Vatican's claim to speak for the entire Christian world. To the Muslim faithful, the standing of the Roman Catholic Church in the region is further marred by the history of the Crusaders, who are reviled as Islam's barbarous enemies.

But it is the Israeli-Vatican relationship that is the most charged, because of the Jewish roots of Christianity and the Christian roots of anti-Semitism. The assumption on all sides here is that when the Palestinians declare statehood, Vatican recognition will be almost automatic -- in sharp and, to Israelis, hurtful contrast to the 45 years it took for the Holy See to acknowledge Israel's existence.

For Catholics, Paul VI, who made the first papal pilgrimage to the Holy Land in 1964, may have been an ecumenically minded reformer in the tradition of his predecessor, John XXIII. But Israelis could not forget that Paul, the first pope to visit their country -- in a side trip from Jordan -- never once uttered its name.

Still, as Shlomo Ben-Ami, the scholarly security minister, reminded an Israeli audience the other day, it was the theological revolution under Paul VI that opened the door to John Paul's embrace of Israel.

No longer were Catholics taught that the "perfidious" Jews had been collectively punished for Jesus' crucifixion with banishment from the Holy Land. Instead the Vatican declared in 1965 that the death of Jesus "cannot be charged against all the Jews then alive, without distinction, nor against the Jews of today." Going further, it explicitly embraced Christianity's Jewish heritage and condemned anti-Semitic acts "at any time and by anyone."

Correction: March 26, 2000

Because of an editing error, an article on Thursday about the pope's relations with Israel and the Palestinians misstated the number of Roman Catholic institutions and "sacred places" in Israel that are guaranteed administrative autonomy and state protection under a 1997 agreement between Israel and the Vatican. It is 130, not 1,130.

The TimesMachine archive viewer is a subscriber-only feature.

We are continually improving the quality of our text archives. Please send feedback, error reports, and suggestions to archive_feedback@nytimes.com.

A version of this article appears in print on March 23, 2000, on Page A00008 of the National edition with the headline: THE POPE IN THE HOLY LAND: THE MISSION; Visit Casts Pope as Ally To 2 Sides In Mideast.

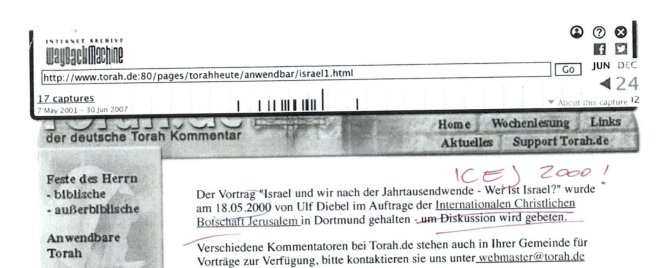
der deutsche Torah Kommentar

Home | Wochenlesung | Links
Aktuelles | Support Torah.de

Feste des Herrn
- biblische
- außerbiblische

Anwendbare
Torah

ICEJ 2000 !

Der Vortrag "Israel und wir nach der Jahrtausendwende - Wer ist Israel?" wurde am 18.05.2000 von Ulf Diebel im Auftrage der Internationalen Christlichen Botschaft Jerusalem in Dortmund gehalten - um Diskussion wird gebeten.

Verschiedene Kommentatoren bei Torah.de stehen auch in Ihrer Gemeinde für Vorträge zur Verfügung, bitte kontaktieren sie uns unter webmaster@torah.de

Israel und wir nach der Jahrtausendwende
Wer ist Israel?

In den letzten 52 Jahren, nach der Gründung des Staates Israel, ist dieses kleine Land immer mehr in das Zentrum der Schlagzeilen in den Medien der Welt gerückt. Leider sind dies häufig keine schönen Bilder. Religiöser Fanatismus, Straßenschlachten, Terror, Landstreitigkeiten und Kriege werden als alltägliches Bild in Israel dargestellt. Dabei bleiben wir als Christen nicht unberührt, sondern beziehen Position.

Die Frage jedoch ist... welche Position?

Stellen wir uns auf die Seite der Medien? Der Ankläger? Der Moslems? Der Seite Israels? Oder stellen wir uns als Christen auf die Seite Gottes, der seinen Standpunkt in seinem Wort geoffenbart hat?

Als Christen und wahrhafte Nachfolger unseres Herrn Jesus sollten, ja müssen wir uns auf das Wort Gottes stellen, wenn es um Israel geht.

Aber was sagt denn die Bibel zum Thema Israel?

Zunächst müssen wir einmal festhalten, das Israel einer der am häufigsten genannten Hauptwörter in der Bibel ist. Die Begriffe YHVH, König und Israel sind zusammen über 8000 mal in der Bibel erwähnt.

Wenn etwas so häufig in der Bibel genannt wird, dann muß es etwas damit auf sich haben. Es ist nicht nur wichtig diese drei Begriffe zu verstehen, sondern man muß auch eine Offenbarung Gottes bekommen um sie in aller Tiefe zu begreifen und die Erkenntnis die man daraus gewinnt praktisch umzusetzen.

YHVH

ist der Schöpfer der Himmel und der Erde und allem was darin ist. Er ist es, der alles durch das Wort seines Mundes erschuf und sich ein Volk zum Eigentum rief. Die Namen YHVH's sind vielfältig und spiegeln seinen Charakter wieder. YHVH ist Gott der Allmächtige, Herr der Heerscharen, Adonai, Elohim, Jehovah, Jahwe. Er ist unser Arzt, unser Versorger, unsere Burg, unser Fels. Er ist Liebe und Zorn. Er ist ein eifersüchtiger Gott, aber vor allem ist er unser Vater, den wir Abba nennen dürfen. Er ist der Vater unseres Herrn Jesus, dem König der Könige.

Ein König steht im Mittelpunkt der Schrift. Dieser König ist Jesus, der von Anbeginn aller Zeiten auserwählt worden war, um über einem Volk von Heiligen zu regieren.

Dieses Volk wurde von Gott Israel genannt und wir werden uns nun anschauen, wer oder was Israel ist, was Gott mit diesem Israel vor hat und was wir tun können, damit das Israel Gottes in seine Bestimmung hineingelangt.

Woher kommt der Name Israels?

Wir alle kennen die Geschichte Jakobs. Der Enkel Abrahams, der sich sein Erstgeburtsrecht mit einer Linsensuppe erkaufte und den Segen seines Vaters erschlich. Er floh von seinem Bruder Esau und arbeitete 14 Jahre für seine geliebte Rachel. Nachdem er dann von seinem Onkel Laban mit seiner gesamten Habe floh und nach Jahren wieder in seine Heimat zurückkehren wollte, stand er wieder seinem Bruder Esau gegenüber. In der Nacht vor der Begegnung mit seinem Bruder, wurde er von Gott in die Enge getrieben und am Fluß Jabbok kämpfte er mit dem Engel.

„Da sagte er: Laß mich los, es sei denn, du hast mich vorher gesegnet. Da sprach er zu ihm: Was ist dein Name? Er sagte: Jakob. Da sprach er. Nicht mehr Jakob soll dein Name heißen, sondern Israel; denn du hast mit Gott und mit Menschen gekämpft und hast überwältigt." Genesis 32:27-29

Was für eine Antwort auf die Frage nach einem Segen! Merkwürdig nicht war? Aus Jakob, dem Fersenhalter und Betrüger wird Israel, der Kämpfer Gottes.

Gott nahm sich viel Zeit um Jakob in Israel zu verwandeln, aber was Gott sich vornimmt vollbringt er auch. Er verwandelte Jakob in einen Gläubigen, der am Ende seines Lebens verstand worauf es ankam. Nicht den Segen zu stehlen, sondern andere zu segnen und ein Zeugnis, ein Kämpfer zu sein für Gott. Als Jakob stahl er den Segen seines Bruders, aber als Israel segnete er nicht nur seine 12 Söhne, die Patriarchen, sondern auch den Pharao, den damals mächtigsten Mann der Welt.

Mit der Verwandlung von Jakob in Israel, gingen alle Verheißungen und alle Bünde die Gott mit seinen Vätern Abraham und Isaak gemacht hatte auf Israel über und nicht nur diese, sondern auch die Verheißungen die Gott schon vorher Jakob gab.

„Ich bin der HERR, der Gott deines Vaters Abraham und der Gott Isaaks; das Land auf dem du liegst, dir will ich es geben und deiner Nachkommenschaft. Und deine Nachkommenschaft soll wie der Staub der Erde werden, und du wirst dich ausbreiten nach Westen und nach Osten und nach Norden und nach Süden hin; und in dir und in deiner Nachkommenschaft sollen gesegnet werden alle Geschlechter der Erde. Und siehe, ich bin mit dir, und ich will dich behüten über all, wohin du gehst, und dich in dieses Land zurückbringen; denn ich werde dich nicht verlassen, bis ich getan, was ich zu dir geredet habe." Genesis 28:13-15

Die Verheißungen an Israel waren:

·   Deine Nachkommen werden wie der Staub der Erde

·   Du wirst dich überall hin ausbreiten

·   In Israel und seiner Nachkommenschaft sollen alle Geschlechter der Erde gesegnet sein

·   Gott ist mit Israel überall wohin er/es geht

·   Gott wird Israel nicht verlassen

·   Gott wird Israel in das Land bringen

Zuerst erhielt Abraham diese Verheißungen, diese ging dann aber nicht an seinen Erstgeborenen Ismael über, sondern an seinen Jüngeren Sohn Isaak. Das Erbe und die Verheißungen Isaaks gingen ebenfalls nicht an den Erstgeborenen Esau, sondern an den Jüngeren Jakob.

An wen ging denn nun das Erbe Israels, seine Verheißungen und sein Vermögen? An Ruben seinen Erstgeborenen? Nein, denn dieser entehrte das Bett seines Vaters in dem er mit der Nebenfrau seines Vaters schlief und wurde „enterbt".

Das Erbe Israels wurde aufgeteilt!

Das Erbe in der Bibel umfaßte drei Teile:

1.) den Namen des Vaters

2.) einen doppelten Anteil am Erbe vor allen anderen Brüdern

3.) die Regentschaft über das Vaterhaus

Anstelle seines erstgeborenen Sohnes Ruben, erhielt sein Lieblingssohn Joseph den doppelten Anteil des Erbes, denn anstelle Josephs traten seine Söhne Manasse und Ephraim, die jeweils in der späteren Landvergabe ein eigenes Erbteil bekamen.

Aber wer erhielt den Namen des Vaters und wer die Regentschaft?

„Und Joseph nahm sie beide; Ephraim mit seiner Rechten zur Linken Israels und Manasse mit seiner Linken zur Rechten Israels und brachte sie zu ihm. Da streckte Israel seine Rechte aus und legte sie auf Ephraims Kopf – obwohl er der Jüngere war – und seine Linke auf Manasses Kopf; er legte seine Hand über Kreuz. Denn Manasse war der Erstgeborene. Und er segnete Joseph und sprach: Der Gott, vor dessen Angesicht meine Väter, Abraham und Isaak, gelebt haben, der Gott, der mich geweidet hat, seitdem ich bin, bis zu diesem Tag, der Engel, der mich von allem Übel erlöst hat, segne die Knaben; und in *ihnen* werde mein Name genannt und der Name meiner Väter, Abraham und Isaak, und sie sollen sich vermehren zu einer Menge mitten auf der Erde!" Genesis 48:13-16

„Juda, du dich werden deine Brüder preisen! Deine Hand wird auf dem Nacken deiner Feinde sein, vor dir werden sich niederbeugen die Söhne deines Vaters. Juda ist ein kauernder Löwe; vom Raub, mein Sohn, bist du hochgekommen. Er kauert, er lagert sich wie ein Löwe und wie eine Löwin. Wer will ihn aufreizen? Nicht weicht das Zepter von Juda, noch der Herrscherstab zwischen seinen Füßen weg, bis das der Schilo kommt, dem gehört der Gehorsam der Völker. An den Weinstock bindet er sein Eselsfüllen, an die Edelrebe das Junge seiner Eselin; er wäscht im Wein sein Kleid und im Blut der Trauben sein Gewand; die Augen sind dunkel von Wein und weiß die Zähne von Milch." Genesis 49:8-12

Ephraim erhielt durch Adoption und den freien Entschluß Gottes den Namen Israel und Judah erhielt die Regentschaft über seine Brüder.

Während der Name auf unbegrenzte Zeit an Ephraim gegeben wurde, wurde die Regentschaft bis zu einem bestimmten Zeitpunkt vergeben, nämlich bis der Schilo kommt. Der Schilo ist der verheißene Messias, dem der Gehorsam der Völker anhängt.

„Das Heil kommt aus den Juden" (Johannes 4:22) sagte Jesus und bestätigt damit nicht nur die Prophetie über Juda, sondern stellt sich selbst als den Regenten dar, der die Welt richten wird.

Jesus ist der Nachfolger dem David verheißen wurde, als Gott zu ihm sprach das ein Nachkomme Davids auf dem Thron sitzen würde für ewig.

Nun stellen sich weitere Fragen: Ist Juda in der Zwischenzeit Israel geworden? Sind die Juden Israel? Wer ist Israel heute? Hat Juda auch heute noch das Zepter?

Um diese Fragen zu beantworten, müssen wir wieder in die Vergangenheit schauen und in das Wort Gottes, welches uns die Vergangenheit besser erleuchtet als jeder Geschichtsprofessor.

Die Kinder Israels wuchsen heran und wurden zu einem starken Volk, welches so an Größe zunahm, das der Pharao es mit der Angst bekam und Israel unterdrückte. Er versklavte die Kinder Israels und diese schrien zu Gott um Errettung. Gott erweckte Mose um der Versprechen und der Bünde wegen, die er mit Abraham, Isaak und Jakob geschlossen hatte.

Als Mose nun das Volk herausführte, erfahren wir in Exodus 12:37-38, daß neben den Söhnen Israels auch viel Mischvolk (Fremde, Nicht-Israeliten) aus Ägypten zog. Diese gesamte Ansammlung von Menschen, direkte Nachfahren Israels, Sklaven, die mit Geld gekauft wurden und Fremde die sich aus den verschiedensten Beweggründen Israel anschlossen, nannte man *das Haus Israel.*

Dieses Haus Israel wurde von Gott als sein Volk erwählt und Gott und das Volk schloß einen Bund am Berg Sinai. Eine Bundeserneuerung fand dann mit der zweiten Generation in der Wüste statt. Aus 5.Mose 29:9-14 geht hervor, das nicht nur die Fremden ein Teil des Bundes zwischen Gott und Israel waren, sondern sogar zukünftige Generationen

Nachdem das Haus Israels dann in das verheißene Land eingezogen waren, begann ein Kampf um die Vorherrschaft über das Volk, vorauf sich das Volk in zwei Häuser teilte: das Haus Judah mit den Stämmen Judah, Bejamin und den Leviten und das Haus Israel unter Ephraim und allen anderen Stämmen.

David als einer der Schatten auf den zukünftigen Messiahs hin, war der Erste und Einzige, der beide Häuser, Israel und Judah vereinigen konnte, die dann schon durch seinen Enkel Rehabeam wieder auseinander fielen.

Von da ab verfielen sowohl Judah, als auch Israel immer mehr in Götzendienst und verließen den Weg ihrer Väter. Am schlimmsten der beiden Häuser jedoch trieb es Israel, die nicht nur tiefsten Götzendienst betrieben, sondern auch noch genau so sein wollten wie die Nationen um sie herum.

Daher ließ Gott Propheten aufstehen, die über die beiden Häuser prophezeiten. Einer davon war Hosea, der gegen das Haus Israel sprach:

„Und er sprach: Gib ihr den Namen Lo-Ammi (Nicht-Mein-Volk)! Denn ihr seid nicht mehr mein Volk, und ich ich will nicht euer Gott sein.

Doch die Zahl der Söhne Israel wird wie Sand am Meer werden, den man nicht messen und nicht zählen kann. Und es wird geschehen, an der Stelle, an der zu ihnen gesagt wurde: Ihr seid nicht mein Volk!, wird man zu ihnen gesagt werden: Söhne des lebendigen Gottes." Hosea 1:9-2:1

Gott verspricht Israel das es in alle Winde verstreut werden wird und nicht nur das, Israel würde nicht mehr das Volk Gottes sein, bzw. als solches erkannt werden. Es würde nicht mehr als Volk Gottes gelten. Israel, welches so sehr sein wollte wie die Nationen, mit all ihrem Götzendienst und ihren Befleckungen, wurde schließlich so, wie sie es wollte.

Im Jahre 722 vor Christus fielen die Assyrer in das Nordreich ein und entführten alle Bewohner, bzw. töteten eine beträchtliche Anzahl. In diesem Jahr hörte Israel auf zu existieren.

Was blieb war Judah im Süden. Aber auch Sie konnten den Anforderungen Gottes nicht genügen und würden in die Gefangenschaft weggeführt. Zurück aus Babylon wurden sie von den verschiedensten Mächten regiert und schließlich im Jahre 135 n.Chr. erneut vollkommen zerstört und in alle Winde zerstreut.

Wer übernahm den nun die Regentschaft und den Namen?

Die Regentschaft übernahm Jesus der Christus und die Kirche übernahm den Namen „das wahre Israel".

Schon sehr früh in den Anfängen der Christenheit kam die sogenannte Ersatztheologie auf, die bis heute noch in sehr vielen Köpfen regiert.

Diese Theologie besagt, das Gott die Juden, als das Israel der Bibel, verstoßen hätte. Die Juden wurden als Gottesmörder bezeichnet und waren deshalb weniger wert als Vieh, mit dem man machen konnte was man wollte. Alle Segnungen der Bibel warn von nun an ausschließlich für das „wahre Israel" – der Kirche und alle Flüche für das fleischliche Israel – die Juden.

Im Namen des Kreuzes und unseres Herrn Jesus wurden in den letzten 1900 Jahren Verbrechen begangen, die sich in Worten kaum wiedergeben lassen. Das Haus Judah wurde verfolgt, verbrannt, vergast, enteignet, gefoltert, aufgespießt, in Stück zersägt, aufgeschlitzt, zwangsgetauft, gebrandmarkt, gepfählt, gerädert, Man machte sie nach außen hin kenntlich, indem sie einen Stern oder eine bestimmte Mütze tragen mußten. Sie wurden in Ghettos gesteckt und sobald sie sich angesiedelt hatten wieder vertrieben.

Das letzte Jahrhundert hat diesen Verbrechen gegen Gott und dem Haus Judah die Krone aufgesetzt. In unserem zivilisierten Deutschland wurden aufgrund „christlicher" Lehren Luthers durch den Katholiken Adolf Hitler und einem „christlichen" Deutschland 6 Millionen Juden systematisch auf bestialische Art und Weise vernichtet.

Warum nur? Wie kann diese Schande jemals wieder gut gemacht werden? Hätten wir vor 50 Jahren auch unseren Herrn und Heiland Jesus vergast? Wo waren wir denn besser gegenüber denjenigen, die damals Jesus an das Kreuz schlugen?

Die Vergangenheit ist schrecklich und für mich, der in Israel lebt manchmal lähmend, besonders dann, wenn ich mit den Überlebenden des Horrors spreche.

Was haben wir als Christen falsch gemacht? Was kann ich als einer der diese Zeit noch nicht einmal erlebt hat überhaupt tun?

Das erste ist die Lüge mit der Wahrheit zu bekämpfen und damit im eigenen Haus anfangen. Mein Haus ist das Haus Israel. Bin ich ein Jude? Nein.

Ich glaube das zu einem mir unbekannten Punkt in der Geschichte die Gemeinde und hinterher ganz besonders die Organisation die sind Kirche nennt einer großen Lüge auf den Leim gegangen ist. Die Kirche hat nicht Judah mit Israel ersetzt und ist damit „mehr wert", sondern die Gemeinde ist durch die Gnade Gottes (wieder) zu einem Teil Israels geworden und war dafür verantwortlich, das Haus Judah zu Eifersucht zu reizen, um es zu ihrem Messiahs zu führen.

Die Gemeinde ist Israel und Judah ist Israel. Der eine Teil glaubt an den Messiahs, der andere Teil nicht. Judah ist nicht unsere „älterer Bruder", sondern unser „noch-nicht-erretteter Bruder".

Halt, Halt, Halt, werden sich einige jetzt denken. Will er uns etwa sagen das wir tatsächlich Israel sind?

Jawohl das will ich sagen. Und damit bin ich nicht allein, sondern habe die Zeugen der Schrift mit mir.

1.Petrus 2:9-10

Ihr aber seid eine auserwähltes Geschlecht, ein königliches Priestertum, eine heilige Nation, ein Volk zum Besitztum, damit ihr die Tugenden dessen verkündigt, der euch aus der Finsternis zu seinem wunderbaren Licht berufen hat. Die ihr ein "nicht-mein-Volk" wart, jetzt aber Volk Gottes seid, die ihr einst „nicht Barmherzigkeit empfangen hattet", jetzt aber Barmherzigkeit empfangen habt.

Petrus schriebt diesen Brief an Nicht-Juden, an die Fremdlinge in Galation, Klein Asien und andere heidnische Provinzen und bezeichnet die Empfänger als diejenigen zu denen Gott im ersten Kapitel des Hoseabuches spricht. Petrus sieht diese HeidenChristen als Israel!

Jakobus 1:1

Jakobus, Knecht Gottes und des Herrn Jesus Christus, den zwölf Stämmen, die in der Zerstreuung sind, seinen Gruß.

Welche zwölf Stämme? Die existierten doch schon seit über dreihundert Jahren nicht mehr! Jakobus schreibt an die Gläubigen und bezeichnet diese nicht mehr und nicht weniger als Israel, die in alle Winde verstreut wurden.

Paulus in seiner Einleitung zum Thema Israel und die Nationen benutzt die gleiche Stelle des Hoseabuch wie Petrus:

Römer 9:24-26

Uns, die er auch berufen hat, nicht allein aus den Juden, sondern auch aus den Natinen. Wie er auch in Hosea sagt: ich werde Nicht-Mein-Volk mein Volk nennen und die Nicht-Geliebte Geliebte." Und es wird geschehen, an dem Ort, da zu ihnen gesagt wurde: Ihr seid nicht mein Volk, dort werden sie Söhne des lebendigen Gottes genannt werde."

Die Einleitung Paulus mündet in dem Gleichnis des Ölbaums aus Kapitel 11.

Der Ölbaum ist Israel und sowohl das Haus Juda, die Juden als auch die gläubig gewordenen Heiden, ein Teil des Hauses Israel, werden durch den Glauben an den Juden Jesus in den Stamm – Israel eingepflanzt. Jeder muß durch den Glauben eingepfropft werden!

Israel unser Stammvater trägt jeden der durch Glauben eingepfropft ist. Jude oder Heide. Dabei ist uns die weit größere Gnade zuteil geworden, da wir Gott einst ablehnten und erst wieder durch Jesus zu ihm zurückfanden.

„Denn wie ihr einst Gott nicht gehorcht habt, jetzt aber Erbarmen gefunden habt infolge ihres Ungehorsams *(weil das Haus Judah Jesus nicht vollständig akzeptieren wollte)*, **so sind jetzt auch sie dem euch geschenkten Erbarmen gegenüber ungehorsam gewesen, damit auch sie jetzt Erbarmen finden. Denn Gott hat alle zusammen in den Ungehorsam eingeschlossen, damit er sich aller erbarmt. O Tiefe des Reichtum, sowohl der Weisheit als auch der Erkenntnis Gottes! Wie unerforschlich sind seine Gerichte und unaufspürbar seine Wege? Denn wer hat des Herrn Sinn erkannt, oder wer ist sein Mitarbeiter gewesen?" Römer 11:30-35**

Haben sie Gottes Sinn mit dieser Welt erkannt? Gott hat es gefallen in Israel alle Geschlechter der Erde zu segnen. Israel sind nicht nur die Juden aus dem der Messias nach Fleisch kam, sondern jeder der an den auserwählten Messias glaubt, also jeder wiedergeborene Christ.

Gott möchte die Welt durch sein Volk Israel segnen und uns in eine gemeinsame Zukunft mit unseren Brüdern aus dem Hause Judah führen.

Wollen wir doch einmal schauen was das Wort Gottes über unsere Zukunft sagt:

Hesekiel 37:16-25

Und du Menschensohn, nimm die ein Stück Holz und schreibe darauf: „Für Juda und für die Söhne Israel, seine Gefährten."

> *Anm.*:Das Südreich umfaßte sowohl den Stamm Judah, als auch diejenigen, die sich von den Söhnen Israels in den Süden begeben hatten, als die Assyrer kamen. Die Söhne Israels aus allen 12

Stämmen wurden Teil des Hauses Judah, waren aber sowohl vorher als auch nachher leibliche Nachfahren Jakobs.

Und nimm noch ein anderes Stück Holz und schreibe darauf:"Für Joseph, das Holz Ephraims und des ganzen Hauses Israel, seiner Gefährten."!

*Anm.:*Mit Ephraim ist das ganze Haus Israel, also nicht nur die Söhne Israels. Das Haus umfaßte sowohl Hausgeborene, für Geld gekaufte und diejenigen, die sich freiwillig dem Haus angeschlossen hatten. Das Haus ist eine wesendlich größere Gruppe als nur die Söhne und beinhaltet auch Heiden, die sich dem Gott Israel anschließen. Da Ephraim so werden wollte wie die Nationen, wurde er so wie die Nationen und Menschen aus den Nationen wurden seine Gefährten.

Und füge sie dir zusammen, eins zum anderen, zu einem Holz, so daß sie eins werden in deiner Hand! Und wenn die Söhne deines Volkes zu dir sagen:"Willst du uns nicht mitteilen, was dies bedeutet?", so rede zu ihnen: So spricht der Herr, HERR: Siehe, ich nehme das Holz Josephs, das in der Hand Ephraims ist, und die Stämme Israels, seine Gefährten; und lege auf es das Holz Judahs und mach sie zu einem Holz, so das sie eins werden in meiner Hand. Und die Hölzer, auf die du geschrieben hast, sollen in deiner Hand sein vor ihren Augen. Und rede zu ihnen: So spricht der Herr, HERR:

Siehe, ich nehme die Söhne Israel aus den Nationen heraus, wohin sie gezogen sind, und ich sammle sie von allen Seiten und bringe sie in ihr Land. Und ich mache sie zu <einer> Nation im Land, auf den Bergen Israels, und ein einziger König wird für sie alle zum König sein; und sie sollen nicht mehr zu zwei Nationen werden und sollen sich künftig nicht mehr in zwei Königreiche teilen.

Und sie werden sich nicht mehr unrein machen mit ihren Götzen und mit ihren Scheusalen und mit all ihren Vergehen. Und ich werde sie retten aus all ihren Treulosigkeiten, mit denen sie gesündigt haben, und werde sie reinigen; und sie werden mir zum Volk und <ich> werde ihnen zum Gott sein. Und mein Knecht David wird König über sie sein, und sie werden alle <einen> Hirten haben;

und sie werden in meinen Rechtsbestimmungen leben und meine Ordnungen bewahren und sie tun. Und sie werden in dem Land wohnen, das ich meinem Knecht Jakob gegeben habe, in dem eure Väter gewohnt haben; und sie werden darin wohnen, sie und ihre Kinder und ihre Kindeskinder, bis in Ewigkeit; und mein Knecht David wird ihr Fürst sein für ewig.

Wann dies sein wird weiß ich nicht. Vielleicht ist es schon in Naher Zukunft, oder erst wenn Jesus wiederkommt und als König regiert. Jedoch eins weiß ich sicher. Gott beurteilt jeden einzelnen von uns wie er Mit seinem Bruder umgeht oder umgegangen ist.

Wie stehen sie zu Israel und ihren Brüdern den Juden?

Ich glaube das es unverzichtbar ist dem anderen Teil der Familie beizustehen. Jeder einzelne von uns ist berufen unseren Bruder zur Eifersucht zu reizen. Dies kann durch Gebet geschehen. Beginnen sie Israel zu segnen und für die Errettung des ganzen Hauses Israel. Beten sie für den Frieden Jerusalems.

Es kann aber auch durch Ihre Person geschehen, indem sie nach Israel gehen und Jesus vorleben. Predigen können sie ihn nur selten, da er durch die Taten der sogenannten Christen gehaßt wird. Aber sie können ihn vorleben und andere mit der Liebe Gottes lieben, die durch den Heiligen Geist in ihnen ist. Oder sie können an diejenigen geben, die eines von beidem tun. Wie z.B. die Christliche Botschaft in Jerusalem

Nach dem Motto tröstet Tröstet mein Volk, arbeitet die ICEJ seit 20 Jahren in Jerusalem und hat duzende Vertretungen auf der ganzen Welt, wie auch diese hier in Deutschland. In ihrem Hauptquartier in Jerusalem arbeiten derzeit etwa 60 Volontäre, die durch ihre Gaben in die Lage versetzt werden vor Ort unseren Brüdern praktisch zu helfen.

Die praktische Hilfe geschieht durch verschiedene Sozialprogramme, Einwanderungshilfen, Ärztlicher Hilfe und anderen tatkräftigen Unterstützungen. Wir stehen als Vertreter Jesu vor Ort und Zeigen unseren Brüdern die Liebe Christi.

Diese Arbeit hat zu einem Wandel in dem Herzen Judahs geführt und ich glaube fest daran, das es eines Tages zu dem Tag kommen wird von dem der Prophet Sacharja sagte:

Aber über das Haus David und über die Bewohnerschaft von Jerusalem gieße ich den Geist der Gnade und des Flehens aus, und sie werden auf mich blicken, den sie durchbohr haben, und werden bitter über ihn weinen, wie man bitter über den Erstgeborenen weint.

„An jenem Tag wird für das Haus David und die Bewohnervon Jerusalem eine Quelle geöffnet sen gegen Sünde und gegen Befleckung.

Und es wird geschehe an jenem Tag, spicht der HERR der Heerscharen, da rotte ich die Namen der Götzen aus dem Land aus, daß sie nicht mehr erwähnt werden, und auch die Propheten und den Geist der Unreinheit werde ich aus dem Land wegschaffen." Sacharja 11:10 + 13:1-2

Nehmen Sie aktiv an der Segnung Judahs teil und erinnern sie sich an die Worte Jesu der sagte:

das was ihr einem der geringsten meiner Brüder getan hab, das habt ihr mir getan.

Torah.de wird von Israel Monthly unterhalten. Gestaltung: ics4u.
Verantwortlich für den Inhalt: Ulf Diebel.
Kommentare jeglicher Art sind ausdrücklich erbeten!

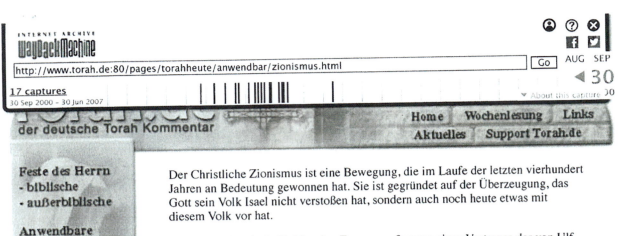
torah.de
der deutsche Torah Kommentar

Home   Wochenlesung   Links
Aktuelles   Support Torah.de

Feste des Herrn
- biblische
- außerbiblische

Anwendbare Torah

Der Christliche Zionismus ist eine Bewegung, die im Laufe der letzten vierhundert Jahren an Bedeutung gewonnen hat. Sie ist gegründet auf der Überzeugung, das Gott sein Volk Isael nicht verstoßen hat, sondern auch noch heute etwas mit diesem Volk vor hat.

Der nachstehende Artikel ist eine Zusammenfassung eines Vortrages der von Ulf Diebel am 27.07.2000 in Jerusalem gehalten wurde.   27.7.2018 22:22

Verschiedene Kommentatoren bei Torah.de stehen auch in Ihrer Gemeinde für Vorträge zur Verfügung, bitte kontaktieren sie uns unter webmaster@torah.de

Christlicher Zionismus

Wenn wir über Christlichen Zionismus reden, dann müssen wir uns die Frage stellen, ob es sich hierbei um eine politische Erscheinung handelt, oder ob es zu diesem Thema eine Basis in der Heiligen Schrift findet. Im Laufe des Abends werden wir feststellen, dass Christlicher Zionismus sehr wohl sein Fundament in der Bibel hat und somit im Grunde genommen als biblisch-christlicher Zionismus bezeichnet werden müsste.

D.h. aber nicht, dass dieser christliche Zionismus nicht zeitweise mit dem politischen Zionismus übereinstimmt, da es sich beim Zionismus als solches ja um ein bestimmtes Land und um eine bestimmte Gruppe von Menschen handelt – Israel.

Christlicher Zionismus hat zum Inhalt die Wahrheit Gottes bezüglich seines Wortes zu verkündigen, welches er das erste Mal zu Abraham sprach:

Genesis: 13:14-18

Und der HERR sprach zu Abram, nachdem Lot sich von ihm getrennt hatte: Erheb doch deine Augen, und schaue von dem Ort, wo du bist, nach Norden und nach Süden, nach Osten und nach Westen! Denn das ganze Land, das du siehst, dir will ich es geben und deinen Nachkommen für ewig.Und ich will deine Nachkommen machen wie den Staub der Erde, so daß, wenn jemand den Staub der Erde zählen kann, auch deine Nachkommen gezählt werden. Mache dich auf, und durchwandere das Land seiner Länge nach und seiner Breite nach! Denn dir will ich es geben. Und Abram schlug seine Zelte auf und ging hin und ließ sich nieder unter den Terebinthen von Mamre, die bei Hebron sind; und er baute dort dem HERRN einen Altar.

Aber Gott gab dieses Versprechen nicht nur einmal, sondern immer und immer wieder, selbst in den Zeiten, wo das Volk Israel durch Ungehorsam in die Verbannung gehen musste. Gott erklärte, dass selbst dieser Ungehorsam, das ewige Versprechen an Abraham nicht aufgelöst worden sei.

Deutoronomy 30:1-6

Und es wird geschehen, wenn all diese Worte über dich kommen, der Segen und der Fluch, die ich dir vorgelegt habe, und du es dir zu Herzen nimmst

unter all den Nationen, wohin der HERR, dein Gott, dich verstoßen hat, und du umkehrst zum HERRN, deinem Gott, und seiner Stimme gehorchst nach allem, was ich dir heute befehle, du und deine Kinder, mit deinem ganzen Herzen und mit deiner ganzen Seele, dann wird der HERR, dein Gott, dein Geschick wenden und sich über dich erbarmen. Und er wird dich wieder sammeln aus all den Völkern, wohin der HERR, dein Gott, dich zerstreut hat. Wenn deine Verstoßenen am Ende des Himmels wären, selbst von dort wird der HERR, dein Gott, dich sammeln, und von dort wird er dich holen. Und der HERR, dein Gott, wird dich in das Land bringen, das deine Väter in Besitz genommen haben, und du wirst es in Besitz nehmen. Und er wird dir Gutes tun und dich zahlreicher werden lassen als deine Väter. Und der HERR, dein Gott, wird dein Herz und das Herz deiner Nachkommen beschneiden, damit du den HERRN, deinen Gott, liebst mit deinem ganzen Herzen und mit deiner ganzen Seele, daß du am Leben bleibst.

Gott, der aufgrund des Ungehorsams der Isareliten das Volk dreimal zerstreute, (722 BC, 586 BC und 70 AD), brachte es immer wieder zurück und gab Ihnen Ihren Besitz wieder.

Jeremiah 30:10 Hört das Wort des HERRN, ihr Nationen, und meldet es auf den fernen Inseln und sagt: Der Israel zerstreut hat, wird es wieder sammeln und wird es hüten wie ein Hirte seine Herde!

Jesaja 11:11 Und an jenem Tag wird es geschehen, da wird der Herr noch einmal seine Hand erheben, um den Überrest seines Volkes, der übrigbleibt, loszukaufen aus Assur und Ägypten, aus Patros und Kusch, aus Elam, Schinar und Hamat und von den Inseln des Meeres.

Die Aufgabe des Christlichen Zionismus ist es diese Wahrheit zu verkündigen, indem wir als Zeugen über die Treue und Glaubwürdigkeit Gottes dastehen, der seinen Bund und sein Wort hält, egal wie sich Menschen verhalten.

Nun gibt es einige Strömungen in der Christenheit, die der Überzeugung sind, das diese Ansicht überholt sei, da sie ja nur aus dem „Alten" Testament belegt werden kann. Nicht nur das sich diese Geschwister, bezüglich der Zuverlässigkeit des Wortes Gottes auf sehr sehr dünnes Eis begeben, es ist daneben noch schlichtweg falsch.

Lukas 21:21-24

Dann sollen die in Judäa auf die Berge fliehen und die, die in seiner Mitte sind, daraus entweichen, und die, die auf dem Land sind, nicht dort hineingehen. Denn dies sind Tage der Rache, daß alles erfüllt werde, was geschrieben steht. Wehe aber den Schwangeren und den Stillenden in jenen Tagen! Denn große Not wird auf der Erde sein und Zorn gegen dieses Volk. Und sie werden fallen durch die Schärfe des Schwertes und gefangen weggeführt werden unter alle Nationen; und Jerusalem wird zertreten werden von den Nationen, bis die Zeiten der Nationen erfüllt sein werden.

Jesus selbst spricht in einer seiner beiden großen Endzeitreden, von der Zerstreuung und Wiedersammlung des Volkes Israels. Das Gleichnis des Feigenbaums folgt hier in den Versen 30ff des gleichen Kapitels und weist auf eine zukünftige Wiedersammlung hin.

Wir haben darüber hinaus mehrere Stellen des Apostel Paulus, der immer und immer wieder darauf hinweist, das Gott Judah nicht verstoßen hat.

Römer3:1-4

Was ist nun der Vorzug des Juden oder was der Nutzen der Beschneidung? Viel in jeder Hinsicht. Denn zuerst sind ihnen die Aussprüche Gottes anvertraut worden. Was denn? Wenn einige untreu waren, wird etwa ihre Untreue die Treue Gottes aufheben? Das sei ferne! Vielmehr sei es so: Gott ist wahrhaftig, jeder Mensch aber Lügner, wie geschrieben steht: «Damit du gerechtfertigt werdest in deinen Worten und den Sieg davonträgst, wenn man mit dir rechtet.»

Römer 11:25-32

Denn ich will nicht, Brüder, daß euch dieses Geheimnis unbekannt sei, damit ihr nicht euch selbst für klug haltet: Verstockung ist Israel zum Teil widerfahren, bis die Vollzahl der Nationen hineingekommen sein wird; und so wird ganz Israel errettet werden, wie geschrieben steht: «Es wird aus Zion der Erretter kommen, er wird die Gottlosigkeiten von Jakob abwenden; und dies ist für sie der Bund von mir, wenn ich ihre Sünden wegnehmen werde.» Hinsichtlich des Evangeliums sind sie zwar Feinde um euretwillen, hinsichtlich der Auswahl aber Geliebte um der Väter willen. Denn die Gnadengaben und die Berufung Gottes sind unbereubar. Denn wie <ihr> einst Gott nicht gehorcht habt, jetzt aber Erbarmen gefunden habt infolge ihres Ungehorsams, so sind jetzt auch sie dem euch geschenkten Erbarmen gegenüber ungehorsam gewesen, damit auch <sie> jetzt Erbarmen finden. Denn Gott hat alle zusammen in den Ungehorsam eingeschlossen, damit er sich aller erbarmt.

Christlicher Zionismus ist aber nicht nur eine Einstellung, sondern verlangt Aktion.

Wir sollen Israel segnen: Genesis 12:3, 27:29, Numeri 24:9
Wir sollen Israel trösten: Jesaja 40:1-2
Wir sollen für Israel beten: Psalm 122:6 und Jesaja 62:6-7
Wir sollen Israel finanziell unterstützen: 1.Korinther 16:1-3
Wir sollen Israel helfen: Matthäus 25.45

Glaube und Aktion gehen Hand in Hand und es die Aktion die Gott von uns erwartet um unseren Glauben auszudrücken.

Ist christlicher Zionismus nun etwa Anti-Arabisch, nur weil es Pro Israel ist? Selbstverständlich nicht, denn dies wäre gegen Gottes Wort. Auch Araber brauchen unsere Liebe und Zuwendung und vor allem die gute Botschaft, damit sie genauso wie jeder Andere auf dieser Welt unseren Herrn Jesus kennen lernen können.

Dennoch müssen wir ganz klar erkennen, das es im Heilsplan Gottes unterschiedliche Aufgaben zwischen Israel und Arabern gibt. Christlicher Zionismus unterstützt somit Gottes Absichten in der Welt auch in Hinblick auf Araber, denn erst, wenn auch die Araber Gottes Absichten mit Israel erkennen, kann es zu einem dauerhaften Zusammenleben kommen, wie es in Jesaja 19:22-25 beschrieben ist:

Und der HERR wird die Ägypter schlagen, schlagen und heilen. Und sie werden sich zum HERRN wenden, und er wird sich von ihnen erbitten lassen und sie heilen. An jenem Tag wird es eine Straße von Ägypten nach Assur geben. Assur wird nach Ägypten und die Ägypter nach Assur kommen, und die Ägypter werden mit Assur dem HERRN dienen. An jenem Tag wird Israel der Dritte sein mit Ägypten und mit Assur, ein Segen inmitten der Erde. Denn der HERR der Heerscharen segnet es und spricht: Gesegnet sei Ägypten, mein Volk, und Assur, meiner Hände Werk, und Israel, mein Erbteil!

Das Interessante am Arabisch-Israelischen Verhältnis ist, dass es ein Familienverhältnis ist, da sie ja den gleichen Stammvater, nämlich Abraham haben. Aber wie es in jedem Familienverhältnis ist, es kann nur dann funktionieren, wenn jeder Teil der Familie, den von Gott gegebenen Platz einnimmt. Ist die nicht der Fall regiert Unverständnis, Hass, Chaos und Uneinigkeit.

Also nur weil Christlicher Zionismus Pro – Israelisch ist, heißt es nicht, das er direkt auch Anti-Arabisch ist.

Wenn wir uns also die endscheidenden Passagen in unserer Bibel anschauen, müssen wir feststellen, das die Christenheit in der Allgemeinheit versagt hat. Anstatt auf Gottes Seite mit Israel zu stehen, wurden Teile, insbesondere der Paulinischen Lehre aus Römer 9-11 entweder ganz, oder teilweise verworfen.

Die als Ersatztheologie bezeichnete Lehre hat zum Gegenstand, dass die Kirche, oder die Gemeinde, Israel ersetzt hat. In mehr oder weniger schwerwiegender Form existiert heute die Lehre, das Israel und ganz besonders das jüdische Volk keinerlei Anspruch auf irgendwelche Verheißungen Gottes mehr hat. Diese Verheißungen sind durch Jesus auf die Kirche übergegangen und damit gehört nun aller Segen der Kirche, Israel aber ist unter einem Fluch.

Diese Theologie hat nicht nur zu den Jahrhunderten andauernden Vertreibungen, Verbannungen, Progromen, Zwangstaufen, den Kreuzzügen und anderen Greultaten geführt, sondern letztendlich auch zum Holocaust, der mit theologischen Äußerungen von u.a. Martin Luthers gerechtfertigt wurde.

Damit hat diese Ersatztheologie eine Entscheidende Rolle gespielt, eines der größten Taten Gottes zu unterminieren.

Nichtsdestotrotz, hat Gott sein Wort gehalten, und sein Volk in das Land ihrer Väter zurückgebracht. Obwohl damit der Kampf um dieses Land noch nicht zu Ende ist, ist jedoch der Grundstein zu einem Prozess gelegt, der letztendlich in der Wiederkunft Christi und seiner Herrschaft münden wird.

Eine weitere Aufgabe des Christlichen Zionismus ist es also gegen diese unbiblische Ersatztheologie vorzugehen, indem sie die Wahrheit der Bibel verkündet.

Nachdem wir also das biblische Fundament des Christlichen Zionismus gesehen haben, aber auch die Fehler der Vergangenheit durch die Hand derer, die im Namen Christi das Volk Gottes verfolgt und getötet haben, ist es die größte Aufgabe des Christlichen Zionismus Heilung zu bringen.

Denn durch die Fehler der Vergangenheit, ist es für einen Juden fast unmöglich in Jesus den verheißenen Messias zu sehen. In dem Moment, wo ein gläubiger Christ anfängt Zeugnis zu geben, denkt ein Jude nicht an Erlösung, Liebe oder ewiges Leben, sondern an Jahrhunderte Verfolgung, Folter, Vergewaltigung und Gaskammern.

Dennoch spricht die Prophezeiung von Hesekiel 36ff von einem Volk, welches in ein dürres Land zurückgebracht wird, letztendlich jedoch mit Gottes Geist erfüllt wird und somit Gerechtigkeit empfängt. Diese Gerechtigkeit und das erfüllt werden mit dem Heiligen Geist kann nur durch Yeshua Ha'Mashiach kommen, wie Jesus auf Hebräisch heißt.

Nur wenn das Volk durch Jesus wieder zu Gott findet, kann neben der physikalischen Wiederherstellung, die sich in der Rückkehr zum Land der Väter äußert, auch eine geistige Wiederherstellung stattfinden, die von Gott gewollt und vorangetrieben wird.

Der Christliche Zionismus hat also die große Aufgabe, Gott bei seiner Aufgabe „zu helfen". Christliche Zionisten waren es, die schon seit dem 16.Jahrhundert für das Volk Israel aufstanden und Heilung zwischen Juden und Christen brachten.

1587 wurde ein Mann namens Francis Kett in England bei lebendigem Leib verbrannt, weil er öffentlich verkündigte, das Gott die Juden wieder nach Israel bringen würde.

1607 veröffentlichte Thomas Brightman ein Buch mit dem Titel Offenbarung der Offenbarung in dem er ganz klar zu Ausdruck brachte, das es selbstverständlich sei, das alle Propheten der Bibel über eine Heimkehr der Juden nach Israel sprachen.

Über die letzten vierhundert Jahre verteilt, gab es gläubige Bischöfe, Staatmänner, Politiker und Laien, die für Israel aufstanden und die Gründung eines israelisch-jüdischen Staates vorantrieben.

Unter diesen war u.a. William H.Hechler, Kaplan der Britischen Botschaft in Wien, der sehr eng mit Theodor Herzl an der Gründung eines Traumes arbeitete, der 1948 mit der Gründung des Staates Israel Wirklichkeit wurde.

Nachdem wir unseren Fuß nun schon in das 21. Jahrhundert gesetzt haben, sind aus den wenigen die Vielen geworden, ja Tausende kommen alleine zum jährlichen Laubhüttenfest nach Jerusalem um ihre Tiefe Verbundenheit und Unterstützung zu Israel auszudrücken.

Werke wie z.B. die Internationale Christliche Botschaft in Jerusalem, haben durch ihre Arbeit das Herz dieses Volkes bewegt und Vorurteile gegen Christen und damit auch gegen ihren eigenen Messias Jesus abgebaut.

Doch damit ist es nicht genug, denn der Kampf um das Land und das Volk Gottes geht weiter und nimmt an Intensität sogar noch zu. Es ist nicht mehr lange hin, bis Jerusalem ein Stemmstein für alle Nationen werden wird und sie sich daran wund reißen werden.

Deswegen müssen Sie sich die Frage stellen „Auf welcher Seite stehe ich?"

In dieser Sache gibt es keine Neutralität. Denn entweder stehen sie auf der Seite Gottes und damit auf seinem Wort und mit Israel, oder sie stehen dagegen.

Es gibt keine Grauzone, entweder oder.

Torah.de wird von Israel Monthly unterhalten. Gestaltung: ics4u.
Verantwortlich für den Inhalt: Ulf Diebel.
Kommentare jeglicher Art sind ausdrücklich erbeten!

Feste des Herrn
- biblische
- außerbiblische

**Anwendbare
Torah**

Islam – Religion des Friedens?

Bevor wir uns ein wenig mit den Glaubensinhalten der Religion beschäftigen, die ein Hirte aus Mekka vor ca. 1400 Jahren in-s Leben rief, möchte ich kurz eine Begebenheit mit einem ehemaligen Nachbarn von mir erzählen.

Vor einigen Jahren besaß meine Familie ein Haus in Krefeld, dessen Garage an einen neu eröffneten Kebab Shop grenzte. Drei Brüder, die schon lange in Deutschland lebten und aus der Türkei kamen, hatten den Schritt in die Selbständigkeit gewagt. Der eine war ledig, einer mit einer Türkin verheiratet und der Dritte mit einer zum Islam übergetretenen Deutschen. Im Grunde genommen waren es sehr säkulare Moslems, die weder in eine Moschee gingen, noch beteten. Es waren sehr liebe, nette und zuvorkommende Nachbarn. Ihr Geschäft florierte und schon nach kurzer Zeit benötigten sie eine Ausbaumöglichkeit. Da wir unsere Garage nicht <u>nutzten</u>, boten wir <u>sie</u> den drei Brüdern zum Kauf an.

Von diesem Zeitpunkt an wurden wir fast richtige Freunde. Wir unterhielten uns über Jesus und Glaubensgespräche waren ein elementarer Bestandteil eines jeden Döner-Ggenusses.

Die<u>s</u> änderte sich nach und nach, als direkt gegenüber ein deutsch-türkischer Kulturverein eröffnete. Wie Pilze schossen diese Vereine in den letzten Jahren in der Düsseldorfer Gegend aus dem Boden. Der Verein in Krefeld besaß einen riesigen Versammlungsraum und innerhalb weniger Wochen kamen zum Freitagsgebet weit über 200 moslemische Männer.

Nun konnte ich beobachten wie der Hodscha (eine Art türkisch-moslemischer Pastor) immer öfters in die Kebabbude meines Nachbarn ging. Bei einem offenen Gespräch mit einem der drei Brüder wurde klar, das der Hodscha auf einem „Deal" bestand. Der Hodscha machte meinem Nachbarn klar, dass wenn er die Kundschaft von 200 hungrigen Moslems am Freitagmittag wünschte, dann habe auch er in die „Gemeinde" zu kommen. Und so fingen meine drei Nachbarn an, in die Moschee nebenan zu pilgern. Nur knapp ein Monat verging und man begann den Laden zu Mittags zu schließen, um sich auf dem Teppich Richtung Mekka zu verneigen. Wieder ein paar Wochen später begannen die Frauen der Brüder Kopftücher zu tragen und sich zu verschleiern.

Bei meinem letzten Besuch bei meinem Nachbarn, kurz bevor wir nach Israel gingen, gab ich meinem Lieblingsnachbarn ein Neues Testament. Der zweite Bruder stieß dazu und gab es mir mit den Worten zurück „Das brauchen wir nicht, das kannst da als Klopapier verwenden, denn mehr ist es nicht wert."

Aus den lieben und netten Nachbarn waren gläubige „friedliebende" Moslems geworden und ein Dialog war nicht mehr möglich.

Auch über einen der Todespiloten, der an einer Universität in Hamburg studierte, wurde gesagt, es sei ein netter und freundlicher Mitschüler. Der Direktor und Kommilitonen fielen aus allen Wolken, als sie erfuhren, dass dieser nette Schüler, Teilnehmer der Islam-—AG der Universität und weltoffener Moslem, mitverantwortlich für den Tod von über 5000 Menschen war.

Bei all dem müssen wir uns fragen, ob wir richtig über die Ziele und Glaubensgrundlagen des Islams informiert, sind.

Der Islam ist einfach kein Thema, weder in der Gemeinde, noch in der Politik. Schlimmer noch, wenn man darauf aufmerksam macht, dass Islam eine dämonische Religion ist, welche die Zerstörung des Menschen sucht, wird man als Ausländerfeind angesehen.

Bei einer Pressekonferenz vor einigen Jahren im King David Hotel in Jerusalem, hatte ich die Möglichkeit, unseren ehemaligen Außenminister Kinkel zu sehen, der folgende Äußerungen verlauten ließ:

„Yassir Arafat ist einer der wichtigsten Partner der Europäischen Union"

„Die Bundesregierung hatte niemals das Ziel zu erfahren was Moslems glauben, wir haben keine Ahnung worum es ihm Islam geht."

Glauben sSie lieber Leser (und Leserin), dass Präsident Bush weiß, worum es geht? Oder gar Bundeskanzler Gerhard Schröder, der es als erster Kanzler ablehnte, bei seiner Vereidigung auf Gott zu schwören, weil er ein gottloser Humanist ist?

Machen wir uns nichts vor. Unserer Regierenden haben keine Ahnung, ja viel schlimmer noch, sie versuchen alles in ihrer Macht stehende, um den Islam als friedliebende Religion darzustellen und ein Miteinander der Religionen zu fördern.

Oder wissen sie vielleicht doch worum es geht, aber sie haben Angst, dass die in unseren Ländern lebenden Moslems als fünfte Kolonne unsere westliche Kultur, unsere Lebensweise, unseren Wohlstand und unsere Demokratie zerstören könnten?

Ich bin mir an dieser Stelle bewusst, dass die von mir getätigten Äußerungen von einigen Lesern als sagen wir „störend" empfunden werden. Jedes Mal, wenn ich es mir erlaubte, etwas gegen Moslem zu sagen, gab es böse Zuschriften und man bezichtigte mich der Lieblosigkeit und gar der Unchristlichkeit. Einige meinten auch, ich würde Hass gegen andere schüren. Bevor mir also jemand wieder eine dieser unfreundlichen Mails zuschickt, bitte ich darum, getätigte Aussagen auf Fakten aufzubauen und nicht auf Wunschdenken.

Wunschdenken ist in diesem Fall, dass Leute davon überzeugt sind, das es möglich ist, mit Moslems auf Llange Sicht gesehen in Frieden leben zu können. Man meint, Werte wie Toleranz und Menschenrechte im Umgang mit Moslems anwenden zu können.

Fakt ist es jedoch, dass der Islam (einen Heiligen) Krieg gegen den Westen erklärt hat und die Werte Toleranz und Menschenrechte zwar bei uns vorkommen, aber nicht im Islam.

Ich kann mich noch an einen Spruch erinnern, den ich abn und zu in der Schule hörte. "Stelle dir vor es ist Krieg - und keiner geht hin!".

Der Westen ist derzeit nicht gewillt zu kämpfen. Ja, man ist bereit, ein vollkommen unterentwickeltes Land in Grund und Boden zu bomben, aber man ist nicht bereit, die Problematik im eigenen Land zu lösen. Und weil wir uns nicht vorstellen können, zu einem Krieg zu gehen, wird der Krieg zu uns kommen. Und so wie es aussieht, eher als wir glauben.

Warum?

Weil der Islam eine kriegerische, friedensfeindliche, unterdrückende Religion ist, die daran glaubt, den gesamten Erdkreis zu unterwerfen.

Was bedeutet Islam?

„Die wortwörtliche Bedeutung von Islam ist Frieden, nämlich Aufgabe des eigenen Willens, was bedeutet, sich selbst für die Sache Gottes zu verlieren und

seine eigenen Freuden für die Freuden Gottes aufzugeben" [1]

Der Ausdruck Frieden hat im Islam also nicht die gleiche Bedeutung wie bei uns. Frieden hat für <u>uns</u> die Bedeutung des „Shaloms" aus der Bibel. Frieden ist für uns das Wohlergehen an Leib, Seele und Geist, im Islam jedoch die Unterwerfung unter Allah.

Wer ist Allah?

Allah ist die Person, die im Koran, (wörtlich: dem viel zu lesenden Buch) als Allmächtiger Gott dargestellt wird. Jedoch spricht Allah nie selbst zu Mohammed, dem Empfänger der Offenbarungen, sondern Gabriel.

Dieser Gabriel gibt Mohammed Visionen und erklärt Allah als den höchsten aller Götter.

Allah war der Mondgott des arabischen Stammes Mohammeds und einer der 360 Götzen, die zur Zeit Mohammeds in der Kaaba in Mekka standen. Der Ruf „Allah akbar", der von jeder Moschee fünf Mal am Tag zu hören ist bedeutet nicht etwa „Gott ist der Größte" sondern vielmehr „Allah ist größer". Größer als was? Größer als alle anderen 359 Götzen die auch noch in der Kaaba waren.

Der Beweis für die Größe und Stärke Allahs ist die unangefochtene und unaufhaltsame Eroberung ganzer Erdteile. Innerhalb von 100 Jahren eroberten die arabischen Streitmächte die gesamte arabische Halbinsel, Nordafrikas und Teile Europas. Man spricht daher auch vom Schwert Allahs, denn entweder unterwarf man sich Allah (Islam) oder man wurde getötet. Und überall, wo Allah seine Herrschaft aufrichtete errichtete man Gebäude mit seinem Zeichen, dem Halbmond, das Zeichen das Mondgottes.

Allah hat keinen Sohn! Während der Gott der Bibel seinen einzigartig geborenen Sohn gab, damit jeder an ihn glaubt nicht verloren geht, sondern das ewige Leben erlangt, regiert Allah alleinig und keiner neben ihm. Es gibt keine Liebe für die Welt, sondern nur Forderungen, die zu erfüllen sind. Damit offenbart sich Allah als Gegenspieler Gottes. Allah ist NICHT der Gott der Bibel.

Wer ist also Allah? Allah ist nichts anderes als die derzeit mächtigste dämonische Kraft der Welt.

2 Korinther 11:14

Und kein Wunder, denn der Satan selbst nimmt die Gestalt eines Engels des Lichts an;

Es war Satan, der sich über den Thron Gottes erheben wollte, um sich selbst als Gott anbeten zu lassen.

Jesaja 14:12-14

Wie bist du vom Himmel gefallen, du Glanzstern, Sohn der Morgenröte! Wie bist du zu Boden geschmettert, Überwältiger der Nationen! Und du, du sagtest in deinem Herzen: Zum Himmel will ich hinaufsteigen, hoch über den Sternen Gottes meinen Thron aufrichten und mich niedersetzen auf den Versammlungsberg im äußersten Norden. Ich will hinaufsteigen auf Wolkenhöhen, dem Höchsten mich gleich machen.

Es ist wahrhaftig traurig, dass Christen ihre Bibel nicht kennen und falschen Göttern auf dem Leim gehen. Nur weil der Islam monotheistisch ist, hat dies noch lange nicht zu sagen, dass es sich um den gleichen Gott der Bibel handelt.

Was ist Salam?

Obwohl im allgemeinen angenommen wird, dass Salam, der „Friedengruß", ebenfalls Frieden bedeutet, so ist dies ebenfalls falsch. Unser Konzept von

Frieden, welcher der Vorstellung der Bibel über Frieden entspricht, existiert im Islam nicht. Salam ist nichts weiter als der Wunsch eines Moslems, dass der Begrüßte unter dem Islam leben wird, d.h. den „Frieden" der vollkommen Unterwerfung unter Allah erleben wird.

An was glaubt ein Moslem?

Wie in jeder religiösen Strömung, so gibt es auch im Islam die verschiedensten Sekten. Ein Beispiel dafür ist z.B. die Herrscherfamilie in Syrien, die der Sekte der Alawiten angehöret, einer Geheimgruppierung des Islams, die vollkommen losgelöst von allen anderen Gruppierungen ist.

Grundsätzlich unterscheidet man im Islam aber zwei Hauptgruppen, den Sunniten und den Schiiten. Während die Sunniten versuchen den Lebensweisen und Vorbildern Mohammeds folgen wollen (arabisch dafür „sunna"), leben die Schiiten nach den Vorbildern eines Imam, eines Absolutheits-Herrschers, der die letzte Autorität bei allen religiösen Fragen hat.

Beiden gemeinsam ist der Glaube an die fünf Säulen des Islams:

1.) Das Glaubensbekenntnis: „Allah ist Gott und Mohammed sein Prophet" muss für (vor?) mindestens zwei erwachsenen männlichen Moslems ausgesprochen werden.

2.) Das Die fünfmal täglich stattfindenden Gebete.

3.) Die mindestens einmal im Leben zu absolvierende Wallfahrt nach Mekka.

4.) Das Geben von Almosen.

5.)   Das ca. 30-tägige Fasten zu Ramadan von Sonnenaufgang bis Sonnenuntergang.

Neben diesen noch recht „harmlosen" Glaubensgrundsätzen muss der Moslem unter „Sharia" leben, dem islamischen Gesetz. Dieses Gesetz basiert aber nicht nur auf dem Koran, sondern vor allem den Hadidsch, den mündlichen Überlieferungen und Erzählungen, die angeblich aus dem Mund Mohammeds gekommen sein sollen. Da es Zehntausende von diesen Hadidsch gibt, bemühen sich Koranschulen um die Auslegung, Sammlung und Ordnung dieser Überlieferungen. Je nach dem, wie ein Schule veranlagt ist, gibt es mehr moderate, oder auch mehr extreme Auslegungen. Je nach Grundeinstellung dieser Lehrer, gewinnt auch das, was von vielen als die sechste Säule des Islams bezeichnet wird, immer mehr an Bedeutung – der Dschihad.

Was ist Dschihad?

Zunächst einmal bedeutet Dschihad nur „Bemühung" oder auch „Anstrengung" und zwar im Zusammenhang mit Allah, was bedeutet, dass jemand, der sich im Dschihad befindet, bemüht uns sich anstrengt, die Wege Allahs zu gehen.

Und genau hier beginnen die Probleme. Denn was will Allah?[2]

Sure 66:9

Prophet! Führe Krieg gegen die Ungläubigen und die Heuchler und sei hart gegen sie! Die Hölle wird sie aufnehmen – ein schlimmes Ende!

Sure 61:4

Wahrlich, Allah liebt diejenigen die für seine Sache kämpfen und in Reihen stehen, als wären sie solide Bauwerke.

Sure 9:5

Töte Ungläubige (Mushrikun, gemeint sind Polytheisten, Christen und sonstige

Nicht-Moslems), wo immer du sie finden kannst, fange sie ein und belagere sie und lege dich in einen Hinterhalt und warte auf sie. Aber wenn sie umkehren und As-Salat halten (öffentliches Gebet mit Moslems) und Almosen geben, dann lasse sie frei gehen. Allah vergibt oft und ist gnädig.

Sure 8:14

Und wer immer Allah und seinen Gesandten wiedersteht und beleidigt, diesen wird Allah wahrlich streng bestrafen. Das ist deine Qual, schmecke es; und ganz sicher für den Ungläubigen ist die Folter im Feuer.

Sure 8:65

Oh Prophet Mohammed dränge die Gläubigen (Moslems) dazu zu kämpfen.

Sure 2:216

Dschihad ist für dich bestimmt

Sure 5:51

Oh alle, die glauben (Moslems), nehme dir weder einen Juden noch einen Christen als deinen Freund oder als deinen Beschützer. Sie (sind?) doch Freunde und Beschützer untereinander. Und wenn du dich zu ihnen wendest, wirst du einer von ihnen.

Sure 9:29

Kämpfe gegen alle, die nicht an Allah glauben, noch an den Letzten Tag, noch diejenigen, die nicht das verbieten, was durch Allah und seinen Gesandten verboten ist, aber auch diejenigen aus den Leuten der Schriften (Juden und Christen), die nicht an die wahre Religion (Islam) glauben, bis sie die Jizyah (besonders hohe Steuer für all die Juden und Christen die nicht zum Islam konvertieren wollen) bereitwillig zahlen und sich selbst unterwerfen.

Allah will, das alle Menschen zum Islam übertreten und wenn nicht freiwillig, dann mit Gewalt. Dieser kleine Auszug aus Koranversen soll genügen, um zu zeigen, dass der Koran dazu auffordert, Juden und Christen umzubringen. Weiterhin wird ebenfalls eine reiche Belohnung, bestehend aus zahlreichen Jungfrauen und einem Leben in Saus und Braus demjenigen versprochen, der im Kampf gegen die Feinde Allahs sein Leben verliert. Auch das ist ausdrücklich im Koran festgehalten.

Praktisch hat das dazu geführt, dass die Islamische „Theologie" die Welt in zwei Häuser einteilt. Das Dar al Islam und das Dar al Harb.

Die beiden Häuser in der Welt

Das Dar al Islam ist das Haus des Islams und ist der Teil der Welt, der die schon für Allah gewonnen wurde. Dabei spielt es keine Rolle, ob jeder in diesem Haus Moslem ist oder nicht. Es geht einzig und allein um Territorium. Dem Islam geht es nicht um Individuen, sondern darum, ganze Länder für Allah zu gewinnen.

Das andere Haus ist das Dar al Harb, das Haus des Krieges. Jeder Teil der Welt, der nicht unter der Herrschaft des Islams steht, muss mittels Dschihad an das Haus des Islams angegliedert werden.

Erst wenn die ganze Welt dem Islam unterworfen ist wird es keinen Dschihad mehr geben.

Die bisher genannten Vorstellungen sind grundsätzlich Lehrsätze bei allen Moslems. Der Unterschied besteht nur in der Durchführung der Ziele. Die sogenannten gemäßigten Moslems sind der Ansicht, dass Dschihad eine Art Missionierung ist, die auf „friedlichem" Weg durchgeführt werden kann. Auf diese

Art der „friedlichen" Islamisierung haben die Moslems bisher ungemeine Erfolge gehabt.

In Frankreich haben Moslems in einigen Gebieten die Bevölkerungsmehrheit. Nach dem Katholizismus gehört der Islam zu zweit-stärksten Religionsgruppe. In England sind schon Hunderte von Kirchen in Moscheen verwandelt worden und auch dort zählt der Islam hinter der Anglikanischen Kirche zur zweitgrößten Religionsgemeinschaft.

Deutschland hat mittlerweile Millionen von moslemischen Gastarbeitern und Asylanten, die überall Moscheen errichten. In dem Moment, wo der Ruf des Muezzin zu hören ist, gehört das Land Allah und geht in das Dar al Islam über. Schon beginnen in Dortmund, entgegen dem bestehenden Gesetz Moscheen zur Mittagszeit zum Gebet auszurufen. Dortmund gehört damit offiziell dem Islam!

Durch die versprochene Belohnung im Falle des Ablebens im Kampf für den Islam, ist es also durchaus wahrscheinlich, dass auch in Deutschland Selbstmordattentate stattfinden können. Wie es der Anschlag auf das WTC gezeigt hat, sind bereitwillige Mörder schon jetzt mitten unter uns, um mit sich, auch Unzählige andere mit in den Tod zu ziehen.

Das israelische Problem!

In seinem erklärten Kampf gegen den Terrorismus hat George W. Bush eine internationale Koalition zusammengestellt, die auch verschiedne islamische Länder umfasst. Und obwohl Israel tagein tagaus unter islamischem Terror leiden muss, ist Israel nicht in diese Koalition aufgenommen? Warum? Weil man die „Gefühle" der islamischen Staaten nicht verletzten möchte.

Wo liegt das Problem mit Israel?

Israels Problem ist, dass es existiert!

Bis 1917 war Israel in alleiniger Herrschaft des Islams. Und auch noch als die Briten das Mandat für das Gebiet Palästina übernahmen (Wwelches damals auch noch das gesamte Haschemitische Königreich Jordanien umfasste), war es auch noch akzeptabel, da die Briten die Araber in ihrem Kampf gegen die einreisenden

Im Verständnis des Islams ist es vollkommen unmöglich, auch nur ein einziges Stückchen Land zu verlieren, wdas vorher in der Hand Allahs war. Der Gott Israels ist aber für die Moslems nicht Allah (ganz im Gegensatz zur Vorstellung von einigen Juden und Christen, die meinen, Allah wäre nur ein anderer Name für ein und den gleichen Gott).

Es ist daher nicht akzeptabel, dass der schon längst besiegte Gott der Juden, Allah auch nur einen Quadratzentimeter Land abnehmen kann. Es spielt keine Rolle wie viele Menschenleben die Befreiung des Landes Allahs kosten wird, Israel muss im Verständnis des Islams unter allen Kosten wieder in seinen Besitz zurück und die Juden, die in dem Koran als Affen und Schweine bezeichnet werden, müssen getötet werden.

Was nun?

Das Problem des Islams ist geistlich. Wie uns Paulus schon im Epheserbrief mitteilt, ist unser Kampf nicht gegen Fleisch und Blut, sondern gegen die Gewaltigen, gegen die dämonische und unsichtbare Welt Satans. Dennoch ist es nicht immer vermeidbar, dass sich dieser Kampf auf die natürliche Welt ausweitet. Die Kräfte hinter dem Islam haben keinen Respekt vor menschlichem Leben überhaupt.

Der Kampf ist im vollen Gange und es wird alles eingesetzt, was der Teufel an Waffen hat. Lüge, Angst, Verführung, Krieg.

Die Geschichte hat es gezeigt, dass der Islam nur durch eine militärische Niederlage zum Stillstand gebracht werden kann. Aber in wie weit eine militärische Niederlage derzeit realistisch ist, ist wahrhaft fragwürdig, da der Westen weder den Willen, noch ein Konzept hat den Islam zu bekämpfen. Sobald sich in Deutschland Menschen gegen die Ausübung des Islams erheben werden, werden sie die volle Macht des Islams zu spüren.

Es ist also anzunehmen, dass wahre Christen in der Zukunft arge Probleme bekommen werden und sich unsere westliche Gesellschaft in jeder Beziehung stark verändern wird.

Leider kann ich auch nicht behaupten, dass es eine Hoffnung gibt, dass sich plötzlich alle Moslems zu Jesus bekehren und eine Erweckung ausbricht, dies würde ich eher als Wunschdenken bezeichnen, denn als biblische Realität.

Unsere einzige Möglichkeit, gegen den Islam zu kämpfen, ist die Waffe der Wahrheit und der Liebe. Wir müssen aufklären und jedem die nötigen Informationen zur Verfügung stellen, um das wahre Gesicht des Islams aufzudecken.

Und wir müssen jede Möglichkeit nutzen, um unseren moslemischen Nachbarn die Liebe Jesus zu zeigen, die im Islam vollkommen unbekannt ist. Nur durch die Liebe ist es möglich, die Menschen aus dem Islam zu erretten, die für das Reich des Christus vorher bestimmt sind.

[1] Übersetzung aus dem Englischen aus http://www.islam.com/introislam.htm, erster Satz

[2] Nachfolgende Suren sind Übersetzungen aus dem Englischen und entsprechen nicht unbedingt einer "offiziellen" Übersetzung

Torah.de wird von Israel Monthly unterhalten. Gestaltung: ics4u.
Verantwortlich für den Inhalt: Ulf Diebel.
Kommentare jeglicher Art sind ausdrücklich erbeten!

(handwritten) ➔ wof = uef = p/c = 1.1.1 / 33.77

Binyamin Ze'ev Kahane

Binyamin Ze'ev Kahane (hebräisch בנימין זאב כהנא; * 3. Oktober 1966 in New York City; † 31. Dezember 2000 in Kfar Tapuach) war ein orthodoxer Rabbiner und extremistischer Zionist. Er war der Sohn von Rabbi Meir Kahane.

Binyamin Ze'ev Kahane

Leben

Binyamin studierte an der Jeschiwa Merkas HaRaw Kook und gründete zusammen mit seinem Vater 1987 die Yeshivat Ha Ra'yon Ha Yehudi in Jerusalem. Nachdem sein Vater 1990 bei einem Attentat getötet worden war, spaltete sich die Kach-Bewegung in die sich ähnelnden Parteien Kach und Kahane Chai auf. Kach wurde von Baruch Marzel weitergeführt. Binyamin stand der extremistischen Partei Kahane Chai bis zu deren Verbot 1994 vor. Er wurde mehrere Male wegen anti-arabischer Straftaten zu Haftstrafen verurteilt[1].

Am 31. Dezember 2000 wurden Binyamin Ze'ev Kahane und seine Frau Talya auf dem Rückweg von Jerusalem in Kfar Tapuach erschossen und fünf ihrer sechs Kinder schwer verletzt. Bewaffnete Palästinenser feuerten mehr als 60 Maschinengewehr-Salven in ihren Kleintransporter. [2]

Weblinks

- http://www.mfa.gov.il/MFA/Terrorism-%20Obstacle%20to%20Peace/Memorial/2000/Binyamin%20Zeev%20Kahane
- https://www.theguardian.com/news/2001/jan/09/guardianobituaries.israel

Einzelnachweise

1. www.mfa.gov (http://www.mfa.gov.il/MFA/Terrorism-%20Obstacle%20to%20Peace/Memorial/2000/Binyamin%20Zeev%20Kahane), Jerusalem Post. 1. Januar 2011 (http://www.mfa.gov.il/MFA/Terrorism-%20Obstacle%20to%20Peace/Memorial/2000/Binyamin%20Zeev%20Kahane), Jerusalem Post. 1. Januar 2011 (http://info.jpost.com/C002/Supplements/CasualtiesOfWar/2000_12_31.html) am hane, wife killed by terrorists (https://web.archive.org/web/20110415003339/http://info.jpost.com/C002/Supplements/CasualtiesOfWar%2F2000_12_31.html) am .01. Archiviert vom Original (https://tools.wmflabs.org/giftbot/deref.fcgi?url=http%3A%2F%2Finfo.jpost.com%2FC002%2FSupplements%2FCasualtiesOfWar%2F2000_12_31.html) . Abgerufen am 14. Februar 2011.
15. April 2011 ⓘ Info: Der Archivlink wurde automatisch eingesetzt und noch nicht geprüft. Bitte prüfe den Link gemäß Anleitung und entferne dann diesen Hinweis.

Abgerufen von „https://de.wikipedia.org/w/index.php?title=Binyamin_Ze'ev_Kahane&oldid=176736050"

(handwritten) 11/2000   TORAH.DE

Meir Kahane

Meir Kahane (hebräisch מאיר כהנא; * 1. August 1932 in Brooklyn als *Martin David Kahane*; † 5. November 1990 in Manhattan) war ein orthodoxer Rabbiner, israelischer Politiker und Gründer der Jewish Defense League, sowie der Kach-Bewegung. Dabei vertrat er eine eigene Richtung des radikalen religiösen Zionismus, die als Kahanismus bezeichnet wird. Seine erklärten Ziele waren die Beseitigung der liberalen Demokratie in Israel zugunsten einer jüdischen Theokratie, die Vertreibung der meisten Nichtjuden aus Israel und den besetzten Gebieten sowie die Errichtung von Großisrael.[1][2] In den Augen demokratischer Israelis war er der Vorkämpfer eines jüdischen Rassismus.

Inhaltsverzeichnis

I en

Früher Werdegang

Schon der Vater von Meir Kahane, Charles Kahane, war orthodoxer Rabbiner und ein radikaler Zionist. Er galt als amerikanischer Unterstützer der Irgun, einer Untergrundorganisation, die im Palästina vor der israelischen Staatsgründung Terroranschläge gegen die britische Besatzung sowie gegen die arabische Zivilbevölkerung verübte.[3] Den Sohn schickte der Vater in die von Wladimir Zeev Jabotinsky gegründete Betar-Jugend. Sein dortiger Jugendführer war der spätere israelische Verteidigungsminister Mosche Arens. Da die Betar-Jugend dem jungen Kahane jedoch noch nicht radikal genug war, trat er 1952 den Bne Akiwa bei.[4] Laut seiner Frau Libby soll Kahane in seiner Jugendzeit ein guter Schüler und Sportler gewesen sein.[3] Ein für ihn wichtiges Hobby war Baseball.[5] Laut Kahanes Angaben gab es in seiner Nachbarschaft nur wenige Juden, und er habe oft mit nichtjüdischen Jungen kämpfen müssen.[5]

Als Erwachsener ließ sich Kahane zum orthodoxen Rabbiner ordinieren und nahm den Vornamen Meir (hebr., „Der Erleuchtete") an. 1956 heiratete er Libby, mit der er vier Kinder hatte.[3] 1958 wurde er der Rabbiner des Howard Beach Jewish Centers in Queens. Die Gemeinde galt als weniger strikt orthodox. Anfänglich gelang es ihm dort, viele der jungen Gemeinde-Mitglieder davon zu überzeugen, eine orthodoxere Lebensweise zu führen. Als er die Mechiza – die Trennung von Männern und Frauen in der Synagoge – einführen wollte, stieß er jedoch auf Widerstand. Sein Vertrag wurde nicht erneuert, und so veröffentlichte er den Artikel *End of The Miracle of Howard Beach* in der orthodox-jüdischen Zeitung *Jewish Press*. Dies war sein erster Artikel in dieser Zeitung, und er schrieb für sie bis zu seinem Tod 1990.[6]

Von Ende der 1950er bis Anfang der 1960er Jahre war Kahane als FBI-Informant tätig. Als dieser unterwanderte er zeitweise die John Birch Society.[3] Er operierte zu dieser Zeit unter dem Decknamen *Michael King* und gab sich als Christ aus.[4]

Jewish Defense League
→ *Hauptartikel: Jewish Defense League*

In ' USA gründete Kahane 1968 die Jewish Defense League (JDL). Die JDL war eine paramilitärische Organisation, die sich primär gegen afroamerikanische Gangs richtete, die laut Kahanes d. iger Begründung die Juden bedrängten und antisemitisch seien. Angriffsziel der JDL waren auch Repräsentanten der Sowjetunion, um für die Auswanderungsfreiheit der russischen Juden zu demonstrieren.[4] 1971 ging Kahane nach Israel.[7]

Kach und Kahane Chai
→ *Hauptartikel: Kach und Kahane Chai*

In Israel gründete Kahane 1971 die Kach-Partei. Zu den Zielen gehörten unter anderem die Forderung nach Errichtung von Großisrael und eine fünfjährige Gefängnisstrafe für Juden und Nichtjuden in einem Liebesverhältnis. 1980 wurde Kahane zu sechs Monaten Haft verurteilt, weil er in einen Plan verwickelt war, der einen provokativen Sabotageakt auf dem Tempelberg in Ostjerusalem vorgesehen hatte.[2]

1984 erreichte die Kach-Partei einen Sitz im israelischen Parlament (Knesset). Beliebt war Kach vor allem unter jungen israelischen Wählern. Kahane veranstaltete damals eine in Israel aufsehenerregende Siegesfeier in Jerusalem, bei der ein arabischer Markt und Passanten überfallen wurden.[2] Kahane wurde Abgeordneter der Knesset und erklärte, keine Regierung zu unterstützen, die nicht befürworte, die Araber zu vertreiben. 1988 wurde seine Wahlliste wegen Verstößen gegen das neu erlassene Wahlgesetz („Aufstacheln zum Rassismus") nicht mehr zugelassen.[8] Der israelische Publizist Uri Avnery charakterisierte Kahane als „jüdischen Nazi" und Kach als „Nazipartei".[4]

Siehe auch: Kahanismus

Ermordung

Kahane kam 1990 bei einem Attentat in Manhattan ums Leben.[9][10][11] Der Hauptverdächtige, El Sayyid Nosair, wurde nach einem Schusswechsel mit der Polizei festgenommen, später aber vom Vorwurf des Mordes freigesprochen.[12] Nosair war in den Bombenanschlag auf das World Trade Center 1993 involviert.[13]

Kahanes Sohn Binyamin Ze'ev Kahane wurde 2000 ebenfalls bei einem Attentat ermordet.

Ansichten über den Islam

Kahanes Anhänger sind häufig islamfeindlich eingestellt. Kahane selbst behauptete allerdings, dass der Islam und Ruhollah Chomeini der jüdischen Religion in bestimmten Hinsichten viel ähnlicher seien als Philosophen oder Politiker der Aufklärung wie Jean-Jacques Rousseau, John Locke oder Thomas Jefferson.[5] Liberalismus und westliche Werte lehnte Kahane als "unjüdisch" und "hellenistisch" ab.[5] Er sah einen Widerspruch zwischen dem Judentum und der westlich-demokratischen Orientierung der israelischen Staatsgründer.[14]

Zitate

„In erster Linie sind es nicht Anstand und Güte, die den Nahen Osten beeindrucken, sondern Stärke."[15]

„Every Jew a Twenty-Two"[16]

„Es ist besser ein Israel zu haben, das von der ganzen Welt gehasst wird, als ein Auschwitz, das von ihr geliebt wird."[17]

„Eines der Probleme der Juden ist, dass sie ein jüdisches Konzept nicht kennen würden, wenn sie nicht darüber stolpertern. Ich berief mich wirklich auf den Talmud. Die meisten Juden denken, dass Judentum ‚Thomas Jefferson' ist. Das ist nicht so!"

Schriften

- *The Jewish Stake in Vietnam* (1968)
- *The Story of the Jewish Defense League* (1975)
- *They Must Go* (1981)
- *Uncomfortable Questions for Comfortable Jews* (1987)
- *Israel: Referendum or Revolution* (1990)

Literatur

- Karen Armstrong: *Im Kampf für Gott. Fundamentalismus im Christentum, Judentum und Islam.* München 2000, ISBN 3-88680-769-X, S. 485ff.
- Rafael Mergui, Philippe Simmonnot: *Israel's Ajatollahs. Meir Kahane and the Far Right in Israel.* Saqi Books, London 1978, ISBN 0-86356-142-X, S. 45.
- Uri Avnery: *Meir Kahane – ein jüdischer Nazi.* In: *Der Spiegel.* Nr. 21, 1986 (online (http://www.spiegel.de/spiegel/print/d-13518550.html)).
- Yitzhak Laor: *Yes, Kahane lives.* (http://www.haaretz.com/print-edition/opinion/yes-kahane-lives-1.298214) *Kahanism is flourishing in Israel's universities.* In: *Ha'aretz,* 25. Juni 2010.

Weblinks

- Porträt Meir Kahanes (http://www.knesset.gov.il/mk/eng/mk_eng.asp?mk_individual_id_t=455) auf der Website der Knesset

Einzelnachweise

1. Meir Kahane: *Uncomfortable Questions for Comfortable Jews,* Lyle Stuart 1987, Part II: *A Jewish State Versus Western Democracy;* Part IV: *Judaism Versus Western Democracy.*
2. Ehud Sprinzak: *Kach and Meir Kahane: The Emergence of Jewish Quasi-Fascism.* (http://members.tripod.com/alabasters_archive/kach_and_kahane.html) The American Jewish Committee.
3. *Carrying a torch.* (http://www.haaretz.com/jewish-world/news/carrying-a-torch-1.267554) Haaretz.
4. Uri Avnery: *Meir Kahane – ein jüdischer Nazi.* In: *Der Spiegel.* Nr. 21, 1986 (online (http://www.spiegel.de/spiegel/print/d-13518550.html)).
5. Philippe Simonnot, Raphael Mergui: *Israel's Ayatollahs: Meir Kahane and and the Far Right in Israel.* Saqi Books, London 1987, ISBN 0-86356-142-X, S. 40–78.
6. ou.org (http://www.ou.org/index.php/jewish_action/article/50163/) Jewish Action Online
7. Victor und Victoria Trimondi: *Krieg der Religionen.* 2006, S. 270.
8. Angaben zu Katach (http://www.mfa.gov.il/MFA/Government/Law/Legal%20Issues%20and%20Rulings/THE%20KACH%20MOVEMENT%20-%20BACKGROUND%20-%2003-Mar-94) Israelisches Außenministerium, 1994
9. Mark Juergensmeyer: *Terror in the Mind of God.* University of California Press, 2003. S. 59.
10. Samuel M. Katz: *Relentless Pursuit: The DSS and the manhunt for the al-Qaeda terrorists.* 2002.
11. Mark S. Hamm: *Terrorism as Crime: From Oklahoma City to Al-Qaeda and Beyond.* NYU Press, 2007, S. 29.
12. Jury Selection Seen As Crucial to Verdict (http://query.nytimes.com/gst/fullpage.html?res=9D0CE5DA1330F930A15751C1A967958260&sec=&spon=&pagewanted=all)
13. Brian Jenkins: *Sheik, others convicted in New York.* (http://www.cnn.com/US/9510/terror_trial/update/) auf: cnn.com, 1. Oktober 1995.
14. Reiner Nieswandt: *Abrahams umkämpftes Erbe. Eine kontextuelle Studie zum modernen Konflikt von Juden, Christen und Muslimen um Israel/Palästina,* Stuttgart 1998, S. 181.
15. Meir Kahane Quotes (http://www.brainyquote.com/quotes/authors/m/meir_kahane.html) brainyquote.com
16. Rabbi Meir Kahane (http://www.jewishvirtuallibrary.org/jsource/biography/kahane.html) jewishvirtuallibrary.org
17. Rabbi Meir Kahane Confronts Protesters At Speech in Minnesota. (https://www.youtube.com/watch?v=866zQ-DFy1E&feature=related) youtube.com

The Ephraimite Error
A Position Paper Submitted to the International Messianic Jewish Alliance
Author: Kay Silberling, Ph.D.

Committee Members and Advisors: Kay Silberling, Ph.D.
Daniel Juster, Th.D.
David Sedaca, M.A.

Introduction

A movement alternately known as the "Ephraimite," "Restoration of Israel," "Two-Covenant Israel," or "Two House" movement has recently gained ground in some areas among ardent Christian Zionists. Proponents of this movement contend that members of the "born-again" segment of the Christian church are, in fact, actual blood descendants of the biblical Israelites who were dispersed as a result of the Assyrian invasion of the ancient kingdom of Israel in 722 B.C.E.[1]

The movement's proponents further argue that these dispersed "Israelites," or "Ephraimites," whose identities have remained undisclosed even to themselves until recent times, primarily settled in areas now recognized as largely populated by Anglo-Saxons. At times they argue that all Anglo-Saxons, and even all of humanity, are descended from these lost Ephraimites. At other times, that only born-again Christians can claim descent. In either case, Christians from Anglo-Saxon lands, such as Great Britain, Australia, Canada, and the United States, can feel assured that they are most likely direct blood descendants of the ancient people of Ephraim.

It is now incumbent upon these members of "Ephraim," they argue, to "accept their birthright" and live as members of Israel.[2] They urge Gentile Christians to keep the Torah[3] in obedience to the Hebrew scriptures, to strive to re-educate Jews and other Christians about their new, "latter-day prophecy," and to work toward the repatriation of the land of Israel by their own number.

Primary among the movement's spokespersons are Batya and Angus Wootten and Marshall, a.k.a. Moshe, Koniuchowsky. The Woottens publish a newsletter entitled the *House of David Herald*, as well as several books. Batya's books include *In Search of Israel*, *The Star of David*, *The Olive Tree of Israel*, and *Who Is Israel? And Why You Need to Know.* Angus' books include *Take Two Tablets Daily*, *A Survey of the Ten Commandments and 613 Laws that God Gave Moses* and *The Messianic Vision.* Other names mentioned by Wootten are Brian Hennessy and David Hargis. Ed Chumney has written a book entitled *The Bride of Christ*, which I was unable to review.[4] Among the Woottens, I will deal only with Batya's writings.

Moshe Koniuchowsky leads a ministry called "Your Arms to Israel." In addition, he has recently formed an organization named "The Messianic Israel Alliance," which, despite its misleading name, has no affiliation with or endorsement by the International Messianic Jewish Alliance or any of its affiliates. The movement is growing to the point that it now has some areas of overlap with the Christian Zionist movement as well as the Messianic Jewish movement. As a result of this, there are several spokespersons in both these groups who advance this teaching while maintaining primary affiliation either as Christian Zionists or as Messianic Jews.

Analysis

Logic and Exegetical Method

Batya Wootten and Koniuchowsky build their theology of "born-again Christians" as Israel on typological and grammatically suspect readings of the stories of the biblical patriarchs and the fall of the northern kingdom of Israel in 722 B.C.E. In doing so, we will see that they create an artificial and contrived analogy between *type* and *reality*. All the patriarchs of the past are models for Wootten's and Koniuchowsky's present. The rhetoric that follows from this, then, is based on typological foreshadowing.

A Multitude of Nations

Starting with the patriarchs, Wootten argues that Jacob's promise to Ephraim in Gen 48:19 predicted the transformation of Ephraim/Israel into Gentiles.[5] The phrase reads, "and his descendants shall become a multitude of nations" (Heb. *v'zar'o yihye m'lo hagoyim*). This is the first instance of a foundational grammatical error on the part of Wootten (also shared by Koniuchowsky) that presupposes that every time the Hebrew word, *goy*, is employed, it is a reference to a Gentile or a Gentile nation.[6] Upon this supposition they will build their case.

This erroneous definition resulting from an inadequate knowledge of Hebrew grammar and syntax is one exegetical problem among many that we shall encounter. In the Hebrew Bible and the Apostolic Writings, the word *goy* (English: people or nation; Greek: *ethnos*) may refer to a Gentile nation, or, just as easily, it may refer to the nation of Israel. Thus a *carte blanche* assumption that the words *goy* or *goyim* always refer to "Gentile" or "Gentiles" in scripture is unwarranted and erroneous. In the Hebrew Bible, Jer 31:36 is especially enlightening in this regard, as it states, "'If this fixed order departs from before me,' declares the LORD, 'then the offspring [lit. "seed"] of Israel also shall cease from being a nation (*goy*) before me forever.'" Exod 19:6 is equally illuminating. It states, "'and you shall be to me a kingdom of priests and a holy nation (*goy kadosh*). These are the words that you shall speak to the *sons of Israel*.'" Other examples of the term being used to refer to Israel or the Jewish people are: Deut 32:28, cf. 32:45; Josh 10:12-13; Isa 1:4; Isa 26:2; Jer 31:36; Zeph 2:9.[7] In the Greek Apostolic Writings, the word *ethnos* refers to the Jewish people in Luk 7:5; 23:2; John 11:48-52; 18:35; Acts 10:22; 24:2,10,17; 26:4; 28:19; 1 Cor 10:18; Phil 3:5. The first contention, then, that *goy* or *goyim* is always translated as Gentile or Gentiles is patently incorrect. It must be determined from the context, and if the context does not call for it, such a translation is unwarranted.

In addition to this, the term "Gentile" is anachronistic as they employ it in this context. At the time of Joseph and Ephraim, the identity of the people was that of a loosely organized kinship group. The concept of "Gentile" as we read it today would have been unknown to the speakers. There was as yet no tribal coalition as we see in the later history of Israel that would have allowed for an in-group/out-group identifier term such as "Gentile." To read that into the text is to read a concept as understood centuries later into the language of the Torah writer.

Koniuchowsky makes the same errors of grammar, logic, and anachronism. In Part I of his four-part article, "The Full Restoration of Israel," he states of Gen 17:5, that the term there, "a multitude of nations" (*hamon goyim*) "literally means a noisy multitude of Gentile nations."[8] Wootten also builds upon the definition of *hamon*, a term which in some contexts can include the concept of a noisy crowd. She ignores the context in Genesis and argues that "Abraham was to father a great multitude of peoples who would cause a tumultuous commotion, or great noise (about God) throughout the world"[9] Her implication is that the evangelistic fervor of Christians

2

is what is referred to in the use of the phrase. The context, however, indicates no such interpretation. Koniuchowsky makes the same argument based on Gen 28:3 but compounds his problems by misquoting the passage. Curiously, although the phrase under discussion is *k'hal 'amim* (assembly of peoples), Koniuchowsky states, "The Hebrew term found in verse three is '*kehelat goyim*' or an assembly of nations or even better an 'assembly of goyim.'" "Somehow," he continues, "the Father will fill the earth with the physical seed of Abraham, Isaac and Jacob by putting together an assembly of goyim."[10] It may be that Koniuchowsky confuses the verse with Gen 35:11 (*k'hal goyim*). Nevertheless, not only does he misquote *both* words in the phrase, but he makes the same broad-brush statement, that the term *goyim* is always translated as "Gentiles," which it is not. His argument is doubly fallacious.

Building on this same promise of *hamon* or *m'lo goyim*, Koniuchowsky lays out his arguments. They go something like this:

ARGUMENT 1:
1-A Abraham and Ephraim are promised that their seed will be a multitude of gentiles.
1-B The Jews are not gentiles.

_____

Therefore:
1-C The promise does not refer to Jews.

ARGUMENT 2:
2-A Abraham and Ephraim are promised that their seed will be a multitude of nations.
2-B Gentiles do make up a multitude of nations.

_____

Therefore:
2-C The promise refers to gentiles.

This is the first of many examples of faulty reasoning and poor logic, in which the conclusion does not follow from the premises. First of all, the reasoning in argument 1 is based on a flawed misreading of the Hebrew, as discussed above. There is no promise of gentiles here, as the concept of what a gentile is will not develop for centuries. The context will not allow for such a translation. Thus premise 1-A is false, rendering Argument 1 false as well. If the premise is false, the conclusion must also be false. Argument 2 is similar, and it is a line of reasoning that both Koniuchowsky and Wootten use. Here, passing over the definition of "gentile" for *goy*, they anachronistically ascribe to the English word "nation" the same meaning that it holds in the modern-day period of "nation-state" or race. Based on this modern notion of "nation," they argue that the social-historical people of Israel is only one nation. Therefore it cannot have fulfilled the promise.

In point of fact, however, a nation in ancient biblical times could be any kind of loose kinship federation, such as the nations of Edom, Ammon or Moab (cf. Jer 48:2). Thus it is entirely consistent that Abraham or Joseph could be foreseeing a future that involved a multitude of kinship groupings centered around a people who call themselves Israel. In the case of Abraham, this is demonstrated by his descendants through the line of Ishmael. But even in the case of Joseph, the kinship groups do not have to include gentiles. Israel itself consisted of a number of kinship groups. This reading of Gen 17:5 and 48:19 has been accepted throughout

3

history by both Jewish and Christian exegetes. For Argument 2 above to be true, it must be ruled out that the other group, Israel, could call itself a multitude of nations. But Israel indeed developed into a multitude of nations, as the term was understood in antiquity to refer to kinship groups. Therefore, Argument 2 is also false. Abraham's and Ephraim's seed was predicted to grow exponentially to a multitude of kinship groups, collectively called Israel, a promise clearly fulfilled in the history of Israel and the Jewish people. It does not require looking outside of the traditional social-historical people of Israel in order for the promise to be "fulfilled."

"Dust of the Earth"

This reading of the text betrays another exegetical problem. One of the hallmarks of Koniuchowsky's exegesis is a hyper-literalist reading of a phrase that precludes the common-sense interpretation of that phrase. For instance, he cites Gen 13:16: "'And I will make your descendants as the dust of the earth; so that if anyone can number the dust of the earth, then your descendants can also be numbered.'" Based on this kind of reading, he argues:

If this promise to Abraham, Isaac and Jacob has been literally fulfilled only through the Jewish people alone, who continue to number only 16 million and can easily and readily be counted, censused (sic) and numbered, then the promise to Abraham, Isaac and Jacob is an outright lie! Yahweh lied! … The promise of physical multiplicity was not fulfilled in Judah alone! That is a numerical and practical impossibility!"[11]

Koniuchowsky goes on to claim:

At the time that this promise [Gen 13:16] is literally and physically brought to pass it will be absolutely impossible for mankind to even count it, or in any way census it, since mankind is totally impotent and unable to count the dust of the earth. This promise is straightforward, needing absolutely no interpretation or explanation. That same seed will inherit the land eventually to be known as Israel…
Whoever this physical seed would turn out to be it would literally have to be more than the dust particles of the sea and the visible stars of the heaven. This promise must be taken extremely and solely on a literal face value. Any tendency to somehow spiritualize this promise is a lack of faith in Yahweh's literal Word. That would be the very opposite of the faith of Abram himself.[12]

Koniuchowsky uses the phrase "dust of the earth" to argue vehemently that the relatively small and theoretically quantifiable people of Israel as known historically cannot possibly be the fulfillment of Gen 13:16. Any group that fulfills the prediction must, he argues, be incapable of being numbered for its sheer vastness. What he ignores is that the Bible is full of hyperbole — expressions or phrases that communicate much more than the idea being expressed. For instance, Gen 8:17, in describing the plagues against Egypt, states that "all the dust of the earth (kal 'afar ha-aretz) became gnats through all the land of Egypt." Clearly this is not meant to be taken literally, to argue that there was not one speck of dust left on the ground in Egypt and that every last speck turned into a gnat. It is a hyperbolic rhetorical style that seeks to get across the point that the number of gnats was vast. 2 Chron 1:9 is even more important for our purposes because it argues that the people over whom King Solomon reigned were "a people as numerous as the dust of the earth." Koniuchowsky has just told us that Israel cannot possibly be meant when referring to "the dust of the earth." He forgot to tell the author of 2 Chronicles, who

4

consciously chose the words of Gen 13:16 to describe his people Israel during the reign of Solomon.

Despite Koniuchowsky's dire warnings, it is not a matter of "spiritualizing" the promises when one recognizes hyperbole in the Bible. It is a matter of being knowledgeable about the rhetorical conventions — the writing styles — used by the biblical writers (see also 2 Sam 22:43; but cf. Isa 40:12).

Wootten betrays a similar ignorance of rhetoric and grammar in her exegesis of Gen 48:4b: "I will make you a company of peoples" (Heb: *v'n'taticha lik'hal 'amim*). She points out that the term for company, or assembly, the Hebrew word *kahal*, is translated elsewhere in the Septuagint into the Greek word *ekklesia*, where it refers to "Congregation or Church."[13] Her point in making this statement is to argue that the "Church" today is physically and materially the same as the ancient assembly of the *b'nei Israel* in the wilderness.[14] Ironically, the LXX (Septuagint)[15] translation here in Gen 48:4 for "company of peoples" is *synagogas ethnwn*, not *ekklesia ethnwn*. To use the word, "Church," is hardly an acceptable way to translate *synagogas*. But the problems with her statement go beyond this. Not only does she incorrectly translate from *kahal* to *synagogas* to Church, but, in addition, she mistranslates the term *kahal* in its own right. The term means "assembly," not church. It can refer to any gathering or company of people and is not even used to refer exclusively to Israel (cf. Ezek 16:40; 23:46). The same goes for the Greek, *ekklesia*, which can refer to any gathering of people for religious, secular, or political purposes. In ancient Greek, a town hall meeting can be an *ekklesia*. The term "Church" was used to translate the Greek *ekklesia* centuries later than the writing of Genesis. It is another example of anachronism and an unwarranted, sweeping application of a single word to all uses of that word, whether or not they are granted sufficient grounds by the context.

Wootten's purpose in recasting *kahal* as "Church," in clear violation of grammar and syntax, is to reinforce the argument that the modern-day Ephraimite Christians, who see themselves as physical Israel, are indeed the selfsame "church" that received the Torah on Sinai. Koniuchowsky elaborates, "Let it be clearly understood that the word "church" is nothing more than the *ekklesia* or assembly of the *Tanach*. It is the *same assembly* [emphasis his] that was receiving Torah on Mt. Sinai (Acts 7:37-38)."[16] Using anachronism and mistranslation, Koniuchowsky has with a dash of the pen superseded the social-historical people of Israel with born-again Christians.[17]

Anachronism

The contentions of Koniuchowsky and Wootten contain many anachronisms and examples of circular reasoning beside those discussed above. Wootten argues that, since "the Shepherd Messiah" said in John 10:27-28, "My sheep hear my voice," and since followers of Yeshua hear his voice, therefore, followers of Yeshua are physical Israel.[18] In another example of misinterpretation of hyperbole, Koniuchowsky interprets Hos 1:10, which states, "Yet the number of the sons of Israel will be like the sand of the sea which cannot be measured or numbered; and it will come about that, in the place where it is said to them, 'You are not my people,' it will be said to them, '*You are* the sons of the living God.'" Based on this verse, Koniuchowsky states,

> This verse further reveals to us just where we are going to find the ten lost tribes or the sand of the sea that cannot be counted. The ones who call themselves and are called by Yahweh children of Elohim! Do you know any modern day group of people that run around referring to themselves and claiming themselves to be children of the living Yahweh![sic] You got it! *The*

5

born-again community of Gentile believers is nothing more than the former dispersed House of Israel [emphasis his].[19]

This conclusion is based on several incorrect premises. The first is another hyper-literalist reference to the "sand of the sea" as being a number so vast that it cannot possibly refer to the historical people of Israel. As in Koniuchowsky's hyper-literalist reading of "all Israel" and "the dust of the earth," so here, he ignores the many instances where the phrase "sand of the sea" is clearly used hyperbolically to refer to a very large and vast number. Examples of this include Gen 41:49, which equates Joseph's store of grain to "the sand of the sea." Isa 10:22 refers to his contemporaries in Israel as "like the sand of the sea." Note that Jer 33:22 refers to the descendants of David and the Levites as comparable in number to "the host of the heaven" which "cannot be counted, and the sand of the sea" which "cannot be measured." Even Koniuchowsky and Wootten are not so bold as to claim that this reference to the descendants of David and the Levites is actually a reference to gentiles! Thus Koniuchowsky's disqualification of social-historical Israel as the referent of Hos 1:10 is, again, not warranted.

The second error in the above citation is his leap from the statement in Hos 1:10 that the revived people will be called "children of the living God." Here, he precludes the obvious, that the renewed and revived social-historical people of Israel will be called "children of the living God" and supersedes the people of Israel by claiming that the reference is to born-again Christians. We will see more evidence of this new supersessionism below.

The final error he makes is to assume that the *only* people referred to in the verse must be those of his own time. Again, this is a hopeful assumption but not demonstrable by the context. His argument is another example of fallacious reasoning:

ARGUMENT 3
3-A Based on Hos 1:10, the children of Israel are those who call themselves and are called children of Elohim
3-B Gentiles call themselves and are called children of Elohim

Therefore:
3-C Gentiles are Israel

Hanging on a Thread
For the argument to be valid and the conclusion (3-C) to be true, he must be able to argue that *no time* and *no people*, present or future, have called themselves or are called by anyone children of Elohim except those that he names. This is patently absurd. We have ample evidence from the post-exilic biblical writers, from the Jewish pseudepigrapha, from the Qumran documents, from the Apostolic Writings, and from the rabbinic literature that Jews during all those periods have called themselves and one another children of Elohim. Further, since Koniuchowsky does not have at his disposal available data about the events of the future, neither can he justifiably disqualify *future* Jewish claimants to the premise 3-A. The conclusion, then, cannot follow from the premises. It is only true if *both* premises provide an irrevocable guarantee for the conclusion. His argument has failed. Instead, all he is left with is a hope — and a hope hanging on a badly unraveled thread.

Parallel Universes

In her book, *The Olive Tree of Israel*, Wootten, drawing her research from the margins of her NIV Study Bible, lays out the history of the northern and southern kingdoms of Israel and Judah.[20] Fundamental to Wootten's argumentation (and shared by Koniuchowsky) is the idea that *"never once did Scripture call them* [the Ephraimites] *Jews* [italics hers]."[21] The purpose of her contention here is to make the argument that the Ephraimites, exiles from the despoiled northern kingdom, could not have joined themselves to the Judahites and the related tribes that populated the southern kingdom in sufficient numbers to keep their corporate identity alive. For her, the exile of the northern kingdom automatically transformed that people into gentiles.[22] This becomes her warrant for the claim that all (or "born-again") gentiles are in fact Israel.

This effort to create a clear and impenetrable boundary between the northern Ephraimites and the southern Judahites is one of the foundation stones of her and Koniuchowsky's argumentation. Koniuchowsky asserts, "this family split is from Him [God]. He ordained it and desired it so that He could bring to pass the promise He made to the patriarchs."[23] If it can be established that the members of the former northern kingdom cannot possibly be called Jews from the post-exilic period on, then it opens the possibility to ask the question as to how God could allow for 10/12ths of God's people to be annihilated. The obvious answer to this is that God could allow no such thing! The stage is then set to attempt to demonstrate that these "lost tribes" are indeed Christians — that they are not lost at all but have been waiting for this end-time prophetic movement to reveal their true natures. As Wootten states, "God allowed them to become lost among the nations. He allowed them to become — *Gentile Israel* [italics hers]."[24]

If, on the other hand, it can be established that a significant remnant of the northern kingdom's subjects reassimilated into the southern kingdom both before its demise and subsequently during the period of the diaspora, and that, based on this assimilation, the Jews today represent "all Israel," then the Woottens' and Koniuchowsky's arguments fail. In fact, "Gentile Israel" in terms of the biblical world of ideas, is an oxymoron.[25]

The truth is, Wootten's and Koniuchowsky's claims about the annihilation of the northern Israelites are exaggerated and unwarranted. Wootten states, "For the people of Israel remain divided. The two houses still exist. This fact is repeatedly proven in Scripture."[26] She quotes Jeremiah and makes much of the fact that he is found "speaking to 'The house of Israel *and* the house of Judah' (Jer 11:10)" as if speaking to two distinct entities.[27] Koniuchowsky adds, "From the original Ephraimites of the north, none stayed in the land and remained (2 Kings 17:18)."[28] As a matter of fact, while there are indeed cases in which Ephraim and Judah are referred to separately, scripture just as often uses the terms "Ephraim" and "Judah" in tandem, employing the two terms ("Ephraim," or "Israel," and "Judah") as a parallelism — a poetic way of speaking synonymously of the two groups. In a parallelism, when two elements are listed separately, such as Israel and Judah, the rhetorical purpose is usually to correlate or equate them. It appears that the source of some of Wootten's and Koniuchowsky's confusion is that they have failed to understand another rhetorical convention — that of biblical poetic parallelism and its literary function.

Poetic parallelism is one of the most common stylistic conventions in the Hebrew Bible. Biblical poets put together synonymous parallel units for the purpose of rhetorical effect. In doing so, they render the meanings of the parallel units interchangeable. Stephen Geller lays out how two parallel motifs are structured in one of the most common types of parallelism — the epithet. He states, "The B Line parallel is a description of or circumlocution for the A Line parallel."[29] An example of this is Deut 32:30, "'How could one chase a thousand, and two put ten thousand to flight, unless their Rock had sold them [A Line parallel], and the LORD had given them up [B Line parallel]?'" In this case, it is clear that the reference to "their Rock" and "the LORD" are parallel epithets, both referring to God. It would be foolish to assume that the reference is to two, distinct deities, one named Rock and one named LORD. But this is exactly the argument that Wootten and Koniuchowsky make with respect to Israel and Judah. Psalm 24:7 gives another example: "Lift up your heads, O gates [A Line parallel], and be lifted up, O ancient doors [B Line parallel], that the King of glory may come in!" Here again, the "gates" and the "doors" are synonyms.

James Kugel points out that the purpose of the parallelism is often to accentuate the idea that the B parallel *completes* the A parallel. He argues, "B *must inevitably be understood as A's completion* [italics his]; A, and what's more, B; not only A, but B; not A, not even B; not A, and certainly not B; just as A, so B; and so forth."[30] Indeed, Israel and Judah are often cited as two elements in biblical parallelism. But for the most part, the purpose is not that of distinguishing the two but of accentuating their selfsameness. Thus when the Psalmist states, "God is known in Judah; His name is great in Israel," the intention is not to differentiate Israel and Judah but to equate them.[31] The post-exilic Judahite prophets considered the return of the southern exiles from Babylon to be a restoration for *all* Israel precisely because they made no sharp distinction between Judah and Israel.

"All Israel"
Jer 30:10, while clearly addressing the Judahite exiles (cf. Jer 29:1, 30-31), addresses them as follows: "'And fear not, O Jacob my servant,' declares the LORD, 'And do not be dismayed, O Israel; for behold, I will save you from afar and your offspring from the land of their captivity. And Jacob shall return and shall be quiet and at ease, and no one shall make him afraid.'" For Jeremiah, the return from Babylonian exile entailed the return of Jacob/Israel to its land. Jer 31:17-20 reports that Ephraim has repented (past tense) and describes Ephraim grieving over its own acts. Ezra 2:70, after naming the genealogical list of returnees from the Babylonian captivity, states of the returned exiles, "and all Israel lived in their cities." Here the author implies that the returnees comprised "all Israel," despite the fact that this author was fully aware that not every last member of Israel had in actuality escaped the dispersion and returned to the land. Neh 5:8 mentions that the returnees had redeemed "our Jewish brothers (*acheinu ha-y'hudim*) who were sold to the nations [pl.]," that is, who were in exile not just in Babylon but in captivity to a number of different nations (cf. Ezr 6:21). Neh 5:17 mentions that Nehemiah had at his table "one hundred and fifty Jews and officials, besides those who came to us from the nations that were around us."

Again, this indicates that the returning exiles' numbers were swelled by refugees from the nations. Zechariah, writing to the same Medo-Persian returnees, addresses them collectively as "Oh house of Judah and house of Israel" (8:13; cf. 8:15) and distinguishes them from the people of the nations who would also be drawn to the rebuilt Temple (Zech 8:23). In doing this, he equates Judah and Israel and makes a distinction between them and the nations — precisely the opposite of how Wootten and Koniuchowsky imagine the events to have been perceived. In fact, in the books of Ezra and Nehemiah, the returnees are called Jews and its derivatives 32 times, but are called Israelites, Israel, children of Israel (*b'nei Israel*), fathers to Israel (*avot l'yisrael*), people of Israel (*'am Israel*), or all Israel (*kal Israel*) 39 times. Add to this the evidence that by the time of the Judahite exile, the Babylonian empire had already swallowed up Assyria and its captive nations. In the year 627 B.C.E., the last Assyrian king, Ashurbanipal, died. In 614

8

B.C.E. Ashur, the religious center, fell. Nineveh fell in 612, allowing Babylon, which had aligned itself with the Median tribes from the northeast, to capture Assyria. In 539 B.C.E., Babylon, in its turn, fell to Cyrus, king of Persia.[32] Thus for the returnees, the restoration of Judah *by definition* entailed the restoration of Israel. All of the former Israelite exiles were as free as were the Judahite exiles to return to the land. It is thus not supported by the biblical record to argue that references to post-exilic Judah are unique to Judah and do not apply to Israel.

Those who returned from exile saw that their numbers included many more than the physical descendants of Judah, Benjamin, and Levi alone.[33] And the returnees, who referred to themselves both as Jews and as the people of Israel, did so not because of tribal affiliation but because they affirmed the theocratic reign of God centered in Jerusalem, the capital of the former kingdom of Judah (*Yehudah*). Wootten argues against the idea that the returnees saw themselves as comprising the collective people of Israel, citing Jer 31:20 to support her position.[34] However, throughout the post-exilic prophetic writings runs the call for the dispersed of *both* Israel and Judah to return to the land. That call continues to this day as those whose community involvement has included a *distinct memory* of being part of Israel continue to yearn for their homeland.

Gentile Israel?

But Wootten has more at stake in her efforts to differentiate Judah and Ephraim. The argument she hopes to establish is that the "lost" Ephraimites as a group became "pagan Gentiles" as a result of their assimilation, this despite the fact that nowhere in scripture is that term used to describe dispersed Israelites.[35] She and Koniuchowsky have a reason for ignoring or obscuring the record of scripture and its tradition as transmitted in both Jewish and Christian history. They want to transform modern-day Christians into Israel using racial and biological categories. But the scriptural record indicates that the returnees from Judah incorporated all from the northern kingdom who wished to join them and thus, as a result, comprised "all Israel." Despite this, Wootten states of the Israelites, "*When scattered, they were Israelites who lived and worked in Assyria. They struck roots in Mesopotamian society. They were absorbed. They became foreigners. Gentiles* [emphasis hers]."[36] But for her, it is not just some who became gentiles…they *all* became gentiles. Koniuchowsky adds to this that "the lost physical sheep of the house of Israel…became the Gentiles and have been living like Gentiles for 2700 years."[37]

While the biblical record confirms that members of the northern kingdom were scattered, it makes no such leap as to declare that Ephraim is now corporately a gentile people. In fact, long before the two kingdoms separated, the various tribes had so integrally mingled together that one would be hard-pressed to make clear definition between any of the tribes at any point in history after the time of the Judges. A cursory analysis of the names listed in the genealogies in Num 26:35-51 and 1 Chron 7:20-27 shows that from the earliest period, Ephraim mingled with many other tribes, especially Asher, Benjamin, and Judah, two of which purportedly comprised the majority of the populace of the southern kingdom generations later.[38] Members of one tribe often lived in the territory of another tribe, even marrying into that tribe. Cultic sites set up in the territory of one tribe were frequented by members of other tribes. H. H. Ben-Sasson notes that in the genealogies can be observed indications "of continual inter-tribal regroupings, the rise and decline of the various sub-units within the tribal frame and their dissolution and eventual merger, as well as the migratory movements of branches to new tribal territories and their frequently distant wanderings from region to region."[39] Wootten counters by arguing that, based on restrictions in land transactions, "surely this restriction limited intermingling."[40] But the

9

evidence is exactly to the contrary. Neither in terms of genealogy nor in terms of territory can clear lines be drawn between one tribe and another. From the time of the earliest confederacy, the tribal groupings offered a way of distinguishing family territorial inheritance, but they did not create the pure, homogeneous racial lines that Wootten and Koniuchowsky imagine. They were never intended to serve such a purpose.

The reason for the intermingling of the various tribes in the period of tribal conquest is a function of the rising and falling fortunes that are recounted during the period of the tribal confederacy. The Danites migrated north from their territories, starting out in the south and ending up at the headwaters of the Jordan river (Jdg 18); the Benjamites suffered defeat at the hands of other confederacy members; Ephraim spread into the territories of Dan and Benjamin and overlapped the territory of Judah.[41] As a result, the genealogy lists show the names of some families and geographic locations that are at one time said to be part of Judah, and, at another time, those very same families and geographic locations are said to be a part of Benjamin, Dan, or Ephraim. The people of Israel, from the earliest period after entering the land, maintained fluid territorial boundaries between tribes that often shifted and fluctuated. However the people themselves intermarried, worshipped together, settled in one another's territories, and generally interacted so closely that all the tribes were justified in calling themselves by the title, "Israel."

Two Houses?

More importantly, the sense of unity fostered by this intermingling was not interrupted, not even by the division into two kingdoms. Koniuchowsky disputes this, declaring fervidly, "Get it fully settled in your minds that after 921 BC there was and still is [sic] two separate houses of Israel!!"[42] But the distinctions are simply not so neat as he desires. The author of 2 Chronicles often makes mention of Israelites from the northern kingdom who lived in the southern kingdom under Rehoboam after the split between the two kingdoms (2 Chron 10:17; 15:9; 31:5-8). It is worthwhile to quote 2 Chron 10:17, which states, "But as for the sons of Israel who lived in the cities of Judah, Rehoboam reigned over them." The importance of this statement is magnified when we read the previous verse, 2 Chron 10:16c, "So *all Israel* departed [from Rehoboam and the southern kingdom] to their tents." In fact, not all Israel departed, but rather many from the northern kingdom remained in Judah, as verse 17 contends. This is merely another example of the rhetorical technique of hyperbole. We have seen that Koniuchowsky sometimes argues for a hyper-literalist reading of the text, disallowing the possibility of this kind of hyperbolic language which is common in scripture.[43] Note also, 2 Chron 11:16, which states, And those from *all the tribes of Israel* [italics mine] who set their hearts on seeking the LORD God of Israel, followed them to Jerusalem to sacrifice to the LORD God of their fathers." This occurred *after* the rise of the northern kingdom — *after* the two kingdoms had separated. In 2 Chron 30:1-11, the southern king Hezekiah invited Ephraim and Manasseh (tribal heads whose names were often used synonymously with Israel to designate the northern kingdom) to celebrate Passover together with his subjects in Jerusalem. Indeed, a great assembly accepted his invitation and came from the north to worship in Jerusalem (2 Chron 30:25; 31:5-6). This unity is underscored as well in 2 Chron 31:1. The Chronicler, in choosing to relay these accounts and not others, did so with a specific purpose. That purpose was to demonstrate the unity of the people Israel around the Jerusalem cultic sites *despite* the tribal split. Daniel 9:11 echoes the sentiment of the Chronicler when he refuses to separate the various tribes in Israel in his prayer of repentance before God.

We have seen that the Chronicler, Jeremiah, and Daniel all portray all Israel as united, during the time of the divided monarchy and after, and despite the fact that the two kingdoms were taken captive in two different periods. This effort of theirs points to the great care that these writers took to portray the exiles from Jerusalem and Judah as nevertheless representative of all the people of Israel. It was not necessary for them that every last Israelite join the southern kingdom in order for Israel to survive as a people. These writers found consequential, and thus worthy of expansion, the information that those who went into the southern kingdom's exile to Babylon in 586 B.C.E. contained a representation of all twelve tribes (cf. Ezra 6:17; 8:35). And for them, this representation was adequate to demonstrate that the whole people had survived as a corporate entity.

The Jerusalem Temple

To those priests who returned with Ezra, the Temple cult mattered most, and integrally tied to Temple practice was the notion that all Israel received the benefits and participated in the activity of the cult — this despite the fact that we have plentiful historic evidence that among the southern kingdom exiles, as well as the northern, many in actuality did not return to Jerusalem upon the decree of Cyrus. Nevertheless, those charged with executing the duties surrounding the Temple cult knew that those duties could not properly be carried out unless they conceived of Israel as a corporate entity. The priests were offering sacrifice for their own people, not for some future imagined people in an age far off in the future. They perceived *their own number* as comprising "Israel" and thus were able to offer sacrifices on behalf of Israel.[44] Offerings made for the community were made "on behalf of the children of Israel" (cf. Num 8:19; Neh 1:6). It is this collective that survived the great destructions of 722 and 586 B.C.E. And this collective called itself Israel. The Bible never refers to the God of the Israelites, only to the God of Israel — the collective people. The reason for this is that Israel has always been an indivisible collective. Thus the people as constituted in any one point in time in the tradition *is* Israel, the *whole* people Israel, irrespective of the number of tribes actually represented (if such a thing could ever be established, which, of course, it cannot).

Not "Not-Judah"

We know that many of the exiles from the southern kingdom elected to stay in Babylon where they developed a thriving and flourishing community that would continue for centuries. Their continuing presence in exile, however, did not render them "not-Judah" or "not-Israel." Rather, it was a witness to the continued state of exile that has been a part of the experience of the people of Israel even to our present day. Only a part of Israel and only a part of Judah went into exile. But the specter of alienation and exile has nevertheless encompassed a significant part of the biblical story as we know it today. In fact, it is this very response to exile that characterizes how Israel is to live and how Israel views itself today.

When Judah returned from Babylon, Ezra made a command concerning the one who did not join with the returnees, that "all his possessions should be forfeited and he himself excluded from the assembly of the exiles" (Ezra 10:7-8). And yet Isaiah and Jeremiah represent a different perspective. They looked forward to the day that the exiles would return in the arms of the God of Israel (Isa 40:11; Jer 46:27). But all three — the authors of Ezra, Isaiah, and Jeremiah, took very seriously the conscious choice to remain a part of the people, demonstrating that membership in Israel has never comprised merely a racial category but has always been primarily a matter of choice — albeit not arbitrary choice.

Thus the phrase "the Jewish people" has become the title for all of Israel. The term *Jew* (Heb. *yehud*), which is derived from the tribe, *Judah*, encompassed all those who were taken into

11

captivity by the time of the Babylonian exile, both former Israelites and Judahites, "the remnant of Israel" (Jer 31:7. Cf. Jer 50:33; Neh 12:47; Dan 9:11; Lam 2:5). This designation was strong enough that by the time of the writing of Esther, the term *Jew*, derived from *Judah*, could refer to someone from the tribe of Benjamin (Esth 2:5). The deuterocanonical book of Tobit relates a story about Tobit, a Naphtalite exiled to Assyria along with the northern tribes. In Tobit 11:17, in a clear reference to the Israelite exiles in the Assyrian capital of Nineveh, it states, "So on that day there was rejoicing among all the <u>Jews</u> who were in Nineveh." What this tells us is that by the Hellenistic period, the term "Jew" was understood as applying to former members of either the northern or the southern kingdom.[45] The book of Tobit reports that the Israelite exiles concentrated in Media, where they were able to maintain group cohesion and thus remained connected corporately to the larger Jewish world.[46] The term had moved beyond a designation of tribal kinship to a designation for a broader social group of adherents to a certain socio-religious entity who desired to be numbered within its boundaries (including gentiles, by the way. Cf. Esth 8:17; 9:27).[47] By the time of the Hellenistic period, the term *Jew* identified those of all the former tribes who dwelt in the diaspora and who affirmed a particular religious system. Nevertheless, the rabbis were and are ever mindful that the term *yehudi* is not completely adequate to describe their people, preferring always to use the terms *am Israel, b'nei Israel, beit Israel, kneset Israel,* or just plain *Israel* for these selfsame Jewish people.[48]

Israel in the Apostolic Age

The Apostolic Writings (New Testament) reflect this Hellenistic usage. The author of Acts describes Peter referring to his Jewish audience members as "all the house of Israel" (Acts 2:36; cf. 4:10). The author continues by referring to the Jewish leaders as the "Council of the children of Israel" (Acts 5:21; cf. also 10:36; 21:28). Acts 13:24 refers to John's proclamation of his baptism of repentance "to all the people of Israel." His audience was comprised of Jews, not gentiles. The apostolic record is reinforced by the later rabbinic evidence that the Jewish people in the rabbinic period also saw themselves as comprising "all Israel." In Acts 26:7, Paul refers to the hope of "our twelve tribes." We notice also that Luke 2:36 mentions Anna as being from the tribe of Asher. Paul states that he himself is of the tribe of Benjamin (Rom 11:1; Phil 3:5). Thus some members of non-Judahite tribes still maintained a memory of their original tribal affiliations. Yeshua claims that his followers are to sit on twelve thrones judging the twelve tribes of Israel (Matt 19:28; Luke 22:30). Their function here is that of representatives of the full twelve tribes.

James (Ya'akov), the apostle sent *to the circumcision*, according to Paul (Gal 2:9), that is, to the Jewish people, not to the gentiles, addresses his epistle "to the twelve tribes who are dispersed abroad" (Jas 1:1). Yet Koniuchowsky, making a circular argument, states of Jas 1:1, "If the ten tribes remained lost and nowhere to be found why would James write to them and call them brethren of faith in verse 2 of James chapter One?"[49] Why indeed? Because Ya'akov considered the Jewish people of his day to represent all twelve tribes. But Koniuchowsky's conclusion *requires* the premise that the ten tribes are lost. Ya'akov himself, by addressing the twelve tribes, indicates precisely the opposite.

In fact, the Apostolic Writings make no mention whatsoever of a gathering of lost Ephraimites. Instead, they portray the gathering of gentiles as a *novum*, an unexpected move in the history of redemption. Never are the gentiles referred to as Ephraim. Moreover, these gentiles are not called upon to receive circumcision, neither at the time of the writing nor in the future. If they were Israelites, they would be expected to receive circumcision. There could be no discussion of a gradual easing into circumcision. When Abraham was given the sign of circumcision, he himself had come out of paganism just as Paul's converts had. But as soon as God had given him the command, he went "in the very same day" and circumcised himself, his son, and all his male servants (Gen 17:23). As gentiles, those who became followers of Yeshua were not required to undergo circumcision precisely because they had no known physical connection to Abraham.

When Ya'akov in Acts 15:15-18 cites Amos 9:11-12, he is referring to a promise for a future age when all the gentile nations will accept the jurisdiction of the Tabernacle of David. For Ya'akov, the future kingdom has broken into the present with Jews and gentiles experiencing a foretaste of that Messianic Age through Messiah Yeshua.

In Romans 11:7-14, Paul states that salvation has come to the gentiles in order to make Israel jealous. If gentile believers are Israel, then how can Israel make Israel jealous? Yet in Rom 11:13-14, Paul claims that a major purpose for his ministry to gentiles is specifically to make Israel jealous. He himself makes a clear distinction throughout his writings between gentiles and Jews. Contrast this with the way that Paul's references to Israel and to Jewish people are interchangeable.

In Romans 15:8-12, when Paul cites scripture to encourage his readers about the unity of Jews and gentiles in Messiah, he does not quote passages dealing with some future regathering of the northern Israelite tribes, although, if Koniuchowsky and Wootten were correct, one would expect him to do precisely that. Instead, he quotes passages that refer to the eschatological renewal of the gentiles. In v. 8, the work of Messiah on behalf of the circumcision is "to confirm the promises to the fathers." What is the purpose of the Messiah's work on behalf of the gentiles? "To glorify God for his mercy" (Rom 15:9). There is no reference to any promise to the gentiles' fathers. This work of Messiah is a foretaste of the Age to Come, when all the nations of the world will acknowledge the God of Israel.

Thus the Ephraimite message undermines the great power of the message of the Apostolic Writings. It makes a message of hope and comfort for all peoples regardless of their heritage, regardless of their station in life, into a racist and race-based plan of salvation for those with the proper bloodlines.

Demonstrating deep ignorance of rhetorical devices such as hyperbole and parallelism, of proper grammar, syntax, and context, of the historical record of the experience of the post-exilic people of Israel, Wootten and Koniuchowsky have made their case. When the exegetical, syntactical, and interpretive data are surveyed more closely, however, the data reinforce the contention that the promises to Israel were not transferred to gentiles because of the "lost tribes." Rather, significant numbers of northern Israelites assimilated with the Judahites, both during the period of the southern kingdom and during the post-exilic period, when large numbers of Israelites who had maintained their identity as Israel, even in Assyrian captivity, returned to the land and joined with their kinfolk from the south to perpetuate the covenant community of Israel.

Not My People

The book of Hosea is important for Wootten's and Koniuchowsky's arguments. Hosea prophesied to the northern kingdom shortly before, during, and after its fall. Hosea described the awful judgment to be meted out against Israel and its final eschatological restoration. In Hos 1:9, Hosea's wife gives birth to a son whom God commands to be named *Lo-ammi*, "Not my people." Wootten combines this verse and others in Hosea that describe Israel's dispersion in Assyria to claim, "Therefore the Lord decreed that they would become indistinguishable from the Gentiles

— He said they would become, *Lo-Ammi — Not A Recognizable People* [italics hers]."[50]   The scripture does not state, however, that *Lo-Ammi* means "Not a Recognizable People." Wootten adds those words herself. According to Wootten, the collective people of Ephraim, that is, northern Israelites, have ceased from being a people before God but continue to exist as individual members of Israel — individuals who are now gentiles but for whom the promises to Israel continue to stand.

The problem here is again twofold. On one hand, Wootten and Koniuchowsky are selective in their choices of scripture. They cite verse 1:9, "for you are not my people and I am not your God," in support of the idea that Ephraim has ceased to have a corporate identity until the time of the final restoration of all things. However, they ignore other verses such as Jer 31:36, "'If this fixed order departs from before me,' declares the LORD, 'then the offspring of Israel also shall cease from being a nation (Heb. *goy*) before me forever.'" Hosea and Jeremiah are responding to the tragedy of exile in two different ways. And yet the difference is not so great as may appear at face value. For Hosea's call for the restoration of Israel is not limited to the distant future. In Hos 14:1-8, speaking prophetically, Hosea calls out to the Israel of his *own day* to repent and offers full restoration to them. The promise is not to some future time, but to Hosea's present and to Hosea's own people. Jeremiah also expects that from among the exiles would come those who desire to repent. It is not uncommon to see this kind of alternation among the prophets between calls for repentance among their own kinsfolk as well as an eschatological call for a future age of full restoration (cf. Jer 29:31-30:24).

This expectation of full restoration has been a product of the experience of exile from the time of the prophets into the modern period of rabbinic Judaism. The call is for a future time when all Israel, many of whose members are scattered to this day throughout the globe, returns to the land and to gather together under the anointed Redeemer figure. Such a call does not, however, demand that those scattered peoples must now be gentiles. For Jews who have had strong, centuries-old traditions and memories of their communities' sojourns in Persia, in Egypt, in Yemen, and in Africa, this hope has reigned supreme since the time of exile. Much more evidence than what has been brought forward based on Hosea's prophetic naming of Ephraim as "Not my people," must be given in order to claim that God has eradicated 10/12ths of Israel. Jer 31:36 precludes such a reading. To be sure, such hyperbolic language is used against Judah as well. Isa 22:4b states concerning Judah, "'Do not try to comfort me concerning the destruction of the daughter of my people." And yet the book of Isaiah is full of words of comfort for future restoration. Jeremiah, who lamented the destruction of Judah, stated prophetically about it: ""And I will scatter them among the nations, whom neither they nor their fathers have known; and I will send the sword after them until I have annihilated them" (Jer 9:16). Words of harsh judgment and annihilation ring out repeatedly in scripture against *both* the northern and the southern kingdoms. Neither Israel's sin nor its punishment was any greater than Judah's. In fact, Jer 3:11 states, "Faithless Israel has proved herself *more* righteous than treacherous Judah." Jeremiah goes on to call out to northern Israel to repent and promises that God will receive them one-by-one to the restored post-exilic Jerusalem: "'Return, O faithless sons,' declares the LORD; 'For I am a master to you, and I will take you one from a city and two from a family, and I will bring you to Zion' (Jer 3:14)." Other verses that indicate that Judah's sin is just as grievous as northern Israel's include Jer 3:10; 5:11, 20-31; 11:10, 17; 12:14; 15:7; 32:30, 32; 36:2; 44:11; Ezek 9:9; Hos 5:5, 9-14; 8:14; 11:12; 12:1-2; Mic 1:5, 9; Zech 12:1-9. The sheer number of these verses clustered together in the exilic and post-exilic prophets demonstrates that there is a motif of judgment that incorporates *both* northern Israel and southern Judah, and thus the attendant restoration includes them both together as well. In fact, in Jer 9:26, both Judah and northern Israel are named among the *uncircumcised* who will be punished. Jeremiah addresses his audience in Judah as the "House of Israel" (Jer 10:1). And his promise of restoration to the land after exile is for *both* of them. Note Jer 30:3-4: "'For, behold, days are coming,' declares the LORD, 'when I will restore the fortunes of my people Israel and Judah.' The LORD says, 'I will also bring them back to the land that I gave to their forefathers, and they shall possess it.' Now these are the words which the LORD spoke concerning Israel and concerning Judah." This promise was fulfilled with the return to the land under Ezra and Nehemiah (cf. Jer 33:7).

Yet although the diaspora has been a part of the experience of Israel since the times of the two captivities (722 B.C.E. AND 586 B.C.E.), Koniuchowsky argues that the diaspora occurred only in 70 C.E. with the destruction of the Jerusalem Temple.[51] This is incorrect. Even during the time immediately preceding the destruction of the Temple, the people did not have autonomy in the land and were controlled by the Romans. The experience of the diaspora is much older than Koniuchowsky claims. This historical error causes Koniuchowsky to attribute to northern Israel and them alone the continued statements about exile that are found in the prophetic writings, when, in fact, we know from biblical, epigraphic, textual, and archaeological evidence that thousands of Jews were living all over the known world by that time.

History

But how do they claim it happened? How did the Ephraimites turn into gentiles? Much of their argumentation is circular as we have seen above. God promised Abraham and Joseph that their descendants would be as numerous as the sand of the sea. Jews do not fulfill that promise (they assert). Therefore the promise must be for gentiles. Or there is the argument that God promised that Israel would call upon God. Jews do not call upon God (implicit in their argument). Christians do call upon God. Therefore Christians are Israel. God promised that Israel would be "Not My People" and at the same time promised Israel's restoration. Israel assimilated into the nations and became gentile. Therefore the promised restoration is to the gentiles. All of these circular arguments have been treated above.

However, Wootten and Koniuchowsky also attempt to give some historical basis for their fantastic claims. As mentioned above,[52] the split between Israel and Judah during the time of the monarchies precipitated this great historical drama. They argue that northern Israel began to adopt pagan customs, ignoring the fact that the record of the whole history of Israel, beginning with the time of the exodus from Egypt, includes accounts of idolatry, and yet the people never lose the designation, "Israel." Nevertheless, Wootten and Koniuchowsky construct a scenario in which the idolatry of northern Israel was so extensive that they became "Ephraimite pagans."[53] This group of pagans, argues Koniuchowsky, "would one day become hidden as individuals within the Christian Church through Yahweh's program of the regathering of Ephraim through Messiah Yahshua."[54] But how did we get from here to there? Koniuchowsky explains by describing the global dispersion of these northern Israelites. "Thus," he claims, "was born the ten lost tribes of Israel."[55] Koniuchowsky sees no hope for a corporate identity for the northern Israelites until the time of Yeshua (or "Yahshua" as Koniuchowsky addresses him). Again, working with circular arguments, Koniuchowsky claims that the statement of Yeshua in Matt 15:24, "'I was sent only to the lost sheep of the house of Israel,'" indicates that non-Jewish followers of Yeshua are in fact Israel. Koniuchowsky boldly states, "*In other words Paris, London, Hong Kong, Tehran, Beirut, Tokyo, New York, Boston, Philadelphia etc., are all considered cities of Israel by our Heavenly Father...the globe is 'His Israel* [emphasis his]."[56]

15

Yet, Yeshua was clear when giving instructions to his disciples in Matthew 10:5-6. He specifically *ruled out* the gentiles *and* the Samaritans, whom Wootten and Koniuchowsky claim as their own, saying, "*Do not go* in the way of the gentiles, and *do not enter* any city of the Samaritans; *but rather* go to the lost sheep of the house of Israel." In saying this as Matthew reports, Yeshua, during the time of the Second Temple, made a clear distinction between those of the house of Israel (Jews) on one hand and the gentiles and Samaritans on the other.

While there is ample evidence that post-exilic Israel saw itself as the sole heir of the title "Israel," there is further evidence that, not only Yeshua, but also the post-exilic prophets continued to see a distinction between Israel and the nations. Wootten and Koniuchowsky argue that the gentiles *were* Israel after the Assyrian captivity in 722 B.C.E. Yet the author of Isaiah, in 11:12, writes that God will assemble Israel and Judah, but offers no such promise to the nations in that particular context. Instead, in the same verse, he writes that "he [God] will lift up a standard to the nations." Israel and Judah are restored, but the nations are not in need of restoration as they were never part of the people of God in the first place. To be sure, God cares about the nations, and God will gather the nations, but not for repentance and restoration as he does for Israel. Rather, God's concern for the nations is for salvation (cf. Isa 49:6).

In the mission speech of 10:5-6, Matthew records Yeshua sending his twelve disciples only to other Jews. And even in the case when Matthew writes of gentiles, we do not see evidence that those gentiles became Yeshua's followers or disciples. The magi in Matt 2 return to their homeland. It is never recorded about the Centurion in Matt 8 that he becomes a disciple. The same is even true of the Centurion who acknowledged Yeshua as Son of God in Matt 27:54. Those in Yeshua's immediate circle of followers were Jews. This is the reason that the conversion of Cornelius in Acts 10 caused such an uproar — because it was a *novum*, unprecedented during the time of Yeshua's earthly ministry.

Who Is Israel?

Wootten and Koniuchowsky give contradictory evidence as to how all believing Christians throughout history could be physically descended from the ancient northern Israelite exiles. At times, they argue that all people on *earth* are physically descended from Israel. Koniuchowsky declares that "*you can rest assured that almost everyone on this planet has a drop if* (sic) *Israelite blood since Yahweh'* (sic) *blessing of physical multiplicity would fill the globe through Ephraim's banishment and subsequent intermarriage and assimilation* [emphasis his]."[57] Wootten adds, "While we are asleep, for all we know, He could be turning the whole world into the seed of Abraham."[58] At other times, Koniuchowsky back-peddles, conceding only that the believing followers of Yeshua may only include "perhaps some true Gentiles."[59] Still other comments are made in which believing followers of Yeshua are designated "another 'sect' of Judaism," without any explanation as to how they can be a sect of Judaism and not Jews![60]

Wootten changes direction and argues a different angle when she declares that when Paul spoke of gentiles being "grafted in" to the olive tree of Israel (Rom 11:17-24), "they became natural branches *at that time!*" From this she reasons that "any children born to these people [to whom Paul wrote] were born of *natural branches!* Furthermore, if *you* [the modern-day Christian reader] are one of their descendants, *you are a natural branch!* [italics hers]"[61] Thus Wootten and Koniuchowsky wildly contradict themselves in their efforts to explain how non-Jewish Christians today can be natural descendants of ancient Israelites. On the one hand, all people are physical Israelites; on the other hand, Israelite status is conferred only when one is "grafted in" to the olive tree of Israel.

16

Wootten tries to put the argument to rest by quoting Paul in Gal 3:29,[62] "If you belong to Messiah, then you are Abraham's *seed* [sperm], heirs according to *the* promise." This portion of Galatians is where Paul makes the case theologically how it can be possible for gentiles to join in the blessings reserved for the people of Israel. Paul, too, shares a biologically-based understanding of the blessing of the *sperma* of Abraham. But rather than arguing that *all* followers of Yeshua are in themselves direct physical descendants of Abraham, as do Wootten and Koniuchowsky, Paul states the following: "'Now the promises were spoken to Abraham and to his seed. He does not say, 'And to seeds,' as *referring* to many, but *rather* to one, 'And to your seed,' that is, Christ.'" Thus Paul specifically refutes the notion that the gentiles gain entrance into the people of God through "seeds"... "as referring to many, but rather to one, ...that is, Messiah" (cf. Gal 3:19). Paul argues that it is only through their standing in Messiah that gentiles can claim acceptance into the people of God. That acceptance is not based on any hint of physical descent from Abraham by any individual except Messiah Yeshua in whom the gentiles have obtained an inheritance. And neither is it a claim to physical descent to have standing "in Messiah," any more than our sitting "in the heavenlies" (Eph 2:6) means that we are sitting on clouds!

Abraham — the Second Adam

Koniuchowsky makes Joseph the typological paradigm for his gentile/Israel. He argues that just as Joseph's brothers did not recognize him, so Jews today do not recognize those formerly gentiles, now Israel.[63] Again, this is no argument. It is typological and no doubt inspiring to Mr. Koniuchowsky, but it does not demonstrate how it can be that gentiles are Israel.

What about genealogy? Is it statistically possible that everyone on earth is descended from one man? Only if that one man be Adam. Their theory would require that no one but Abraham had ever produced offspring that survived — that Abraham indeed be the "new Adam." For any offspring that were produced before or during Abraham's life, including all their descendants throughout history cannot exist according to Wootten's and Koniuchowsky's theory. Wootten desperately tries out another angle to this genealogical argument, contending that since the earliest followers of Yeshua were Jewish and Samaritan (hence Ephraimite), and since those early followers certainly produced offspring, then today's followers of Yeshua, although considered gentiles, are actually offspring of those early Jewish and Samaritan believers.[64] Thus, she reasons, even if the reader were to discount her other arguments, the reader must accept that today's Christians, as "descendants" of the earliest believers are indeed physical Israel. Again, the contention is statistically and historically untenable. We have numerous accounts from the patristic writers that the early Christian message was widely accepted by thousands and thousands of former pagans. How then, can today's Christians be heirs, not of those former pagans, but only of the earliest Jewish (or Samaritan) followers? The argument is patently weak. Secondly, descendants of Jews, by Wootten's own definition, are not descendants of Ephraim. Finally, as we will see, Wootten and Koniuchowsky discount the Middle East as the source of these Israelite descendants and claim that they are found primarily in the West. Yet, if one were to follow the logic of this argumentation of Wootten's, if any Christians today can make the claim to physical descent from the early Jewish followers of Yeshua, it should be Christians of North African, Egyptian, Syrian, and Palestinian descent, for all of which there is indeed evidence of the presence of Jewish or Jewish-influenced communities that followed Yeshua from the second century onward.[65] However, Wootten and Koniuchowsky ignore the people from these geographic areas and, moreover, have only harsh words against the Palestinians.[66] They

17

are the enemy to be vanquished by this new Israel. Koniuchowsky states that "the Jewish people will never ever conquer the Palestinians, Arabs, Edomites and sons of Esau [all the most likely candidates for his pseudo-genealogy, but all non-white], until they are reunited with one heart...into one massive army...with non-Jewish Israel [!]"[67]

Crypto-Jewish Ephraimites?

Koniuchowsky even makes the case that the crypto-Jews of Spain, known to have come from Jewish descent, are in reality Ephraim. He does not explain how self-proclaimed Jews could become Ephraimites in 10th through 16th century Spain, but he claims them as his own regardless.[68]

Koniuchowsky tries another angle when he quotes Don Isaac Abarbanel, a medieval Jewish philosopher. Koniuchowsky accepts as literal the rabbinic Jewish metaphorical designation of the church as Edom. From there, he argues that the Christians of European descent, as Edom, are part of this same Ephraimite people, despite arguing, as quoted above, that the Edomites are the enemy! He states that the European churches "were made up of many very lost Ephraimites and Edomites."[69] But although we know that the references to the church as Edom in rabbinic Judaism are metaphorical, Koniuchowsky accepts this designation as historically valid.[70]

Both Koniuchowsky and Wootten visibly struggle to make the case for this physical inheritance. Yet, like their exegetical arguments, their "historical" arguments tend to be circular, unhistorical, contrived, and based on false or unproven premises. It may be that they sense the weakness of these arguments, for ultimately, they both have to resort to the *argumentum ad ignorantiam* (argument to ignorance), the classic logical fallacy. This fallacious argument is that because a claim cannot be *proven* false; therefore, it is true. However to make such an argument is by definition to fail to substantiate that same argument. The burden of proof is on Wootten and Koniuchowsky. It is their responsibility to come up with solid arguments to support their claims. Yet Wootten's reply to the challenge to demonstrate her claim that non-Jewish followers of Yeshua are Israel is, "No one can prove that they are —- and *no one can prove that they are not!* [italics hers][71] This is no argument.

Ultimately, the argument made is purely subjective — if you *feel* that you are Israel, then you are. Wootten illustrates: "It will be as it was when you were born from above: You knew in your 'knower.'...So it is regarding the truth of your heritage: You cannot prove it. But neither can any man *disprove it* [italics hers]."[72] Koniuchowsky adds, "Genealogy is an issue of faith in who you think you are."[73]

This *pseudo*-genealogy that Wootten and Koniuchowsky have created is ultimately a desperate and contrived one — one that exists if you "know it" in your heart. This differs drastically from kinship groups that have shared communal memories of kinship that are supported by a rich history of literature, archaeology, and epigraphic evidence. Wootten and Koniuchowsky are unable to see a difference. But the differences are striking. One has a subjective, "touchy-feely" base; the other is based in history, memory, kinship, and shared traditions.

British Israel

We still have to answer the question as to how these physical descendants of Abraham made their way from ancient Canaan through ancient Israel to places as far-flung as Australia and Canada. Our authors have already explained the dispersion of the northern Israelites to other nations — primarily Assyria. But it is a long trek from Assyria to Australia! Koniuchowsky takes his clues from Hosea 12:1 and 13:5, which state that Ephraim will pursue or be swept up by an "east wind" (Heb. *kadim*). The east wind, as it sweeps into Israel from the deserts of the east, is a hot, dry wind that scorches and leaves the land parched and barren. It is often used as a metaphor for God's judgment, as in Psa 48:8 [English: 48:7], Job 27:21, and Jer 18:17, where it refers to the *southern* kingdom being expelled "on the day of the east wind" (*bayom kadim*). This is significant in light of Koniuchowsky's later contention that the Judahites did *not* experience global dispersion.[74] But the term can also be a reference to vacuousness and emptiness, as in Job 15:2. To argue directly from this phrase that the Ephraimites would, following the westerly wind currents, migrate to *Great Britain* is again to argue for a conclusion that simply does not follow from the evidence. The cryptic references to the east wind in Hosea 12:1 and 13:5 are merely references to the severity of the judgment. They make no geographical claims about Israel.

But pursuing this line of reasoning, Koniuchowsky then adds that Zech 10:8-9 states that the people of Ephraim will be summoned by Yahweh from "all the western nations where they have been sowed (sic).[75] These verses, however, make no mention of "western nations," stating only that Israel will remember him "in far countries" (Heb. *merkhakim*). Yet Koniuchowsky, based on these verses, boldly asserts that "all land today west and northwest of Israel such as the Americas, North, Central & South, as well as Europe and the British Isles are all locations of major population centers of Ephraimites."[76] Wootten contends that these lost Ephraimites would by now exist in all the nations, but she adds, "Of necessity, these nations would primarily, but not exclusively, be located in the West."[77] It is significant to note that the areas that Koniuchowsky names are primarily populated today by white anglo-Saxons, although Koniuchowsky does concede that Russia is another area of settlement, an area also, conveniently, populated by white, although Slavic, people.[78] In fact, when Koniuchowsky quotes Rashi to argue that the reference to "Sinim" in Isa 49:12 is to the south, he skips China and Africa completely and argues that it refers to Australia![79] Further, according to his theory, any follower of Yeshua who is of the descendants of Esau or Edom or Ishmael is disqualified, since Koniuchowsky "nullif[ies] any claims by Islam and Ishmaelites."[80] This will become significant as we compare this movement to the eighteenth-century Anglo-Israelite movement. Koniuchowsky goes on to construct a convoluted history of development based on questionable etymologies and obscure geographic references to support his claims.[81]

Rabbinic Attestation

Koniuchowsky argues vigorously that rabbinic tradition supports his claim. This bold contention flies in the face of 2,000 years of rabbinic history. Koniuchowsky interprets rabbinic expectation for the regathering of the people to be consistent with his own theology. However to do so is to ignore the whole corpus of rabbinic literature. Throughout rabbinic literature, the reference to the Jewish people interchangeably as *b'nei Israel, Israel, kal Israel, kneset Israel, am Israel, klal Israel*, et al, are too numerous to list. The perception during the rabbinic period of the people of Israel as united was not shaken by the political rise or fall of kingdoms during the biblical era. The rabbis perceived the people Israel as a whole people. The election of one entailed the election of all. The destruction of those destined for perdition only allowed for the survival of the corporate group. Thus developed the idea that "all Israel be surety for one another" (*Israel 'aravin ze l'ze*) as a way of demonstrating the "wholeness of the nation."[82] The early rabbis believed that punishment of the sinner released the corporate people from punishment. According to Urbach, virtually all of the Tannaitic Midrashim contain the homily,

19

"And that soul shall be cut off from among his people — then his people will be at peace."[83] The multitude of attestations of this saying indicate the strong sense of unity and wholeness that has pervaded rabbinic tradition. For the rabbis, "Israel was 'as one body, as one soul.'"[84] The rabbis of the Talmud and Mishnah demonstrated no concern for any supposed lost Ephraimites — if any former Israelites had been cut off in ages past, it was for the purpose of the remnant being at peace. Nor did the rabbis view Christians as Ephraim. In fact, as stated above, the preferred designation for Christians was Edom, not Ephraim. They did not equate Christians with pagans either. The *halachot* (rabbinic interpretations of biblical laws) that the rabbis developed for Christians differed from that which they developed for pagans.[85] To argue, as Koniuchowsky does,[86] that the rabbis support his position, is to ignore the vast body of rabbinic evidence to the contrary as well as the whole of rabbinic history.

Parallels to Anglo-Israelism and Racial Theory

Where have these ideas of Wootten's and Koniuchowsky's come from? The sources they give are few. Koniuchowsky cites Yair Davidy as a major source,[87] but attributes to him few specific citations. Neither he nor Wootten make any mention of another probable source, the writings produced during and after the eighteenth century movement called Anglo-Israelism or British-Israelism. And it is for good reason that these sources are not mentioned, as they are popular among some American anti-Semitic groups for their pro-white, racial claims to being Israel. Wootten and Koniuchowsky make the same pro-white, racial claims, although they do not cite any Anglo-Israelite authors. Nevertheless, the parallels between their teachings and those of Anglo-Israelism are uncanny and should be discussed.

One of the best known proponents of Anglo-Israelite theology was Herbert W. Armstrong, whose "Worldwide Church of God," based in Pasadena, California, grew into an international movement. Although Armstrong is now deceased, the church recently gained media attention when it repudiated its former teachings and joined the mainstream evangelical movement. However, the Anglo-Israelite movement originated in England with a man named Richard Brothers (1757-1824).[88]

Both Wootten and Koniuchowsky share many theories with traditional Anglo-Israelite teachings, although they acknowledge no dependence on them. I will list several parallels that are striking in their agreement.

Both groups (Anglo-Israelites and Ephraimites) build their theories on the mythic story of the ten "lost tribes" of the northern kingdom. However, there is one significant difference between the two groups, and that is that the "Ephraimite," or "Two House" movement rejects the Anglo-Israelite claims that Jewish Israel is under a divine curse.[89] Nevertheless, Wootten and Koniuchowsky share with Anglo-Israelites the concern to distance the two tribal groups, Israel and Judah. As Herbert W. Armstrong, stated,

> This distinction [between Israel and Judah] is vital if we are to understand prophecy...The next place where the term 'Jew' is mentioned in the Bible, the House of Israel had been driven out in captivity...and the term only applies to those of the House of Judah. There are no exceptions in the Bible.[90]

Both groups put great store by suspect etymologies — and often their contrived etymologies are identical, pointing to direct dependence. For instance, both argue that the term "British" is derived from the Hebrew *b'rit* (covenant) – *ish* (man), thus "man of the covenant (Wilson)" or "covenant of man (Koniuchowsky)."[91] However, the problem is that the Hebrew *b'rit ish* cannot be correctly translated either way. Both are nonsensical grammatically. It is thus no surprise that I have been unsuccessful in finding any etymologically sound dictionary that makes any mention of such derivation. Martin adds that "every major work on the subject of English derivatives reveal a total absence for support for the Anglo-Israelite contention that there is a connection between the Anglo-Saxon tongue and the Hebrew language."[92]

The Anglo-Israelites focus strongly on the biblical passage that states that Joseph made the younger son, Ephraim, first-born, making Ephraim preeminent among the tribes. John Wilson wrote in 1877, "The Birthright or heirship to the Promises made to the Fathers was given to the GENTILES in a way in which it was never bestowed upon the people called Jews."[93] I shall quote extensively from Wilson, who wrote sixty responses to questions posed to Anglo-Israelites. There he based his argument on Gen 48:19 and compared it to Rom 11:25, as do Wootten and Koniuchowsky, even making identical errors of interpretation.[94] Wilson also argued that the salvation of "all Israel" must entail the salvation of the "lost" Israelites.[95] He made a distinction between "backsliding *Israel*" and "treacherous *Judah* [italics his], as do Wootten and Koniuchowsky.[96] Like Koniuchowsky, Wilson invites the Jews to join with him and enjoy the "privileges of Ephraim," when he states,

> Our view facilitates the conversion of the Jews, because it enables us to approach them upon greater terms of equality, and not as magnifying them in the flesh, which must always be a hindrance to their embracing Christianity, whereby they lose that very *caste* on account of which they are valued. It is surely better to invite 'the Jew' to join the commonwealth of Israel — to partake of the privileges of Ephraim, '*My Firstborn*' — of being set among '*the children*' of Joseph, whose is '*the Birthright* [italics all his]."[97]

His peculiar reference to "the Jew" in the singular to refer to Jewish people at large is parallel to Wootten's writing, where she peppers her book, *The Olive Tree*, throughout with references to "the Jew,"[98] using the term as a disembodied, abstract singular to reference an impersonal and thus removed "other." Koniuchowsky also uses the term in this manner.[99] Wilson, Wootten, and Koniuchowsky all point to the area north of Israel as the locus of the ancient forebears of the Saxons.[100] Like Wootten and Koniuchowsky, Wilson equates the British Isles with the Isles of Tarshish (Psa 72:10).[101] Wilson shares the same exegesis of Hos 1:10 with Koniuchowsky.[102] Both groups share an innate hostility toward Roman Catholicism. Wilson depicts the "Church of Rome" which cut itself off, as opposed to the "churches of the Reformation which were of Israel."[103] Koniuchowsky's references are even more inflammatory. He refers to "the Roman Church and her daughter hookers," "the Roman Church and her harlot offspring,"[104] "the church and her Roman Pontiff," "the Pontiff Maximus (Supreme Divine King)," "the unholy father in Rome, and his disciples," "the unregenerate pope," and "false apostate Roman ecclesiastical heresy" and "this breakaway, illegal, and renegade flock."[105] He even accuses the Vatican of secretly plotting to move its headquarters to Jerusalem.[106]

Both proclaim that the teaching they propound is a "mystery" revealed only through their teachers who are relieving the rest of God's people from a state of blindness.[107] Wootten states, "The absolute truth about ones (sic) physical heritage remains hidden to humanity."[108] Wootten sees the "time of the end" as the time when, people will gain "latter-day insight," citing Daniel and proclaiming, "'Those who have *insight* will shine brightly' (Dan 12:3)."[109]

White Supremacy

Of most concern about the Anglo-Israelite and the "Two House" theory (I use the singular because the two theories are virtually identical — the differences are minimal) is the racial element found in both. Wilson, lauding the accomplishments of the anglo-Saxon "race," states,

> Let us consider what provision God, in His good providence, has made towards this glorious result: the various blessings we possess — physical, mental, spiritual, artistic, mechanical, commercial, political, and literary; our remarkable position in regard to other races all around the globe; our responsibilities as rulers and missionaries; as civil, naval, and military servants…Let us fill up our destiny of being for Blessing to all nations….Soon may Ephraim indeed possess and exercise the spirit of the Firstborn![110]

The arguments of Wootten and Koniuchowsky focus entirely on race as well, especially in their focus on white, Anglo-Saxons as comprising the majority of these Israelites. Wootten makes mention of "blood-line Israelites" and the promise that the scattering of the northern Israelites "did not dilute the bloodlines."[111] She refers to Jews today as "biological Jews."[112] There is no recognition on her part or on the part of Koniuchowsky that the issue of God's relationship with Israel is not racial. Yet the social-historical people of Israel have never claimed racial priority as the basis for their covenant relationship to God. Throughout the recorded history of Israel and the Jewish people, outsiders have been welcome into their ranks, receiving full acceptance in the process. Jewish identity is based, not on racial deliberations but on a shared communal memory and on choice. Each generation is called upon to remember Sinai as if its own members stood at the foot of the mountain along with their ancient forebears. This is true whether you are an Israeli Jew or a Chinese Jew. Jewish identity is not racial — it is based on memory and choice.[113]

Wilson's glowing racial panegyric can perhaps be excused as a product of his time, the late nineteenth century, when nationalist ideas were fresh and hopeful, and the idealism of the post-Enlightenment period had not yet been trampled under Nazi Storm-trooper's boots. But in this post-Holocaust world, to excuse the race-based theology of Wootten and Koniuchowsky and their reduction and limitation of God's grace to nationalist and racial criteria is to be remiss in our concerns for the welfare of our communities.

The most striking parallel between the two groups is their focus on white, Anglo-Saxons as the locus of the majority of the people of Israel. Both argue that the lost tribes migrated to areas where they became known as Scythians and eventually Saxons. Both groups make mention of the nobility of anglo-Saxons as evidence for their biblical, Israelite heritage. Citing a rabbinic commentary on 1 Sam 1:1, Wilson quotes, "Ephrati is taken to mean someone from the tribe of Ephraim and of noble birth."[114] Based on the same verse, Koniuchowsky states that "these rabbis understood that …the House of Joseph…would turn up in the west as nobles, aristocrats and monarchs." "The ancient sages," he adds "understood that the ten tribes would flourish as noblemen every where (sic) they went. Nowhere is this truth found more than in the former British Empire and her colonies."[115] Wootten adds, "To be Israel is to rule with the Almighty. Thus, the 'Who is Israel?' question, of necessity, is also asking, '*Who* will rule with the Almighty?'"[116]

Citing Obadiah 1:20, Koniuchowsky calls Germany the land of the Canaanites and Zarapheth he labels France and Britain![117] Both groups argue forcefully that the people of Israel are in the West.[118] The significance of this is that it indicates the dependence of Wootten and Koniuchowsky on classic Anglo-Israelite theology despite their protestations.[119]

Koniuchowsky is right to be sheepish about his dependence because of the primarily anti-Jewish stance of the Anglo-Israelites. Our extant textual, historical, archaeological, and epigraphic evidence universally points away from the west toward Persia, modern Iran and Iraq, Egypt, Asia Minor, North Africa and Syria as areas of significant populations of exiles. But these areas are primarily populated with non-whites. In the face of such overwhelming evidence, why would these two groups, the Anglo-Israelites and "Two House" theorists, purportedly unrelated to each other in their teaching, both argue for white Anglo-Saxons as the true descendants of Israel unless there was indeed dependence of the latter [Wootten and Koniuchowsky] upon the former [Wilson et al]?

Koniuchowsky works vigorously to separate himself from the teaching of "replacement theology." In Part 3 of his series, "The End Time Solution to Replacement Theology," he puts the full blame for this theology on the Roman Catholic church, sometimes overlooking the serious role played by post-Reformation Protestants in the church's history of anti-Judaism. He also overlooks the strong history of anti-Jewish thought that goes back to the pre-Roman period, the second century, with Justin Martyr and the Epistle of Barnabas.[120] Filled with vituperation and sarcasm, Koniuchowsky "protesteth too much." He speaks with great vehemence and passion, admitting that his "blood is boiling."[121]

"Babylon is Fallen"

But in his effort to distance himself from his Anglo-Israelite forebears, he presents a hysterical and caricatured portrayal of the church's treatment of the Jews. Certainly there is much in Christian history to condemn, but rather than an even-handed and scholarly treatment, Koniuchowsky presents a tirade of confused and confusing accusations. At one point the Protestants are Israel, at another point, the Reformer upon whose teaching so much of Protestantism is based, Martin Luther, is excoriated.[122] Certainly Luther deserves excoriation for his anti-Jewish remarks, but the inconsistency in Koniuchowsky is unnerving. He calls "Dominion Now" or "Kingdom Now" theology, which is a recent Pentecostal theological development, a *"papal farce, designed to enlist Protestants in a new age attempt to liquidate the Jewish race, by theology rather than by a sword* [emphasis his]."[123] He does acknowledge, grudgingly, that there may indeed be "Israelites" in the Roman Catholic Church,[124] but he makes no mention of Rome's repudiation of their anti-Jewish stance since the time of the Second Vatican Council — no mention of the Lutheran repudiation of Martin Luther's anti-Semitic statements. Instead, with biting sarcasm, Koniuchowsky denounces the "so called 'church' system" and its "second covenant law, which is love, baby, love," this "man made ecclesiastical organization started, funded,, (sic) and headquartered in Rome," which "now wants to force their (sic) paganized Christendom down the throats of the worlds (sic) populace."[125] Engaging in further speculative pseudo-etymology, he claims that for these Christians, "a pagan blonde haired, and blue eyed European, pork eating Jesus (the English translation of the sun diety Zeus), has replaced Yahweh the Father as LORD (from the pagan deity Lourdes), over his 'church' (from the pagan circular ritual conducted by the Celts)."[126]

23

Messianic Replacement Theology?

The final irony is that in one broad sweep, Koniuchowsky indicts Messianic Jews as major players in this "replacement theology" debacle as well. He argues that Messianic Jews are the unwitting pawns of these evil conspirators in that they accept the notion that the church is not social historical Israel. His argument in this section is filled with mischaracterizations, not only of Christian theology, but clearly of Messianic theology as articulated by any known Messianic spokesperson. For those who know Messianic theology, it would be unimaginable for a Messianic teacher to claim that the church has replaced Israel. But Koniuchowsky is not daunted in his accusations. There is none that escapes his scorching condemnations. He even has words for Hebrew Christians, calling their movement "a dying dinosaur if there ever was one."[127] As the article progresses, the bold print and underlined sections of his treatise threaten to dwarf the normal font. Koniuchowsky's cry to Christians is to call them "BACK INTO THE COMMONWEALTH OF ALL ISRAEL, HER MESSIAH, AND HER ETERNAL PRECEPTS! [emphasis his]."[128]

Koniuchowsky argues that those Christians and Messianic believers who accept the church as a viable entity along with the Jews are "enflam[ing] the nefarious fires of replacement theology...guarantee[ing] its survival."[129] He accuses Christians and Messianic Jews of fostering the idea of "spiritual Israel."[130] He wrongly imputes "replacement theology" to those who do not teach it. Christian and Messianic theologians today teach that the church has status as "grafted in" to Israel (Rom 11:17) and are members of "the commonwealth of Israel" (Eph 2:12) or the "Israel of God" (Gal 6:16). But they do not conceive of this membership in racial terms. Koniuchowsky ignores this in his efforts to mischaracterize his opponents. In doing so, he creates a false "straw man" that he can knock down in righteous indignation. The straw man, I am afraid, does not exist in most Roman Catholic, Protestant, or Messianic Jewish circles, all of whose noted theologians have repudiated replacement theology and the notion of the church as spiritual Israel.[131]

The same exegesis, the same contrived etymologies, the same constructed histories, the same white, Anglo-Saxon racial focus, the same arguments against the church — the parallels are unmistakable and undeniable. Without leveling the formal charge of plagiarism, it indeed appears that Wootten and Koniuchowsky have built their "Two Houses" on the shifting sand of Anglo-Israelite theology. The concerns that this raises for Jews, whether Messianic, rabbinic, or secular, and for non-Jewish Christians are evident.

Anti-Jewish Elements in the "Two House" Theology

Certainly Wootten and Koniuchowsky are not Jew-haters. But the words of Lloyd Gaston are worth citing here. He states:

> Perhaps I should make clear what I mean when I speak of antisemitism or anti-Judaism in this connection [of Christian interpretive tradition about the Jews]. Just as individuals can be relatively free of personal prejudice and still participate actively in a system of racism, so anti-Judaism has to do with the *objective effect* [italics mine] of the word used, whether or not the people who speak them subjectively hate Jews.[132]

Thus despite the fact that Koniuchowsky may be Jewish (we have not verified this), and despite his vigorous and at times comic protests, there is indeed a great deal of anti-Jewish rhetoric in his claims. It is to Wootten's credit that she is more discretionary in this regard. However, even in Wootten's case, the implications of her teaching are of grave concern to those of us in the Jewish community. Wootten warns that current theologies about Jews and Gentiles "can produce feelings of superiority [among Messianic Jews]." She goes on to say, "Believing they are 'natural' sons (sic), descended from the 'Chosen race of the Jews,' some contend they are 'Twice Chosen.'" She continues by accusing Jews of a "false racial pride."[133] Following what has become a typical motif among Christian critics of Messianic Judaism, Wootten raises the specter of Jewish attitudes of superiority without citing any actual evidence for it. In all my own 18 years in the Messianic Movement, I have yet to find any Messianic Rabbi arguing for a superior stance for Jewish over non-Jewish believers in Yeshua. It is a charge that has no foundation. Despite that, however, the charge persists in Christian circles and is now taken up and repeated by Wootten.

In this, Wootten and Koniuchowsky, in their grand claims to have solved the issue of racial pride, have done so by replacing an old racial argument with a new one. Those who can count themselves among the redeemed are the racial Ephraimites. Among those who cannot, Wootten and Koniuchowsky include rabbinic and secular Jews as well as the rest of the nations, who, purportedly, will experience a lesser status during the Messianic age. In all cases, race and "bloodline" is the determining factor.

Functional Supersessionism

Both Wootten and Koniuchowsky are careful to denounce "Replacement Theology."[134] But their efforts to distance themselves from it is drawn, not so much out of a concern for the Jewish people, but from the fact that it is a rival theology of Israel that cannot coexist along with their own. Ultimately, however, their own theology functions in the same way as replacement theology. Rather than *supplant* social-historical Israel, they argue that their standing as physical Israel is *in conjunction with* social-historical Israel. As we will see, however, this stance is a Trojan Horse to allow them to establish the idea that they, as physical Israel, are owed a 10/12th percent of the land of Israel. The end result is that indeed they *do* supplant those of social-historical Israel that are not followers of Yeshua. Both the writings of Wootten and Koniuchowsky lack any reference to the eternal nature of the covenant with any Jews except Messianic Jews.

Certainly redemption is through Yeshua, but this does not do away with the eternal nature of the covenant with all Israel. We as Jewish believers in Yeshua are still in a covenant relationship with Jews who do not know Yeshua. We believe that God will ultimately be faithful to that covenant and draw our rabbinic and secular sisters and brothers into relationship with him through Yeshua. But in our claims, we give full recognition to the assertion that God's covenant with Israel as a corporate people is eternal. It is not in any way supplanted by the church. How are Wootten's and Koniuchowsky's claims any different from the former supersessionists who also claimed that only those among the Jewish people that were believers in Messiah could participate in the blessings of the kingdom? There is no difference.

It appears that the existence of Messianic Judaism may provide an "out" for those who want to deprive the members of social-historical Israel of their rightful blessings as covenant partners with God. The blessings of social-historical Israel, claim Wootten and Koniuchowsky, are bestowed upon Messianic Jews alone.[135] Compare Ruether's words as she describes the church's tradition of supersessionism:

> Essentially, there is one covenant, *promised* to Abraham, *foretold* by the prophets, and *fulfilled* in the gentile Church, who accepted the Messiah promised to Israel... The message of election

25

refers to a believing people. The Jews proved through their history that they are not this people. So the believing people becomes a historical reality only with the gentile Church.[136]

The only difference between this statement describing traditional supersessionism and that of the "Two House" theorists is that the latter group can point to modern-day Messianic Jews and argue that because they accept Messianic Jews, they have not supplanted Israel. Messianic Jews have become their "out" to recast supersessionism and to continue to deny to rabbinic and secular Jews a place in God's redemptive history. As a result of this, the net result of their teaching is not functionally or effectively different from the results of replacement theologies — theologies that also fully embraced Jews as long as they joined their ranks. It is functional supersessionism. It functions in the same way as does supersessionism. Even their use of Gen 17:5, God's promise to make Abraham "a father of a multitude of nations," calls to mind the church's history of anti-Jewish rhetoric that seeks to prove that Abraham's promised descendants are gentiles, not Jews.[137] It appears that what we have here is nothing really new.

Wootten and Koniuchowsky make much of "Ephraim's jealousy of Judah,"[138] which is Wootten's code for what she perceives as the jealousy of non-Jewish followers of Yeshua toward Jewish followers. While arguing that her teaching is the key to the end of such jealousy (because, purportedly, all sides will follow her teaching and will thus be in agreement), she nevertheless implies that her own proponents are "vexed" because Jews do not recognize them as fellow members of physical Israel.[139] This "vexation" and alienation from Jewish people, from Messianic as well as secular and rabbinic Jews, shows up often in Wootten's and Koniuchowsky's rhetoric. Koniuchowsky writes of "a battle royal over the title of who is Israel!"[140] And of course, it is only when all accept his own definition that the battle will be resolved.[141] He builds his case typologically on the inability of Joseph's brothers to recognize him and argues that the biblical story is a type for Jews' inability to recognize the "Ephraimites."[142] In all of this, there is noticeably absent any effort on the part of Wootten or Koniuchowsky to ameliorate the problems that they perceive save by calling all parties to submit to their own teaching.

What is equally interesting is that, despite their charged rhetoric against historical Christianity, despite their purported abandonment of classical Christian antinomianism, Wootten and Koniuchowsky have nevertheless internalized much of those Post-Reformation Christian scriptural exegetical traditions that are inherently anti-Jewish. For instance, Wootten argues that "Jewish Israel seek[s] justification by the Law of righteousness."[143] This is a standard post-Reformation reading of Rom 9:30-32 (cf. Gal 2:16; 5:4), which ignores the overwhelming evidence that first-century Judaism (as well as any Judaism since) did not look to the law for justification. It follows that any reader that attributes this interpretation to Paul misunderstands him.[144] Thus while claiming a positive view of social historical Israel, Wootten nevertheless internalizes the Church's history of distorting Jewish texts.

Wootten goes on to create an expansion upon Rom 11:1, "Has God rejected his people?" However, she is careful not to cite the passage specifically, possibly because she takes very real liberties with the text here.[145] Her discussion is interesting, however, because it gives an example of her selective reading of the term "Israel" in scripture and especially in the Apostolic Writings. For when her topic is Israel as not "saved," then Israel equals the Jews. Otherwise the term equals the Ephraimites. "Brothers," she freely paraphrases, "my heart's desire and prayer to God for *Jewish* Israel is that they may be saved [italics mine] (cf. Rom 10:1)."[146] For her, Israel as not "saved" is Jewish Israel. Israel as "saved" is Ephraimite Israel (read: non-Jewish followers of Yeshua). Moreover, she repeats the oft-cited but inaccurate accusation of "Judah's

26

rejection of Messiah,"[147] She would do well to note that Paul never uses the term "Israel" without a modifier to describe the church. For Paul, Israel *means* the Jews and as such needs no modifier. For Wootten, Israel *means* the non-Jewish church and *only* needs a modifier when it refers to the Jews. Something is upside-down. Thus in Wootten's writings, as well, we see evidence for functional supersessionism. For the "Ephraimites," references to Israel's ultimate redemption are now appropriated to themselves."[148] As Ruether notes about this tradition, "By dividing prophetic wrath from prophetic promise, one makes the Old Testament a text for anti-Judaism, on the one hand, and for ecclesial triumphalism, on the other."[149] This is indeed a kind of supersessionism.

Law or Grace?

Most striking is Wootten's internalization of and acceptance of the Law/Grace dichotomy of the post-Reformation interpretive tradition. In her apocalyptic vision of the end times, she reinterprets the two witnesses of Rev 11:3-4 as "a Judahite and an Ephraimite."[150] And their "two-fold message is: The Lord has a Law, yet for the lawbreakers, He offers Grace. Two witnesses. Law and Grace."[151] Thus, for Wootten, Jews are equated with Law...Christians are equated with Grace, or, in her words, "One only knows the Law, the other only knows Grace."[152] This is a patent misunderstanding of Jewish approaches to law and grace and demonstrates her dependence on the anti-Jewish exegetical traditions of Christianity for her ideas.[153] In point of fact, as Gaston notes, for Paul, the problem of legalism —of doing works in order to be counted righteous — is a distinctly gentile problem and not a Jewish problem at all.[154] Wootten magnifies her Reformation-based theological bent by accepting the neoplatonic hierarchy common among church fathers, which portrays Christians in a higher realm than Jews. Thus she states, "In Elementary school [i.e., from the Jews] we learned the basics about the Law. In High school [i.e. from the Christians] we learned the basics about Grace."[155]

"Blind Jews"

Another motif that crops up often in Wootten's and Koniuchowsky's writings is the motif of the "blind Jews," again, a long-standing, standard motif of Christian anti-Jewish rhetoric.[156] Wootten states, "They cannot hear. They cannot see. Until the Lord lifts the veil..."[157] Messianic Jews are repeatedly the targets of demands to accept their viewpoint.[158] Koniuchowsky admonishes Messianic Jews to "take off your blinders."[159] Thus ultimately, Wootten's call to "let each [Jews and "Ephraimites"] begin to hear the other," rings false and empty.[160] She and Koniuchowsky show no desire to "hear" the perspective of Jewish people. Instead, she scolds Jews, demanding that they "must accept" her own viewpoint.[161] Wootten and Koniuchowsky demand to set the vision for Messianic Jews today. What both do not understand is that they must give to the people of Israel the right to define themselves and to set their own vision without being defined by Wootten's and Koniuchowsky's "mystery."[162] Wootten argues that it is only when Jews follow *her* teaching that they will be obedient to God, "for only then," she promises, "will you be what the Father called you to be..."[163]

The Elder and the Younger Brother

Even their message of the "Two Houses," or two peoples, is only mildly different from the church's tradition of contrasting the rival sons Isaac and Ishmael, Jacob and Esau as two peoples.[164] Now it is Joseph and his brothers or Ephraim and Judah. The function of the typology is the same — it allows Christians to make claims to status of primacy vis-à-vis the

Jews. In order to support the church's supersessionist claims, Maximinus, writing in his treatise *Contra Judaeos*, listed many of the same sibling rivalries as do Wootten and Koniuchowsky. The first that he lists is Cain and Abel.[165] Compare Koniuchowsky's accusation against Jews as having "the murderous vexing, (sic) spirit of Cain."[166] In this, Wootten and Koniuchowsky have not moved far from the church's tradition of creating a dichotomy between the Jews and "the nations," which, argues Ruether, was "the heart of the *adversos Judaeos* tradition."[167] The message, ultimately, is still one of substitution — perhaps not total substitution as before, but substitution nevertheless.

Wootten castigates the church and the Messianic world for making a distinction between Jews and non-Jews within the body of believers in Yeshua.[168] In this, she fails to understand current Christian and Messianic treatments of the Pauline doctrine of the people of God. In arguing for different *functions* and different *callings* between Jewish and non-Jewish believers, Messianic Jews are in no way arguing for a "spiritual Israel" vs. a "physical Israel," nor are they arguing for separate status in God's sight, nor for a hierarchy of Jews over gentiles or gentiles over Jews. The Christian church has also largely repudiated the notion of the church as "spiritual Israel." But as Lloyd Gaston has stated, "Paul (and the whole Christian movement before Justin Martyr) continues the Biblical distinction between Jews and non-Jews, Israel and Gentiles."[169] In fact, for Paul it is a fundamental distinction (cf. Gal 2:15). To make a distinction, then, between Jews and non-Jews with respect to calling and purpose while affirming their equal standing before God is a very Pauline thing to do. In Gal 2:7, Paul mentions two gospels, one to the circumcised and one to the uncircumcised. And just as the gospel to the circumcision was a beautiful thing, so the gospel to the uncircumcised was also glorious. It stated that gentiles can share in the blessings of Israel without physically *becoming* Israel. This is the great theological moment for which Paul is responsible. Paul never uses the phrases "new Israel" or "spiritual Israel," and neither do Messianic Jews (nor do most Christians today).

The "Final Solution"

With an irony that Koniuchowsky seems to be unaware of, he refers to his solution for the problem of Jewish and Christian relations as "the biblical final solution."[170] As with many in the past history of the church who have come forth with a new message for Israel, so Wootten and Koniuchowsky appear originally to have been enthusiastic about the expected response of Messianic Jews to their message. But Koniuchowsky, especially, shows that his reaction is classical and typical when Messianic Jews do not accept his teaching.[171] His charged rhetoric is filled with name-calling and accusations. For instance, he states that "saved Judah's carefree, careless attitude towards trying to discover where in the world the rest of his lost physical family really is, is nothing more than a colossal case of a self centered mindset!"[172] Dripping with sarcasm, he chides, "Could it be that Ephraim is just as chosen as Judah? Does that burst your bubble? Poor thing!"[173] He accuses Messianic Jews of keeping "'saved Ephraimites' in perpetual second class adopted chains worshiping at the throne of Judaism instead of His Son."[174] He chastises Messianic Jews with the admonishment, "Shame on you for believing the party line birthed in fear rather than in the faith of Yahweh."[175]

Koniuchowsky's sarcasm and personal attacks extend to the Messianic Jewish Alliance as well. In thinly veiled terms, he condemns those "man made steering committees…who continue to tell so called 'Gentile believers', (sic) that they are…at worst associate members, who cannot vote."[176]

28

We do not need another "final solution," such as the one offered by Koniuchowsky. The Jewish people barely survived the last one. Koniuchowsky's and Wootten's statements speak for themselves. All of these statements of theirs are of concern to the Jewish world as well as to the Christian world. What we see here may not be the same as past anti-Jewish theologies, but it draws its life-spring from them and, ultimately, results in functional supersession.

Dangers of the Movement

Notwithstanding this heated rhetoric, both Wootten and Koniuchowsky try elsewhere to apply a thin veneer of philo-Semitic rhetoric. However, despite their efforts, Wootten's and Koniuchowsky's words elicit the gravest concern in the images they construct for the future. For as physical Israel, they expect (and Koniuchowsky claims to be aggressively working toward) their full reintegration into the political and territorial picture of the modern State of Israel — which integration includes their claim to Ephraim's ancient territorial possessions — 10/12th of the ancient tribal boundaries of Israel. Wootten states:

> The heirs of the patriarchs [among whom she of course numbers the "Ephraimites"] are to *possess*, to *yaresh* the Land (the verb is *lareshet*). They are to occupy, by driving out previous tenants and possessing in their place. They are to seize, inherit, expel, impoverish (literally), ruin, cast out, consume, destroy, disinherit, and dispossess the enemy. They are called to succeed — utterly.[177]

Who is the enemy about which she speaks in such ruthless and pitiless terms? We are left to wonder. However, given Wootten's strong claims to the land and her assertion of Ephraim's territorial rights, we must conclude that the "enemy" includes any people now living in regions once occupied by the ancient tribal groups, hence, thousands of Jews along with other ethnic groups. In evidence for this, she cites Hos 1:9-10, "This declaration was made *on the hills of Ephraim*. And to those hills Ephraim will yet return."[178] Wootten also cites Zech 10:10 as referring to her own "Ephraimites." She states, "At that time [during the eschaton], the people of Ephraim will return in great numbers, 'Until no room can be found for them' (Zech 10:10)."[179] Given this kind of supersessionist rhetoric, this should cause some alarm to the Israeli Jewish community. For in the pages of both Wootten's and Koniuchowsky's writings lies a strong assumption, sometimes stated explicitly, sometimes implicitly, that the land belongs to them (along with the Jewish people, of course). Writing of the eschaton, Koniuchowsky describes "the 'catching away,' where millions of Methodists, Baptists, Presbyterians, Nazarenes and other regathered born again folk, are supernaturally caught up and airlifted to Israel on His Almighty wings to, (sic) be returned *to their land forever more* [italics mine]."[180] For the "Two House" proponents, the land of Israel is "their land." Koniuchowsky also writes "about returning Ephraim as born again Israelite-Christians (non-Jewish believers) and Christian Zionists, who will rebuild the Hekal, or the third temple on Mt. Moriah!" He adds that this return *must* occur before Jewish people can be regenerated: "By definition the Jews cannot return to Israel physically and Messiah spiritually, without a simultaneous revival of the other House of Israel."[181] He states that believers are "legitimate saved physical citizens of the Commonwealth of Israel," by which he means the State of Israel.[182] Here we have people with no social or historical connection to the Jewish world making claims that the land of Israel is theirs.

The Next Middle-East War

And as if this were not serious enough, they anticipate that such taking of the land will not be without a fight. Without any context of changing times and places, without any sense of pity, they are preparing for a role as combatants in a future, eschatological war, when "the enemies of Judah are cut off."[183] Lest we have any doubt about who the chief of these "enemies of Judah" might be, Wootten supplies the answer: "their ancient enemy, the Philistines."[184] We can assume that she interprets the Philistines of ancient times as the Palestinians of today, for she also calls for "the complete destruction of the Palestinians and Babylon."[185] Koniuchowsky elaborates: "The Jewish people will never ever conquer the Palestinians, Arabs, Edomites and sons of Esau [all of whom, if anyone, are statistically most likely to be made up of former "Israelites"], until they are reunited with one heart…into one massive army, through this reconciliation of Jewish Israel with non-Jewish Israel."[186]

This militaristic, aggressive, and warlike stance is unnerving in light of the volatile powder-keg that currently exists in the Middle East. But it is even more unnerving when we read that Koniuchowsky is mapping out his own future territory. He states, "Scripture talks about the Mountains of Ephraim (Samaria), that will produce the watchmen [Christian followers of Yeshua] of the last days."[187] It is unclear how aggressively Koniuchowsky is pursuing efforts to work with those groups who are attempting to rebuild the third Temple; however, he makes glowing reference to them more than once.[188] His words also cause the reader to question the motives of the many Christian Zionists who flock to Israel. "Christian Zionists," he states, "long to return home. [People in the government of Israel] openly welcome Christian Zionists, their monies, and their tourist pilgrims with open arms. *This is no doubt a major first step to full restoration!*" [italics mine][189] He dismisses those who oppose him by quoting the Pauline statement, "they are not all Israel who claim to be Israel."[190]

Here again, the acorn has not fallen far from the tree. Traditionally, Anglo-Israelite thinking has also included an expectation that the land would be theirs as physical Israel.[191] It evokes for us memories of the Crusaders of the 11th through 13th centuries, who also, based on the claim to be heirs of Israel, sought to take their "rightful place" as dwellers of the land through conquest and warfare.

Conclusion

Through this analysis of the writings of two major "Two House" spokespersons, we can observe that, for them, everything rests on their reinterpretation of the phrase, "multitude of nations," in Gen 17:4-5 and 48:19 and on their contention that post-exilic Israel did not formally include the former northern kingdom of Israel. These two propositions have been shown to be flawed due to faulty logic, poor grammar, inadequate knowledge of the sociology and history of ancient tribal groups, and subjective, pseudo-genealogies.

Moreover, we have observed that this teaching is fraught with inconsistencies and contradictions. On the one hand, we have seen them argue that every person on earth has some Israelite blood. On the other, the claim is made that only followers of Yeshua have Israelite blood. At one point it is stated that the former Ephraimites are concentrated in Western, Anglo-Saxon areas. But we know that the total number of Asian, African, and South American believers outnumbers the number of white, Anglo-Saxon believers. What of them? Further, Wootten claims that direct descendants of the early *Jewish* followers of Jesus are the Ephraimites, a contradiction in itself – and that somehow all Christians today are biological descendants of those early Jews. But she compounds the confusion by arguing that Palestinians and Syrians, who have the greatest claim to direct descent from these earlier followers, are the enemy and are to be utterly destroyed. Elsewhere we read that Ephraimites will take over the land of Israel (at least 10/12ths of it). But there are hundreds of millions of Christians in the world. How will they fit? How can these "Ephraimites" take over the Galilee and lands now owned by Israelis without dispossessing them? And when is this conquest to take place? At one point it is stated to be before the expected revival breaks out among Jews; at another point it is during the Messianic age. This confusion is an indication of the imprecision of thinking that is the hallmark of this movement.

Finally, Wootten and Koniuchowsky never explain to us what this new racial identity adds to any believer in Yeshua. What is lost to non-Jewish believers who do not see themselves as part of Ephraim? Do they experience less of the grace of God? Do they experience less of the presence of God…less of the acceptance of God…less of the blessing of God? In all of these cases, the answer should be a resounding "No." Yet Wootten and Koniuchowsky create false accusations against Messianic Jews of fostering "second-class status" and feelings of inferiority among non-Jews that have no basis in fact in their attempt to stir up envy and discontent among today's Christians. The fact is, gentiles are free to participate fully in Messianic congregations; they are free to celebrate biblical holidays and shabbat; they are free to live a life consistent with the Torah as a free-will expression of their love for God. The only thing that non-Jewish followers of Yeshua cannot claim is a legitimate claim on the land of Israel. Can it be that this claim to the land is driving this movement?

Or can it be that the movement is driven by racist, race-bating motives in people who demand to be "first-born," who demand to have spiritual primacy and to see themselves as the center of the plan of God based only on their bloodline? This racial element is perhaps the most disconcerting component of this teaching. For while the promises to Abraham were indeed made to his physical heirs, the door has never been shut to extending that promise to all who come and to all who believe, irrespective of their nationality. The Apostolic Writings reinforce this idea, opening the doors to all the nations by not requiring the covenantal obligations that Israel had taken upon itself. Ultimately, the message is anti-gentile because it finds no validation in the non-Jew unless that person is physically an Israelite. For while inconsistent in this matter, both Wootten and Koniuchowsky admit that there are those among the followers of Yeshua who cannot claim physical descent from Abraham or Joseph. Such individuals have no solid basis for justification in the Ephraimite camp. Finally, it is anti-Jewish for its attacks on Jews, its perpetuation of anti-Jewish stereotypes, and its claims of Jewish blindness.

The position of the I.M.J.A., then is that the Ephraimite, or "Two House" movement is in error for the following reasons:

1) flawed, unwarranted, and dangerous interpretation of scripture
2) inconsistent logic and contradictory positions
3) racist and race-based theology
4) supersessionist theology
5) historically inaccurate depiction of Israel
6) dangerous, false, and militant claims to the land which threaten the stability of the current State of Israel

It is not unusual for a group to construct a false genealogical myth, that is, one that is empirically unfounded, in order to create for itself a new story, a new mythic purpose in the world, a new ideology and sense of rootedness. It appears that this may be the impulse that gave birth to this teaching. What it tells us is that Messianic Jews have an important task ahead to offer to the Christian world a clearly-articulated theology of Israel. We should not forget that, up until the time of the Holocaust, the only formally developed theology available to Christians was a supersessionist theology. Since the time of the Holocaust, several Christian theologians have made important efforts to contemplate the theology of the Apostolic Writings in light of a sincere and open dialogue with the Jewish world.[192] The Messianic world would do well to encourage the dissemination of these theological works to the Christian world as well.

[1] Moshe Koniuchowsky, in "Your Arms to Israel: Updated Doctrinal Statement Reflecting Kingdom Restoration Views of the Ministry of *Your Arms to Israel*" (www.teshuvah.com/yati/articles/full_restoration1.htm) states, "the Jewish people have been the identifiable representatives and offspring of Judah. Non-Jewish followers of Messiah from all nations have been up to now the unidentifiable representatives and offspring of Ephraim (Zechariah 8:23)." It should be stated that Koniuchowsky would not use the term "Christian." See Moshe Koniuchowsky, "The Full Restoration of All Israel: Part 3," 8. Please note that for purposes of research, I printed out all four parts of the series, and my page number references are to that of the final printout. Because of the size of the document, I determined that it was important to have more detailed reference than just to the document as a whole.

[2] Batya Ruth Wootten, *Who Is Israel? And Why You Need to Know* (St. Cloud, FL: Key of David, 1998), 55.

[3] However, Batya Ruth Wootten, "House of David Herald: Muddled Doctrines" (http://www.mim.net/hod/hod0160/rf0160.htm), 6, states that for followers of Yeshua, the "emphasis of circumcision" is moved "to that of the heart."

[4] For more information on this book, go to hebroots.org, a website that primarily posts general Christian Zionist material.

[5] Batya Ruth Wootten, *The Olive Tree of Israel* (White Stone, Virginia: House of David, 1992), 31. Cf. also *Who Is Israel?*, 16-17, 28.

[6] Wootten, *Who Is Israel?*, 82-83, acknowledges that it sometimes refers to Israel, but she asserts that by the time of the conquest of the land by Israel, the name referred primarily to the foreign nations. This is not the case, however, for the exilic and post-exilic prophets continued to use the term to refer to Israel. Add to this the common usage of the Greek term *ethnos* in the Apostolic Writings to refer to Jews. Moreover, she constructs her doctrine precisely upon the use of the term *goy* in the *pre*-conquest period, during the time of the patriarchs.

[7] Koniuchowsky, "The Full Restoration of All Israel: Part 2," 7, argues that these references reinforce his point that Israel is Gentile. The reasoning is circular and begs the question.

[8] Moshe Koniuchowsky, "The Full Restoration Of [sic] Israel: Part 1 of a Series," 1.

[9] Wootten, *Olive Tree*, 32.

[10] Koniuchowsky, "The Full Restoration of Israel: Part 1," 2. Cf. also Wootten, *Who Is Israel?*, 3.

[11] Koniuchowsky, "The Full Restoration of Israel: Part 1," 9.

[12] *Ibid.*, 1.

[13] Wootten, *Olive Tree*, 32, 33. In the footnote to the above passage, she concedes that "this does not mean the 'Greek westernized cultural Christianity' implied by the word today," but we will see that her qualification here is not to contradict her argument above but to safeguard her group's rhetorical stand against modern-day Christianity. See below.

[14] Wootten, *Who Is Israel?*, 6.

[15] The Septuagint (LXX) is the Greek translation of the Hebrew Bible, completed late third century B.C.E.

[16] Koniuchowsky, "Full Restoration: Part 1," 7.

[17] whom he contends to be physical Israel *along-side* with the Jewish people who comprise the tribe of Judah.

[18] Wootten, "Muddled," 3.

[19] Koniuchowsky, "Full Restoration: Part 1," 6.

[20] pp. 41-43. Koniuchowsky, "Full Restoration: Part 1," 5 shows a lack of facility in dealing with historical data as well. He calls the Assyrian king "Tilgat Pilsger III" (his name was Tiglath-pileser III).

[21] Wootten, *Olive Tree*, 42.

[22] *Ibid.*, 43.

[23] Koniuchowsky, "Full Restoration: Part 1," 5.

[24] Wootten, *Olive Tree*, 43.

[25] Wootten, *Who Is Israel?*, 93, calls the term, "Gentile Christian" an oxymoron, but has no problem using the term "Gentile Israel." Cf. *Olive Tree*, 43.

[26] *Ibid.*, 50.

[27] Wootten, "Muddled," 12.

[28] Koniuchowsky, "Full Restoration: Part 4: What Judaism Really Says About Joseph's Seed!" 7.

[29] Stephen A. Geller, *Parallelism in Early Biblical Poetry* (Missoula, MT: Scholars Press, 1979), 36.

[30] James L. Kugel, *The Idea of Biblical Poetry: Parallelism and its History* (New Haven: Yale Univ. Press, 1981), 13.

[31] Examples of the use of parallelism to demonstrate that Israel and Judah are synonymous (the list is far from exhaustive) are Ps 114:2; Isa 5:7; Jer 23:6; 50:20; Hos 5:12-14; 8:14; 11:12; 12:1-2; Mic 1:5; Mal 2:11.

[32] W. Lee Humphreys, *Crisis and Story*, 2nd edition (Mountain View, CA: Mayfield, 1990), 152.

[33] Koniuchowsky, "Full Restoration: Part 2, 1, does acknowledge that "both houses" contain representatives from all the tribes, but he does not see this representation as adequate for redemption. The record of the post-exilic prophets belies this conclusion. Further, Wootten, *Olive Tree*, 51, also admits to references to the post-exilic people as "all Israel." ironically, however, she insists that while it may be said that "all Israel" returned, because the term does not really represent every last northern Israelite, it does not tell us anything about the post-exilic status of Israel. But what it does tell us is how post-exilic writers in the Hebrew Bible *interpreted* Israel's status after the exile. As writers of scripture, their interpretation of events is crucial for the modern theologian. And according to their interpretation, the residual people of Israel who had returned represented "all Israel." Cf. Wootten, *Who Is Israel?*, 24, 109.

[34] Wootten, *Olive Tree*, 49.

[35] Wootten, "Muddled," 12.

[36] Wootten, *Olive Tree*, 42-43.

[37] Koniuchowsky, "Full Restoration: Part 1," 7.

[38] "Ephraim," *Encyclopaedia Judaica*, 1971 ed., 807. See H. H. Ben-Sasson, Ed., *A History of the Jewish People*, trans. George Weidenfeld and Nicolson Ltd. (Cambridge: Harvard Univ. Press, 1976), 65-67, for examples of genealogies that list identical chains of names (i.e., identical father to son to grandson, etc.) in differing tribes, including evidence of admixture with non-Israelites as well.

[39] Ben-Sasson, 63.

[40] Wootten, *Who Is Israel?*, 25.

[41] *Ibid.*

[42] Koniuchowsky, "Full Restoration: Part 1," 5.

[43] For other examples of such hyperbolic language that is clearly not meant to be taken hyper-literally, cf. 2 Chron 13:15; 16:6; 35:18; Jer 13:19; 20:4; 44:14; Ezra 10:9. On the Jeremiah references, cf. Jer 39:10; 40:11-12; 40:4-7. Also see above, p. 4.

[44] In response to this, Wootten, *Who Is Israel?*, 112, using characteristically racial categories argues, "Prayer cannot change Israelite genetics." However, the practice of the Temple cult in the post-exilic period is evidence for how the people during this time viewed themselves. In turn, this viewpoint, then, was recorded and affirmed by the prophets and writers of scripture.

[45] Richard Bauckham, "Anna of the Tribe of Asher (Luc 2:36-38)," *Revue Biblique* 410 (1997), 169, states, "Despite their origins in the northern kingdom, many (if not all) of the exiles of the northern tribes in the Second Temple period adopted the same kind of Judaism as their fellow exiles from the southern tribes in Babylonia, i.e. they acknowledged the Jerusalem temple and its form of the Torah."

[46] *Ibid.* See Tob 1:9; 3:15; 4:12-13.

[47] Cf. Robert M. Seltzer, Ed., *Judaism: A People and its History* (New York: Macmillan, 1989), 121.

[48] *Ibid.*, 122.

[49] Koniuchowsky, "Full Restoration: Part 1," 10.

[50] Wootten, *Olive Tree*, 46; *Who Is Israel?*, 38. For an example of the use of this verse in Christian anti-Jewish tradition, see Rosemary Ruether, *Faith and Fratricide: The Theological Roots of Anti-Semitism* (Eugene, OR: Wipf and Stock, reprt. 1997), 140.

[51] Koniuchowsky, "Full Restoration: Part 1," 10.

[52] p. 7.

[53] Koniuchowsky, "Full Restoration: Part 1," 5.

[54] *Ibid.*

---

[55] *Ibid.*

[56] Koniuchowsky, "Full Restoration: Part 2," 2.

[57] Koniuchowsky, "Full Restoration: Part 1," 8-9. He also states (*Ibid.*, 3), *"there will be virtually no one in the earth that is not somehow belonging to the seed of Ephraim."*

[58] Wootten, *Olive Tree*, 112.

[59] Koniuchowsky, "Full Restoration: Part 1," 6. But Wootten, *Olive Tree*, 107, remains steadfast, arguing, "It is very probable that these former Gentiles actually descend from the scattered Ephraimites that Yahveh said He would regather…Though their background may appear to be that of a Gentile, in reality, they probably are physical Israelites."

[60] Wootten, "Muddled," 7.

[61] Wootten, *Olive Tree*, 106.

[62] She wrongly cites the verse as Gal 2:29 in *Olive Tree*, 114. See also Koniuchowsky, "Full Restoration: Part 2," 5.

[63] Koniuchowsky, "Full Restoration: Part 1," 11.

[64] Wootten, *Olive Tree*, 9, 106. See also "Muddled," 8; *Who Is Israel?*, 97.

[65] Koniuchowsky, "Full Restoration: Part 4," 6, indeed acknowledges the significance of Syrian Antioch for the growth of the early communities of followers of Yeshua. However, he does not develop the logic of his contention, which would point to today's Syrian Orthodox Church as a major center for his theory of physical Ephraimites in today's churches.

[66] Cf. n.184 and 185.

[67] Koniuchowsky, "Full Restoration: Part 4," 8.

[68] *Ibid.*, 9-10.

[69] *Ibid.*, 12.

[70] *Ibid.*

[71] Wootten, *Olive Tree*, 117. Cf. Koniuchowsky, "Full Restoration: Part 2," 11.

[72] *Ibid.*, 119.

[73] Koniuchowsky, "Full Restoration: Part 2," 11.

[74] Koniuchowsky, "Full Restoration: Part 2," 9. He argues there that Judah's dispersion was confined only to Babylon.

[75] *Ibid.*, 8.

[76] *Ibid.*

[77] Wootten, *Olive Tree*, 49; *Who Is Israel?*, 74.

[78] Koniuchowsky, "Full Restoration: Part 4," 3, adds New Zealand and South Africa to the areas populated by former Israelites. No doubt his reference is to the *white* populace of South Africa.

[79] *Ibid.*, 4. Although he does very briefly mention "Black Israelites" on p. 5. He never elaborates, though.

[80] Koniuchowsky, "Full Restoration: Part 1," 2. But contrast his statements in n. 69.

[81] *Ibid.*, 6.

[82] E. E. Urbach, *The Sages: their Concepts and Beliefs* (Jerusalem: Magnes Press), 1979, 539.

[83] Cited in Urbach, 539.

[84] *Ibid.*

[85] Cf. Lawrence H. Schiffman, *Who Was a Jew? Rabbinic and Halakhic Perspectives on the Jewish Christian Schism* (Hoboken, NJ: Ktav), 1985.

[86] Koniuchowsky, "Full Restoration: Part 4."

[87] Koniuchowsky, "Full Restoration: Part 2," 12.

[88] Walter R. Martin, *The Kingdom of the Cults* (Minneapolis, MN: Bethany Fellowship, 1965, rev. 1968), 297.

[89] Cf. Martin., 298.

[90] cited in Martin, 299. Cf. also John Wilson, *Sixty Anglo-Israel Difficulties Answered: Difficulty One* (http://www.abcog.org/wilson2.htm), 2; *Difficulty 18*, 10.

[91] Wilson, *Difficulty One*, 2; Koniuchowsky, "Full Restoration: Part 4," 10.

[92] *Ibid.*

[93] *Ibid.*, 1. Wilson adds (2), "The 'Jews' have their own place in prophecy, but not that of the 'Firstborn,' which belongs to the descendants of Ephraim, …the people contemplated by our Lord when He said to the Jews, *The kingdom of God shall be taken from you, and given to a nation bringing forth the fruits thereof* (Matt. 21:43)." Wootten and Koniuchowsky do not share the idea that the entire kingdom will be taken from the Jews — only 10/12th of the kingdom, as we will see below.

[94] *Ibid.* and *Difficulty 13*, 3. Cf. Wootten, *Olive Tree*, 31-32.

34

---

[95] Wilson, *Difficulty One*, 1. Cf. Wootten, *Who Is Israel?*, 86.

[96] Wilson, *Difficulty One*, 2.

[97] Wilson, *Difficulty 2*, 3. Cf. Wootten, *Who Is Israel?*, 15.

[98] Wootten, *Olive Tree*, 6, 77, 81 *et passim*. See also, her "Muddled Doctrines" and *Who Is Israel?*, 91, 92.

[99] Koniuchowsky, "Full Restoration: Part 3," 2.

[100] Wilson, *Difficulty 3*, 5.

[101] Wilson, *Difficulty 4*, 5.

[102] Wilson, *Difficulty 8*, 7. Cf. n. 19.

[103] Wilson, *Difficulty 12*, 2.

[104] Koniuchowsky, "Full Restoration: Part 3," 3.

[105] Koniuchowsky, "Full Restoration: Part 2," 5; Part 3, 3-5.

[106] Koniuchowsky, "Full Restoration: Part 3," 3.

[107] Wilson, *Difficulty 14*, 6.

[108] Wootten, "Muddled," 5.

[109] Wootten, *Olive Tree*, 14-15. Cf. also 71, 77, 79-83; *Who Is Israel?*, 83-88.

[110] Wilson, *Difficulty 13*, 4.

[111] Wootten, *Olive Tree*, 52; "Muddled," 5; *Who Is Israel?*, 73.

[112] Wootten, "Muddled," 4.

[113] Nevertheless, Wootten, *Who Is Israel?*, 97, accuses others of "separat[ing] Christians and Jews based on genetic heritage." But because of her singular focus on race and genetics as the only valid category, she even questions the Jewish status of converts to Judaism (Wootten, *Who Is Israel?*, 98).

[114] Wilson, *Difficulty 13*, 4.

[115] Koniuchowsky, "Full Restoration: Part 4," 2.

[116] Wootten, *Olive Tree*, 22. Cf. Wootten, *Who Is Israel?*, 6.

[117] *Ibid.*, 9.

[118] Wilson, *Difficulty 19*, 12; cf. above, n. 74, 75 *et passim*.

[119] Koniuchowsky, "Full Restoration: Part 2," 10, states, "We do not need Herbert W. Armstrong, Mormons *the replacement theologians of British Israelism* [italics mine], or the American Indians to tell us where to look for …the Tabernacle of David."

[120] Koniuchowsky, "Full Restoration: Part 3," 1. Cf. n. 103. For more information on the church's tradition of anti-Jewishness, see Ruether.

[121] Koniuchowsky, "Full Restoration: Part 3," 3.

[122] *Ibid.*, 1.

[123] *Ibid.*, 1-2.

[124] Koniuchowsky, "Full Restoration: Part 4," 11. But he adds, "Yahweh help us!"

[125] Koniuchowsky, "Full Restoration: Part 3," 2.

[126] *Ibid.*

[127] *Ibid.*

[128] *Ibid.*, 10.

[129] *Ibid.*

[130] *Ibid.*, 12.

[131] For an excellent Catholic theological treatment of the Jewish people, see Clemens Thoma, *A Christian Theology of Judaism* (New York: Paulist Press, 1980). For a Protestant theology, see R. Kendall Soulen, *The God of Israel and Christian Theology* (Minneapolis: Fortress Press, 1996).

[132] Lloyd Gaston, *Paul and the Torah* (Vancouver, Univ. of British Columbia, 1987).

[133] Wootten, *Olive Tree*, 2. Cf. also "Muddled," 10; *Who Is Israel?*, 104-105.

[134] *Ibid.*, 7. See also n. 119.

[135] Cf. Wootten, "Muddled." 2, where citing Isa 11:13 she makes the threat against Jews who are not Messianic, stating, "And those who harass Judah *will be cut off*." Cf. 11.

[136] Ruether, 137.

[137] Ruether, 138, n. 70 cites *Ep.* Barn. 13, 7; Just. *Dial.* 119; Ter. *Adv. Jud.* 2; Euseb. *D. E.* I, 2, 15; Cyp. *Test.* I. 5; Aph. *Dem.* II, 4; 13, 8; 16, I; Iren. *Haer.*, IV, 7, 2; Max. *C. Jud.* 5; Prud. *Apo.* 363-5; *Dial. A.-Z.* (Conybeare, *Expositor* 45, p. 447).

[138] Wootten, *Olive Tree.*, 54. See also Koniuchowsky, "Full Restoration: Part 1," 7.

---

[139] Wootten, *Olive Tree*, 54; *Who Is Israel?*, 135. She indicts modern-day Messianic Jews because of events described in 2 Sam 19:41-43, 3,000 years ago! She goes on to accuse rabbinic Jewish treatment of modern-day Messianic Jews as an example of Judah vexing Ephraim (*Who Is Israel?*, 138). When it is convenient for her, Jewish followers of Yeshua are Ephraim; when it is not, they are Judah. She cannot have it both ways.

[140] Koniuchowsky, "Full Restoration: Part "Part 1," 4; cf. "Part 3," 11. Cf. Wootten, "Muddled," 13: "There is a war between Jew and Christian over the title of Israel."

[141] *Ibid.*

[142] *Ibid.*, 11.

[143] Wootten, *Olive Tree*, 74.

[144] On this, there is a wealth of current scholarship. Cf. Terence L. Donaldson, *Paul and the Gentiles* (Minneapolis: Fortress, 1997); Gaston; and E. P. Sanders, *Paul, the Law, and the Jewish People* (Philadelphia: Fortress, 1983), 17. There is an excellent bibliography in Donaldson for further research on the topic.

[145] Wootten, *Olive Tree*, 74-75.

[146] *Ibid.*, 74.

[147] *Ibid.*, 76.

[148] Cf. the treatment of Hos 2:21-23 in Koniuchowsky, "Full Restoration: Part 1," 6 and of Obad 1:20 in "Part 4," 9.

[149] Ruether, 132.

[150] Wootten, *Olive Tree*, 85. Cf. "Muddled," 14.

[151] *Ibid.*, 85-86. Cf. also 88.

[152] *Ibid.*, 92.

[153] Nowhere is the tradition of the parallel contrasts, Jew/Gentile and Law/Grace, more overt than in Marcion, who posited the existence of two gods with two distinct characteristics, also representing two modes of operation in the world.

[154] Gaston, 25.

[155] *Ibid.*, 119.

[156] Cf. Ruether, 121, 135. In 135, she reminds us that the cathedrals built during the Medieval period often included statuary images of two women, representing Church and Synagogue. The one representing the Church looked alive and full of power. The one representing the Synagogue looked sad and always wore blindfolds over her eyes. For an example of this identical motif in Anglo-Israelism, see Wilson, *Difficulty 15*, 6.

[157] *Ibid.*, 92.

[158] Koniuchowsky, "Full Restoration: Part 1," 8; "Part 3," 10, 11; "Part 4," 5, 12.

[159] Koniuchowsky, "Full Restoration: Part 2," 6.

[160] Wootten, *Olive Tree*, 124. Cf. Wootten, *Who Is Israel?*, 142-143, for her treatment of the blindness of the Jews.

[161] Wootten, *Olive Tree*, 124.

[162] Cf. Gaston, 34.

[163] *Ibid.*, 125. Cf. also Koniuchowsky, "Full Restoration: Part 3," 6.

[164] Cf. Ruether, 133.

[165] Cited in Ruether, 133.

[166] Koniuchowsky, "Full Restoration: Part 2," 6.

[167] Ruether, 137. She writes (133), "The Church especially seized on the line in Genesis 25:23 where it is said that 'two nations' are in the womb of Rebekah and 'the one shall be stronger than the other, the elder shall serve the younger.' Unquestionably, this refers to the Church, the gentile people, who came after the Jews but overcame them, while the elder people, the Jews are made to 'serve' the younger people, the Church." This motif of the younger brother is also used by Wootten in proclaiming "Ephraim" to be the prodigal son of Luke 15:11-32 while the Jews are the elder brother" (Wootten, *Who Is Israel?*, 130-134).

[168] Wootten, *Who Is Israel?*, 147-155.

[169] Gaston, 6.

[170] Koniuchowsky, "Full Restoration: Part 3," 4.

[171] For a discussion on the history of Jewish converts to Christianity turning on their fellow Jews when their message was not accepted, cf. Sander L. Gilman, *Jewish Self-Hatred: Anti-Semitism and the Hidden Language of the Jews* (Baltimore: Johns Hopkins, 1986), 53-67.

[172] Koniuchowsky, "Full Restoration: Part 1," 9.

[173] *Ibid.*, 10.

[174] *Ibid.*, 11.

[175] Koniuchowsky, "Full Restoration: Part 3," 11.

---

[176] *Ibid.*, 6.

[177] Wootten, *Who Is Israel?*, 13.

[178] *Ibid.*, 175.

[179] Wootten, *Who Is Israel?*, 179. On p. 76, she states, "Yahveh…promised to give 'the land to them and to their 'seed' after them.' These two blessings —*fruitful multiplication* and the *land* are the heart of all His blessings. And they are first to be taken in a *p'shat*, literal, sense." In the Prologue to *Olive Tree*, she writes with regard to Ephraim, "And I [God] will bring them back, each one to his own inheritance, each one to his own land." In *Olive Tree*, 67, she cites Isa 9:1 and Matt 4:15, "Galilee of the Gentiles," implying by such a citation that the area of the Galilee belongs to her "Ephraimites." Later (69), she writes, "The Galilee was the area where the Samaritans lived." Still later (72) she castigates Jewish returnees who "continued to scorn those who lived in the Galilee." Here I will cite H. H. Ben-Sasson, who writes (135), "As only a section of the population [of Galilee] was deported [in 733-732, when Tiglath-pileser annexed Galilee] and a considerable Israelite element remained, it is not at all clear whether Galilee was resettled with foreign colonists. In any case, we have no evidence of a new ethnic entity consisting of a mixture of Israelites and colonists coming into being in Galilee, as was the case in Samaria."

[180] Koniuchowsky, "Full Restoration: Part 2," 5.

[181] Koniuchowsky, "Full Restoration: Part 4," 5.

[182] *Ibid.*

[183] Wootten, *Olive Tree.*, 54.

[184] *Ibid.*

[185] *Ibid.*, 36. Here her concerns for all the supposed lost "Ephraimites" among the Palestinians and Babylonians, peoples among whom one would statistically expect them to be most concentrated, is not anywhere evident.

[186] Koniuchowsky, "Full Restoration: Part 4," 8.

[187] Koniuchowsky, "Full Restoration: Part 4," 10.

[188] Koniuchowsky, "Full Restoration: Part 4," 12, 13. He contends that the greatest supporters of the Temple Mount Faithful are not traditional Christians, not Messianic Jews, but "Ephraimites."

[189] Koniuchowsky, "Full Restoration: Part 4," 13. We must keep in mind, however, that the great majority of Christian Zionists do not subscribe to this teaching.

[190] *Ibid.*

[191] Wilson, *Difficulty 3*, 4, contended that the land is lying desolate without them and looked forward to the time when "the mountains were to shoot forth their branches, and bear their fruit for the people of Israel." Cf. also *Difficulty 20*, 13.

[192] Cf. n. 131 above.

15.11.2002

The International 'Christian Embassy' in Jerusalem and Its Terrorist Connections

by Michele Steinberg

On Oct. 11, President George W. Bush delivered a videotaped address to a Washington, D.C. meeting of the Christian Coalition, the organization founded by televangelist billionaire "Diamond Pat" Robertson. The Coalition conference gathered thousands of Christian Zionists for a "Unity With Israel" rally, whose major theme was, that there will never be a Palestinian state on the Biblical land of Israel, which, for them, includes the West Bank of the Jordan River and all of the Palestinian territories occupied by Israel during the 1967 war. The United Nations Security Council, with U.S. support, has passed numerous resolutions demanding that Israel leave. That the President of the United States would address such a gathering is a scandal, and the White House is keeping the President's remarks under wraps.

As *EIR* warned on Oct. 25, in "Separation of Church and Mental State Needed," President Bush's leading speechwriter, Michael J. Gerson, is a Christian fundamentalist, who is seeding Bush's speeches with Biblical references designed to appeal to a Christian Zionist "Armageddon Army," which is calling for war with Iraq, and wants to capture the White House and bring the United States into a global war against Islam. The following report goes much further into mapping the penetration of these Christian Zionist networks into the White House, Defense Department, and Congress.

'Project Jerry Falwell'

When televangelist Jerry Falwell blasphemously labelled the Prophet Mohammed a "terrorist," on the Oct. 6 edition of CBS News' "60 Minutes," it was a calculated move to shift U.S. policy to an overt war against Islam, but it goes much further than politics following the Sept. 11, 2001 irregular warfare attack. Falwell's attack was more than 20 years in the making. Falwell's role, as the semi-fallen leader of the once-mighty Moral Majority, is to mouth the most outrageous, indefensible remarks, on behalf of the entire Christian fundie/Christian Zionist network, for which he then can "apologize," while his colleagues, such as Pat Robertson, Gary Bauer, Tim LaHaye, and Rev. Ed McAteer, sit back in smug silence. If Falwell gets away with it, the others will soon follow suit. In CIA parlance, it might be called "plausible deniability." Falwell's insult to Muslims is designed to show the world how much clout the right-wing Christian fundies in the United States, particularly the *Christian Zionists*, have.

For Falwell, the war on terrorism *is* the "Clash of Civilizations," the plan for global anti-Muslim war authored by British intelligence operative Prof. Bernard Lewis. The outline was filled in by Harvard's Samuel Huntington in a 1993 *Foreign Affairs* article, and in a 1996 book, *Clash of Civilizations and the Remaking of World Order*. And despite contrary statements ritually delivered by George W. Bush and other members of the Administration, that U.S. policy is *not* a Clash of Civilizations—Reverend Falwell answers to a "higher authority" about what the policy of the United States is, and should be. Don't be fooled into thinking that that higher authority for Falwell is God—it's actually some combination of Reverend Moon, Israel's Benjamin Netanyahu, and an Anglo-American imperial network that is hell-bent on starting World War III in the Middle East.

In 1980, Falwell was honored as a Christian savior for the State of Israel by the Likud Party's first Prime Minister, Menachem Begin, who came into office in 1977. Begin was himself a former Irgun terrorist and follower of Vladimir Jabotinsky, an admirer of Benito Mussolini whom Israeli founding father David Ben-Gurion heaped scorn upon as "Vladimir Hitler." Begin arranged for Falwell to receive an award in honor of Jabotinsky. Begin also arranged for Falwell to be presented with a gift of a Lear Jet, in appreciation for his "service to Israel," reports former U.S. Rep. Paul Findley in his book, *They Dare to Speak Out*. (This is also reported in the September/October 2002 issue of *Mother Jones* magazine.)

The anointing of Falwell was pursuant to a study by Israel's Ministry of Religious Affairs in 1977-78, profiling Christian fundamentalists in Europe and, especially, the United States. Begin's group then cultivated these "fundies" to become the allies of the Likud, in order to implement the territorial, expansionist grab known as "Eretz Israel," which has always been the program of the Likud.

The 1982 Israeli invasion of Lebanon, and the plan to permanently take over the West Bank, Gaza Strip, Syrian Golan Heights, and Egypt's Sinai Peninsula, have always been part of that Likud program—kept secret because of U.S. opposition, with the memory still fresh of President Dwight D. Eisenhower's threatened sanctions against Israel's seizure of the Suez Canal in 1956. In order to eliminate the danger of U.S. opposition—which would mean sudden death economically for the State of Israel—a project of several decades was

Jerry Falwell (at podium) has emerged as the loud-mouthed spokesman for the Christian fundamentalist/Christian Zionist alliance in support of Israel's Ariel Sharon (inset). Here, in November 1994, Falwell meets with Anti-Defamation League National Director Abe Foxman (seated left), Rabbi James Rubin of the American Jewish Congress (seated right); and Rabbi Yechiel Eckstein, president of the International Fellowship of Christians and Jews (standing left).

begun, to expand Israel's already formidable political clout in America by forging the Christian Zionist/Jabotinskyite alliance.

In 1978, a Ministry of Religious Affairs grant led to the publication of *American Fundamentalism and Israel: The Relation of Fundamentalist Churches to Zionism and the State of Israel,* by Yona Malachy. Also funding the book-length study, which appeared in English, were the Jacob Blaustein Fund for American Studies, and the Institute of Contemporary Jewry of the Hebrew University of Jerusalem. The book features a detailed profile of Protestant denominations in the United States.

EIR's Scott Thompson reports that the Malachy book, though couched in academic terms, appears to be the first-approximation field map of Christian fundamentalism, drawn up for the purpose of launching cultural warfare and political intelligence operations, by the Ministry of Religious Affairs (MRA), and other members of Begin's government and its intelligence organs. "The Ministry is an institution that has been notorious for overpoliticization," noted the Jewish Telegraphic Agency in January 2000, when the MRA was shut down at the initiative of then-Justice Minister Yossi Beilin of the Labor Party. In the last months of Ehud Barak's Labor-led government, in which Beilin served, the MRA was reopened, but, it was kept under watch, because of the record of abuse of its powers by right-wing religious parties. Today, in Ariel Sharon's Likud-led government, the reopened MRA's role as a right-wing tool continues under Asher Ohana of the Shas Party, who is in touch with Christian Zionist Pat Robertson, regarding the creation of a "New Jerusalem Foundation."

As the Malachy book implies, Darbyist "dispensational millennialism" was the most immediately favorable ideology for the Likud agenda, just as Darbyism had proved enor-

mously useful to British imperial schemes since aristocrat John Nelson Darby began preaching in 1830s England. Darby was the first to construct the "dispensation" notion, which says that God dealt with mankind by granting "dispensations" at different times, and that the world is approaching the last of these, the "End Times." The central feature of the "End Times" is the return of the Jews to Zion and the rebuilding of the Temple in Jerusalem, as Darby recounted in *The Hopes of the Church of God in Connexion with the Destiny of the Jews and the Nations as Revealed in Prophecy.* Darby taught that the apocalyptic battle will be fought "on the plains of Megiddo" in Israel/Palestine, at which time Christ will come with His army to end this battle. There will be a "Tribulation," but the "true Christians" will be "raptured"—physically carried into Heaven, thus missing the Tribulation. Fundamentalist Christians therefore joyfully welcome the prospect of Armageddon—including nuclear confrontation—originating in the Middle East.

What do the American Christian fundies' Zionist interlocutors make of this doctrine? When confronted with the fact that the only place for Jews in the Darbyite belief structure, is to be converted, or be killed *en masse* and eternally damned, Zionists of America leader Morton Klein said sarcastically, "I am willing to make this deal: If they continue to support Israel's prosperity, security and survival, then if Jesus comes back in the future, I will join their parade. . . . Hey, if I was wrong, no problem" (*Mother Jones,* September/October 2002). Abe Foxman, head of the Anti-Defamation League of B'nai Brith (ADL), is more slick, saying that the "End Times" predictions are "speculative," and therefore are no immediate threat to Judaism.

Religious figures in Israel *do not* see it that way. In the daily *Ha'aretz* on Oct. 16, reporter Yair Sheleg wrote and

Rev. Sun Myung Moon is in the thick of the Christian Zionist networks. Here he embraces Jerry Falwell, whom he bailed out of bankruptcy.

article, entitled "Christian Generosity Becomes a Rabbinical Nightmare," reporting that U.S.-ordained Rabbi Yechiel Eckstein and his Chicago-based "International Fellowship of Christians and Jews," along with Ralph Reed, the former head of the Christian Coalition, are under the gun from top Israeli rabbis. A four-member committee has been appointed by the Chief Rabbinical Council in Israel to investigate Eckstein's Jerusalem Friendship Fund, which gathered $15 million in the past year to resettle Jews from the former Soviet Union and Argentina, to Israel. The funds, all provided by U.S. Christian fundies, are also used to set up soup kitchens and other charities among the poorest Jewish communities, including one that "removes bodies and body parts after terror attacks."

The issue of Eckstein (about whom there is more below,) was raised by Israeli Rabbi Simcha Hacohen Kook, the chief rabbi of Rehovat, who said, "I am ashamed that this kind of money [from the evangelicals] is currently being accepted by Torah-observant Jews." Rabbi Kook is concerned, in the words of *Ha'aretz*, that "accepting evangelical money is wrong because it comes from people who believe, according to their Messianic vision, that Israel will ultimately disappear with one-third of world Jews converting to Christianity and the other two-thirds being destroyed." Eckstein tried to counter this by producing a "poll" with Ralph Reed (who is also chairman of the Georgia State Republican Party), allegedly showing that *only 10%* of evangelicals support Israel because of "their vision of end days." The other 90% allegedly support Israel's "democratic values" and "war against terrorism."

'The International Christian Embassy of Jerusalem'

There is no question that "Project Jerry Falwell" came out of the MRA's Malachy study, but Falwell is just a small (if corpulent) piece of the picture. The *global* operation, mostly centered in the Israeli Embassy in Washington, and aimed at the White House, is the International Christian Embassy of Jerusalem. The ICEJ is currently the central coordination point for Christian Zionism, and has its tentacles into George W. Bush. It is the ICEJ networks, in the coming months, that will run the American side of political cover for the most dangerous Israeli hard-line policies — from the expulsion and/or assassination of Palestinian President Yasser Arafat, to genocide against the Palestinians, to the possibility of an Israeli nuclear strike against Iraq — either in tandem with Bush's war, or in a "breakaway ally" scenario.

ICEJ founder Jan Willem ven der Hoeven shares a common agenda with Likud wildman Moshe Feiglin (see below), and with the U.S.-based National Unity Coalition for Israel (a Jabotinskyite/Christian Zionist operation of which the ICEJ is a part): Since Ariel Sharon has been ineffective and weak, the time is now for cruel war against the Palestinians. How they are doing this, and how they intersect the insane war crowd controlling George Bush's teleprompter, is the next subject of this report.

The "Christian Embassy" was founded by Dutch evangelical Jan Willem van der Hoeven and five colleagues, in 1980, in an action that was a slap in the face of international law, which recognized Tel Aviv as the capital of Israel. After 13 embassies moved their offices out of West Jerusalem to Tel Aviv, to protest Menachem Begin's annexation of Arab East Jerusalem, van der Hoeven — with Begin's blessing — moved directly into the vacated building of the Chilean Embassy. The "Christian Embassy" was symbolic, and became a rallying point for the drive to overturn the United Nations resolutions saying that Israel and its neighbors should reach peace agreements, after which Israel should return to the borders that existed prior to the 1967 Arab-Israeli war. Falwell was involved with the Christian Embassy from the outset (the same year that he received his Jabotinsky award) and became one of the lobbyists for the United States to move its embassy to Jerusalem.

Van der Hoeven writes about himself that he is "the founder of different ministries in Israel and Holland . . . born in the Netherlands where his father was private secretary to Queen Juliana. He studied in London where he obtained his Bachelor of Divinity Degree from the London University.

"Jan Willem has lived in the Middle East for more than 35 years, and currently resides in Jerusalem. . . . Both his children have served in the Israeli Army."

But there is a murkier story here — of Nazis, faith healers, and European oligarchs. According to an article, "De heilige Juliana" ("The Saintly Juliana") by Rene Zwaap in the Dutch newspaper, *De Groene Amsterdammer* of June 3, 1998, Queen Juliana was advised by a female faith-healer, Greet Hofmans, the power behind the throne (1948-56), who apparently even counselled Juliana to divorce Prince Bernhard, a former Nazi. The Prince staged a coup: "All the sympathizers of Greet Hofmans and her 'pacifist clique' [were purged] . . . including the personal secretary of the Queen, . . . Baron W J. Heeckeren van Molecaten, his wife and his mother, three

The late Israeli terrorist Vladimir Jabotinsky. Israeli Prime Minister Menachem Begin arranged for the Jabotinsky Award to be awarded to Jerry Falwell in 1980, for his "service to Israel."

intimates of the Queen. To take the place of the Baron, there came J. van der Hoeven, a man with an NSB [Dutch Nazi Party] past."

So the former Nazi Bernhard, fresh from starting the Bilderberger Group and about to co-found the World Wildlife Fund with Britain's Prince Philip, put the ex-Nazi van der Hoeven in as the Queen's private secretary.

The younger van der Hoeven left the ICEJ in 1999, but remained head of one of its projects, the International Christian Zionist Center.

The operational profile of the ICEJ includes the following:

The Manfred R. Lehmann Foundation. Based in New York City, this charitable foundation's head, the late Manfred Lehmann, was a German Jew, who had been active in the United States procuring weapons for the Jewish Underground in Palestine in 1948. Before his death in the late 1990s, Lehmann used his foundation to promote and support the murders of Israeli Prime Minister Yitzhak Rabin, and of innocent Palestinians. A 1996 communiqué on the Lehmann Foundation's website says, "Dr. Baruch Goldstein's Memory should be rehabilitated. . . . Dr. Goldstein's act [machine-gunning more than 200 Palestinians during Friday worship in Hebron, killing at least 29, in February 1994] was not an unprovoked act of violence, but a pre-emptive strike against a looming Arab pogrom of the Jewish population of Hebron."

Another communiqué from M.R. Lehmann praises van der Hoeven: "Rev. Jan Willem van der Ho[e]ven, head of the International Christian Embassy in Jerusalem, recently completed a two-week, grassroots tour, with successful addresses to pro-Israel Christian audiences in Tennessee, Massachusetts, Washington, D.C., California, and Texas. He has also undertaken to help Moshe Feiglin, the courageous Israeli civil rights activist, who, as head of the non-partisan civil rights group, Zo Artzeinu, is now being indicted by the leftist Israeli government—with the threat of a long jail term—under the accusation of 'sedition.' "

Moshe Feiglin. A 42-year-old Australian emigré, Feiglin is the self-anointed head of a Likud Party splinter, linked to the banned terrorist group Kahane Chai (founded by Jewish Defense League terrorist Meir Kahane). In 1995, Feiglin was in the middle of propaganda operations that set up the assassination of Yitzhak Rabin, telling *Haaretz*, "Hitler also rose to power in democratic elections. . . . Rabin is the [Judenrat] putting us on the trains." Feiglin founded Zo Artzeinu (This Is Our Country) with **Rabbi Benny Alon,** of the Moledet party. Alon is no stranger to radicalism and American money: He headed the Beit Orot Yeshiva, located in a Palestinian neighborhood in Jerusalem, which had been bought up with money from Miami-based billionaire Dr. Irving Moskowitz, a Likud supporter. The Feiglin/Alon group organized massive civil disobedience in Israel, traffic blockades, and violent sieges of the offices of Palestinians. Feiglin even directed these activities from a rented helicopter. Alon and Moledet refer to Palestinians as a "disease," which must be surgically removed from Israel.

Alon is now a Member of the Knesset (parliament), and was in the Washington on Oct. 11-12 to attend the Christian Coalition's meeting, and pick up some more fundamentalist money from the groups allied to the Christian Embassy. In televangelist style, Alon aroused the crowd with chants against the Palestinian state, while Christian Zionists organized, from the podium, the ritual blowing of the *shofar* (ram's horn).

Rev. Ed McAteer is the founder of the U.S. Religious Roundtable, and public relations man for the **National Unity Coalition for Israel** (NUCI). Working directly for the Office of Interreligious Affairs, at the Israeli Embassy, McAteer organizes evangelicals from all over the United States to come to the Embassy—at their own expense—and hear him speak. The contact man for the last several years has been Moshe Fox, the Embassy's Minister of Public Affairs. That "old-time religion" is provided by the Christian Elmer Gantrys, but Fox quotes from the Old Testament, telling the assembled Christian fundamentalists, that "God promises the Jews a land flowing with milk and honey," in the words of *Mother Jones* magazine, before he tells them to "help turn this divine promise into reality."

The job that McAteer and NUCI took up in early 2001, was to threaten the White House, and begin a drumbeat against Secretary of State Colin Powell with the message: *"Lay off Ariel Sharon."* On July 30, 2001, McAteer and Jewish groups, including the Zionists of America and American Friends of Likud, had a White House meeting with Administration officials to deliver the message, that the Christian Right had mobilized millions of voters for Bush, who *could* lose this vote, if the White House tries to rein in Sharon by calling for a cease-fire or sending an international observer force with U.S. backing. This assessment of the meeting came from Herb Zweibon, president of Americans for a Safe Israel,

Rabbi Meir Kahane, the American terrorist who was assassinated in 1990. Rabbi Mordecai Eliayahu gave the eulogy for Kahane—and has been named as one of seven Israeli right-wing rabbis who later issued a decree calling for the death of Israeli Prime Minister Yitzhak Rabin.

who was a participant. The entire meeting was directly organized by the Christian Embassy Washington office.

For the 15 months since that meeting, the groups behind the ICEF have continued to put pressure on Bush, to end all assistance to *any kind* of Palestinian administration in the Occupied Territories, and to abandon all support for a state of Palestine. The ICEJ/NUCI gaggle also wants Bush to expel the Palestinian Authority from the United States, and declare the P.A. and Arafat to be terrorists. They have demanded that the United States back an Israeli plan to flatten every structure and asset in the Palestinian territories, the same way that U.S. airpower flattened Afghanistan.

So far, the Christian Zionists have not succeeded, but with a new Republican Party majority in the House and Senate, they plan to "collect" their payment, and expect to be able to push Bush over the edge. However, the Oct. 30 collapse of the Sharon government, may have robbed them of that opportunity. For, while Sharon has filled his interim Cabinet with right-wing fanatics, factions in the Labor Party and other pro-peace Israeli elements have renewed a campaign to return to the Rabin peace plan, and are shaking up the Democratic Party, and the Jewish pro-peace camp in the United States, to get the job done.

The Strange Rabbi Eckstein

One of the key weapons the Christian fundamentalists intend to use to force Bush into line behind their insane agenda, is the strange Rabbi Yechiel Eckstein, the Chicago-based

rabbi with no congregation, whom Sen. Joseph Lieberman (D-Conn.) calls "the best-kept secret in the United States."

Until 1983, Eckstein was the co-director of interreligious affairs for the Anti-Defamation League, the organized-crime-linked spy organization in the United States (see *EIR*'s book, *The Ugly Truth About the ADL*, 1992). He left the ADL to create the International Fellowship of Christians and Jews (IFCJ), where he claims to have become the world's leading Jewish expert on Christian evangelicals, and boasts of breaking "new ground with [Christian fundie] groups that formerly had no contacts with Jews."

Like Falwell and the Christian Embassy, Eckstein has a "Moonie connection," through Philadelphia-based Rabbi David Ben-Ami. Ben-Ami is director of one of Eckstein's 1998 spin-offs, the Institute for Religious Values, which ran an operation with Eckstein's board member, Gary Bauer, to organize hundreds of American rabbis to influence Jewish Senators, to ensure that President Clinton's veto of a bill banning so-called late-term abortions would be overridden. Ben-Ami is well known to both the Moonies, and to Israeli fanatics. When Moon was jailed in the United States for tax fraud, Ben-Ami rushed to defend the sex pervert. In Israel, Ben-Ami's links to terrorists go back to the early 1980s, when he was laundering money for the so-called American Forum for Jewish-Christian Understanding to the operatives who were planning to blow up the al-Haram al-Sharif holy places in Jerusalem (known in English as the Temple Mount), so that the Third Temple of Solomon could be built, and fulfill Darbyite prophecy. In that scheme, Ben-Ami worked closely with Meir Kahane's chief contact in the Washington area, Rabbi Herzl Kranz, of Silver Spring, Maryland.

Here, another detail from Eckstein's ongoing row in Israel with the Chief Rabbinate should raise alarms about his connections to Israelis who protect these Jewish fascist terrorists and assassins. In defense of his alliance with the Christian fundies, Eckstein cites a letter from the late Rabbi Mordecai Eliayahu, a former Chief Rabbi of Israel, who happened to be the mentor of terrorist Meir Kahane. When Kahane was assassinated in 1990, Eliayahu gave the eulogy. More horrifying is the fact that Eliayahu is named as one of the seven right-wing rabbis who reportedly issued the religious ruling of *din rodef*, opening the door to the murder of Yitzhak Rabin, on the grounds that he had exposed Jews to life-threatening harm and loss, by negotiating the Oslo peace accord. While the charges against Eliayahu were not investigated at the time, the Rabin case is still open, with the prosecution of an informant for the Shin Bet domestic intelligence service going on in Israel at the present time.

Meanwhile, part of the $65 million that Eckstein gets from the U.S.-based fundies, has gone to Eliayahu's son.

Though he moved to Israel two years ago in the religious/political act of return, or *aliyah*, Eckstein is more active in the United States than ever, with connections that not only go into the Senate, but to the White House itself.

On Oct. 19, Eckstein and his co-director Ralph Reed pulled together the "Stand for Israel" prayer meeting, which was reportedly a flop compared to projected participation, but which pulled together the leading names of Darbyism in the United States. While it is easy to drown in the "alphabet soup," of like-sounding Christian Zionist efforts, the Eckstein/Reed combo gathered the "generals" of this crackpot crusade to hijack U.S. policy. The endorsers were: Pat Robertson, now head of the Christian Broadcasting Network; Rev. Jerry Falwell; Rev. John Hagee of the Cornerstone Church in San Antonio, Texas (where Benjamin Netanyahu preaches about the divine right of Israel to control Palestine;) Chuck Colson of the Prison Ministries; Tim LaHaye, author of the "End Times" best-selling novels; and Richard Land of the Southern Baptist Convention, which has recently been embroiled in a a scandal over anti-Muslim statements. And not to be left out, Gary Bauer, former Republican Presidential candidate in 2000, is on the Board of Eckstein and Reed's International Fellowship of Christians and Jews.

This was the second pro-Israel mass rally held by the fundies this Fall. On Oct. 12, the Christian Coalition, held the "Unity for Israel" rally in Washington. Rabid speeches given by Gary Bauer, House Majority Whip Rep. Tom DeLay (R-Tex.), Benny Alon from the Moledet Party, and Jerusalem Mayor Ehud Olmert, all said the same thing: There will be no peace agreement between Israel and Palestine; the Bible says God gave the land to Israel only; peace will come only when Palestinians are transferred out of the Occupied Territories.

The Christian Zionists and their neo-conservative allies are now "crunching the numbers" to prove that Bush and the GOP had better pay close attention to this bloc, because the 2004 Presidential election is "just around the corner."

But, for the moment, more insidious are the cronies that the Eckstein/Reed/ICEJ network have *in place* in the White House and the Defense Department. Among the "Chicken-hawks" that *EIR* has identified as gunning for war against Iraq, otherwise known as the "Wolfowitz cabal," one is of particular importance: Assistant Secretary of Defense for Policy Doug Feith. *Mother Jones* magazine reported in October, that Feith had been the honorary policy chairman of the National Unity Coalition for Israel, which, as identified above, is a project of the "Christian Embassy." *Mother Jones* also noted that Feith "has said the Israelis should reoccupy all lands ceded to the Palestinian Authority, even though 'the price in blood would be high.' " Feith, a second-generation Jabotinskyite, not only expresses these divided loyalties, at odds with Bush's stated policy on Israel, but, he also runs a Pentagon-based "parallel" intelligence agency, plotting a war on Iraq, in league with Defense Secretary Donald Rumsfeld, Deputy Defense Secretary Paul Wolfowitz, and Richard Perle, head of the Defense Policy Board.

The other agent in place is even closer to Bush—chief White House speechwriter Michael Gerson, an evangelical who has a degree in theology from Wheaton College in Illi-

nois, a center of Darbyism. Gerson's ties to Eckstein are multiple: His former boss, Sen. Dan Coats (R-Ind.), was the co-chairman, with Joe Lieberman, of Eckstein's front group for Congress, called the Center for Jewish and Christian Values. Coats, who gave Gerson his Washington credentials, ran Eckstein's Oct. 7, 1997 "Christians in Solidarity with Israel" conference on Capitol Hill, which featured the Israeli Ambassdor to the UN, Dore Gold, a pro-Sharon lunatic. Eckstein's event was designed to undermine President Clinton's efforts to put pressure on then-Prime Minister Netanyahu, to continue negotiations on the Oslo Accords. Another of Gerson's former employers is Chuck Colson, who is also a co-sponsor of Eckstein's operations.

Much has been written in the U.S. press about Gerson, who controls Bush's teleprompter, but few note how important Wheaton College is for his connection to Bush. Dan Coats, who is now Bush's Ambassador to Germany, is a Wheaton graduate, as is evangelist Billy Graham, the man who is credited in many media accounts with bringing George W. Bush into the "Born Again" fold. Gerson and Eckstein have also drawn from the same stable for their operatives. While William Kristol, the neo-conservative editor of the *Weekly Standard*, who favors a unilateral American "empire," serves on Eckstein's board, Gerson has frequently employed Kristol's protégés as White House speechwriters for Bush.

The Jerusalem Declaration on Christian Zionism

in media [1]

> THE JERUSALEM DECLARATION ON CHRISTIAN ZIONISM html m79465fc4.jpg [2]

It is with concern that we note the negative opinions about Christian Zionism voiced by certain church clerics in Jerusalem in a recent statement entitled, "The Jerusalem Declaration on Christian Zionism" (view entire statement below). Using inflammatory language they have expressed views that are far from the truth.

The truth is:

1. Christian Zionism is a theological position that sees a future destiny for Israel in the land of her forefathers. A Christian Zionist believes in a literal interpretation of the Bible and rejects replacement theology that definitely played a pivotal role in the persecution of Jews through the centuries, and under girded the Holocaust. Christian Zionism is not heretical; in fact, Christians from all traditional backgrounds have held such a view for two thousand years. Simply put, a Christian Zionist is one who believes that God, by a sovereign choice, gave the Land of Canaan as an everlasting possession to the Jewish people, for His kingdom purposes. (Genesis 17:7-8).

2. Christian Zionists believe that while God loves all people equally, He has chosen the Jewish people to bring redemption to mankind. Our Messiah and King, Jesus Christ, was born of Jewish parents, into a Jewish society, thus making the Jewish people our 'royal family', to be honored because the King was born to them. Christian Zionists reject hatred of any people group.

3. Christian Zionists do not base their theological position on end-time prophecy, but on the faithful covenant promises of God given to Abraham some four thousand years ago. They do not have a "thirst for Armageddon," and do not claim to know the sequence of events that will lead to it.

4. Christian Zionists recognize that Israel has a right to exist in peace and security. Moreover, there are biblical considerations that regulate Israel's national existence and these have to do with the issues of justice and righteousness and her treatment of the stranger within her midst. Christian Zionists fully recognize this and stand for these.

→ Ephraim

5. Christian Zionism is not a threat to anybody, but instead seeks to be a blessing. The Christian Zionist organizations in Israel have given millions of dollars of aid and care to all the population groups in the land, including Israeli and Palestinian Arabs, Druse and others.

We pray for peace. But we note with sadness that the present Palestinian Government is totally dedicated to the destruction of Israel and its charter declares it. So, the problem in the region is not as simple as the Jerusalem Declaration makes out!

6. Sadly there have been no meetings between the Jerusalem clerics and their Christian Zionist counterparts. We invite such a dialogue and consider it a biblical prerequisite. We are distressed that a public denunciation has occurred first. We feel that we have been treated with disrespect and disdain, and attacked by the issuing of these public declarations. They present themselves as lovers of justice, mercy, truth and peace! This public attack seems lacking in these qualities.

We find the paper unbalanced and notably one-sided. It totally ignores the jihadist goals of the Hamas government and turns a blind eye to terrorism perpetrated by this regime. Everything is attributed to "occupation and militarism", meaning Israel is the only problem. We think not! This one-sided unbalanced view of the conflict is in fact unhelpful to the peace process and contributing to its failure!

So, in closing, we Christian Zionists call upon Christians and Churches everywhere not to remain silent, but to break their silence and speak for reconciliation with justice in the Holy Land. To pray for the peace of Jerusalem, to affirm Israel's right to live in peace and security, free from the threat of liquidation by Islamic Jihadists who definitely seek to 'colonize' the Jewish State by bringing it into the Empire of Islam. We reject all forms of discrimination.

Signatures

Rebecca Brimmer
International President, Bridges For Peace

Ray Sanders
Executive Director, Christian Friends of Israel

Malcolm Hedding
International Christian Embassy Jerusalem

guilty of genozid

"THE JERUSALEM DECLARATION ON CHRISTIAN ZIONISM"

Statement by the Patriarch and Local Heads of Churches In Jerusalem

"Blessed are the peacemakers for they shall be called the children of God." (Matthew 5:9)

Christian Zionism is a modern theological and political movement that embraces the most extreme ideological positions of Zionism, thereby becoming detrimental to a just peace within Palestine and Israel. The Christian Zionist programme provides a worldview where the Gospel is identified with the ideology of empire, colonialism and militarism. In its extreme form, it places an emphasis on apocalyptic events leading to the end history rather than living Christ's love and justice today.

We categorically reject Christian Zionist doctrines as false teaching that corrupts the biblical message of love, justice and reconciliation.

We further reject the contemporary alliance of Christian Zionist leaders and organizations with elements in the governments of Israel and the United States that are presently imposing their unilateral pre-emptive borders and domination over Palestine. This inevitably

leads to unending cycles of violence that undermine the security of all peoples of the Middle East and the rest of the world.

We reject the teachings of Christian Zionism that facilitate and support these policies as they advance racial exclusivity and perpetual war rather than the gospel of universal love, redemption and reconciliation taught by Jesus Christ. Rather than condemn the world to

the doom of Armageddon we call upon everyone to liberate themselves from the ideologies of militarism and occupation. Instead, let them pursue the healing of the nations!

e call upon Christians in Churches on every continent to pray for the Palestinian and Israeli people, both of whom are suffering as victims of occupation and militarism. These discriminative actions are turning Palestine into impoverished ghettos surrounded by exclusive Israeli settlements. The establishment of the illegal settlements and the

construction of the Separation Wall on confiscated Palestinian land undermines the viability of a Palestinian state as well as peace and security in the entire region.

We call upon all Churches that remain silent, to break their silence and speak for reconciliation with justice in the Holy Land.

Therefore, we commit ourselves to the following principles as an alternative way:

We affirm that all people are created in the image of God. In turn they are called to honor the dignity of every human being and to respect their inalienable rights.

We affirm that Israelis and Palestinians are capable of living together within peace, justice and security.

We affirm that Palestinians are one people, both Muslim and Christian. We reject all attempts to subvert and fragment their unity.

We call upon all people to reject the narrow world view of Christian Zionism and other ideologies that privilege one people at the expense of others.

We are committed to non-violent resistance as the most effective means to end the illegal occupation in order to attain a just and lasting peace.

With urgency we warn that Christian Zionism and its alliances are justifying colonization, apartheid and empire-building.

God demands that justice be done. No enduring peace, security or reconciliation is possible without the foundation of justice. The demands of justice will not disappear. The struggle for justice must be pursued diligently and persistently but non-violently.

"What does the Lord require of you, to act justly, to love mercy, and to walk humbly with your God." (Micah 6:8)

This is where we take our stand. We stand for justice. We can do no other. Justice alone guarantees a peace that will lead to reconciliation with a life of security and prosperity for all the

peoples of our Land. By standing on the side of justice, we open ourselves to the work of peace - and working for peace makes us children of God.

"God was reconciling the world to himself in Christ, not counting men's sins against them. And he has committed to us the message of reconciliation." (2 Cor 5:19)

His Beattitude Patriarch Michel Sabbah
.tin Patriarchate, Jerusalem

Archbishop Swerios Malki Mourad,
Syrian Orthodox Patriarchate, Jerusalem

Bishop Riah Abu El-Assal,
Episcopal Church of Jerusalem and the Middle East

Bishop Munib Younan,
Evangelical Lutheran Church in Jordan and the Holy Land

Source URL: https://int.icej.org/media/jerusalem-declaration-christian-zionism

Links:
[1] https://int.icej.org/category/main-menu/media
[2]
https://int.icej.org/sites/icej.org/files/THE%20JERUSALEM%20DECLARATION%20ON%20CHRISTIAN%20ZIONISM_html_m79465fc4.jpg

PRÄDESTINATION

Die Lehre von der Gnadenwahl und Vorherbestimmung Gottes[1]

PRÄAMBEL

Gibt es einen freien Willen oder nicht? Bestimmt Gott alles im Voraus oder entscheidet der Mensch autonom? Weiß Gott schon, wer in den Himmel kommt, oder ist das alles noch offen? Und: hat Gott mich erwählt oder kann sich alles noch ändern? Diese Fragen bewegen Christen, solange sie die Bibel lesen und über Gottes Weg mit den Menschen nachdenken.

Bei uns im BFP ist die Prädestinationslehre Calvins in den letzten Jahren verstärkt in den Interessenfocus gerückt. Der große Reformator verfasste im 16. Jahrhundert eine erste umfassende evangelische Dogmatik, aus der insbesondere der konsequent durchdachte Erwählungsgedanke weit über den Bereich der Theologie hinaus Wirksamkeit entfaltet hat. Geschult durch ein gründliches juristisches Studium und mit dem ihm eigenen scharfsinnigen Verstand formt Calvin eine Gedankenkette, die von der Souveränität und Allmacht Gottes ihren Ausgang nimmt und sich bis zur doppelten Prädestination zum Heil und zur Verdammnis erstreckt. Richtungsweisend wirkte dabei die Theologie des katholischen Kirchenlehrers Augustinus. Mit der Wiederentdeckung seines Gnadenverständnisses griffen die Reformatoren hinter die mittelalterliche Werkgerechtigkeit zurück und rückten den handelnden Gott wieder in den Mittelpunkt des Heilsgeschehens.

Bei aller Zustimmung zum Gnadenverständnis und der Alleinwirksamkeit Gottes im Heil sind die finalen Schlussfolgerungen Calvins nie unwidersprochen geblieben. Die Vorstellung eines Gottes, der Menschen willkürlich zur Verdammnis oder zum Heil vorbestimmt, wird im Widerspruch zu universalen Gnadenbekundungen in der Heiligen Schrift gesehen. So ist das Lebenswerk der Reformatoren als enormer Fortschritt zu würdigen, und doch bleibt ihr Denken durch die Gegebenheiten ihrer Epoche begrenzt.

---

[1] Veröffentlicht durch den Theologischen Aussschuss des Bundes Freikirchlicher Pfingstgemeinden (BFP) im Auftrag des Präsidiums des BFP, Erzhausen, Juni 2009..

Die Lehre von der Gnadenwahl und Vorherbestimmung Gottes

Unsere Arbeit mit der Bibel sowie die Forschung in der Theologie und Kirchengeschichte erlauben uns die Zusammenfassung unserer Überzeugungen in folgenden Sätzen:

Gnade. Wir betonen die Gnade Gottes als einzige Grundlage unseres Heils. Kein Mensch kann aus eigener Kraft oder Entschlossenheit etwas zu seiner Rettung beisteuern oder sich Gottes Gnade verdienen. Rettung ist ein Geschenk Gottes.

Allerdings folgen wir nicht der Schlussfolgerung, diese Gnade müsse sich zwingend und ausschließlich in der Vorherbestimmung zum Heil wie zur Verdammnis (Supralapsarismus[2]) Ausdruck verschaffen, so als könne sich die göttliche Gnade nicht anders manifestieren. Gnade wirkt und ereignet sich im Hören der Gebote Gottes wie auch des Evangeliums (als Ruf zum Umkehr), als Schöpfungsgnade[3] und Erlösungsgnade[4]. Es ist Gnade, auf den Ruf Gottes eingehen und sich bekehren zu können.

Eph. 2,8-9[5]: *Denn aus Gnade seid ihr errettet durch Glauben, und das nicht aus euch, Gottes Gabe ist es; nicht aus Werken, damit niemand sich rühme.*

Glaube. Wir sind überzeugt, dass der heilsaneignende Glaube ein Geschenk Gottes ist. Durch Seine Gnade ermöglicht Gott es dem Menschen, zu glauben und somit gerettet zu werden.

Allerdings verstehen wir Glauben nicht als vorherbestimmtes und damit zwanghaftes Ereignis, sondern als Resultat Seiner vorlaufenden Gnade[6]. Diese Gnade erreicht den gefallenen und in Sünden versklavten Menschen im Wort des Evangeliums und dem Ruf zur Umkehr. Sie versetzt ihn überhaupt erst in die Lage, eine Entscheidung für Gott treffen zu können. Glaube ist Vertrauen in Gott und Annahme des Heilswerkes Christi durch einen bewussten Schritt der Entscheidung.

Röm. 3,28[7]: *Denn wir urteilen, dass der Mensch durch Glauben gerechtfertigt wird, ohne Gesetzeswerke.*

Allwirksamkeit. Wir bekennen, dass Gott der allein Handelnde ist, der die Initiative zur Rettung der Menschen ergriffen und alle Voraussetzungen für die persönliche Heilsaneignung geschaffen hat. Damit widersprechen wir auch jeder Form des Synergismus[8], die dem menschlichen Vermögen einen eigenen von der Gnade losgelösten Beitrag zu Bekehrung und Wiedergeburt zuerkennen will.

---

2   Supralapsarismus ist die theologische Vorstellung, dass bereits der Sündenfall von Gott vorherbestimmt war. Auch der bis dahin sündlose Mensch des Paradieses habe damit keine Wahl gehabt und musste in Sünde fallen.

3   Die Schöpfungsgnade besteht darin, dass der Mensch seine ganze Existenz einem Gnadenakt Gottes, der Schöpfung, verdankt. Darin ist der Mensch auf Gott hin angelegt, da er aus Gott seine Existenz als Geschöpf Gottes erhält.

4   Die Erlösungsgnade ist die Erweckung des Menschen zum Glauben und seine Errettung durch den Glauben. Bei der Errettung wird der Mensch durch die Verkündigung des Evangeliums unter der Wirkung des Heiligen Geistes zum Glauben erweckt, gibt Gott in diesem Glauben Antwort und wird dadurch aus der Gottesferne zur Gottesgemeinschaft errettet. Hierbei erfährt der Mensch die Wiedergeburt und die Gewissheit seines Heils in Christus.

5   Weitere Verse: Röm. 3,24; Röm. 11,6; Tit 3,7.

6   Die vorlaufende Gnade ist die Wirkung Gottes am unerretteten Menschen, wodurch der Mensch befähigt wird, Gott im Glauben zu antworten. Hierbei geht es nicht um den freien Willen des Menschen, sondern um den befreiten Willen infolge von Gottes Gnadenwirken am bislang unerretteten Menschen.

7   Weitere Verse: Hab. 2,4; Röm. 1,17; Gal. 2,6.

8   Synergismus ist die theologische Überzeugung, dass der Mensch zum Heil seinen eigenen Teil beitragen muss. Somit ist nicht Gott der allein Wirkende, sondern der Mensch ist in Bezug auf sein Heil der Mit-Wirkende.

Allerdings können wir der Ansicht nicht folgen, die Entscheidung des Menschen für Gott im Glaubensgehorsam könne den Anstrich eines verdienstlichen Werkes annehmen. Denn die menschliche Entscheidung erfolgt nur aufgrund und infolge der vorlaufenden Gnade, die sich in der Botschaft des Evangeliums konkretisiert. Indem ein Mensch auf den Ruf zur Umkehr eingeht, handelt er nicht aus eigener Kraft und eigenem Vermögen, sondern antwortet verantwortlich auf die Gnade Gottes.

Phil. 2:12-13[9]:   ... bewirkt euer Heil mit Furcht und Zittern. Denn Gott ist es, der in euch wirkt sowohl das Wollen als auch das Wirken zu seinem Wohlgefallen.

Heilsunfähigkeit. Wir wissen um die Gottesferne und Heilsunfähigkeit des natürlichen Menschen. Aufgrund seines gefallenen Zustandes ist er verderbt und verloren; es gibt nichts Gutes im Menschen, das in Fragen der ewigen Seelenrettung Gewicht beanspruchen könnte.

Allerdings können wir nicht zustimmen, wenn hieraus gefolgert wird, der Mensch könne auch nicht glauben oder gehorchen, also müsse der Glaubensakt als vorherbestimmt und zwanghaft gelten. Die Verderbtheit des Menschen erfordert nicht eine Zwangsvorherbestimmung in unwiderstehlicher Gnade. Vielmehr hat Gott durch das Opfer Seines Sohnes die Voraussetzung der Rettung geschaffen und öffnet jetzt durch die Evangeliumsverkündigung den Zugang zum Heil durch Glauben. Dieser Ruf zum Glauben ist ein Wirken der Gnade am Willen des Menschen, den der Heilige Geist von seinem Verlorensein überführt.

Es wäre ein Irrtum, diese Auffassung als humanistisch misszuverstehen. Der Humanismus verkörpert einen schrankenlosen Glauben an das Gute im Menschen. Jede Selbsterlösung oder gar das Bestreiten einer Erlösungsnotwendigkeit überhaupt bewegt sich außerhalb der Bibel. Wo dieser naive humanistische Optimismus trotz seines Scheiterns an der Wirklichkeit von Geschichte und Gegenwart immer noch das Denken beherrscht, findet sich die Antipode zum biblischen Menschenbild. Daher wäre es auch ungerechtfertigt, bibelgläubige Christen als Humanisten zu verdächtigen, weil sie etwa eine doppelte Prädestination ablehnen.

Röm. 3:10-12[10]:... wie geschrieben steht: Da ist keiner, der gerecht ist, auch nicht einer. Da ist keiner, der verständig ist; da ist keiner, der nach Gott fragt. Sie sind alle abgewichen und allesamt verdorben. Da ist keiner, der Gutes tut, auch nicht einer.

Alleinwirksamkeit. Wir unterstreichen, dass Christi stellvertretender Opfertod am Kreuz grundlegend und entscheidend für das Heil ist. Gott allein handelt in der Hingabe Seines Sohnes; Christus allein konnte als sündloses Lamm Gottes Opfer sein. In diesem historischen Ereignis liegt die Basis für die Rettung des einzelnen.

Allerdings können wir nicht nachvollziehen, wieso dieses Bekenntnis zur Wirksamkeit des Opfers Christi ein partikularistisches Erlösungsverständnis erfordern soll.[11] Potenziell hat Christus das Heil für alle erworben, auch wenn es nur durch die aktive Annahme im Glauben persönlich wirksam wird. Das Heil wird in der Evangeliumsverkündigung allen als echte und wirksame Rettungsmöglichkeit angeboten, tritt aber erst durch Glaubensgehorsam des einzelnen für ihn in Kraft.

Titus 2:11: Denn die Gnade Gottes ist erschienen heilbringend allen Menschen.

1 Tim. 2:4:   Gott will, dass alle Menschen gerettet werden und zur Erkenntnis der Wahrheit kommen. Denn einer ist Gott, und einer ist Mittler zwischen Gott und Menschen, der Mensch Christus Jesus, der sich selbst als Lösegeld für alle gab.

---

9   Weitere Verse: Röm. 2,4; Eph. 2,1-5.

10   Weitere Verse: Jes. 53,6; Röm 3,23; 1Joh. 1,8.

11   Der Partikularismus behauptet, Christus sei nicht für alle Menschen, sondern nur für die zuvor Erwählten gestorben. Im Englischen spricht man von limited atonement, dem begrenzten Sühneopfer Christi, im Unterschied zum universalen Verständnis Seines Heilswerkes für alle.

| 1Joh. 2:2: | *Und er ist die Sühnung für unsere Sünden, nicht allein aber für die unseren, sondern auch für die ganze Welt.* |

Souveränität. Wir unterstreichen die Souveränität und Allmacht Gottes. Er allein ist es, dem jeder Gerettete sein Heil verdankt, und von dem der Mensch überhaupt Rettung erwarten kann. Gott ist auch der Herr der Geschichte, der Seine Pläne und Heilsabsichten mit der Welt und den Menschen zum Ziel führt.

Allerdings folgen wir nicht der Deutung, dass diese Wahrheit eine willkürliche Festlegung einzelner Persönlichkeiten zum Heil oder zur Verdammnis nach sich ziehen müsse. Vielmehr erkennen wir, wie die Bibel den persönlichen Heilszuspruch infolge der verantwortlichen Entscheidung des Individuums zu Glauben und Gehorsam geschehen lässt. Diese Entscheidungsmöglichkeit ist Geschenk der Gnade, die der souveräne Gott Seinen Geschöpfen bietet.

Auch können wir nicht nachvollziehen, wieso Gottes Souveränität nur dann gewahrt bliebe, wenn sie sich in einer doppelten Prädestination[12] äußern dürfe. Wir sehen die biblische Selbstoffenbarung des menschenliebenden Gottes, der Sein Leben für Sünder gab, durch diese Behauptung verdunkelt und gefährdet.

| Röm. 11:33-36: | *O welch eine Tiefe des Reichtums, beides, der Weisheit und der Erkenntnis Gottes! Wie unbegreiflich sind seine Gerichte und unerforschlich seine Wege! Denn „wer hat des Herrn Sinn erkannt, oder wer ist sein Ratgeber gewesen?" Oder „wer hat ihm etwas zuvor gegeben, daß Gott es ihm vergelten müßte?" Denn von ihm und durch ihn und zu ihm sind alle Dinge. Ihm sei Ehre in Ewigkeit! Amen.* |

Erwählung. Wir bekennen die göttliche Erwählung des Menschen zum Heil und seine Bestimmung für die ewige Gottesgemeinschaft.

Allerdings erkennen wir in der Bibel keine parallele Struktur von Erwählung[13] und Verwerfung[14], auch keine Stütze für einen dogmatischen Charakter der Prädestinationslehre und ihre Verankerung in der vorweltlichen Ewigkeit. Diese Gefahr besteht immer dann, wenn man Gottes Willensbekundungen philosophisch abstrakt „vor" den Entscheidungen Seines geschichtlichen Handelns denkt. Doch Gottes ewiger Wille und Sein geschichtliches Handeln sind eins. Weil Er außerhalb, ja oberhalb aller Zeit steht, verwirklicht sich Sein Wille in der Geschichte. Andernfalls träte ein Parallelismus von Erwählung und Verwerfung zutage, den die Bibel aber nicht kennt, und das Weltgeschehen würde in ein schematisches Korsett der Kausalität[15] gezwängt.

| 2Thess. 2:13: | *Gott hat euch von Anfang an erwählt zur Errettung in Heiligung des Geistes und im Glauben an die Wahrheit.* |

Erwählung „in Christus". Wir bekennen die Erwählung der Gemeinde und der Heiligen zur ewigen Rettung „in Jesus Christus". In dieser souveränen Entscheidung Gottes liegt der alleinige Grund für die Möglichkeit der persönlichen Heilsaneignung.

---

12 Unter der doppelten Prädestination (gemina praedestinatio) versteht man Gottes aktives erwählendes und verwerfendes Handeln. Gott erwählt die einen Menschen zum Heil und bestimmt die anderen zum Unheil. Hierbei ist es allein Gott, der die einen errettet und die anderen verwirft.

13 Erwählung bedeutet die Gnadenwahl Gottes, wodurch er den Menschen zum Heil bestimmt.

14 Verwerfung ist die Konsequenz von Gottes Gericht über dem sündigen Menschen. In der Vorstellung der doppelten Prädestination jedoch wird der Mensch, der von Gott nicht zum Heil erwählt ist, von vornherein von Gott verworfen. Verwerfung ist hier also die logische Folge des Nichterwähltseins.

15 Kausalität ist der gesetzmäßige Zusammenhang von Ursache und Wirkung. In der Vorstellung der doppelten Prädestination bedeutet dies, dass aufgrund der aktiven Erwählung Gottes auch auf die aktive Verwerfung Gottes geschlossen werden müsse.

Allerdings wollen wir festgehalten wissen, dass diese Erwählung „in Christus" erfolgt ist. Ihr Akzent liegt damit nicht auf der Vorzeitlichkeit, sondern auf der Lebensverbindung mit Christus, die allein das Heil garantiert. Insofern ist sie auch eine ewige Erwählung vor Grundlegung der Welt, weil der Entschluss Gottes, die Menschheit durch Seinen Sohn Jesus Christus zu retten, eine ewige Entscheidung ist. Hierin zeigt sich auch das völlig andere Verhältnis Gottes zur Zeit. Sein ewiges Wollen und Sein Handeln greifen ineinander und unterscheiden sich nicht. So ist das, was dem Menschen als Aufeinanderfolge vorkommt, in Gottes ewigem Wesen eins, da Er außerhalb jeder Zeit steht.

Eph. 1:4,13: *In Christus hat Gott uns auserwählt vor Grundlegung der Welt, dass wir heilig und tadellos vor Ihm seien ... In Ihm seid auch ihr, nachdem ihr das Wort der Wahrheit, das Evangelium eures Heils, gehört habt und gläubig geworden seid, versiegelt worden mit dem Heiligen Geist der Verheißung.*

I Petr. 1:20-21: *Er ist zwar im voraus vor Grundlegung der Welt erkannt, aber am Ende der Zeiten geoffenbart worden um euretwillen, die ihr durch Ihn an Gott glaubt, der Ihn aus den Toten auferweckt und Ihm Herrlichkeit gegeben hat, damit euer Glaube und eure Hoffnung auf Gott gerichtet sei.*

Bedingungslose Erwählung. Wir bekennen, dass die Erwählung des Menschen durch keine Voraussetzung in seiner Person begründet ist. Es gibt nichts, durch das sich ein einzelner Gott gewogen machen könnte oder wie er durch eigene Leistung Gottes Gnade auf sich ziehen könnte.

Allerdings öffnet sich diese Wahrheit nicht dem Verständnis, in Glaube und Entscheidung des Menschen Bedingungen der Gnade sehen zu müssen. Dieser Glaube ist Antwort auf den Ruf des Evangeliums. Im Glaubensgehorsam wird das Heil als Geschenk der Gnade angenommen. Weil die Gnade überhaupt erst in den Stand der Entscheidungsfreiheit setzt, ist Glaube und Bekehrung kein verdienstliches Werk. Weil die Gnade aber durch die Evangeliumsverkündigung wirkt und einer Antwort bedarf, ist sie nicht als zwangsweise oder unwiderstehlich zu verstehen.

Joh. 3:16[16]: *Denn so hat Gott die Welt geliebt, dass Er Seinen eingeborenen Sohn gab, damit jeder, der an Ihn glaubt, nicht verloren geht, sondern ewiges Leben hat.*

Allwissenheit. Wir unterstreichen die Allwissenheit Gottes, ausdrücklich auch im Hinblick auf alle Entscheidungen und Handlungen des Menschen sowie auf ihre finale Rettung oder Verdammnis hin.

Allerdings versagt sich die Bibel unserer Auffassung nach einem Erwählungsverständnis aufgrund von Vorherwissen, so als erwähle Gott diejenigen, deren Entscheidung Er voraussehe. In diesem Falle könnte die Glaubensentscheidung als eine Bedingung missverstanden werden, die mit freier Erwählung nicht in Einklang stünde. Tatsächlich aber ist die Entscheidung Folge der Gnade und des Rufes zur Umkehr. Erwählung geschieht durch die bedingungslose Liebe Gottes und ist durch nichts auf Seiten der Erwählten motiviert, auch nicht durch Vorherwissen seiner Entscheidungen.[17]

Hebr. 4,13+16 *... und kein Geschöpf ist vor ihm unsichtbar, sondern alles bloß und aufgedeckt vor den Augen dessen, mit dem wir es zu tun haben. ...*
Lasst uns nun mit Freimütigkeit hinzutreten zum Thron der Gnade, damit wir Barmherzigkeit empfangen und Gnade finden zur rechtzeitigen Hilfe!

---

16   Weitere Verse: Röm. 5:8; Röm. 10,17.

17   Nirgends zeigt sich das deutlicher als bei dem hartnäckigen Widerwillen, mit dem sich auch die Erwählten (z.B. Israel) den Plänen des Ewigen verweigern können.

Heilsgewissheit. Wir glauben und bekennen in großer Dankbarkeit, dass Gott die Seinen für die ewige Rettung zu bewahren weiß. In Seiner Gnade, mit der Er uns erwählt und errettet hat, wird Er uns auch hindurchtragen und zum Ziel führen. Heilsgewissheit ist das Geschenk Gottes an alle gläubigen Christen.

Allerdings ist unter Heilsgewissheit keine Bewahrung zu verstehen, die ein Mensch ungeachtet seines Lebensstils oder Glaubensgehorsams beanspruchen könne. Vielmehr gehört zu einer verantwortlichen Glaubensentscheidung auch die Möglichkeit der Abkehr vom Glauben. Das Neue Testament lässt seine Leser nicht im Unklaren über einzelne Christen, die sich trotz eines guten Starts vom Weg des Glaubens abgewandt haben und jetzt Gericht und Verdammnis entgegengehen.[18] Gnade und Heilsgewissheit dürfen nicht zum Vorwand genommen werden, die Ermahnungen der Nachfolge und die Gebote der Heiligung zu vernachlässigen oder gar zu ignorieren. Der Mensch kann die Gnade ausschlagen und sich durch bewusste Entscheidung oder konkludentes Handeln aus der Lebensbeziehung mit Jesus Christus und der Heilsgemeinschaft der Gemeinde lösen.

2Petr. 2:1: *Es waren aber auch falsche Propheten unter dem Volk, wie auch unter euch falsche Lehrer sein werden, die verderbenbringende Parteiungen heimlich einführen werden, indem sie auch den Gebieter, der sie erkauft hat, verleugnen. Die ziehen sich selbst schnelles Verderben zu.*

Hebr. 12:14: *Jagt dem Frieden mit allen nach und der Heiligung, ohne die niemand den Herrn schauen wird.*

Bibel. Wir achten die Bibel als die einzige Erkenntnisgrundlage in allen Fragen des Heils und der Erwählung und bekennen unsere Ehrfurcht vor Gott und der Heiligen Schrift, wie sie Gott als den Allmächtigen und Rettenden offenbart.

Allerdings betonen wir ausdrücklich: Christen, die eine doppelte Prädestination, ein begrenztes Sühneopfer (Partikularismus), die unwiderstehliche Gnade oder die These von der Unverlierbarkeit des Heils ablehnen, stehen zur Souveränität Gottes und bestreiten keinesfalls die Allmacht Gottes im Wirken des Heils. Ein Humanismusvorwurf oder der Verdacht verdünnter Bibeltreue wäre gänzlich unangebracht, da das Gnadenhandeln Gottes in keiner Weise geschmälert wird.

2Tim. 3:16-17: *Alle Schrift ist von Gott eigegeben und nützlich zur Lehre, zur Überführung, zur Zurechtweisung, zur Unterweisung in der Gerechtigkeit, damit der Mensch Gottes richtig, für jedes gute Werk ausgerüstet.*

Das reformatorische Anliegen. Wir teilen das reformatorische Anliegen, den Heilsgewinn der menschlichen Verfügbarkeit zu entziehen und ihn stattdessen ganz der Gnade Gottes anheim zu stellen. Dabei anerkennen wir das positive Anliegen Calvins, die Souveränität Gottes bei der Erwählung des Menschen zu betonen.

Allerdings folgen wir der Erwählungslehre Calvins da nicht mehr, wo sie Thesen beinhaltet, die nicht mit der Bibel in Einklang zu bringen sind und die vor allem das Wesen und den Charakter Gottes zu verzerren drohen. Denn das Motiv, Synergismus zu vermeiden und gleichzeitig Gottes Alleinwirksamkeit im Heil zu bewahren, zwingt nicht zu Partikularismus, Supralapsarismus und Heilszwang. Nehmen solche Thesen eine zentrale Bedeutung an, rückt auch das Gesamtgebäude ins Zwielicht. Das Werk der Erlösung ist und bleibt alleine Gottes Geschenk, das der Mensch anzunehmen durch die Gnade Gottes in Stand gesetzt wird, ohne sich dessen rühmen zu können. Kurz gesagt: Wird er gerettet, dann ist es ausschließlich Gottes Werk; geht er verloren, war es seine eigene Schuld. Die Bibel lehrt eine echte eschatologisch[19] relevante Verantwortung. Hierin

---

18   Hymenäus, Philetus, Alexander, Demas (1Tim. 1:19f; 2Tim. 2:17f, 4:10,14).

19   Die Eschatologie ist die „Lehre von den letzten Dingen". „Eschatologisch" bedeutet, in Bezug auf die endzeitliche Vollendung gesehen. Diese Vollendung ist der Inhalt der Hoffnung, die wir in Christus haben.

liegt die Dialektik[20] und Komplementarität[21] der biblischen Gnadenlehre. Diese Spannung muss ausgehalten werden, auch wenn sie unbefriedigend erscheinen mag.

Ein geschichtliches Erwählungsverständnis „in Christus" und eine komplementäre Quantentheologie[22] der Prädestination kann mit dem polaren Spannungsfeld von göttlicher Souveränität und menschlicher Freiheit umgehen. Die Alleinwirksamkeit Gottes und die Verantwortung des Menschen bleiben erhalten, aber sie stehen nicht gleichwertig nebeneinander. Menschliche Freiheit ist Gnade, die der souveräne Gott ermöglicht. In Gottes Willen und Gnade ist der Spielraum des Menschen eingeschlossen, in den Gott durch Sein geschichtliches Handeln in Christus und durch den Ruf des Evangeliums hineintritt, um das individuelle Heil zu verwirklichen. Sowohl Synergismus als auch Heilszwang, Allversöhnung oder doppelte Prädestination halten wir für hilflose Übergriffe auf den Ratschluss Gottes. Alle Versuche, das dimensionale Ineinander von Gottes Allwirksamkeit und unserer Eigenverantwortung zu lösen, führen an die Grenzen des Denkvermögens. Das Reden von der Vorherbestimmung Gottes hat da seine Berechtigung, wo es das reformatorische *sola gratia*[23] und den unverdienten Charakter der Rettung wahren will. Es wird da anmaßend, wo es in ahistorischer Spekulation zu Partikularismus und Verdammungsurteil kommt.

Dem doxologischen[24] Charakter der Prädestination entspricht die Heilsgewissheit. Durch kein Versagen des Christen wird sich Gott in Seiner durch Christus am Kreuz erwiesenen Treue beirren lassen. Der biblische Erwählungsgedanke will nicht Anlass zu einer spekulativen Lehre sein, die entweder Angst oder Sorglosigkeit auslösen könnte, sondern drückt die Dankbarkeit, Heilsgewissheit und Freude des Gläubigen aus. Seine Rettung hängt nicht von ihm selbst ab und wird auch nicht durch vielerlei Umstände aufs Spiel gesetzt, sondern entspricht dem Willen Gottes. Er darf sich in dieser gottgewollten Gottesgemeinschaft für ewig geborgen wissen.[25]

---

20 Dialektik bedeutet, dass sich zwei scheinbare Gegensätze in konstruktiver Spannung gegenseitig ergänzen und zu einer ganzheitlichen Sicht führen. So darf die Gnade und die Verantwortung des Menschen nicht gegeneinander ausgespielt werden. Der Mensch wird aufgrund der Gnade zur Verantwortung gerufen. Verantwortlich handeln kann der Mensch aber nur, weil ihn Gott durch die Gnade dazu befähigt.

21 Komplementarität. In den scheinbaren Gegensätzen biblischer Aussagen stößt die Theologie auf die Komplementarität der biblischen Gnadenlehre. Komplementär werden in der Physik Phänomene genannt, wenn zwei unterschiedliche Experimente unterschiedliche und einander – vordergründig betrachtet – widersprüchliche Ergebnisse hervorbringen, die aber beide die identischen physikalischen Dinge untersuchen. Das bekannteste Beispiel ist der „Welle-Teilchen-Dualismus" des Lichts.

22 Siehe mcw-Prädestination-C Abschnitt II.7. Den Begriff „Quantentheologie der Prädestination" führt der Verfasser ein, um die Gleichzeitigkeit und das Nebeneinander zweier biblischer Wahrheiten zu illustrieren. Einerseits gilt nämlich die Herrschaft Gottes über die Geschichte, deren von Gott geplanter Ausgang durch menschliche Entscheidungen weder verhindert noch gefördert werden kann. Andererseits ist damit die Entscheidungsmöglichkeit des einzelnen nicht geleugnet. Wie im Bild der Quantenphysik werden auf der Makroebene Gottes Pläne unwiderstehlich zustande kommen, ohne dass damit jede Entscheidung auf Mikroebene vorweggenommen ist. Die Wahlfreiheit des durch das Evangelium angesprochenen Menschen ist nämlich Teil des umfassenden Rettungsplanes Gottes. Damit steht einerseits der durch die Gnade befreite Wille des Menschen vor den Optionen von Gehorsam oder Unglauben, während andererseits der souveräne Gott, der Sein Weltregiment zum Ziel bringen wird, darin die Freiwilligkeit des Menschen eingeschlossen hat.
Veröffentlicht in: Wolff, Matthias C. *Von Ewigkeit erwählt. Neues Licht auf alte Fragen – Die Lehre von der Gnadenwahl und Vorherbestimmung Gottes.* Herausgegeben von Bundes-Unterrichts-Werk. 2010. Erzhausen.

23 *Sola gratia* bedeutet: Allein aus Gnade. Dabei wird betont zum Ausdruck gebracht, dass allein die Gnade Gottes und keinerlei Mitwirken des Menschen das Heil bewirkt.

24 Doxologisch, Doxologie bedeutet: Lobpreisung Gottes.

25 Unvergessen bleibt die einfache Illustration eines theologischen Dozenten, der das Rettungsgeschehen mit einem Tor verglich, das auf der Außen- und Innenseite zwei unterschiedliche Aufschriften trägt. Außen liest der schuldbeladen eintretende Sünder „Herzliche Einladung!", und sobald er das Tor durchschritten hat, erkennt der nunmehr von seiner Sündenlast Befreite die Worte „Von Ewigkeit erwählt!"

Die Ergebnisse im Überblick:

I. Worüber Konsens besteht	II. Was modifiziert werden muss	III. Was nicht mitgetragen wird
• Verderbtheit, *Depravity*; Sündenzustand, die Verderbtheit des Menschen, der zu seinem Heil nichts beitragen kann. • Alleinwirksamkeit Gottes zum Heil, uneingeschränkt und bedingungslos. Die Erwählung von Menschen zum Heil durch Gottes persönlichen Ratschluss wird in der Schrift ausdrücklich bezeugt.	• Völlige Verderbtheit, *total depravity*; der Mensch ist zwar völlig heilsunfähig, was die Bibel aber nicht so versteht, dass er dem Ruf Gottes nicht gehorchen könne und deshalb zwangserwählt und – gerettet werden müsse.	• Doppelte Prädestination *(Gemina praedestinatio)*; die Erwählung zum Heil und zur Verdammnis. Parallele Struktur von *vocatio et reprobatio*, Erwählung und Verwerfung, wird von der Bibel nicht gelehrt. Verwerfung setzt immer eigenes Verschulden voraus und liegt damit nicht im Ratschluss Gottes. • Supralapsarismus; die Vorherbestimmung des Sündenfalls.
• Unfreier Wille und vorlaufende Gnade *(gratia praeveniens)* • Der Wille der Menschen ist in der Tat nicht mehr frei, sondern von der Sünde versklavt, … • Bedingungslose Erwählung, *unconditional election*; Berufung und Erwählung als Gnadenwirken Gottes. • Keine Prädestination durch Vorherwissen (Präszienz).	• … doch darf die vorlaufende Gnade, die die Annahme des Heils ermöglicht, weder mit Vorherbestimmung noch mit souveräner Entscheidungsfreiheit des Menschen verwechselt werden.	• Partikularismus, *limited atonement*, begrenztes Sühneopfer; Christus sei nur für die Erwählten gestorben. • Unwiderstehliche Gnade, *irresistable grace*; Heilszwang. • Beharren der Heiligen, *perseverance oft the saints*; Verneinung des Abfalls der Erwählten; „once saved – always saved" („einmal gerettet – immer gerettet").

Published on ICEJ International (https://int.icej.org)

Home > Printer-friendly

Ephraimite theory an 'unsound doctrine'

By David Parsons

10/2010

in None [1]

As Christians in unprecedented numbers seek to stand with Israel today and recapture the Jewish roots of our faith, one potential pitfall of this movement is the "Ephraimite doctrine."

Based largely on a flawed interpretation of the prophetic vision of the two sticks of Judah and Ephraim being joined back together in Ezekiel 37, this is a mystical belief that many Christian Zionists today are actually descended from the "Lost Ten Tribes of Israel." They 'sense' God is drawing them back to the Jewish fold through Christ and their heart-felt love for Israel.

Taken to its extreme, some Ephraimite teachers maintain that, as blood descendants of the ancient Israelites, adherents must observe the Law, thereby departing from the core New Testament belief that salvation is by faith. Some also teach a limited atonement; that Jesus only came for the "lost sheep of the House of Israel."

The doctrine also has elitist strains, as many believe the Lost Ten Tribes are to be found today among white European Christians, since they are more 'blessed' and prosperous than other nations. They often tend to separate themselves from mainstream Evangelicals, believing they are the "True Church." They also can tend to have a superior attitude towards the Jewish people, who after all still reject Jesus – thus they are also the "True Israel."

No doubt they have tapped into a long line of shaky 'scholarship' which purports to trace the movement of the lost tribes into Western Europe. In past generations, this false teaching was known as British Israelism, among other monikers.

In Israel today, some Jews are intrigued by this phenomenon, seeing it as a sign of expected mass conversions of Gentiles to Judaism or the Noahide laws in the "last days." Some on the Right also see it as a way of strengthening the settler movement, as these Christian Zionists tend to be strong proponents of keeping all the land. They have even proposed that Ephraimites be allowed to take up residence in the settlements.

But overall, most Israelis aware of the Ephraimite movement see it as yet another reason to question the beliefs and motives of Christian Zionists.

IN EXAMINING this teaching, it can first be stated that the "myth" of the Lost Ten Tribes is just that – a myth. Nowhere does the Bible state that the Ten Tribes of the northern Kingdom of Israel were totally lost. Scattered? Yes! But they are still largely accounted for in Scripture (save for the ultra-rebellious tribe of Dan, which indeed was lost to history).

It is the Jerusalem Talmud which is the source of the myth, and even that cannot be used to support Ephraimite thinking. One passage speaks of a remnant of the ten tribes still living in self-imposed exile "beyond the Sambayton River." This mystical river, whose name is derived from Shabbat, referred to a voluntary separation from the Jewish mainstream by removing themselves "beyond" Sabbath observance and other Jewish customs.

doubt, a small portion of the northern ten tribes likely drifted off to lands unknown, but the Bible does account for the vast majority, who went through a sifting process whereby the faithful ꞈ absorbed back into Judah.

After the northern Kingdom of Israel broke away from the southern Kingdom of Judah, the books of Kings and Chronicles repeatedly tell of many from the northern ten tribes defecting to the south, even well before the Assyrian assault on Samaria in 722 BC (recounted in 2 Kings 17 and 18).

Many were still loyal to Jerusalem as the center of worship and pilgrimage, rather than the rival temple set up on Mount Gerizim. Others believed the true successor to King David was in Judah, while Israel's kings were falling into apostasy. These defections accelerated whenever civil war erupted between the divided kingdoms.

Thus, for instance, 2 Chronicles 15:9 says that many "fell to him [Judah's King Asa] out of Israel in abundance, when they saw that the Lord his God was with him." (See also, 2 Chronicles 11:13-17 and 19:4)

The army of Judah grew exponentially in this period to over one million warriors (compare 1 Kings 12:21 with 2 Chronicles 14:8 and 17:14-18), while King Ahab eventually could only muster 7,000 from the "children of Israel" (1 Kings 20:15).

Then as the Assyrians laid siege to the northern tribes, many more fled southward. Archeologists have verified that Jerusalem itself grew ten times in population in this brief period due to the influx of Israelite refugees, and a new outer wall was hastily erected to enclose them – a section is still visible along Nablus Road near the US Consulate in eastern Jerusalem.

Then in the 135 years between the Assyrian invasion of the north and the Babylonian siege of Jerusalem in 586 BC, more drifted south from the ten tribes. This was because conquerors in those days would only take away the nobles and learned and skilled workers into exile, while leaving the leaderless peasantry to work the land and pay tribute (see the similar fate of Judah in 2 Kings 24:10-14).

In his dissertation studies on the subject, author Jack Carstens notes that, curiously, the Encyclopedia Judaica recites that only 27,290 Israelites were carried off by the Assyrians to beyond the Euphrates.

Of those left behind, some joined lots with Judah while others intermingled with foreigners brought in to colonize the area, giving rise to the shunned Samaritans of the Gospels.

The Bible confirms many Israelites were left in the land and that the Kings of Judah even came north and took control of their cities. In 2 Chronicles 30, for example, King Hezekiah invites the remaining Israelites to keep Passover with Judah (See also 2 Chronicles 31:1 and 35:17).

Later, when elements of both Israel and Judah were in captivity, they stayed in contact with each other and all the royal edicts allowing the return to Zion were passed on to the northern tribes in exile. The books of Esther, Ezra and Nehemiah attest to such interaction and begin to use the terms Jews and Israelites interchangeably. The noted Jewish historian Josephus F᠎꞉ᵗus also documents their contacts in exile and is still able to account for the ten tribes as of the First Century.

Thereafter, the New Testament writers both assume and affirm that the Jewish people of their day contained significant remnants from all 12 tribes. They also treat the terms Jews and Israel as synonymous.

In one clear example in Acts 26:7, the Apostle Paul uses the present tense in telling King Agrippas: "To this promise our twelve tribes, earnestly serving God night and day, hope to attain."

James also addresses his epistle to the "twelve tribes which are scattered abroad" (1:1). Again, they are dispersed but still accounted for!

Leading Jewish researchers into the fate of the 'lost' Ten Tribes, such as the late Rabbi Eliyahu Avichail, have concluded that some indeed drifted west and blended back into the Jewish mainstream, while others drifted eastward and live today in isolated communities stretching from the Kurdish areas of northern Iraq over to Kashmir and Tibet. They number several million, share a strong self-identity as Israelite descendants, use certain Hebrew names and phrases, and often keep certain Jewish traditions, such as the Pashtun tribes in Afghanistan who light two candles on Friday evenings.

Even so, these scholars concur that the bulk of the Houses of Ephraim (Israel) and Judah were later exiled together by the Romans into the Jewish Diaspora, half of which has now have been gathered back together in the Land, forming "one nation… on the mountains of Israel" – just as the Hebrew prophets all agreed they would (Ezekiel 37:22; see also Isaiah 11:12-13; Jeremiah 3:18, 23:6-8 and 31; Zechariah 8:13). From the perspective of the divided and warring kingdoms of their day, this is an amazing accomplishment.

THERE ARE TWO sobering lessons to take from all this. The first is that people can cut themselves off from the move and purpose of God of their own volition. He gave ample chances for the northern Kingdom to repent and stay with the remnant He was preserving over time, and yet some chose otherwise.

The second is that we should not take Scriptures with plain meaning and read into them mysteries that are not there. Both the letters of Timothy and Titus exhort us to teach "sound doctrine." Clearly, the Ephraimite theory does not make the grade.

Source URL: https://int.icej.org/news/none/ephraimite-theory-%E2%80%98unsound-doctrine%E2%80%99

Links:
[1] https://int.icej.org/category/news/none

MALCOLM HEDDING

The Ephraim Doctrine

> "Now the Spirit expressly says that in the latter times
> some will depart from the faith, giving heed to deceiving
> spirits and doctrines of demons."
> 1 Timothy 4:1

Search _

Essentially the Ephraim Teaching, that continues to plague so many Israel supporting Christians, is false as it is rooted in historical inaccuracy and the irresponsible exposition of the scriptures. Of course those enamored with all things Jewish see in this teaching an opportunity to identify themselves as Jews! The Ephraim teaching is a form of replacement theology in that by virtue of its older manifestation as British Israelism it asserts that the British Commonwealth of nations are indeed the so called lost ten tribes of Israel. They just don't know it but if they studied their history they would discover this as the word "British" actually means "Covenant Man". The British Royal Family is thus said to be the perpetuation of David's Throne since after the destruction of Jerusalem in 586 BC Jeremiah supposedly brought the "Crowning Stone", otherwise known as the "Stone of Scone", and the royal Princesses to the British Isles.

In its more recent form this doctrine takes the names of "The House of Joseph" or that of "The Ephraim Teaching." To support this theory two scenarios are posited:

1. That Christians replace the Ten Tribes of the once Northern Kingdom of Israel and are thus very much part of Israel and as such have the right to make Aliyah. (Return to the land of Israel and resettle in the Biblical heartland.) They assert that the Northern Kingdom was judged and exiled because of their rebellion against God and subsequently cast away.

2. That Christians are the ancient house of Israel and that Jesus' atoning work only extends as far as them. Fully misunderstanding Jesus' mission; in that the Kingdom had to first be offered to Israel, they wrongly apply Matthew 15:24 (Jesus says; "….I was only sent to the House of Israel.') to themselves and thereby believe in a limited atonement. Jesus did not die for every man on the face of the earth (Hebrews 2:9) but only for the house of Israel. Thus a Zulu man living in the one thousand hills of Kwazulu-Natal in South Africa, if he comes to faith in Jesus, proves that he is in fact a descendant of the ancient house of Israel! How he got there they cannot tell you!

All of this turns Paul's references to the Gentiles in the New Testament upside down. They are in fact Israel Gentiles! Jesus never really died for real Gentiles, like those in the Amazon jungle, as He only came for the lost sheep of the House of Israel. This also makes nonsense of the Great Commission and the fact that one day in Heaven there will be people from every tribe and nation gathered at the great Throne of God. (Matthew 28:19-20; Revelation 5:9-10) And yet, this false doctrine continues to take root everywhere deceiving the untaught and unsuspecting Christians. It brings the valid biblical ministry to Israel into disrepute and ministers are rightly scared to move in this direction because they fear that the Ephraim crazies may well move in and affect their flocks with their nonsense.

The truth is:
1. The tribes of Israel were integrated by division and dispersion.
That is; with the division of the Davidic Kingdom into two entities after Solomon's reign a mass migration from the Northern Kingdom of Israel to the Southern Kingdom of Judah took place because of the Temple at Jerusalem and the significance of the city itself. To stop this migration Jeroboam, the Northern King, built a rival Temple in Samaria with pagan rituals. Scripture affirms that he caused Israel to sin thereby. (1Kings 12:25-33) Therefore in the south the tribes mingled, lived together and finally integrated. Slowly but surely the term Jew became a generic term for all of Israel.

In 722 BC the Northern Kingdom is conquered by the Assyrians and taken into exile. This exile is to the north and east of Israel meaning that when the Southern Kingdom was conquered by the Babylonians in 586 BC the people were carried off into the same region. Here again they mingled and integrated and became finally known as Jews. (Esther 3:6; Nehemiah 1:6) So, the ten tribes of the Northern Kingdom were lost only in the sense that they lost their tribal identity. They were never lost in the sense that they vanished from history. Proof of this is that Jesus recognized that in preaching to the Jews of His day He was in fact preaching to all of Israel. (Matthew 10:6; Matthew 15:24) Also, James addresses his epistle to the…"twelve tribes which are scattered abroad." He would not write in this way if the twelve tribes were lost! Actually these twelve tribes were Jews who had believed in Jesus as the early apostolic preachers went from Synagogue to Synagogue preaching Jesus. (Acts 13:5)

The Jews that have returned to Israel today are indeed the twelve tribes of Israel and truly as Ezekiel predicted they have returned to the land of their forefathers as "one stick" and not two! (Ezekiel 37:15-19)

2. The Book of Hosea is incorrectly expounded by Ephraim Teachers.

Hosea warns Israel that she will be judged for her iniquity and that a people who were never God's people (not my people) will be invited into fellowship with the God of Israel. (Hosea 2:23) Ephraim teachers wrongly assert that these "not my people" are Christians called to replace Israel or at a later date, some 2030 years later, are the lost tribes recovered in the Christian Church! This is sheer nonsense.

Our understanding of what Hosea meant is not open to conjecture as Paul clarifies this for us in his Epistle to the Roman Church. The Northern Kingdom's rebellion against God and sin removed its people, for a period, from the grace of God. To make them jealous God will call a people to a place of faith and salvation who historically were never His people. (Romans 9:30) These people are real gentiles from all over the world according to Paul. They are not Israelites and never were and they are not a replacement of them. They are gentiles called out of darkness into the great light of Jesus and they share in Israel's spiritual things. (Romans 9:25-26, Romans 15:27) Moreover, they are grafted into Israel's spiritual tree of salvation and are thus first class citizens of the Kingdom of God and do not have to prove that somehow they are Jewish or Israel. (Romans 11:17-22)

So then to infer that the Gentile believers are somehow the lost ten tribes of Israel or a replacement of them and thus having a secret identity is a blatant contradiction of Paul's teaching. Enough said; the argument is over! Indeed the Gentile believers in Jesus are the fulfillment of God's promise to Abraham when He told him that he would be the father of all nations. (Romans 4:13)

3. The New Testament itself bears testimony to the fact the Jews in the dispersion are in fact the twelve tribes of Israel.

The Ephraim teaching is offensive to Jews as it constitutes yet another attempt to rob them of their identity. The doctrine is a deception built on the falsification of history and the twisting of the Word of God. It attacks the notion that God loves the whole world (John 3:16) and that He gave His Son to die for it. It also undermines the completeness of Jesus' work as its disciples begin to keep Jewish rituals, Sabbaths and feasts. All of this is warned against by Paul. (Colossians 2:6-10; 11; 16-19)

Jesus knew that by preaching to the Jews of His day He was in fact preaching to the twelve tribes of Israel and He sent His disciples out to do the same thing and said as much. (Matthew 10:6) James writes to the Jews in the dispersion and calls them the twelve tribes (James 1:1) and Peter does the same by addressing his first epistle to the "pilgrims of the dispersion." (1Peter 1:1) These were Jews or Israel as the gentiles were never "pilgrims of the dispersion" as he puts it.

In closing let me say that the Jews today are a people comprising all the original tribes of Israel and that the term "Jew" then has become an inclusive designation of all the tribes. These tribes are not lost by any means as, apart from a great multitude from all tribes and peoples that will appear at the Throne of God in the end, there will also be the saved twelve tribes of Israel. (Revelation 7:4-12) God seals them and numbers them! The message could not be clearer.

Malcolm Hedding

©Malcolm Hedding Ministries

28.8.2018

8/2011

CHRISTIAN ZIONISM 101

BIBLICAL ZIONISM

ISRAEL'S CALLING

ISRAEL AND JESUS

ISRAEL AND CHRISTIANS

TRENDS IN THE NATIONS

THE EGYPTIAN TERRITORISM

THE EPHRAIM FABLE

THE EPHRAIMITE FABLE
A Speculative and Divisive Theology

By Malcolm Hedding

The Ephramite teaching has infiltrated the Christian Zionist movement and threatens to bring it into disrepute. Essentially, it is a misguided attempt to identify Gentile believers in Jesus with the half-tribe of Ephraim, which later in Scripture became synonymous with the Northern Kingdom of Israel exiled to Assyria in 722 BC. These Ten Tribes are deemed to be lost but now rediscovered in the Church! There are three versions of this error.

7/2011

15.01.2014 → IAMCS Report
on 26.5.2014 ⎤
20.1.2018 ⎦ DANIEL 12 and   **USA**

1335 days of "ABOMINATION of DESOLATION" of Daniel 12.11 + 12.12
take place

INTERNATIONAL ALLIANCE OF MESSIANIC CONGREGATIONS AND SYNAGOGUES
(IAMCS)

A JUDGEMENT of the
"Synagoge of Satan" named - IAMCS -

→ # One Law, Two Sticks: ←

A Critical Look at the Hebrew Roots Movement

**A position paper of the International Alliance of Messianic Congregations and
Synagogues (IAMCS) Steering Committee**

1/15/2014

← LIAR

SLANDER/LIES/DESTRUCTION as 1 2014 !!

X	Eddie Chumney
	Scott Diffenderfer

X Victims   2012 in Berlin @
Ulf Diebel's House

2 Pastor / DREAMSTREAM

Michael Jay Solome

Ulf Diebel

take all to COURT!
22.9.2018

Business partner
Dreamstream

Table of Contents:

<u>**One Law, Two Sticks:**</u>
A Critical Look at the Hebrew Roots Movement

I.

<u>**Introduction**</u>:

Preface:

We, as Messianic Jewish leaders, have become increasingly concerned that there are a growing number of individuals and groups today promoting the idea that all the world's believers in the Messiah - Jewish and Gentile alike - ought to be keeping the Torah, *→ Mt. 5.17 -20* particularly the Shabbat, the feasts, and kosher diet. The doctrine which is the subject of this paper has been around since the day of the Apostles, in different forms, but today it has come to be known as "One Law One People" or just "One Law," for short. It insists upon Gentile Torah observance universally. Most of those who teach it, also promote false theories about Israel identity as well. Recently, some of the more prominent One Law teachers have banded together and begun using the label "Hebrew Roots" to *Rooted in* describe themselves as a movement. This nomenclature is regrettable from our point of *Ephraic :-)* view, since it causes confusion. *Since A'coficgfk*

Obviously, the roots of the biblical faith are Jewish. Thankfully, many non-Jewish believers worldwide recognize the fact that their faith is rooted in a Jewish Messiah, Jewish Apostles, and a Jewish gospel. We note that many precious, well-meaning Gentile believers are drawn to Messianic Judaism because they wish to connect with Israel; they want to understand the Bible in historical context, or they simply have a desire to enrich their faith by acquiring a more Jewish understanding of the Lord.

Therefore, we wish to be clear up front that not everyone who uses the label "Hebrew Roots" is necessarily part of that "Hebrew Roots" camp which is the cause for our concern. Since we don't invent the names for these movements, we are resigned to have to use the names and labels which they apply to themselves.

One Law Doctrine:

One Law doctrine is based on the idea that everybody everywhere ought to be keeping the Torah given to the Jews at Sinai. In their view, the law wasn't intended just for Israel, but for everyone. Moreover, neither the coming of Messiah, nor the atonement provided in the New Covenant changes anything in terms of what they see as the universal human need to relate to God through the laws of Moses.

Accordingly, One Law teachers, as embodied today in the Hebrew Roots movement, are highly critical of what they see as the historical error of the Gentile church in not keeping the laws which God gave to Moses and Israel at Mount Sinai. Of particular concern to them seem to be the laws pertaining to Shabbat and festival observance, as well as the

2

dietary laws. Those Gentile Christians who don't necessarily see the need to follow such laws are considered as "pagans."

One Law doctrine holds that the true "Hebrew roots" of the faith are to be found in keeping the laws of Moses given at Mt. Sinai. Their mission, as it seems, is to promote observance of the law as the means of restoring the body of Messiah to the supposed true Hebrew roots of the faith, which are to be found in the Sinai covenant. This mission takes on particular urgency in the end-times. One Law proponents advocate, therefore, the urgent need for all Gentile believers to depart from "paganism," and to return in zeal to the "true Hebrew roots" of their faith, which is supposedly to be found in the legal observance of Torah.

In recent years, they have bombarded the internet with their teachings. Some of them are very savvy when it comes to this.

The Issue:

Followers of "One Law One People" insist that everybody ought to be keeping the Torah. Since everybody does not keep the Torah, they typically see their Torah observance as some kind of evidence of their chosen-ness. Not only does this breed a sense of legalistic pride, but there are deeper concerns.

Almost inevitably, "One Law One People" teaching is associated with the idea that people who keep the Torah given to Israel actually ARE Israel. This idea is usually advanced by myths about the "lost tribes." The followers of "One Law" typically begin to identify Israel in Bible prophecy as somehow pertaining to them. Most of them think of themselves as belonging to the northern kingdom of Israel, as represented in the prophecy of the two "sticks" referenced in Ezekiel 37. Thus, they see Torah observance as their duty as members of the people Israel.

The question of Israel identity always seems to be related to this doctrine of One Law. Thus, not only is it wrong on its face, theologically, but it is deeply and intimately intertwined with replacement theology.

Obsession with the Torah, and with Israel identity, has caused many Hebrew roots groups to take on the external look and feel of being Jewish. In Hebrew roots conferences and in local congregational groups, for example, it is commonplace to hold meetings on Shabbat and during the Levitical feasts. In their meetings, they typically employ traditional articles of Jewish worship like davidic dancing, Jewish liturgical prayers, and shofar-blowing. It is common for people to be wearing kippot and tzitzit, using Hebrew slogans on their banners, displaying the magen David, and even processing Torahs.

We don't disagree generally with the use of Jewish symbolism and expression by non-Jews. However, such usage by legalistic, non-Jewish groups, many of whom think they are the true Israelites, and who are often critical and divisive toward the Gentile church, can cause much offense and/or confusion in both the Jewish and Christian community. Both the Jewish and Christian communities may not be able to see the distinction between the Messianic Jewish community and the Hebrew Roots camp. Due to their external appearance, and the imitation of Jewish expression, there is potential that the practices and beliefs of these Hebrew Roots groups could wrongfully be attributed to Messianic Jews.

Our Purpose in This Paper:

By issuing this paper, we wish to identify and describe One Law theology and the related Hebrew Roots movement, both historically and today, and to give an informed opinion as to the errors as well as the inherent dangers of it.

We in the messianic Jewish movement also wish to make clear the fact that we are opposed to One Law theology, and to any doctrine which advocates, as One Law does, the idea that New Covenant faith among the Gentiles is to be fulfilled by embracing the Sinai covenant. We do not seek the fulfillment of God's plan for the salvation of Israel through the Sinai Covenant, but rather, through the gospel. If our own Jewish people have not been reconciled unto God by the Sinai covenant, then this must also certainly be true for the Gentiles, who were not given the Sinai covenant to begin with.

While many aspects of Torah are found in messianic Judaism as a unique expression of our Jewish faith in the Messiah, we do not believe that the Gentile church, or Gentile Christians universally, are called to the same expression as us. In fact, it is the unity of Jew and Gentile in Messiah, *in spite of* our cultural diversity, which glorifies God in the body of the Lord, via the one new man. (Eph. 2:15). In our view, therefore, it is wrong to admonish Gentile believers universally to think that they need to observe the Torah. It is clear, furthermore, that the Apostles dealt with this precise question of Gentile Torah observance and answered it on point in Acts 15. All of this will be discussed further in this paper.

At this point, we wish to be clear about our purpose and our heart's intent: In what we say in this paper, we are not in any way speaking against the many precious Gentiles who fellowship in messianic synagogues in response to a call from the Lord. Many non-Jews come into the messianic Jewish fold with the desire of knowing the Lord through the Jewishness of the scriptures, and in the ancient way of life, which was Yeshua's own culture and heritage, as preserved in the life of the Jewish people. We, in Messianic Judaism, have always welcomed and encouraged non-Jews to fellowship with us, to celebrate Messiah together, and help us restore Israel to faith in Yeshua. Our concern is with those who advocate legalism.

4

<u>**Definitions**</u>

What do they mean by "Torah"?

In addressing the errors of One Law theology, it will be necessary to frequently refer to the term "Torah." At times, this can be rather ambiguous, as the term "Torah" (law), of course, has different meanings depending on context. For example, there is not just the law given at Sinai. But there is the law which tells us how God created mankind and the universe in Genesis. There are the testimonies in the Torah of how Joseph was reunited with his brothers, how God fought with Israel against the Canaanites, how Aaron's rod budded, or how God split the Red Sea through Moses. Even when we talk about the actual legal part of Torah, there are 613 commandments. Many have to do with the service of the Temple.

Generically, the term "Torah" is often thought of as a set of laws providing a moral code for right living. Although there are such commandments in the Torah, the moral law is a very limited part of Torah, and is not a good basis for understanding what Torah is. While the Torah does contain certain moral laws given to Israel, it was not in fact, given in order to be the ultimate moral statement and standard of God to humanity for ethics and basic right v. wrong living. The Torah does not purport to be such a statement. While there clearly are universal moral laws in the Torah, there are many aspects of the Torah that have nothing to do with morality, and which therefore are not intended to be universal. For example, the commandment to Israel to wear tzitzit (Num. 15:38), or to be circumcised (Lev. 12:3).

The Torah does not approach being an exhaustive, all-encompassing, moral code. In fact, Paul's assertion in Romans 2:14 states:

"Indeed, when Gentiles, who do not have the law, do by nature things required by the law, they are a law for themselves, even though they do not have the law."

The scripture acknowledges that there is at least a basic sense and assertion of morality in all of the world's cultures. Most societies eschew murder, stealing, adultery, rape, abuse of the weak and helpless, et cetera. There is a moral sense in the conscience of man that to some extent parallels that of scripture, but is able to discern right and wrong even in spite of never having read or heard the Torah which God gave to Israel.

The gift of the Torah to the Jewish people at Sinai, therefore, was not revelatory in the sense of the moral aspect of it. Noah was an "ish tzadik" or "righteous man" (See Gen. 6:9); and Abraham obeyed God's statutes and commandments (Gen. 26:5), even long before the law at Sinai was even given.

Torah is not a revelation of morality. Nor is the moral aspect of it unique in any way. A basic understanding of moral law is already embedded by God in the understanding of mankind. God did not appear to Israel at Sinai to present a moral code.

God gave the law at Sinai, creating a unique nation. There are things given in the Torah which are unique to Israel. Above all, the actual revelation at Sinai was not the law, but rather, the lawgiver. In fact, God not only gave the law at Sinai, but God revealed Himself unto the people Israel. (See Ex. 19 and 20). The Jews from the most ancient times have understood this.

Hence, the controversy over "Torah observance," as engendered by One Law teachers, does not involve questions of defining moral and ethical commandments. No one would argue whether moral laws, such as those found in Torah or anywhere else, are universal in application. Of course, prohibitions against murder, sexual immorality, theft, coveting, etc., are universal. Morality, as expressed in the Torah, is universal. It is incumbent upon all mankind to be moral. But one need not learn morality from the Jewish Torah in order to be moral. Morality as a standard is not the unique revelation of the Torah.

In the context of "One Law" theology, the "One Law" teachers have established a presence on the internet, where they often publish condemnations of the Gentile church for its alleged failure to keep "Torah." The implication is that failing to "keep the Torah" is a moral failure, which renders the Gentile church either unrighteous, unholy, or both, in the eyes of God. If in fact we were talking about breaching moral laws, then such accusations might hold water. However, that is not the case.

In fact, there are three major areas of the Torah in which the "One Law" teachers seem to feel that the Gentile church is at fault for failing to obey God: 1) The Sabbath, 2) the Levitical feasts, and 3) the dietary laws. To a lesser extent, some would also find fault in Gentile believers who do not obey ceremonial laws such as circumcision and wearing tzitzit (fringes). These Torah commands, which do not pertain to issues of morality, are the main focal point of the "One Law" controversy. Why these?

We note that the commandments in Torah which tend to be the main topic of controversy with One Law teachers are the laws which stand out as being uniquely identified with Israel. Not only the church today, but all civilized cultures, even going back to Egypt and Rome have had laws against murder and theft, but only the Jews have had laws pertaining to Yom Kippur or Passover. Thus, the issue is not with laws that are clearly universal, but with those that are Israel-specific.

"One Law" as Replacement Theology:

The idea behind "One Law" theology, whether stated or implied, is that he who keeps the law given to Israel, therefore IS Israel. Accordingly, "One Law" theology is simply a form of replacement theology. By keeping the laws which are specific to Israel, one thereby presumes to be Israel. This incorrect desire to "keep Torah" in order to become Israel is a deception that dates back to the time of the Apostles. (1 Tim. 1:4, Titus 3:9).

III.   **History and Background**:

"One Law" doctrine of the 21st century has been greatly popularized in recent years by the emergence of the Hebrew Roots movement. But it is important to point out that the Hebrew Roots movement and its accompanying legalistic doctrine is not something new. We find in Paul's warning to Timothy, that in their time, too, there were Hebrew roots teachers who taught myths about Jewish genealogy and sought to promote themselves as expert Torah teachers, even though they had no idea what they were talking about. (1 Tim. 1:4-8). Paul describes the doctrine of such teachers as "meaningless talk." He further describes them:

> *"They want to be teachers of the law, but they do not know what they are talking about or what they so confidently affirm."* (1 Tim. 1:8)

In order to understand and explain the errors of the Hebrew Roots camp of today, it is necessary to consider its historical predecessors. While the whole matter can be traced back to the day of the Apostles, for our purposes here, we will go back to the 19th century, and mention a few key religious movements in America which are most clearly the parents and grandparents of the modern Hebrew Roots movement. This will include the Millerite and Sabbatarian movements of the 19th century. From that came forth the 20th century Sacred Name movement, and the Worldwide Church of God (WCG), of Herbert W. Armstrong.

The Millerites – Origins of legalisitic, end-time fanaticism:

William Miller was a Baptist lay preacher who began preaching in the 1830's that the return of the Messiah was imminent. Up until that time, there was little teaching or discussion about the return of the Messiah or end-time prophecy in American churches. Most Christians never thought about the idea of Messiah literally coming back to set up a Kingdom and reign on earth. What we know and believe to be biblical fact today regarding the Lord's return was not being preached in America's churches. With the rise of new mediums of communication, like the high speed printing press, and the telegraph, a free marketplace of religious expression arose, independent of the mainstream church. This allowed for biblical expression that might otherwise not have been taught in church, but it also opened the door to fanaticism.

Miller not only insisted that Messiah would return to earth to set up a Kingdom, but he insisted that such return was imminent, and even narrowed it down to a date certain in 1844. Based on a combination of the Karaite Jewish calendar and the 2300 days of

Daniel (Dan. 8:14), Miller and his followers were expecting the Messiah to return specifically on Yom Kippur, Oct. 22nd, 1844.

In 1840, Miller's end-time prophetic doctrine was transformed from being an obscure, local teaching to a national religious movement known as the "Millerite" movement. It was also referred to as "Adventism," since it was characterized by a certain obsession with the idea that the Messiah would return to earth a second time. The impetus for this change occurred mainly due to the help of Miller's alliance with a Boston Pastor who was an able and experienced publisher. Miller's magazine, *Sign of the Times*, soon began appearing in major cities all over America and Canada. During the 1840's alone, millions of copies were distributed.

The fanaticism created by the Millerites spread all the way to Great Britain and Australia. We note that Miller's Adventist theology was one of the first national religious movements in America to effectively make use of the mass media in widely disseminating fanatical beliefs based on a false interpretation of prophecy.

Adventists and Sabbatarianism:

Thousands of Millerite followers were literally waiting in the fields to see the Lord return on Oct. 22nd, 1844. When it did not occur, this resulted in what came to be known as the "Great Disappointment," in which countless Millerites were discouraged and disillusioned. Though the Lord did not return on schedule, the fanaticism created by the Millerites continued, and it found a new outlet of expression.

In the aftermath, many Millerite leaders began to proclaim that it was necessary for Christians to start keeping the Sabbath to be prepared for the final return of the Lord. Not the Sunday Sabbath, but the Sabbath of Israel.

The hook for the Sabbatarian idea is the belief that there is an end-time crisis at hand, in which a great controversy is brewing over God's concern with mankind not keeping the Sabbath. As it is presented, the implication is that those who keep the Sabbath of Israel, ARE Israel. And those who do not, are outside of the covenant people. They are under condemnation for their unbelief and disobedience to God.

Accordingly, it should be understood that there is a strong connection between Sabbatarianism and Adventism. Those who insist upon the need to keep the Sabbath (and other laws), will typically motivate their followers thru fanaticism, obsession, and false claims related to end-time prophecy.

In the wake of the fanaticism created by the Millerites, many people were already primed and ready to accept the idea that God was separating the "true Israel" from the rest of humanity over the issue of Sabbath-keeping. The acceptance of this belief gave rise to the Sabbatarian church movement of the latter part of the 19th century, which is based in a form of "One Law" theology and more closely resembles the modern Hebrew Roots movement in terms of its belief that Gentiles must keep the law of Moses to please God.

Seventh Day Adventist Church:

One Millerite who became a key advocate of the need to keep the Sabbath was Ellen White, one of the founders of the Seventh Day Adventist (SDA) church. White wrote:

> *"I saw that the holy Sabbath is, and will be, the separating wall between the true Israel of God and unbelievers; and that the Sabbath is the great question to unite the hearts of God's dear, waiting saints."* [1]

The SDA church today, which continues to preach Sabbath observance as the mark of a true christian, boasts a membership of over 16 million members worldwide. Under "fundamental beliefs," it states the following on its website:

> *"(The Sabbath) is a symbol of our redemption in Christ, a sign of our sanctification, a token of our allegiance, and a foretaste of our eternal future in God's kingdom. The Sabbath is God's perpetual sign of His eternal covenant between Him and His people."* [2]

Since SDA sees Sabbath-keeping as a sign of both salvation and of holiness, it further considers itself to be the "covenant people." Consequently, SDA has no vision whatsoever for the salvation of Jewish people or the birth of the Jewish State. It sees the State of Israel today as if it is in no way connected to anything in scripture. For example, in a major SDA publication, entitled "How Should Christians view Israel," it states:

> *"The 1948 establishment of the State of Israel, an outgrowth of the Nazi Holocaust in which 6 million Jews were killed, is viewed by Adventists as a political, not a prophetic event."* [3]

It should be understood that those who would compel Gentile Christians to keep the Sabbath, and other such laws given specifically to Israel at Sinai, will typically assign

---

[1] Ellen G. White, *Early Writings*, p. 33, : www.gilead.net/egw/books2/earlywritings/ewindex.html

[2] http://www.adventist.org/beliefs/fundamental/index.html

[3] Mark Kellner, *"How Should Christians view Israel?"* (2007), http://www.adventistreview.org/article/1456/archives/issue-2007-1531/how-should-christians-view-israel

unto themselves the identity of being the "chosen people." This is necessary in order to provide their followers with a motive to think it necessary to keep the law. Their "chosen-ness" is thus confirmed by their presumed keeping of the commandments of God. Accordingly, they will challenge the true identity of Israel, and replace it, theologically, with themselves.

Hence, in this skewed, legalistic approach to the prophetic scriptures, Israel has nothing to do with the Jewish people, but it has everything to do with Gentiles observing laws that were once given to the Jews. The Jews, of course, broke those laws, and incurred God's wrath. Therefore, the Jews are replaced by one more worthy to be God's nation. Thus, Israel is no longer the Jewish nation, but rather, it is an end-time remnant of Gentile Sabbath-keepers. These Sabbatarian Christians are the true "Israel of God." Or so they seem to think.

In this Sabbatarian model, we see not only a poor understanding of prophecy but obvious replacement theology too. For the unfortunate gentile christian who is deceived by Sabbatarian teaching, the message comes across loud and clear: Salvation is not only by grace through faith, but also by the law; for the sign of the true gentile believer is seen in the keeping of the Sabbath.

By the 20th century, and still today, SDA grew to become the largest Adventist/ Sabbatarian denomination in America, and in the world, spreading their beliefs and practices among Christians in every country.[4] But there were many others that arose in the wake of the Millerite fiasco of 1844, which did not accept the prophetic claims of Ellen White, and instead, founded their own Sabbatarian groups. Most non-SDA Adventist/Sabbatarian groups, which rejected Ellen White, came to be known as "Church of God", in one form or another. [5] Two of the "Church of God" denominations which shall be discussed in this paper are "Church of God (Seventh Day), and also the "Worldwide Church of God."

The impact of SDA and related Sabbatarian groups through the late 19th and early 20th century, particularly in America, was quite significant. The widespread promotion of the idea of Gentile Torah observance set the stage for what was to come later.

Sacred Namers:

By the early 20th century, many Sabbaterean Christians began to concern themselves not only with keeping the Sabbath, but also with the Lord's name. A new movement thus

---

[4] J. Gordon Melton, *Encyclopedia of Protestantism,* Infobase Publishing, (Jan. 1, 2005), p. 478

[5] Richard Nickels, *History of the Seventh Day Church of God,* Giving and Sharing Publications, (1999), pp. 11-12.

emerged within Sabbatarianism that came to known as the "Sacred name" movement. It arose particularly during the 1930's.

Based on the premise that true Christians must return to their Hebrew roots by keeping the law, Sacred-namers insisted that it was necessary to keep not only the 4th commandment (the Sabbath), but also the 3rd commandment (You shall not take the Lord's name in vain). In their view, the mainstream church was in error, and out of favor with God, not only in regard to their non-observance of the Sabbath, but also because they pray to God in the wrong name.

The problem with praying to God by His so-called "sacred name," was that nobody was really quite sure what it was. Some said it was "Jehovah," while others decided it was "Yahweh," and there were other forms as well. Some Sacred-namers also advocated keeping the feasts of Lev. 23. The unifying factor among them was this abiding concern over using the "correct" Hebrew name of the Lord.

Origins of the Sacred Name Movement:

Although there were various contributing persons, the rise of the Sacred Name movement seems to have emerged largely out the efforts of key pioneer, Clarence Orvil Dodd. [6]

Dodd was an elder in a particular Church of God Sabbatarian church known as Church of God (Seventh Day). The Church of God (Seventh Day) was one of the major Millerite/ Sabbatarian churches that arose during the 1850's, after "the Great Disappointment". Church of God (Seventh Day) actually arose at the same time as the SDA church, but remained separate from SDA because its leaders rejected the writings of Ellen White. [7]

The Church of God (Seventh Day) made its mark on the Adventist/Sabbatarian movement beginning in 1863 when it began publication of its official magazine called *Hope of Israel*. The same is known today as *Bible Advocate*. (See: http://baonline.org).

A colleague of Dodd's in the Church of God (Seventh Day) was one Herbert W. Armstrong. Both Dodd and Armstrong were dis-fellowshipped from the Church of God

---

[6] J. Gordon Melton, *The Encyclopedia of American Religions*, McGrath Publishing Company, (1978), p. 476.

[7] Richard Nickels, *History of the Seventh Day Church of God*, Giving and Sharing Publications, (1999), pp. 10-12.

(Seventh Day) based on their dispute with the church over doctrinal issues, although for different reasons. In Dodd's case, the dispute was over the issue of the feasts of Lev. 23.[8]

Many Sabbatarian churches, including SDA, in spite of their insistence on keeping the Sabbath, did not believe it was necessary to keep the feasts of Lev. 23. But for a growing body of Sabbatarians in the 1930's, keeping the Sabbath wasn't enough. Now they wanted to keep the feasts too. Dodd was one of them.

In 1937, Dodd began publishing a magazine called "*The Faith,*" in which he advocated not only use of the Sacred name, but also keeping of the feasts of Lev. 23. His ideas were widely published through the magazine. It has been said that no single force in spreading the Sacred Name movement was as important as *The Faith* magazine. [9]

Also important in advancing the movement was publication of the Sacred Name bible, by Angelo "A.B." Traina. A disciple of Dodd, Traina published Sacred Name editions of the scriptures. First, Traina published the *Holy Name New Testament* in 1950, and then the *Holy Name Bible* in 1962. These bibles were a major contribution to spreading the Sacred name doctrine and legalistic mindset.

Other sacred name groups which shared the same theology, such as the Assemblies of Yahweh, began to organize and help Dodd to promote the Sacred-name movement.

Problems with Sacred-name Beliefs:

Sacred-namers claim that it is wrong for people to pray in the "pagan" Greek-influenced name of "Jesus" or "the Lord." They insist upon using the "correct" Hebrew name. As previously mentioned, they do not agree universally on what that name should be. However, most Sacred-namers generally claim it is "Yahweh" as the presumed Hebrew name of the Lord in the Old Testament. They add to that, the name "Yahshua" as the supposed Hebrew name for "Jesus." This interpretation continues today even though in both cases their Hebrew is wrong.

Yet, Sacred-namers stubbornly insist upon the need to use these two names, staking their claim based on the third commandment:

> "*Thou shalt not take the name of the LORD thy God in vain: for the LORD will not hold him guiltless that takes his name in vain.*" Ex. 20:7.

---

[8] *Sacred Name Movement History,* Yahweh's Assembly in Yahshua (2008) p. 1, available at: http://www.sacrednamemovement.org

[9] J. Gordon Melton, *The Encyclopedia of American Religions,* McGrath Publishing Company, (1978), p. 476.

The correct way to pronounce the tetragrammaton (יהוה), remains a mystery even to Jewish scholars to this day. There are varying ideas about how to pronounce the name, what it may mean, or if it is even meant perhaps to be an acronym. The reality is that nobody knows. Yet, if anyone did know, it would likely be the Jewish people.

In fact, among the millions of indigenous, Hebrew-speaking Jews, both in Israel and in the diaspora, no one knows definitively how to pronounce the name. Among the Jewish people, therefore, the common accepted practice is to say "Adonai," which means "Lord," rather than build a theology of speculation on how to pronounce the tetragrammaton.

The error of the Sacred-namers is far more serious than simple ignorance and misconstruction of the Hebrew language. The gist of the sacred name movement was to stake their claim upon the use of the name as evidence of their being "chosen."

Sacred-namers suggest that people who use the "true name" are part of the true Apostolic congregation, in fact, a continuation of the tradition of the first century congregation. Their mission, therefore, was to restore the body to its true roots, as it once was in the day of the Apostles, as if the mystery of the Holy Spirit, and the power in which the Apostles ministered the gospel, was connected to their knowledge and use of the true Hebrew "sacred name."

Sacred-namers insist not only upon use of the name "Yahweh," but they further insist that one must also use the Messiah's correct Hebrew name, which according to them is *Yahshua* (יהשע). This is another error. It was obviously created to try and conform to a theology, that "YAHshua" is the son of "YAHweh." However, the name "Yahshua" (יהשע) makes no sense linguistically in Hebrew. Nor is such a name anywhere to be found in the Old Testament.

Hebrew version New Testaments, created for the purpose of reaching Hebrew-speaking Jews with the gospel, typically use the name "Yeshua" (ישוע). Thousands of Hebrew-speaking Messianic Jews are living today in Israel who pray in the name of Yeshua (not Yahshua). Before them, Hebrew-speaking missionaries and Jewish Christians living in the land used the name "Yeshua," as it is written in Hebrew New Testaments.

Of course, there are no known original books of the New Testament written in Hebrew. All Hebrew versions of the New Testament are translated from the Greek. However, the correct Hebrew translation of the Greek "Iesus" is not a mystery. It is well-established by Jewish and Christian scholars, historians, and linguists that the correct Hebrew name of the Messiah was "Yeshua" (ישוע), which means "Salvation" or "He saves." If you read a Hebrew New Testament, the name of the Lord as written therein is Yeshua (ישוע). Simply put, "Yahshua" is a fabrication popularized in the 20th century by the Sacred-namers.

13

Unfortunately, a number of Hebrew roots adherents to this day still use the name "Yahshua," with insistence that it is the correct Hebrew name of Jesus. It is another example of a false theology being popularized through the use of mass media in the modern era of communications. The Sacred-name errors were widely published not only by Dodd's magazine *The Faith*, but also in a host of different Sacred Name version Bibles that have been in circulation since the 1950's.

The error of the Sacred-namers was not simply a linguistic one. The bigger error of the Sacred Name movement, and its successors who follow their traditions today, is in its legalistic insistence that using a little Hebrew is somehow going to improve a person's relationship with God. Using Hebrew is not indicative of a person's chosen-ness, nor does it increase righteousness, holiness, or intimacy with God. The fact that they use incorrect Hebrew only serves to highlight the error, and exposes the inaccurate nature of the Sacred Name movement.

Herbert W. Armstrong:

As previously mentioned, one of the early disciples of the Church of God (Seventh Day) was Herbert W. Armstrong, who came into it at the prodding of his wife in the late 1920's. Like Dodd, Armstrong identified not only with the Sabbath, but with the idea of keeping the feasts. Armstrong began his Worldwide Church of God (WCG) in 1934, after being dis-fellowshipped from the Church of God Seventh Day. The reason that Armstrong was kicked out was because he had become a proponent of a controversial doctrine which at the time was known as "British Israelism." An explanation of that doctrine is as follows:

British/Anglo-Israelism:

"British Israelism," also known as "Anglo-Israelism," is the theological belief that the Anglo-Saxon and associated cultures of northwestern Europe, and in particular Great Britain, are the actual racial descendants of the tribes of Israel. Thus, by extension, North Americans, including both the U.S. and Canadians, are supposedly composed of the same descendants of the ancient Israelites.

The theology is based on the myth that the 10 northern tribes of Israel wandered into the lands in northwestern Europe and settled there, after being exiled by the Assyrians in the 8th century B.C.. Though there is zero historical, archeological, biblical or any other kind of evidence in support, the theory became quite popular in the 18th and 19th century, as Great Britain became the leading world power.

For many of its proponents, the theory has had a broader application to include not just England, but the people of Germany, who have an historic blood kinship with the British.

14

Others expand it to include most of Protestant northwestern Europe, including the Netherlands and Scandanavia as part of the presumed Anglo-Israelite fold. The great national successes of Britain and Germany as leaders of post-Industrial Revolution Europe in the 19th and early 20th century, was often heralded as a kind of confirmation that the people of northwestern Europe were in fact of Israelite descent, and therefore the chosen people of God, destined to rule the earth.

False doctrine based upon genealogical myths is nothing new. Paul apparently dealt with similar myths in his day. He warned Timothy to take care to teach no doctrine rooted in genealogical speculation:

> *Neither give heed to fables and endless genealogies, which minister questions, rather than godly edifying which is in faith.* (1 Tim. 1:4).

Anglo-Israelism is not only based on genealogical myth and false prophecy, but it is also a kind of replacement theology that is heavily-laced with racism and, in particular, anti-Semitism. Anglo-Israelism in the extreme cases is the driving vision of certain anti-Jewish hate groups such as the ultra-right wing "Christian Identity" movement in America. Christian Identity is a neo-Nazi and white supremacist movement, basing its dogma on classic Anglo-Israelite theory. The Christian Identity movement is listed as a dangerous, anti-Semitic hate group on the website of the Anti-Defamation League (ADL). The ADL says the following about the Christian Identity movement:

> *"Christian Identity is a religious ideology popular in extreme right-wing circles. Adherents believe that whites of European descent can be traced back to the "Lost Tribes of Israel." Many consider Jews to be the Satanic offspring of Eve and the Serpent, while non-whites are "mud peoples" created before Adam and Eve. Its virulent racist and anti-Semitic beliefs are usually accompanied by extreme anti-government sentiments. Despite its small size, Christian Identity influences virtually all white supremacist and extreme anti-government movements. It has also informed criminal behavior ranging from hate crimes to acts of terrorism."* [10]

In its more subtle, mainstream forms, Anglo-Israelism tones down the rhetoric against the Jews. It maintains the claim that the tribes of Israel can be traced to European descent, however, it concedes that the Jews are the descendants of at least one of the twelve tribes, that being Judah. However, mainstream Anglo-Israelism maintains that the fault for rejecting the Messiah is squarely upon "Judah" (the Jews). Of course, the 10 northern tribes of Israel had nothing to do with it, since they were living in Europe at the time, and were not present when Messiah came. Furthermore, in Anglo Israelism, it is Jewish Judah who still remain blind to the Messiah today, and are in need of salvation, while the 10 northern tribes are the true Christian church of our day.

---

[10] http://archive.adl.org/learn/ext_us/Christian_Identity.asp?xpicked=4&item=Christian_ID

15

Worldwide Church of God (WCG) of Herbert W. Armstrong:

By the 1930's, many Gentile Christians in America were ready to embrace Herbert W. Armstrong's Anglo-Israelite message. Armstrong, who first called his church the "Radio Church of God," later changed to "Worldwide Church of God," made full use of the mass media available to him, especially including radio, but also TV and print journalism, to get his message out there loud and clear. And the message was: It is time for American Christians to reclaim their "birthright" as natural-born Israelites. The subtext of this message was that it was therefore necessary for "Israel" to return to the law of the Sinai covenant as the mark of the true church.

Accordingly, Anglo-Israelism is necessarily connected, and inevitably intertwined, with "One Law" theology. Though Armstrong did not become an advocate of the use of the "Sacred Name," he taught the same basic core theology as them, namely, that Gentile Christians need to return to their roots by observing the biblical laws of the Torah. For in Armstrong's world, the true Gentile believer is to consider himself physically descended from Israel. Not just grafted into the olive tree by faith. Not just the seed of Abraham by faith in the Messiah. But, rather, they are the actual, physical descendants of Israel. And if Israel, then they must live as Israel – by the Torah.

Armstrong even claimed that his Torah-keeping Anglo-Israelite followers were the true heirs of the land of Israel. For example, just one month after the State of Israel declared independence and was in the midst of the war for its survival, Armstrong wrote in his June 1948 edition of his magazine *The Plain Truth*:

> "The dying Jacob passed the birthright, and possession of Palestine on through the tribes of EPHRAIM and MANASSEH, sons of Joseph (Gen.48:4-5, 15-16). He names HIS NAME (Israel) on them - Ephraim and Manasseh. It is their descendants today, the American and British people, therefore, who are truly the national Israel. The Jews come from Judah, and belonged to the nation Judah, not the nation Israel . . . the Jews want (the land of Palestine) because they come from Jacob but through JUDAH. Yet it belongs to none of them by divine right. It belongs to Great Britain and America, into whose hands God placed it, but who have been so valiantly trying to get rid of it." [11]

Thus, after the holocaust, as Jews poured into the land of Israel, WCG followers saw this event not as a fulfillment of divine will according to Bible prophecy, but rather, some kind of deception. Armstrong's followers had the idea that the right to possess the land of Israel belonged not to the Jews, but to the Gentile nations of Britain and America, under the banner of Ephraim. They were urged to observe the Sabbath, the feasts, and the biblical dietary laws, as a condition of fulfilling the right to be heirs to the land. This is

---

[11] Herbert W. Armstrong, Plain Truth, Vol XIII, No 02, June 1948, page 8.

16

exactly on all fours with what is currently still being taught today in much of the Hebrew Roots movement by proponents of "One Law" theology.

In both Sacred Name churches and Armstrong's WCG, observance of three major aspects of the Torah was emphasized: the Sabbath, the feasts, and the dietary laws. Keeping those three biblical commandments of the Torah seems to have been a kind of mark of distinction from other Gentile Christians who are, in their minds, still under the "pagan" influence of the church because they meet on Sundays, don't keep the feasts which God gave to the Jews at Sinai, and because they eat "unclean" foods. The controversy over whether Gentile believers should feel compelled to keep the Sabbath, the feasts, and the dietary laws is the exact same controversy that Paul, as the Apostle to the Gentiles, addressed with the Colossians:

> "Let no man therefore judge you in meat, or in drink, or in respect of a holy day, or of the new moon, or of the sabbath days." (Col. 2:16).

From Paul's day, to the Sacred Namers and the WCG, right up to today, we find these Hebrew roots groups "judging" over the exact issues that Paul warned not to judge.

Armstrong's ministry was also characterized by an obsession concerning end-time prophecy. This kind of fanaticism is typical of legalistic groups who seem to think they are separated, chosen, or on a higher plane of holiness with God on account of their observance of the Sabbath, etc.

The eschatological views of legalistic groups such as Armstrong's, often seem to be rooted in the fact that they see their legal observance as somehow indicative of their "chosen-ness" among all others in the end of times. In the wake of the fanaticism, Armstrong declared himself to be a prophet of the Lord, and also God's true apostle. This hearkens back to Miller and to Ellen White.

The Hebrew roots version of end-time prophecy, as presented by Armstrong, replaces the Jews with Torah observant Gentiles. Thus, all scripture concerning Israel's prophetic rebirth is applied to Gentiles that keep the law. Instead of the Jews returning to the land, and instead of the salvation of Jewish people as a sign of the end-time (See, e.g., Ez. 39:27), the Hebrew roots message is that the Lord is preparing the way for His return by restoring Gentile believers to observance of the law. Only then will a "bride" be made ready to be redeemed by the Lord.

By the 1970's, Armstrong's use of television enabled him to publish his messages to millions of people worldwide. Armstrong's broad influence greatly contributed to setting the stage for the kind of legalistic thinking we see today in the modern Hebrew Roots movement. Armstrong's version of the Hebrew roots "true church" message spread more than any other because he made English-speaking white protestants believe that they were the physical descendants of Israel, and therefore entitled to inherit the land of Israel as a matter of race. All they needed to do to perfect their claim was to observe the law.

Hence, by the latter part of the 20th century, the stage was set for a great apostasy in the Gentile church as people embraced the lie that their great hope for deliverance from the upcoming tribulation and final judgment of mankind rests not in their faith in Messiah, but rather, in keeping the Sabbath, festivals and dietary laws of the Torah. This is what Sacred Namers, Armstrong, and their modern day Hebrew Roots successor preach. It is not the gospel handed down by the Apostles. It is a different "gospel."

It should be noted that after Armstrong's death in 1986, his Worldwide Church of God repudiated all of Armstrong's teachings, including Anglo-Israelism, Sabbath and feast observance, etc.[12] What was essentially a religious cult for over 50 years, continues today under the name "Grace Communion International" (GCI), under former elders and former associates of Herbert W. Armstrong, who repented of his teachings. Their own words tell so much about what is wrong with that which we are describing herein:

> *"We have worked hard to inform our members about where we went wrong — and we say "we" honestly, for the current leaders of the church once believed and taught these erroneous doctrines. We have criticized other Christians as false, deceived, children of the devil. We have much to apologize for. We are profoundly sorry that we verbally persecuted Christians and created dissention and disunity in the body of Christ. We seek forgiveness and reconciliation."* [13]

This move, no doubt, came at great cost to the organization, in terms of loss of members and finances. The GCI nevertheless continued to renounce and repudiate Armstrong's core teachings, and removed all of his writings from publication by the church. In fact, GCI has moved into line theologically with mainstream evangelical Christianity, and has even become a member of the National Association of Evangelicals. As of 2009, GCI is reported to have 42,000 members in 900 congregations in about 90 countries.[14]

IV.   The Post-Armstrong era: The Two-House of Israel Movement

After Herbert W. Armstrong passed away in 1986, and with his church having repudiated British Israelism and Torah observance, and having characterized its former founder and Senior Pastor as a cult leader, a great void was formed. The countless masses of people influenced by over 50 years of Armstrong's messages were now looking for new leadership and direction. The barn door was left wide open for others to step into the

---

[12] http://www.gci.org/prophecy/usb

[13] http://www.gci.org/aboutus/history

[14] http://www.youtube.com/watch?v=LWAtvE1xiRk

void left by Armstrong's departure. Thus, a new cast of characters quickly arose on the scene, to carry the baton of Anglo-Israelism through the 1990's and into the 21st century.

From British Israelism to Messianic Israelism - a Change of Name:

After Armstrong's passing, instead of "British Israelism," which was the term favored by Armstrong, the teachers and followers of British Israelite doctrine in the post-Armstrong era began to use a different name to express their vision. Considering the stigma attached to all things associated with Herbert W. Armstrong, this new name may have arisen out of a desire to avoid such associations. Certainly, the doctrinal beliefs did not change.

Consequently, beginning in the late 90's, instead of "British Israelism" or "Anglo Israelism," most folks who followed British Israelite doctrinal beliefs in the post-Armstrong era, began using the name "Messianic Israel" and/or "Messianic Israelites" to describe themselves. That name seems to have been coined by **Batya Wooten** who, as a writer of books, preached in essence the same doctrine as Armstrong in terms of the identity of the northern tribes of Israel. Wooten had a profound impact on carrying British Israelism through the 1990's and into the 21st century. Another major proponent was **Marshall "Moshe" Koniuchowsky**. Both Wooten and Koniuchowsky will be discussed further below.

Followers of British Israelism after Armstrong also became known as "Ephraimites," or, as we generally refer to them, the "Two House" movement.

The Two-house Movement:

In spite of the best efforts of some Two-housers to deny it, there can be no doubt of the direct historic link between the Two-house movement and Herbert W. Armstrong. It is a different name, but it is essentially the same foundation of false theories about the identity of Israel, together with the legalistic message concerning the need to keep the law.

In our official position paper entitled, *The Ephraimite Error*, released by the International Messianic Jewish Alliance in 2000, endorsed and published by the MJAA and IAMCS, Dr. Kay Silberling Smith examined the writings of Batya Wooten in exhaustive fashion, and exposed the errors as well as the connections to Herbert W. Armstrong and British Israelism.[15] Dr. Silberling Smith concisely and accurately describes the Two-house movement as follows:

---

[15] Kay Silberling Smith, Ph.D., *The Ephraimite Error*, 2000, available at: www.mjaa.org/site/DocServer/EphraimiteError.pdf

"Proponents of this (Two-house) movement contend that members of the "born-again" segment of the Christian church are, in fact, actual blood descendants of the biblical Israelites who were dispersed as a result of the Assyrian invasion of the ancient kingdom of Israel in 722 B.C.E.

The movement's proponents further argue that these dispersed "Israelites," or "Ephraimites," whose identities have remained undisclosed even to themselves until recent times, primarily settled in areas now recognized as largely populated by Anglo-Saxons. At times they argue that all Anglo-Saxons, and even all of humanity, are descended from these lost Ephraimites. At other times, that only born-again Christians can claim descent. In either case, Christians from Anglo-Saxon lands, such as Great Britain, Australia, Canada, and the United States, can feel assured that they are most likely direct blood descendants of the ancient people of Ephraim."[16]

We do not at this time, by any means, intend to revisit, nor rehash the theological issues which have already been addressed in *The Ephraimite Error*. However, there are a few developments with the Two-house movement that have occurred since 2000, which need to be mentioned herein.

While Armstrong made use of mass communications available through radio and TV, the Two-housers today are extremely savvy at promoting themselves through the internet. Quite recently, internet TV and video has become the main vehicle of expression for Two-housers.

Other than the name change, and the use of different media for promotional purposes, the Two-housers continue today where Armstrong left off. In spite of slight stylistic differences, and other subtleties, the Two-housers espouse the same British Israelite doctrine as Armstrong, claiming that the Gentile believers are actually the physical descendants of the ten northern tribes of Israel.

Sacred Name meets the Two-Housers:

Two-house groups are also well-known for use of the "sacred name." Among Two-housers, the common language is "Yahshua" and "Yahweh." For Two-housers, the issue of the "sacred name" is part of its repertoire of complaints against the mainstream evangelical church. Many Two-housers see the evangelical church as "pagan" because, among other reasons, it uses the "Greco-Roman" names of "Jesus" and "Lord."

Moreover, the Two-housers insistence upon using the name "Yahshua," instead of the correct Hebrew "Yeshua," has often been used as a way for the Two-housers to distinguish themselves from Messianic Jews. Apparently, because they pray in the true "Sacred-name," they assume to have more favor with God then we do.

---

[16] Ibid, p.1

20

The Sacred-name issue is just one of many issues about which the Two-housers find fault with us. The main reason, however, is because we don't recognize their core theory, specifically, their claim to be the physical descendants of Israel.

A Strange kind of "Zionism":

Zionism is one of the great ideals of the Jewish people. Few things in the Jewish mind and heart are as sacred as the belief in the basic right of the Jewish people to return to Eretz Yisrael (the land of Israel). This dream of the Jewish people, which came at great cost, is at last being realized today, as post-holocaust Jewry has returned to the land.

Two-housers have a warped view of Zionism. As proponents of "One Law One People" theology, they presume to be under a calling to observe the law given to Israel at Sinai. Keeping the law, they believe, serves as confirmation of their identity as Israelites. But, moreover, they presume an even greater incentive to keep the law. For Two-housers, keeping the law of Moses not only proves that they are the true Israel, but they seem to think it confirms a "biblical" right to possess the land which God promised to Israel.

Hence, for Two-housers, as it was for their predecessor, Herbert W. Armstrong, the modern miracle of the Jewish State is not something to be celebrated. Zionism is redefined as pertaining not to just the Jews, but to the Gentile "Israelites" as well. Thus, the imperative of keeping the law is in every way connected to this absurdly skewed misunderstanding of Zionism, which seems to think that Gentile believers have the same relationship to Eretz Yisrael and even the same inherent right to possess and live in the land as do the Jewish people. This doctrine is not only strange, but it is also anti-Semitic.

In the official paper entitled, *The Ephraimite Error*, released by the International Messianic Jewish Alliance in 2000, Dr. Kay Silberling Smith quite accurately characterizes the Two-House movement's concept of Zionsim, as follows:

> *"It is now incumbent upon these members of Ephraim, they argue, to accept their birthright and live as members of Israel. They urge Gentile Christians to keep the Torah in obedience to the Hebrew scriptures, to strive to re-educate Jews and other Christians about their new "latter day prophecy," and to work toward the repatriation of the land of Israel by their own number."* [17]

The bottom line is this: The ultimate goal of "One Law One People" theology, as embodied today in the Two-house movement, is replacing the Jewish people as Israel. With Two-housers, replacement theology goes so far as even to the extent of possessing the land.

---

[17] Ibid.

21

Thankfully, there are millions of Christians in the world today who feel they have a biblical calling to bless the State of Israel. This Christian love shown to Israel is a powerful witness of the gospel to Jewish people. Because of it, thousands of Jews are turning to Messiah Yeshua. However, needless to say, a Gentile group which claims it has some kind of biblical right of its own to possess the ancient Jewish homeland, is not a blessing to Israel. Such a claim is not well-received by Jews. It is nothing but an offense to Israel.

Pioneering the Two-House Movement: Wooten, Koniuchowsky and the MIA

In the late 1990's, Batya Wooten and Moshe Koniuchowsky were the key pioneers of the organized, mainstream post-Armstrong form of British Israelism. There were others who were involved, but we can't possibly address all of them in this paper. A few key players will therefore be discussed herein.

The core of the Two-house movement began with its organization, by Wooten and Koniuchowsky, into a body which they called the Messianic Israel Alliance (MIA). This occurred in about 1998. At that time, Batya Wooten, along with her husband Angus Wooten, were closely allied with Koniuchowsky. Working together, both the Wootens and Koniuchowsky were co-founders of the MIA. The name obviously sounded a lot like the Messianic Jewish Alliance of America.

The MIA was an umbrella organization for a network of Two-house congregations. Through the use of the emerging forum of the internet, the MIA quickly made a splash and became the leading voice for Two-housers at that time. Its rhetoric against the Messianic Jewish movement, and against established organizations such as the Messianic Jewish Alliance of America, as well as the Union of Messianic Jewish Congregations, was often quite vitriolic.

Wooten wrote and published books addressing the topic of Israel's identity with a foundation clearly based in British Israel theology. Her writings, with the help of Koniuchowsky, greatly helped to inspire and organize the Two-house movement during the 1990's.

In *The Ephraimite Error*, it was mainly the teachings of Wooten and Koniuchowsky which were examined and refuted. In spite of their refusals to admit it, their teachings regarding the identity of Israel were practically identical to Armstrong's, as described by Dr. Kay Silberling Smith:

> *"The parallels between their (Wooten and Koniuchowsky's) teachings and those of Anglo-Israelism are uncanny"*[18]

---

[18] Ibid, p. 24.

22

"Both Wooten and Koniuchowsky share many theories with traditional Anglo-Israelite teachings, although they acknowledge no dependence upon them."[19]

Dr. Silberling Smith also quite accurately described the teachings of Wooten and Koniuchowsky as anti-Semitic, and a form of replacement theology.[20]

The errors of Two-house theology have been fully addressed on behalf of the Messianic Jewish movement in Dr. Silberling Smith's excellent paper. *The Ephraimite Error* addresses and exposes a multitude of errors with the Two-house theology. For a full discussion of those errors we would refer the reader to that paper.

We reiterate, there is no need to further address and delineate those theological errors in this paper, nor is it our intent to do so in this paper.

Ralph Messer:

At the time that Wooten and Koniuchowsky were founding and forming the MIA, another key figure in the Two-house movement, who was closely allied with them, was Ralph Messer. In an article critical of Messer, which was published by Batya and Angus Wooten via the Messianic Israelite Alliance website, they describe the relationship with Messer as follows:

> *"As for the MIA and Messer, when we were forming the Alliance in 1999, we invited him to speak at some of our early conferences. As a pastor, Messer offered to help us. Being a fledgling organization, we were happy to receive an offer of help. But, in our opinion, he soon began to try to take over the MIA. When it became apparent that we were not going to yield to his ways, he left and took whoever he could with him. We have not had a relationship with Ralph Messer since 2002."*[21]

Aside from being a Two-house teacher, who apparently is ostracized by his own colleagues in the Two-house movement, Ralph Messer is also widely-known for bizarre religious showmanship that has caused great offense to Jewish people. One of Messer's best-known tactics is a ceremony in which he uses a Torah scroll to wrap a fallen church leader as a symbol of redemption.

---

[19] Ibid, p. 25.

[20] Ibid, pp. 30-31.

[21] Angus and Batya Wooten, *Jewish Leaders Offended by Ralph Messer's Ceremony*, (Messianic Israelite Alliance, 2012). Available at: http://www.messianicisrael.com/m/index.php?option=com_content&view=article&id=1921:offended&catid=13&Itemid=35

Most widely known of Messer's Torah-wrapping ceremonies was the one which he performed upon Bishop Eddie Long of Atlanta. The ceremony was heralded by Messer as not only a sign of Long's restoration, but also a kind of "coronation" of Long.

As media outlets reported the story, it quickly circulated across the internet, causing an outcry from Jewish leaders.[22] Many Jewish leaders, who are not familiar with the antics of the Two-house movement, at first believed that Messer, who claims to be a "Rabbi," was somehow connected to Messianic Judaism. In response, the Messianic Jewish Alliance of America (MJAA) and Union of Messianic Jewish Congregations (UMJC) collaborated in issuing a joint statement condemning Messer's antics.[23]

Koniuchowsky:

By 2002, the Wootens had a falling out not only with Messer, but also with their close ally and MIA co-founder, Koniuchowsky. After the break up with Koniuchowsky, the MIA continued under the Wootens. Meanwhile, Koniuchowsky went on his own path.

In 2003, Koniuchowsky formed a new alliance with another controversial character in the Two-house movement, **James Trimm**. Since the break-up with Batya Wooten, Koniuchowsky and his followers were no longer calling themselves "Messianic Israelites." Instead, together with Trimm, they became the "Nazarene Yisraelites." Koniuchowsky also made another change. Originally a user of the so-called sacred names of "Yahshua" and "Yahweh," Koniuchowsky switched to the new sacred names: "Yahushua" and "Yahuwah."

At the time that *The Ephraimite Error* was published as a position paper of the Messianic Jewish Alliance of America in 2000, Marshall "Moshe" Koniuchowsky was the most vocal of the Two-house leaders. For several years, his bombastic rantings over the internet made him somewhat of a comical figure. His brash, confrontational style caused him to be considered as the mouthpiece of the Two-house movement during the time that he was allied with Wooten.

The RAMYK:

Like Herbert W. Armstrong, Koniuchowsky has begun calling himself "the Apostle." He also uses an acronym for himself - the RAMYK (Rabbi Apostle Moshe Yoseph

---

[22] Associated Press, *Jewish Leaders Offended by Ga. Preacher's Ceremony*, Feb. 2nd, 2012. Available at: http://www.foxnews.com/us/2012/02/02/jewish-leaders-offended-by-ga-preachers-ceremony/

[23] Joel Chernoff, Paul Liberman, Russ Resnik, et al., *UMJC and MJAA respond to Messer Video*, (Feb. 3rd, 2012), available at: http://www.mjaa.org/site/News2?page=NewsArticle&id=7533&security=1&news_iv_ctrl=1581

Koniuchowsky). Moreover, Koniuchowsky has authored a book entitled *The Rebirth of Yisraelite Marriage – Sexual Freedom of Torah*. The subtitle promises that the book will "turn generational hangups into spiritual truths." As one might imagine from the title of the book by the "RAMYK," Koniuchowsky plainly advocates polygamous marriage as the sacred way of life for true believers living by the Torah.[24]

In addition to his book, Koniuchowsky also advocates polygamy in voluminous papers he has published on his website.[25] This advocacy of polygamy apparently has resulted in a split from his "Nazarene Yisraelite" comrade, James Trimm. Trimm responds to Koniuchwosky in a 2008 article entitled *Wolf in the Fold*:

> *"Over the last week we have been flooded with emails, many from persons who had, until now, studied under the teaching ministry of Moshe K. (Koniuchowsky). The common denominator of these emails is that they were all shocked and dismayed by Moshe K's recent actions and teaching. Just this last week, Moshe K. sent out an email soliciting single women to match into polygamous marriages. And all of this is being done in the names of "Messianic" and "Nazarene" ...*
>
> *... My friends, fear not! The "Nazarene" movement will endure this latest trial...*
>
> *... In seeking to promote polygamy, Moshe K. has only succeeded in relegating himself and his ministry to the position of "obscure polygamist cult" and thus to a position of irrelevancy to the movement...*
>
> *... This last week Moshe K. announced an "Emancipation Proclamation of Plural Families" with the following BYSW "Rabbis" overseeing the proclamation: Rabbis' Jenkins, Nolan, Altaf, Aguilar, Thompson and Koniuchowsky and then soliciting "single women" for these polygamous marriages."[26]*

By all appearances, Koniuchowsky's work has degenerated into what would be considered an outright cult by most standards. None of this, however, should come as much of a surprise, considering the same patterns seen now in Koniuchowsky were already established in the forebearer of the Two-house movement, Herbert W. Armstrong.

Eddie Chumney:

---

[24] Koniuchowsky, *The Rebirth of Yisraelite Marriage – Sexual Freedom of Torah, A manual that will turn generational hangups into spiritual truths*, by the RAMYK-Apostle to Yisrael Moshe Yoseph Koniuchowsky, 2010. The book can be accessed for free in pdf at: http://www.yourarmstoisraelglobal.com/the-rebirth-of-yisraelite-marriage.html

[25] http://www.yourarmstoisraelglobal.com/scriptural-marriages.html

[26] James Trimm, *Wolf in the Fold, (July 20, 2008).*

25

One key figure in the Two-house movement beginning in the late 90's was Eddie Chumney. Though he does not appear to be a formal affiliate with the MIA, Chumney has been a regular speaker at their events. On his own behalf, Eddie Chumney has used the internet to broadly publish his writings, proclaiming the Two-house theology. He has thus succeeded to become a major voice in the Two-house movement, somewhat independently of the MIA. Chumney has published voluminous materials, including articles, books, as well as videos espousing the Two-house doctrine, most of which can be found on his website at: www.hebroots.com.

Even though he calls his ministry "Hebraic Heritage Ministries," and even though the terminology "Hebrew Roots" is found all over Chumney's website and materials, Chumney's teachings are heavily focused on Two-house theology. He is unmistakably, and unabashedly, dedicated to preaching and promoting Two-house theology. Other Two-house teachers have also leaned on Eddie Chumney to promote their work and make their voice known in the Two-house movement.

In fact, Chumney uses his website to promote not only himself and his own materials, but several other teachers and their materials. These are individuals who apparently are worthy, in Chumney's view, of being promoted on his Two-house website. As of the date of this writing, featured on Chumney's website as fellow teachers are: **Monte Judah, Bill Cloud, Rico Cortes, Brad Scott, and Avi Ben Mordechai.**

Monte Judah:

Monte Judah is another figure who has made his mark as a key teacher of Two-house theology and a major voice in the Two-house movement. In 2003, Eddie Chumney teamed up with Monte Judah, in an effort to defend Two-house teaching. As a result, Chumney and Judah published a letter that attempted to explain the basic tenets of Two-house theology as being biblical:

> "Monte Judah of Lion and Lamb Ministries, and Eddie Chumney, of Hebraic Heritage Ministries International, actively teach that Yeshua / Jesus, the Messiah, died on the tree (John 10:14-17, 11:49-52) to redeem and restore both houses of Israel (Ephraim and Judah)."[27]

Monte Judah has definitely made his mark as a vocal teacher of Two-house theology, and has quite a significant following via his Lion and Lamb Ministries. Monte Judah has also become known for his controversial teaching which proclaims that the book of Hebrews is not the word of God. In his 2005 ministry newsletter, Monte Judah proclaims:

> Why do we believe that the book of Hebrews is the authoritative Word of God, inspired by the Holy Spirit, and inerrant? It appears that the answer is primarily because it is

---

[27] Monte Judah and Eddie Chumney, *Report to the Body of Messiah*, (2003), available on Eddie Chumney's website at: www.hebroots.org/twohousemeeting.htm

already printed in the Bible, it speaks for the Messiah, and because of the Paradigm. As presently printed in our Bibles, the book of Hebrews in a side-by-side comparison does not accurately reflect the Law of Moses. It appears to misrepresent Hebrew definitions and concepts by willfully substituting Greek definitions and concepts.[28]

On Sept. 9th, 2005, Monte Judah reportedly gave this statement in one of his teachings, aired publicly over the internet, in regard to the book of Hebrews:

> *"The book of Hebrews is written against every messianic believer there is. If you're a messianic believer, the book of Hebrews is intentionally your enemy and against you . . . We've been bullied into this. This is false teaching. Passed off as the word of God."*[29]

Why the attack on the book of Hebrews? Monte Judah, like all Two-house leaders, is a "One Law One People" teacher. They advocate that all people, Jew and Gentile alike, should equally be keeping the Torah. The attack on the book of Hebrews is necessitated by the fact that it is a portion of scripture which totally contradicts "One Law One People" teaching. In fact, the book of Hebrews is a book specifically telling the Jewish people to seek righteousness through the Son of God and not through the Sinai covenant. It presents the Messiah as the Great High Priest, not descended from the Aaronic order, but associated with David, who is not designated a Priest according to the Law of Moses, but according to the order of Melchizedek. As it says in Hebrews 7:11-12:

> *"If perfection could have been attained through the Levitical priesthood—and indeed the law given to the people established that priesthood—why was there still need for another priest to come, one in the order of Melchizedek, not in the order of Aaron? For when the priesthood is changed, the law must be changed also."*

Hebrews presents a way in which not only the Jewish people, but all people, may come to God. It is not through the law given at Sinai, but rather, it is through the Messiah, whose blood cleanses from sin, a Messiah who "ever lives to make intercession" (Heb. 7:25). He is the mediator of "a better covenant, which was established upon better promises" (Heb. 8:6). He did not come to bring people under the Sinai covenant, as the "One Law" teachers say, but rather, He came to pay the penalties of our sins, and thereby to reconcile people unto God. The book of Hebrews is clear: The New Covenant is not like the covenant made previously at Sinai. The book of Hebrews thus presents peculiar problems for those who advocate, in one form or another, adherence to the Sinai Covenant. In any case, we wish to make it clear that Monte Judah's rejection of the book

---

[28] Monte Judah, *The Paradigm of Hebrews*, Yavoh Magazine, Nov. 2005. Available at: http://lionlamb.net/v3/YAVOHArchives/Volume11/11

[29] Boaz Michael, *Answering the Questions regarding the Epistle of Hebrews, A Response to Monte Judah's Questions of Canonicity*, First Fruits of Zion, Oct. 5th, 2005.

of Hebrews is wrong. Needless to say, in our view, Hebrews is in fact the inerrant, authoritative word of God.

From 2007 – 2013, Monte Judah has organized an annual Feast of Tabernacles conference, held in Chandler, Oklahoma, in which the following persons have been regular speakers at the event: **Rico Cortes** and **Eddie Chumney**.[30]

Recorded teachings of both Cortes and Chumney are featured on Monte Judah's website at www.lionlamb.net in the link called "messianic marketplace." These two seem to be Judah's closest associates in the Two-house movement, at least in terms of participating in events sponsored by him. **Brad Scott** also has appeared as a speaker at Judah's 2011 Tabernacles event, and his messages are also available on Judah's website.

Scott Diffenderfer: The MIA after Koniuchowsky:

Considering the vast amount of in-fighting and division within the Two-house camp, it is not so easy to keep up with who's who among them, nor what they are teaching from day to day.

However, soon after the split with Koniuchwosky, the Wootens brought in Scott Diffenderfer. Diffenderfer was soon identified by the MIA as their "Executive Director" and "CEO," as well as a member of what they called the "Shepherd's Council," which operated as sort of a steering committee of the organization. He also was the publisher of a magazine which he called "Messianic Home Magazine," which featured articles written by the Wootens, and other key Two-house teachers, including Diffenderfer himself. [31]

Diffenderfer's commitment to Two-house doctrine goes back to the 1990's. Scott Diffenderfer was the founder of a Hebraic roots fellowship in the Nashville area in 1994, which uses the name "LAMB" (Lighthouse Assembly of Messianic Believers). Here is an excerpt from one of Diffenderfer's articles from 1998:

> *"What a joyful time it will be as YHWH's redeemed people come into the fullness of who they are. As the House of Judah (Jews) and the House of Ephraim (former Gentiles) unite through the power of our Torah observant Messiah Yahshua. They will come running out*

---

[30] Available at Judah's website at: https://lionlamb.net/cgi-bin/lion/search.html? fi=products&st=db&sp=results_b&co=1&sf=category&se=MP3-Events&op=rm&nu=0&sf=prod_group&se=Audio%20Sets&op=&nu=0&ml=50&tf=description&to=r

[31] See, an archive of articles published by Messianic Home Magazine at: http:// messianichome.com/alpha.htm

of the Churches and Synagogues looking for a better way. A way that is unencumbered by the doctrines of man. A way that leads to the Father... Yahshua and His Torah. "[32]

The fact that Diffenderfer is a teacher of Two-house doctrine is well-established by his teachings and by his long history of leadership and involvement with the MIA. Along with Diffenderfer, other key MIA staff members were Daniel Botkin, who was a member of the "Shepherd's Council;" and Ed Harris, the "Director of Community Relations."

In 2012, Diffenderfer split off from the MIA, leaving the Wootens to carry on the MIA without him. Diffenderfer created his own organization, which he calls "Messianic Covenant Community." The name provides no hint of being Two-house in theology. This is a new trend among the Two-house movement, to use names and labels that don't sound Two-house at all. By no means has there been a renouncing of the Two-house doctrine.

Ed Harris and Daniel Botkin, who were Diffenderfer's co-workers in the MIA, both of whom have a long history of teaching Two-house doctrine, have joined Diffenderfer in his new endeavor as the "Messianic Covenant Community." The website lists Diffenderfer as the President and Elder; Ed Harris as Vice President of Community Relations; and Daniel Botkin as an Elder.[33]

Moreover, Diffenderfer is currently listed as the "Director" of an organization called "B'nai Ephraim" (children of Ephraim). The mission and vision of B'nai Ephraim is classic Two-house:

> *"B'nai Ephraim International (BEI) serves as a global advocate and educational resource for the sons of Ephraim, descendants of the ancient tribes of Israel..."*

> *"... to achieve global presence as the premier advocate and resource center for education and community for the returning sons of Ephraim, once dispersed to the nations but now nearing the end of their biblical punishment of exile from Israel...*

> *"We believe that ultimately, this will lead to the foretold restoration of both kingdoms, Judah and Ephraim/Israel, back into the reunited House of Israel as the end of the age approaches."*[34]

---

[32] Scott Diffenderfer, *Redeemed Israel*, Messianic Home Magazine, Fall, 1998, available at: http://messianichome.com/articles/1998/fall/redeemedisrael.htm

[33] See, www.messianiccovenant.com/homepage/our-leadership

[34] See, www.bnaiephraim.com/about-us

We note that B'nai Ephraim was initially a vision of the MIA, which it referred to as "the intial steps toward Ephraim's nationhood."[35] B'nai Ephraim lists as its President, Hale Harris, who was the General Secretary of the MIA during Diffenderfer's reign as CEO. Like Diffenderfer, and the others mentioned, Hale Harris also seems to have left the MIA at this point and is no longer listed as an officer.

Another Name Change – the End of the MIA :

With the departure of Diffenderfer and many other key staff members of the MIA, in 2013, Batya and Angus Wooten changed the name of the Messianic Israel Alliance to the "Redeemed Israel Alliance." Though the name has changed, the preaching of Two-house doctrine clearly has not.[36]

Now that the Wootens are no longer the "Messianic Israel Alliance," certain questions naturally arise. What is the reason for this name change? As Batya and Angus explain it in an article posted on the homepage of their website:

> *"Now is the time for a change in the Messianic Israel Alliance – it is time for a new name that will better depict our renewed call and purpose. We are changing our name to the Alliance of Redeemed Israel – because we feel a need to refocus on our Divine Redeemer."*[37]

Notwithstanding the allusion to a "new call and purpose," the article then goes on to explain how this change somehow is connected to "Ephraim's jealousy of Judah." They claim that Ephraim is destined in the last days to be delivered of this jealousy when he at last "sees the truth of his own Israelite roots." [38] As far as the Wootens and their name changes, it's plain to see: New name, same rhetoric.

---

[35] Batya Wooten, *Celebrating Ten Years of Restoration*, The Herald, July-Aug 2008, Messianic Israel Alliance, available at: http://www.messianicisrael.com/m/pdfs/herald/08julyaug.pdf

[36] See, www.redeemedisrael.com

[37] See, www.messianicisrael.com/m/

[38] Ibid.

V.   The Hebrew Roots Movement

"One Law" Carries On:

In most recent years, with the MIA having split apart and reformed, a new movement has arisen out of the Two-house movement, which carries on the "One Law One People" tradition. This new movement calls itself "Hebrew Roots."

What has happened is that Two-house leaders seem to have made the decision to soften the emphasis on the Two-house message. Indeed, in many cases, it seems, they even try to deny or conceal their identity as Two-house teachers. Though not disavowing or renouncing the Two-house doctrine by any means, they are keeping it on the "down low," presumably in an effort to avoid the great controversy often associated with that teaching, which was the subject of Herbert W. Armstrong's ministry.

Accordingly, it is commonplace today for Two-house leaders to use names and descriptions which do not specifically designate them as Two-house. Whereas, in years past, the architects of the Two-house movement used descriptive names for what they believe such as "Messianic Israelite," Ephraimite, and even "Two-houses of Israel," now these same pioneers are specifically avoiding such overt names and labels. They have found a more subtle way to appeal to the same crowd.

Today, Two-housers are moving and operating under the broader label which they have dubbed: "Hebrew Roots." Whatever names and labels they use, there can be no mistake about it: Hebrew Roots teachers are mainly Two-housers. There has not been an ideological change, it is merely a change of strategy for promoting the same beliefs in regard to Israel identity and the need to keep the law.

The Hebrew Roots Message:

The essential, unifying message of the Hebrew Roots movement is the mistaken belief that all people everywhere – Jew and Gentile alike - should be keeping the law of Moses. This overarching message of "One Law One People" finds perfect favor among those who have an agenda concerning Israel identity issues. This is why the core leadership of the Hebrew Roots movement was formed by, and is occupied by, Two-house teachers.

The Hebrew roots movement of the 21st century is the culmination of years of erroneous teaching concerning Israel's identity, combined with the "One Law" creed, that Torah observance is mandatory for the Gentiles. It is propelled by the common misconception that one law was given at Mt. Sinai for all people, and that the law is the way for people to be reconciled unto God. It holds that all people everywhere should be keeping the Torah. The idea, whether stated or implied, is that if a person keeps Torah, then this confirms their identity as Israelites.

31

A Gospel of Law, an Angry God:

Hebrew Roots teaching suggests that the only hope for the Gentile believer is to get out of the church, and start keeping the Sabbath, the Levitical feasts, and eating kosher along with other Sabbaterean Hebrew Roots "believers." This kind of legalistic message is necessarily connected to a mistaken belief about the identity of Israel. It presumes that the Jews are either not descendants of Israel at all, or that Jews are a people who constitute just one tribe among Israel. In either case, therefore, the only way we can know if a person is Israel or not, is if they are keeping the Torah. Hence, by keeping the law, a person proves that they *are* Israel. This is the Hebrew Roots premise.

Furthermore, as opposed to the gospel of scripture which proclaims the good news of forgiveness of sin, the Hebrew Roots message is a gospel of law; to wit, that man is to be reconciled unto God not by faith in God, but by keeping the Law of Moses. Accordingly, no person can hope to be in a healthy relationship with God unless he or she is keeping the weekly Sabbath, the appointed feasts, and the dietary laws. The scriptures testify otherwise. (Col. 2:16).

In Hebrew Roots, the message is that God is supposedly angry at the Gentile church because they have not kept His law. As if, in their skewed view of the coming judgment, God is going to judge the world, not just because of inhumanity, wickedness, injustice, violence and immorality; but, rather, because the world is eating the wrong foods, and because humans are failing to gather on the correct appointed days.

From the Hebrew Roots perspective, God is presented not as a loving and forgiving God who gave His only Son to die for the sins of all people. But rather, an intolerant God, who rejects all Gentile cultures, and only loves His own Hebraic culture. As if there is no way that a person can be in good standing with God as a Gentile. As if a Gentile must become culturally Jewish in order to come into the fullness of a healthy relationship with God.

The Hebrew Roots message to the Gentiles is that the reason Messiah died on the tree was not to deliver the Gentile from sin, but to deliver the Gentile from being a Gentile. As if being a Gentile would somehow be unacceptable to God. The gospel message therefore, for the Hebrew Roots enthusiast, is that God has sent His son into the world in order to conform people to the image of a Jew. After all, Yeshua is Jewish, so all people must be like Him – not just in character, but in culture. He won't have it any other way, or so they say in Hebrew Roots. In our view, this is entirely wrong. It is the very antithesis of the gospel.

In Messianic Judaism, we believe God loves all people. We believe God accepts people from every tribe and tongue, and that He loves people as they are, and without regard to their culture. While we do welcome all people in messianic synagogues, we do not believe that everybody needs to be in a messianic synagogue, or that everybody needs to become a Messianic Jew, or become culturally Jewish, in order to please God. Nor do we see the Messianic Jewish movement as the model for all.

Hebrew Roots and "One Law":

In Hebrew Roots, whether one is considered physically descended from Israel or not, there is a presumed duty upon every "true believer" in the Messiah, to observe Torah. And if one keeps Torah, then this verifies a person's "chosen-ness," and that means, he or she is an Israelite. In this manner, the Jews are not Israel, but rather, the Jewish people are replaced by a remnant of end-time Torah-keeping Gentiles. Any way you slice it, this is none other than replacement theology.

As in the days of the Millerites, and 19th century Sabbaterean Christianity, the Hebrew Roots movement is fueled by an obsession with end-time events concerning Israel. Much of the teaching has to do with prophecies concerning Israel in the end-time. The most popular Hebrew Roots teachers are often held out as people who have answers regarding end-time prophecy due to some exceptional knowledge or skill they possess, which enables them to reveal "mysteries" that the average Christian Pastor could never see, on account of his non-Hebraic, Greco-Roman orientation. This exceptional skill or knowledge, which is often grossly exaggerated, could be in regard to Hebrew language; Jewish liturgy, Talmud or mystical studies; training from an orthodox Rabbi; lots of trips to Israel; or some special study having to do with the secrets of the Temple.

Although Hebrew Roots groups are characterized by a certain fanaticism about Jewish *stuff*, they have little to no interest in Jewish *people*. Their "vision" is not for Jewish people to come to Messiah, but rather, to push Torah on the Gentiles. They employ Jewish cultural expression in the Hebrew Roots movement merely as a mask to bolster their claim that they are in fact Israel – which is the premise of what they believe.

As has been previously discussed, oftentimes Hebrew Roots has elements that seem anti-Semitic. This can be very subtle. How can people obsessed with Jewish things actually be prejudiced against Jews? What happens is that people who think they are Israel, see actual Jews as the threat to their core beliefs. What stands between them and their "rightful" claim to be Israelites is the Jews. Therefore, though we embrace them as brothers in the Messiah, they reject us, finding fault in us, for not acknowledging them specifically as Israel.

Hebrew Roots is rooted in legalisitic, end-time Sabbatareanism, and British Israelism. The spirit of Hebrew roots, as well as the actual meaning of their doctrine, is simply to replace Israel. That is what "One Law One People" doctrine is ultimately all about, and

33

this is why Two-house and British Israel believers are necessarily associated with "One Law".

The Two-House Connection:

In the so-called "Hebrew Roots" movement, most of the key figures are in fact Two-house teachers with a long established history of preaching that doctrine. Some of them seem to want to conceal the fact that they are Two-house teachers. But their presence is overwhelming and unmistakable. There are a few leaders who are not Two-house teachers, but they are definitely the exception.

We will discuss a few of the key players to show definitively how the Hebrew Roots movement is a legalistic, "One Law" movement which grew out of the Two-house movement, and which is both organized and led by Two-house teachers.

Key Players:

The Hebrew Roots movement of today consists of various popular teachers. It is not possible to discuss all of them. But there are a few of the key players in the Hebrew Roots movement of today that have made their presence known. Some of them have already been discussed herein in the section on Two House leaders – **Batya and Angus Wooten, Moshe Koniuchowsky, Ralph Messer, Eddie Chumney, Monte Judah, Scott Diffenderfer, Ed Harris, Daniel Botkin, and Hale Harris**.

All of these are in one way or another now using the label "Hebrew Roots" to describe themselves. None of them are any more using the once popular moniker of their movement: "Messianic Israelite." It is not to be found in their ministry names or in any of their current literature. But, rest assured, Hebrew Roots is in essence a new name for an old song. Thus many of the lead characters are the same. However, new characters have also arisen, and new organizations. Some of the people and organizations which form the mainstream of the Hebrew Roots movement will be discussed as follows:

Hebraic Roots Network:

If one is looking to find the teachings of many key leaders in the Hebrew Roots movement of today, the easiest way to do that is to connect with the Hebraic Roots Network (HRN), which is found online at their website: www.hebraicrootsnetwork.com.

HRN was founded in 2011. It is designed to be an internet TV site, where many of the popular Hebrew Roots teachers have networked together in order to broadcast their "shows" over internet TV. It features nearly 24/7 live-streaming of video programs, as well as programs on demand, which are recorded by these popular Hebrew Roots teachers. The "shows" can be viewed online just like watching television. Many of the videos seem to be produced specifically for HRN.

For example, one of the most prominently featured teachers on HRN is well-known Two-house teacher, **Eddie Chumney**. The website features "**The Eddie Chumney Show.**"

Another popular show promoted on HRN is "**The Bill Cloud Show.**" For each of the shows, the website offers quite a smorgasbord of teachings available on demand or for purchase on DVD.

As of the date of this writing, the following are currently listed under the "Teachers" link on the Hebraic roots network website, which means their teachings are being aired by HRN, and their materials are being promoted and sold on the website:

Eddie Chumney, Bill Cloud, David Rives, Mordecai Silver, Richard Rives, Brad Scott, Daniel Botkin, Ed Harris, Holissa Alewine, Diana Dye, Rico Cortes, Tony Robinson, and Valerie Moody.

A brief bio is provided for each of the listed teachers by simply clicking on their name.

Under the "Products" link, HRN also provides for each of the featured Hebrew Roots teachers to make available their teaching materials for purchase. This includes CD's, DVD's, books and other items. In addition to the listed teachers, there are other teachers who are not necessarily producing videos to be aired on HRN, but whose materials are nonetheless promoted and made available, including **Scott Diffenderfer**. In fact, Diffenderfer was one of the founding "teachers" involved in the organization of HRN at the outset in 2011.

Most of the "teachers" whose shows are aired over the Hebraic Roots Network are well-known figures from the Two-house movement, with a substantial, established history as teachers of the Two-houses of Israel doctrine. Eddie Chumney, for example, has been discussed already at length. We have also discussed Diffenderfer, Botkin and Harris, who are now promoted as "Hebrew Roots" teachers by HRN, and all of whom have a significant history as former officers of the Messianic Israel Alliance, and years of serving as co-laborers with Batya Wooten in the promotion of the Two-houses of Israel doctrine through the MIA.

It is not possible to evaluate and discuss every one of the individuals listed as "teachers" on HRN. Some of them will be discussed further below, though certainly not all of them. We note first, however, that nowhere on the HRN is there any mention of Two-house teachings or anything associated with it. This clearly seems to be deceptive on the part of HRN. In spite of all the Two-house teachers on board with HRN, there is no mention of the controversial doctrine which they actually teach, and have been teaching for many years. Even Eddie Chumney, nowhere in his bio is there a mention of the Two-house doctrine which he regularly teaches. It is difficult to imagine that this is an unintentional oversight.

The only exception to be found is in the bio of Michael "Mordecai" Silver. Silver's bio tells the story of how he came to be a teacher of Two-house theology. It says of Silver:

> "... several years back he came across the teaching of the two houses of Israel. Finally he saw some of the truth that (had) been hidden away and entered into a new phase in his spiritual walk as part of Judah and as part of Israel. God has been blessing the congregation and drawing in those who are becoming part of those who are one in Messiah and Torah observant. Mordecai views the two house teaching as that, a Biblical teaching, that speaks to the equality of all Believers in Messiah and Torah."

Other than this blurb about Silver, none of the other bios make any mention of the Two-houses of Israel doctrine or movement in spite of strong affiliations, if not overt teachings, associated with many, if not all, of the HRN teachers. (That is not to say that there has been any renunciation or repudiation of the Two-house doctrine by any of the individuals in question).

Revive Conference:

Another key feature of the Hebraic Roots Network website is that it promotes an annual Hebrew Roots conference called "Revive." Since the launching of HRN in 2011, the Revive conference has quickly become an important venue for Hebrew Roots followers. In fact, it is the annual main event for Hebrew Roots at this time. Many of the more prominent advocates of Two-house / Hebrew Roots teachings are at the "Revive" conference. Most of them are the same persons which are featured teachers promoted on the HRN website.

For example, the line up of speakers for the "Revive" 2012 and 2013 conferences has included as follows: **Eddie Chumney, Scott Diffenderfer, Bill Cloud, Brad Scott, Daniel Botkin, Ed Harris, Holissa Alewine, Rico Cortes, Tony Robinson, and Valerie Moody.**

Essentially, it is the same cast as those appearing on the Hebraic Roots Network. There are a few key figures in the Revive conference who are not listed on HRN. One of them is an individual named **Ephraim Judah,** who is a family member of Monte Judah, and is on staff with his ministry. Ephraim Judah is the director of youth ministry for Revive conferences.

There are certain key worship leaders at the Revive conference who have been regulars in providing the worship in the events of the Hebrew Roots movement. **Lenny and Varda Harris** have led worship at Revive conferences. The Harris' are well-known Two-housers, as reflected by the subject matter of their music, which is heavily Two-house, not to mention their years of appearing at major events sponsored by the MIA.

Other key worship leaders at the "Revive" conferences include **Steve Manning**, who is currently the worship director for Scott Diffenderfer's Messianic Covenant Community. An emerging figure is **Mason Clover**, who was a producer and performer, along with Lenny and Varda Harris and Steve Manning, on an album recorded live at Batya Wooten's 2009 MIA conference, and has become quite a regular appearing at Revive conferences and at major Hebrew Roots gatherings over the last couple of years. Like the Harris', over many years, both Manning and Clover have regularly made appearances as worship leaders at Two-house conferences of the Messianic Israel Alliance, organized by Batya Wooten and Scott Diffenderfer. Now they have become key worship leaders at these "Revive" conferences being organized under the new label, "Hebrew Roots."

Many of the teachings, activities and events occurring at the "Revive" conferences are filmed and made available for purchase on HRN's website. Much of it is also plastered all over the internet video sites, including on YouTube. The first Revive conference was held in Jacksonville, Fl. from June 29th – July 1st, 2012. The second was in Dallas, Texas, from June 21st – June 23rd, 2013. Another conference is currently scheduled for June 27th – June 29th, 2014.

Torah Services:

Video footage of a "Torah service" held at Revive 2012, is a pretty good example of what the Hebrew Roots movement is about. When a Torah is displayed and processed in a non-Jewish setting, from our point of view, this raises a "yellow flag" of concern. For one thing, it can be a cause of great offense to Jewish people.

The Sefer Torah (Torah Scroll), which is typically dressed in elaborate covers and decorated with jewels, symbolizes the age-old struggle of the Jewish people to stand committed to Jewish ideals and Jewish calling, even in the face of generations of suffering and persecution. Obviously, the Bible as a whole has meaning and purpose for all people. But the Sefer Torah is a very Jewish symbol that is unique and has been cherished and guarded for generations by people who risked their lives to do so.

Processing the Sefer Torah inappropriately, for the wrong reasons, and/or in the wrong context, or even by people who don't really know what they are doing, can be a source of re-opening wounds for the Jewish people. Ralph Messer's vulgar misuse of a Torah scroll is a good example of the kind of offense that can be caused in the minds of Jewish people in the mainstream.

So why is this being done? What is the message here except to say: "You are Israel!"

Furthermore, from a scriptural point of view, there are other warnings that come to mind, such as 1 Tim. 1:7:

> *"They want to be teachers of the law, but they do not know what they are talking about or what they so confidently affirm."*

By way of comparison, Torah services have a special place in the history and tradition of the Jewish people and that is why they are to be commonly found in Messianic Judaism. In our own Messianic Synagogues and Messianic Jewish conferences, we continue to use much Jewish tradition which comes from the synagogue. We know that the Jewish community often objects to this, but we do it for one simple reason – because we are Jews. We train children to learn Jewish religious customs and we train them to have bar and bat mitzvah ceremonies, not because we believe everybody should be doing the same, but simply because we are Jewish and it is part of our heritage and culture as Jews.

In Messianic Judaism, we have no aversion or objection to Gentiles being involved in Torah services or in Jewish liturgical services. But when these things occur in the setting of a Messianic Synagogue it is an entirely different matter. A messianic synagogue consists of both Jews and Gentiles together in Messiah. Messianic Judaism is a Jewish movement, a messianic synagogue is Jewish, and the revival of Israel, is a Jewish revival. Both Jew and Gentile understand, in messianic Judaism, God is using us together, as One New Man, as a joint witness, *in a Jewish context*. Together we are a light and witness to the Jewish community, to publish the gospel to the Jewish people. That is the calling from God in Messianic Judaism. There is no agenda among us to see the rest of the world's believers holding Torah services or otherwise worshipping and behaving as Jews. It is what we do because it is who we are.

The "Revive" conference, on the other hand, is not a Jewish event. Hebrew Roots is not a Jewish movement. Therefore, when a Torah service is held in that context, in a Gentile organization, and a Gentile worship setting, certain natural questions arise: Why are they doing this? Why are they processing Torahs? Why, in a non-Jewish setting, are they performing the cherished religious traditions of Jewish people? Why are they doing things which are historically done by Jews in the synagogue? Why are they saying Hebrew liturgical prayers for which the people have no traditional relationship?

The natural answer is: Because they think themselves to be Israel. And that is exactly what is going on in Hebrew Roots. The message is: "You are Israel." It is nothing more than a continuation of the Two-house creed. People are being told to keep the law, because, after all, they are the chosen remnant; they are indeed the people Israel.

Rico Cortes, Torah Reader:

The Torah service at Revive 2012 and 2013 was led by **Rico Cortes**. As mentioned previously, Cortes was a regular speaker at conferences sponsored by Monte Judah, going back to 2007. He has also been a key speaker at conferences held by the Messianic Israel Alliance. Rico Cortes' bio, listed on HRN's website, heralds him as a Torah teacher, and a person with certain expertise on the hidden truths of the Temple, and the services in the Temple. Cortes is also held out as a person knowledgeable in Jewish liturgical worship and practices. In addition to being Two-house in ideology, he also is clearly a "One Law One People" advocate. The bio states:

> *"Rico Cortes will challenge you to keep the Commandments that Yeshua/Jesus kept. He specializes in uncovering spiritual truths hidden within the Holy Temple and the services that took place there. His knowledge of the Tabernacle, Holy Temple, priests and procedures combine to bring an incredible prophetic message to us today regarding how we are to reverently approach and be true servants of our Creator YHVH!*
>
> *... Rico's vision is to see all who believe in the God of Abraham, Isaac & Jacob return to the Torah and to be a set apart people who serve our Creator as He has instructed. He travels around the globe sharing the hidden truths that he has uncovered, encouraging believers in the Messiah to keep the Commandments that Yeshua (Jesus) kept."*[39]

Before processing the Torah at the "Revive" 2012 Torah service, Cortes apparently finds it necessary to address the question – "Why are we doing this?" In other words, why is a traditional Jewish Torah service being held in a non-Jewish event, hosted by a non-Jewish organization? Good question. Cortes then explains why Jewish liturgical prayers such as the Amidah are important for all people to recite. Cortes makes reference to the Jewish people as "Judah." Before processing the Torah, Cortes says:

> *"I am going to do my best to try to entice you to understand why we do what we do. Are we trying to learn from our brother, Judah? Absolutely. Because he took from the essence from the Temple and he basically encapsulated it in a little prayerbook, that if you don't have any concentration or meditation on the words, it means nothing. In Hebrew it's called "kavanah." But if you put your heart and your soul and your mind and everything that you have into a prayer or a protocol or a blueprint of how to approach, how to praise, how to exalt, how to uplift, how to handle yourself in the presence of the King of the universe, ladies and gentlemen. Now today, you will have the opportunity, that as one out of seven billion people on the face of the earth, you are a remnant that the Father has*

---

[39] http://www.hebraicrootsnetwork.com/teachers/rico-cortes

called from among the nations to lift, to uphold, to exalt, to praise, to worship, to revere, to exalt the name of the living Elohim."[40]

Obviously, Cortes wants the people to believe that they are the end-time remnant of Gentile Torah keepers, members of the northern tribes of Israel, soon to be united with their "brother Judah." Aside from the Two-houses of Israel message, what Cortes and his colleagues are doing is problematic in other ways as well. It is symptomatic of what is wrong in the Hebrew Roots movement. It is a movement based on pretense and supposition about Israel identity. It is led by teachers who assume they are Israel, and teach others to believe likewise, even though they aren't Jewish. Hebrew Roots is founded, built, and programmed by Two-house leaders who, whether they admit it or not, are teachers of replacement theology.

We note that after the procession of the Torah, the main speaker at the Revive 2012 Torah service was **Bill Cloud**. In June 2013, in Dallas, Texas, a similar Torah service was held at "Revive" 2013, led by Rico Cortes, with **Tony Robinson** as the speaker. **Bill Cloud** was the Friday evening speaker at that 2013 conference. Another "Revive" conference is currently scheduled for June 2014, in Jacksonville.

MIA Conferences:

Beginning in 1999, Batya Wooten and her colleagues in the Messianic Israel Alliance (a/k/a Redeemed Israel Alliance) have been organizing Two-house conferences. These MIA summer conferences have been the main event for Two-housers and have served as a platform for Wooten and colleagues to promote the Two-house ideology. The MIA conferences typically have featured most of the same speakers that are now speaking at "Revive" Conferences and are listed as "teachers" on the Hebrew Roots Network. These same so-called Hebrew Roots teachers have been the regular speakers at Wooten's MIA conferences for many years.

Wooten and Diffenderfer have advertised the MIA conferences in various ways, including their own monthly MIA newsletter called "The Herald." Although these MIA annual conferences go back to 1999, and although there are regional and other specially organized conferences of the MIA, we will only go back as far as 2009, and will only discuss the annual summer conference which has been the main MIA event. We will list some, but not all, of the prominent speakers which are regular speakers for each of these MIA conferences, as advertised by "The Herald":

2009, MIA Tenth Anniversary conference, Orlando, Fl., Sept. 4th - 7th :

---

[40] Rico Cortes, Revive Conference 2012, Torah Service, at video timecode 00:30. Available at: http://www.youtube.com/watch?v=mX855srWJTM

- Speakers: **Bill Cloud, Brad Scott, Daniel Botkin, Scott Diffenderfer, Ed Harris, Angus and Batya Wooten**. [41]

2010: Maryville College, Knoxville, Tn., July 26 - Aug. 1.

- Speakers: **Bill Cloud, Brad Scott, Holissa Alewine, Rico Cortes, Daniel Botkin, Scott Diffenderfer, Ed Harris, Angus and Batya Wooten** [42]

2011: Maryville College, Knoxville, Tn., June 28th – July 4th

Speakers: **Bill Cloud, Brad Scott, Holissa Alewine, Scott Diffenderfer, Ed Harris, Angus and Batya Wooten** [43]

By the year of 2012, the MIA did not hold any more conferences because the organization ceased to exist. The Messianic Israel Alliance that year changed its name to the "Redeemed Israel Alliance." This name change coincided with the advent of HRN, the departure of Diffenderfer and others from the MIA, and the first "Revive" conference held in 2012.

Under the new name, Wooten has held two conferences in Orlando, one in 2012 and another in 2013. These events have actually featured onsite DNA testing, conducted by Dr. Alex and Georgina Perdomo. This is presumably to try and prove biological connection to the people Israel.

Wooten's 2012 and 2013 conferences have not featured the usual speakers, who are now appearing on HRN and in the "Revive" conferences. Has Wooten's organization been trumped in popularity by the Hebraic Roots Network? Has the "Revive" conference surpassed Wooten's annual gatherings as the main event for Two-housers / Hebrew Roots enthusiasts? It would appear so. The only HRN "teacher" to appear at Wooten's 2013 Redeemed Israel Alliance conference, held during Labor Day weekend in Orlando, was **Bill Cloud**. [44]

---

[41] The Messianic Israel Alliance Herald, April, 2009, available at: www.messianicisrael.com/m/pdfs/herald/09april.pdf

[42] The Messianic Israel Alliance Herald, July, 2010, available at: http://www.messianicisrael.com/pdfs/herald/10july.pdf

[43] The Messianic Israel Alliance Herald, Jan. 2011, available at: http://www.messianicisrael.com/m/pdfs/herald/11jan.pdf

[44] http://www.redeemedisrael.com/events-2/

Bill Cloud:

One of the most, if not the most, popular of the Hebrew Roots teachers currently is Bill Cloud. He is not only a featured teacher on HRN, but he seems to make his presence known at every major gathering billed under the title of Hebrew Roots or Two-houses of Israel.

Cloud calls his ministry "Shoreshim" (Roots). The idea is that he is bringing people back to their Hebrew Roots. Cloud, who hails from south Georgia, claims to have studied under a Rabbi, through which Cloud claims to have become an expert on Hebrew language. Whether or not Cloud has actual expertise in Hebrew language is indeed arguable. He is known, however, for using a few key words and phrases in Hebrew in order to build upon in his teachings.

Cloud's claim to have "prolific" Hebrew skills, is a major part of Cloud's teaching style in terms of understanding prophecy. He holds himself out as a revealer of prophetic mysteries in the Bible, which the average English-speaking Christian wouldn't be able to see on his own, due to lack of Hebrew skills. His bio on HRN, which is posted verbatim on his own website as well, states:

> "Bill began studying Hebrew under the tutelage of a local rabbi and has since become quite prolific at reading and writing the Holy Tongue. He has spent many hours studying, not only the Hebrew text, but the Hebraic roots of Christianity as well. This research has been rewarded with a keen insight into Biblical Judaism and its relationship to Christianity.
>
> This interest is tied to Bill's desire to unlock the deep secrets of the Word of God and to teach them, along with our Hebraic roots, to believers in Messiah. Furthermore, this insight has allowed Bill to better understand the prophetic element of Scripture. As a result of this study, Bill has developed a variety of media resources dealing with prophetic themes as well as teachings related to our lost Hebraic heritage."[45]

As far as what Bill Cloud believes and teaches, one of the popular episodes of the Bill Cloud Show currently promoted and made available for purchase on DVD at the HRN website, and also at Bill Cloud's own ministry website, www.shoreshim.org, is a two-part teaching called *The Joseph Factor*.[46] This video consists of about 80 min. of teaching from Bill Cloud, and provides a good example of what Bill Cloud is about.

---

[45] At HRN website: http://www.hebraicrootsnetwork.com/teachers/bill-cloud , also at Shoreshim Ministries website: http://billcloud.org/about-bill

[46] At HRN website: http://www.hebraicrootsnetwork.com/shop/teachings/bill-cloud , and at Bill Cloud's website: http://www.goestores.com/catalog.aspx?storename=shoreshimministries&DeptID=243301&ItemID=10053419&detail=1

In *The Joseph Factor* teaching part I, Bill Cloud addresses the meaning of Gen. 48:19, in which Jacob blesses the two sons of Joseph. That verse is typically a key subject matter in Two-house teachings.[47] It is also typical to do what Cloud does here, which is to try and connect that verse to Paul's words concerning the salvation of Israel in Rom. 11:25-26. Cloud says:

> *"And he places his right hand on Ephraim's head, and he says, and in you, Ephraim, shall be the multitude of nations. The Hebrew phrase is 'm'lo hagoyim', and it, what that means, 'm'lo' – completion or fullness. 'Hagoyim' – the nations, or the Gentiles. In other words, it's the same phrasing that Paul uses in Romans 11. He says, in essence, that in you shall be the fullness of the Gentiles. In other words, when you who have come to Israel looking like pagans, if you will, those of you who have been outside of this family, but who now have been adopted in this family, when you come into the realization that you are part of this family, and consequently should begin to act like part of this family, and you begin to understand that, and how did we come into this family? Because the Messiah made it possible. When you begin to see the fullness of these things, then, it says, that's the completion of the Gentiles, that's that fullness of the Gentiles, that is the key that leads to all Israel being saved."[48]*

So, according to Cloud, Ephraim becoming a multitude does not refer to the Jewish people multiplying, it refers to Gentile believers being the descendants of Israel. This is the premise of British Israelism and Two-houses of Israel theology. Cloud continues, making clear his view that Joseph in prophecy is the Gentiles, and Judah is the Jews:

> *"You and I who are believers in Messiah, perhaps some of us are coming into trying to understand the Hebraic roots of our faith, perhaps asking why is it that just now I am beginning to see these things. Why is it that I didn't see these things long ago, or why is it that generations before me didn't see these things? Because ultimately ladies and gentlemen, it's all part of God's plan. Because there has to be a Joseph. There has to be a Joseph whose Hebraic identity is concealed, for such a time as this. And what is the purpose of it all? So that all Israel might be saved. Because there is coming a day when Joseph - who I believe represents the*

---

[47] Kay Silberling Smith, Ph.D., *The Ephraimite Error,* p. 2, www.mjaa.org/site/DocServer/EphraimiteError.pdf

[48] Bill Cloud, *the Joseph Factor part I*, Time code 35:25 - 36:31, available at: http://www.youtube.com/watch?v=Yv53zui4o5A

body of Messiah at large. And Judah - the Jewish people at large. There is coming a day when these two trees, these two groups, are gonna be reconciled and are going to become one, and thus, all Israel shall be saved." [49]

Cloud's teaching here is classic Two-house teaching. The whole context of Romans 11 is about the salvation of the Jewish people. It foretells how the gospel will go to the whole Gentile world, and Israel will be provoked to jealousy. If the Gentiles coming to faith are actually Israel, then is Israel to provoke Israel? Obviously not. The whole world will hear the gospel, and as Gentiles come to faith, at an appointed time, the Lord will turn his face back to Israel. The Jews brought the gospel to the world, yet, blindness has come upon Israel until the designated time, in which that blindness shall be removed. Messianic Judaism is the living truth and the fulfillment of that scriptural promise of the salvation of Jewish people found in Romans 11.

Yet, Cloud's teaching here tows the party-line for the Two-house movement: He teaches that the salvation of "Israel" spoken of by Paul in Romans 11 is not about Jewish salvation, but it is about the restoration of the houses of Judah and Joseph (Ephraim). He suggests that the salvation of Israel can only occur when the house "Joseph" (Ephraim) at last realizes its hidden identity among the nations where they have become a "multitude," not as Jews, but as Gentiles. Only then can Israel be saved. So, it isn't about the Jewish people coming to Messiah, it is about Gentiles discovering that they are Israel. This is Two-house doctrine. The hope of the Gentiles is in discovering at last what has otherwise been "hidden" – that they are Israelites. And having discovered it, as Cloud says, they must stop being pagan and start "behaving" as Israelites, which means keeping the law.

In part 2 of *The Joseph Factor*, Bill Cloud elaborates on his view that Americans are actually the house of Joseph:

"I'm going to suggest to you that the reason that you and I, and Americans, enjoy so much luxury, so much wealth, is not for the sake of the wealth itself, it's not because we're Americans. It's because all these different nations, this multi-colored coat, is congregated, by and large, in this country, and God is blessing Joseph, because Joseph has a role to play as it relates to our brethren, who are living in the land of Canaan, and who, along with all of us, are one day going to

---

[49] Ibid, time code 38:00 – 39:00.

be threatened with something that is going to originate in the deserts of Saudi Arabia." [50]

So, America is Joseph? How can Gentile believers in America constitute the northern kingdom of Israel? This teaching is straight off the pages of Herbert W. Armstrong and British Israelism. But Bill Cloud builds on it. He continues with his claim that America is Joseph, citing a verse from the book of Obadiah which says:

> *"And the house of Jacob shall be a fire, and the house of Joseph a flame, and the house of Esau for stubble, and they shall kindle in them, and devour them; and there shall not be any remaining of the house of Esau; for the LORD has spoken it."* (Obadiah v. 18)

So according to Cloud, American Gentile believers are actually the "house of Joseph," which will ultimately consume the "house of Esau" on behalf of all of Jacob. He continues:

> *"And so who is God going to use primarily to bring about the destruction of the house of Esau? According to His word, the house of Joseph. Now who is the house of Joseph? If we put all these things together, ladies and gentleman, that we've been discussing, I have to come to this conclusion, the house of Joseph is referring to people like you and me. And if I'm correct, if the largest portion of Joseph is living in this nation, perhaps this is an allusion to the United States."* [51]

As Cloud continues, as further evidence for his claim of America as Joseph, Cloud turns to his Hebrew skills. He claims that the Hebrew word "busha" (bet, vav, shin, hey) found in Obadiah v. 10, which is translated into English as "shame," is in fact a prophetic allusion to America. Cloud claims that since the masculine form of "busha," is "bush," that this word is a prophetic allusion to President Bush. He offers this to make the point that America is the house of Joseph in prophecy, which is destined, according to Cloud, to destroy Israel's enemy, the house of Esau. [52] Of course, all of this reeks of British Israelism and Two-house theology.

---

[50] Bill Cloud, *the Joseph Factor part II*, Time code 32:20 - 32:60, available at: http://www.youtube.com/watch?v=InNCcS4tXmM

[51] Ibid, at timecode: 36:15 – 36:44

[52] Ibid, at timecode: 37:55 – 38:48

Cloud wraps up part 2 of the Joseph Factor with a summation that hammers his point home. According to Cloud, American Gentile believers, being the house of Joseph, can look forward to the promise of being united with the Jews in the land:

> *"You and I have been hidden among the nations. You and I, we've been hidden so well, we didn't even know we were hidden. The reason we were, is so that somebody would come looking for us. And by that I mean our brethren who live in the land of Canaan, because one day there is going to be this restoration of all things that Peter describes in Acts chapter three. There one day is going to be this great reconciliation where these two become one, in the land."*[53]

Jim Staley:

Though Jim Staley is not one of the teachers promoted by HRN, he has made his presence known through the internet, and is clearly one of the most prominent Hebrew Roots teachers at present. Staley's ministry, headquartered in St. Charles, Missouri, he calls "Passion for Truth Ministries."[54] Staley has organized Hebrew Roots conferences of his own, which he called "Final Return" in 2010, and "Final Restoration" in 2011. These events have featured as speakers some of the usual Hebrew roots teachers, including: **Bill Cloud, Rico Cortes,** and **Tony Robinson**.[55]

In addition to using livestream internet videos to promote himself, Staley is quite savvy at marketing his recorded teachings through DVD's and CD's. Staley's website is replete with materials carrying the "One Law" and Two-house message, authored by both Staley and others whom he promotes. Staley makes clear in most of his teachings that he believes every Gentile believer ought to consider it their obligation to keep Torah, especially the Shabbat, the feasts, and the dietary laws.

Not only is Staley an avid "One Law" teacher, but he is also a Two-houser. We note that similar to the current trend of most Hebrew Roots teachers, Staley does not describe himself or his ministry with any labels that might indicate his Two-house doctrinal beliefs. However, even a cursory glance at some of his teaching materials indicates quite plainly that he is in fact a devoted Two-house teacher.

---

[53] Ibid, at timecode: 38:52 - 39:21

[54] See Staley's website at: www.passionfortruth.com

[55] Promo for conference available at: www.youtube.com/watch?v=-EWjUe4McNw

The best example of what Staley teaches is found in one of his popular DVD teachings called *"Identity Crisis – Discovering Your True Identity."*[56] Having been produced in 2011, as of the date of this writing, Staley's website lists the *Identity Crisis* DVD under the subheading "number one teaching."

Hence, it's pretty clear that *"Identity Crisis"* quite vividly represents the heart of what Staley and his ministry stand for. The teaching is 120 minutes long, so this short review is not intended to be a full rebuttal by any means. In any case, there is nothing new in it that hasn't already been addressed in *The Ephraimite Error*. Staley in essence has made his mark by preaching the same points that Batya Wooten has written, the difference being that it's a different medium. What Wooten put in books, Staley is preaching in front of the camera, as Herbert W. Armstrong did.

For our purposes here, we will review a short portion of the *Identity Crisis* DVD, not as a full rebuttal, but simply to reference it, and record it herein, as proof positive of what Staley believes and teaches. Staley is undeniably a part of the Hebrew Roots crowd which in fact is an extension of the Two-houses of Israel movement. While the entire Two-house position is anti-Semitic in nature, many of the Hebrew Roots teachers have tried to tone down the anti-Semitic rhetoric that inheres in the Two-house position. Not so with Staley. Jim Staley, in particular, stands out as one who comes across, quite unabashedly, as anti-Jewish. The promo on the jacket of the DVD states:

> *"For two thousand years we have all been taught that Israel is the Jewish people and the Jewish people are Israel. This misunderstanding has crippled our ability to truly glean from the scriptures all that was originally intended."*

As the promo makes clear, the entire "Identity Crisis" teaching is about the identity of Gentile believers as Israel. It is typical Two-house teaching. Staley, who delivers the entire message standing at a pulpit flanked by two tall banners – one of Judah, the other of Ephraim - begins by listing what he claims are "myths" about the Jewish people. Two of those "common myths" according to Staley are:

- The Jewish people were the chosen people in the Old Testament
- The Torah and the law was given to the Jews[57]

These are actually "myths" about the Jews. According to Staley, another misconception is that the Jews were the people at Mt. Sinai. Staley says:

---

[56] Jim Staley, *Identity Crisis*, available at: http://www.youtube.com/watch?v=BTx5tjNQEvw

[57] Ibid, at time code 8:44.

"How many tribes were at the base of Mt. Sinai when the commandments were given? All twelve tribes. Next question, logical to be asked, is how many were Jewish? One tribe. One tribe was Jewish, which begs the question, where are the other ones? Because if they were given to all of Israel, all the twelve tribes, then they can't possibly be Jewish, or that's just not fair. The Jewish people cannot own the holidays. They're just one tribe."[58]

True to form as a Two-house teacher, Staley makes a big deal about the reference in Genesis 48:19 to Ephraim as a "multitude of nations." He argues just like Bill Cloud, and Batya Wooten, and all other Two-house teachers, that the Hebrew from that verse, "m'lo hagoyim," actually means "fullness of the Gentiles," and therefore it is a reference not to the Jews, but to the Gentile believers. Staley says:

"So the ten tribes were taken into captivity and disbursed all across Assyria, over time they assimilated into the nations and became exactly what the prophecy said of Ephraim, the m'lo hagoyim, the fullness of the nations, they became as Gentiles."[59]

The "m'lo hagoyim" teaching, which cites Gen. 48:19 as supposed evidence that the Gentiles are physical descendants of the ten northern tribes, is classic Two-house. Whether British Israelite, Herbert W. Armstrong, Batya Wooten, or Jim Staley, the teaching is the same. As expected, Staley goes on to try and connect it to Romans 11:26, which, according to their view is a reference to the salvation of the Gentile descendants of Israel.

"That blindness in part has happened to Israel, speaking of the local Israel of that day, in context, the only Israel that existed, the house of Judah, until the fullness of the Gentiles comes in. I told you I would come back to this verse. Do you think that Paul is just making this up by some stroke of genius? He's quoting from the Tanakh. The blessing that went on Ephraim. The fullness of the house of, excuse me, the fullness of the Gentiles. This is what he's talking about. The northern kingdom coming home. Until they all come home. This is what he's talking about. Continuing, and so all Israel will be saved. How many, like me, have always thought at some point all those Jewish people will finally understand, and they'll all get saved? Cause we've defined Israel as the Jewish people. But the reality is that it's all Israel, ladies and gentleman, all twelve tribes will eventually come

---

[58] Ibid, at time code 9:32 – 10:08

[59] Ibid, at time code 28:00 – 28:15.

back, that's what he's talking about. (applause). When the fullness of the Gentiles comes home, that's when all Israel will be saved."[60]

Like most every other major figures in the Hebrew Roots movement, obviously Staley is a Two-house teacher, whose message to the Gentile believer is loud and clear: You are the true Israel. Therefore, you should be keeping the Torah.

Michael Rood:

Of all the figures currently operating under the label of "Hebrew Roots", Michael Rood is in a class of his own. Although Rood does not presently appear to be connected with any of the major figures or events in the Hebrew Roots movement, yet he has made quite a significant impact on the Hebrew Roots movement on his own behalf. He has done this mainly through the use of the internet. In particular, he has used video and internet television.

Based in Charlotte, N.C., Rood's teachings are currently aired, promoted, and marketed through his website at: www.aroodawakening.tv. Similar to the Hebraic Roots Network, Rood also uses a 24/7 internet TV site of his own which he calls "Messianic TV." That site, which is linked to his main website, is found at www.messianic.tv .

Michael Rood's preaching appeals to the typical Sabbaterean Christian in America. Sporting a long, white beard, Rood commonly dresses in robes and head pieces which resemble the garments of Israelite priests in Temple times. The way he dresses, though comical indeed, does not appear to be in jest. It is very much a part of the character which Rood has created for himself. He has cast himself into the role of a doomsday prophet, who has come to decry the sins of the Gentile church in America. To be a Moses or Elijah, one must look and act the part, and Michael Rood does exactly that.

Nearly all of Rood's teachings, which he often refers to as "A Rood Awakening," are about end-time prophecy. His teachings seem to always focus upon inevitable thermonuclear war with Russia, impending judgment upon America, the anti-christ, economic collapse, the beast of Revelation, global conspiracies, the New World Order, etc.. These are all topics of interest to believers today, and many preachers, at times, delve into the same. But in Rood's case, end-time prophecy provides the basis for his urging Gentiles to believe there is a need for them to be keeping the law of Moses, in order to escape God's wrath. In particular, the feasts, the Sabbath, and the dietary laws are promoted by Rood - because God is angry with the "pagan" church, which has failed to keep these things. Rood's style of playing on people's fears concerning real issues such as nuclear war, terrorism, Arab-Israeli conflicts, recession, and global politics, as a backdrop for promoting legalism, is highly reminiscent of Herbert W. Armstrong.

---

[60] Ibid, at time code: 50:36 - 51:41

Rood makes lots of trips to Israel, and many of his videos are shot on location there. He clearly endeavors to produce his videos in a way which associates himself with the land of Israel, and which implies to his followers that he is an Israelite, and so too are they if only they follow his teachings.

Rood insists upon a Karaite version of the biblical calendar which he calls the "*Astronomically and Agriculturally Corrected Biblical Hebrew Calendar*. Rood makes a big issue about the correct calendar being connected to the ripening of the barley harvest in the Spring. He suggests that those who keep Passover at the "wrong" time, following the mainstream, modern Jewish calendar, are not keeping the commandments of God concerning appointed feast days.

Rood's impact upon the Hebrew Roots movement is quite significant, as is his name recognition all over the internet. Unfortunately for the messianic Jewish movement, Rood often refers to himself as a "Rabbi" or even a "Messianic Rabbi," though he is not Jewish by birth, and has absolutely zero history with Messianic Judaism.

Although Rood has mainly used video to make himself known, he has also written books which document his teachings. One of Michael Rood's key writings is a book called, *The Mystery of Iniquity*. This book is in essence the Michael Rood manifesto. It documents the bulk of what he teaches concerning end-time prophecy. The *Mystery of Iniquity* is promoted for sale on his website as of this date.[61] One of the issues Rood presents in that book is his theory of Israel identity. He refers to the end-time remnant of 144,000 from each tribe of Israel, as described in Revelation 7. Who are these 144,000? According to Rood:

> *"These are not 144,000 Jews. The tribe of Judah comprises only one twelfth of those who will be sealed by God. There are 11 other tribes, ten of which have been lost since the carrying away of the northern tribes by Shalmanessar the Assyrian Emperor. That carrying away and dispersal helped to fulfill the prophecy of God to Abraham that from his loins would come many nations. The prophecy of Israel over his twelve sons was also expedited by this dispersion. The lost tribes of Israel have been traced all over northern Asia and Europe. Modern archaeological finds in Europe show the migration of the Hebrew people throughout the continent. Many of the royal families of Europe can still trace their roots back to their forefather, Israel. The ten lost tribes of Israel may not have*

---

[61] Michael Rood, *The Mystery of Iniquity*, Bridge-Logos (2001)

much, if any, pure blood left in their families. The vast majority of them do not even know who they are. Yet!"[62]

It's plain to see from his book that Michael Rood is a believer and teacher of Two-house theology. The claims about the Royal families of Europe and the supposed "modern archeological finds" about Israelite tribes settling in Europe are unmistakable evidence of Rood's British Israel ideology. Rood's orientation in British Israelism is further delineated as he drones on about Britain and America:

> *"When one analyzes the prophecies that were spoken over Joseph's two sons, Ephraim and Mannaseh, there are only two nations that fulfill **any** of these prophecies. In fact, those two nations fulfill **every** prophecy concerning the promises to those tribes in the last days. The two nations are Great Britain and the United States. When one realizes that the Oracles (Words) of God were committed to his people Israel, one can understand why the Bible houses of England and America have published over 90% of all the Bibles in the world. The promises of God have been fulfilled right under the noses of those who do not even know their ancient origins."*[63]

When one reads these words in his book, there can be no doubt that Michael Rood is a proponent of British Israel / Two House theology.

Another example of what Rood teaches is a teaching he calls *"Israel, Judaism and Christianity: Apostasy in the Church, and the Time of Jacob's Trouble."* Here we get a pretty good idea of what Rood is about. In this video, Rood discusses his belief that the "time of Jacob's trouble" (Jer. 30:7) is an historical event, still yet to come, which ultimately causes both Jew and Gentile to return to the land of Israel.

Rood begins the video by appearing in costume at the Kotel (Western Wall) in Jerusalem. Then he cuts to Yad Vashem (one can only wonder how he got permission to film there), where he claims that Islamic nations which hate the Jews are going to start a thermonuclear war, which will destroy the world's economy, and then, this will somehow result in "Israel" at last returning to the land. Rood says:

> *Jeremiah speaks of the day when the Lord God will bring Israel back into the land that he gave unto our fathers. Even though the nation of Israel was born in one day, May 15th, 1948, in fulfillment of Isaiah's prophecy, the multitude of the dispersed Israelites has not even considered returning to the land. Zachariah said*

---

[62] Ibid, p. 213. Note – an earlier edition, pdf version of this book is available at : http://markswatson.com/moi.pdf , p. 128.

[63] Ibid.

51

(quoting Zech. 1:17) that because of prosperity, the tribes would be dispersed for an extended period. But the time of Jacob's trouble will put an end to that prosperity, and force the return of the dispersed sons of Israel.[64]

Rood then continues, with a background of still photos depicting graphic holocaust images. He cuts from one image to the next, explaining how the atrocities which the Nazis committed against the Jews in Europe were actually done in fulfillment of God's word in Jer. 16:16, regarding fishers and hunters, which he claims were the Nazis. The video goes on to show an array of holocaust images: As we see Hitler and the Nazis, scenes of Jewish businesses destroyed, and pathetic figures of Jews in the death camps, etc., a caption suddenly appears at the bottom of the screen which says: *"please consider donating at michaelrood.tv"*.

Then, as we see scenes of the crematoriums, and piles of starved Jewish bodies being tossed into mass graves, Rood explains why all this had to happen. He says:

> *In the end, the modern state of Israel was born out of the labor pains of Judah's great tribulation....*[65]

Hence, the suffering of the Jews in the holocaust, which resulted in the Jews returning to the land of Israel as a consequence, was an event involving only the one tribe of Judah? Not the rest of Israel? Ok, so where was the rest of Israel, who apparently escaped suffering in the holocaust?

Like nearly every other Two-house teacher who operates under the label "Hebrew Roots," Rood teaches that the Jews are Judah, and the Gentiles are Israel. In this skewed view, it was the Judah alone, the "Jewish tribe," which suffered the holocaust. The rest of Israel was living in the cushy empires of America or England, unaware of their descent from the lost tribes – but soon to rediscover their heritage as Israelites.

In fact, according to Rood, Judah is going to have to go through yet another holocaust before being reunited to the Gentile Israelites. Yes, says Rood, the "Time of Jacob's Trouble" (Jer. 30:7), as if the holocaust wasn't enough, is coming again, but to Judah's consolation, this time it will happen to all Israel.
Rood continues:

---

[64] Michael Rood, *Israel, Judaism and Christianity: Apostasy in the Church, and the Time of Jacob's Trouble*, at timecode : 3:07-3:43. Available at: http://www.youtube.com/watch?v=CWZeEnuHHPQ&list=PL3Oc6f4BdE5D4seUz-6EOtL7EPVCHDXB6
Also available at : http://natzrim.blogspot.com/2010/12/time-of-jacobs-trouble.html

[65] Ibid, at timecode: 4:32 – 4:39.

...in the last days it will not be just the time of Judah's trouble, but all of Israel will be tried in the crucible of tribulation, in the time of <u>Jacob's</u> trouble. And just as in days of long past, all of Israel will be saved by the hand of the Almighty. "[66]

Rood's teaching resonates of all the same theories which are typical of Two-house teachers who claim that the only way "all Israel will be saved" (from Romans 11:26), is when the Gentile believers reconnect with their heritage by keeping the law. Only then will they be reunited to their "brother Judah." But in Rood's case, it will take global thermonuclear war to at last cause Gentile believers to wake up to their Israelite descent and come back to their Hebrew Roots. The ones who follow Rood's teachings are ahead of the gang, and getting a jump on the preparations.

Christian Zionism – True Friends of Israel:

As mentioned in the introductory comments of this paper, it is unfortunate that the label "Hebrew Roots" has been used by proponents of the "One Law" message. We wish to make it clear that "Hebrew Roots," "Hebraic Roots," "Jewish Roots," and similar labels do not always mean what is meant by "One Law" proponents. We wish to make this clear because it is not our intent to discourage any believer in Yeshua from searching out and discovering the Jewish character and culture of the Lord.

Hebrew Roots is not to be confused with the growing number of Christians in the world today who have a sincere heart for Israel. Though not really an organized movement, there is a modern-day phenomenon of Gentile Christians who love Israel, often-referred to as "Christian Zionism." This is a work of the Lord.

Whatever it is to be called, there is in fact a biblical, prophetic, Spirit-led response happening today among millions of Gentile Christians worldwide who see Israel's restoration as a promise of God. These are Christians who believe in the right of Jewish people to possess the land of Israel, and who believe in promoting the salvation of the Jewish people. These are Christians who love Israel and want to see Jewish people come to know Yeshua. Many go on tours to Israel, visit Messianic Synagogues, join in prayer for the peace of Jerusalem, and encourage their respective national political leaders to stand with Israel.

Individually, many Christians who support Zionism also seek to enrich their own personal faith by learning the culturally Jewish roots of Christianity. Such Christians, even though planted firmly in evangelical churches, are great friends of Messianic Judaism, and faithful supporters of Messianic Jewish ministries.

---

[66] Ibid, at 4:39-4:56

53

By comparison to what calls itself "Hebrew Roots," Christian Zionism has no agenda to bring anyone under the law, nor cause division in the church. The agenda is to enrich the Gentile Christian's understanding of the Jewish Messiah, and to unite the body into a common bond of support in order to advance the salvation and restoration of Israel.

We note also that some Gentile believers identify with Messianic Jews, and see their congregational home in a messianic synagogue, which we welcome and encourage. These precious brethren who come to us from among the masses of Gentile believers in the world are the exception, not the rule. We do not see Messianic Judaism as the final destiny for all believers in Messiah. We are not the model for the whole world to follow. We are simply who we are in the Body because of the unique calling. Among the masses of Gentile believers in the world, though many are devoted friends of Israel, most do not belong to a Messianic Synagogue, nor do they identify with the calling of Messianic Jews to orient our lives in a Jewish expression of faith in Messiah. Nor do we believe that they necessarily should.

Indeed, many Christians who love Israel simply see their home in the evangelical church. They do not think it necessary to become Torah observant in order to perfect any calling they may have to connect with Israel. Many Christians see God's biblical plan for Israel, and therefore support Messianic Jewish ministries, but they do not necessarily identify the messianic synagogue as a congregational home for themselves and their families. They are perfectly content to be Gentile Christians, serving God as Gentiles, in a Gentile Christian setting. They are confident in who they are, and feel they have the freedom to be whom God created them to be in the Lord. We agree.

By comparison, the Hebrew Roots movement is full of criticism toward non-Torah keeping Gentiles, and demonstrates little to no desire to see Jews come to know Messiah. Rather, their "Israel-obsession" is driven by the common idea, whether stated or implied, that they ARE Israel. The idea is based on replacing the Jews as the true Israel, through the keeping of the law given at Sinai.

VI.   "One Law" Theology and First Fruits of Zion

FFOZ:

First Fruits of Zion (FFOZ). FFOZ is a publishing ministry, which has developed a significant network of customers who purchase their materials through the internet. The organization's founder is Boaz Michael, who started FFOZ in 1992. From the outset, Michael has used FFOZ to mass distribute books, CD's, DVD's, newsletters, study programs for children and adults, and other materials.

FFOZ sees itself mainly as an outreach to Gentiles that have an interest in learning the Torah. At times FFOZ has worked in harmony with the Messianic Jewish movement.

However, from about 2003 – 2009, FFOZ was a major promoter of "One Law One People" teachings. We note that FFOZ was not a promoter of Two-house doctrine, not directly, anyway. FFOZ was a proponent of "One Law One People" teachings which advocate Gentile Torah observance. That approach, as we have seen, almost inevitably results in promoting Two-house beliefs, even if unintended.

In any case, to the credit of FFOZ, after initially promoting and publishing "One Law" teachings on a wide scale, leadership at FFOZ had a change of heart. This change came in 2009, after witnessing the fruit of "One Law" teaching. Consequently, under Boaz Michael's leadership, FFOZ eventually rejected and recanted "One Law" theology.

Therefore, it is an interesting and persuasive case study indeed to review what happened with FFOZ, and examine how and why Boaz Michael came to the conclusion, based on personal experience, that "One Law One People" theology is erroneous. It is our hope that there will be other groups that recant and renounce both "One Law", and the related Two-house theology as well.

It should also be mentioned that Boaz Michael and FFOZ as a ministry, as of the date of this writing, have formally reconciled and re-established a relationship of good standing within the Messianic Jewish movement, including with both the MJAA and UMJC.

As far as what led to the recantation, the following is what we know based on FFOZ's own reports:

FFOZ and Tim Hegg:

In about 2003, FFOZ became allied with outspoken "One Law" advocate Tim Hegg. Although Hegg is no longer much of a voice today, during the time that he was allied with FFOZ, he was given a broad platform to publish his "One Law" teachings. In 2003, as FFOZ started broadly publishing Hegg's materials, almost immediately FFOZ met the resistance of Messianic Jewish leadership, who voiced strong objections to "One Law" theology. The Union of Messianic Jewish Congregations (UMJC) published a paper which confronted Hegg's teachings and refuted "One Law" theology.[67]

Tim Hegg's teachings so strongly stressed the need for Gentiles to observe the Torah, that it often sounded as if Hegg actually equates Torah observance to the gospel itself. To give an example of Hegg's teaching, Hegg argues based on a comparison of two

---

[67] Daniel Juster and Russ Resnik, *One Law Movements*, 2005. Available at: http://www.mjstudies.com/storage/Juster_Resnik_One_Law_Movements.pdf

scriptures, Mat. 5:20 and Mat. 28:19-20 that the purpose of the Great Commission was to bring Torah to the Gentiles.[68] The two scriptures Hegg refers to are as follows:

> *"For I say unto you that unless your righteousness surpasses that of the scribes and Pharisees, you will not enter the kingdom of heaven."* Mat. 5:20.

And:

> *"Go therefore and make disciples of all the nations, baptizing them in the name of the Father and the Son and the Holy Spirit, **teaching them to observe all that I commanded you**, and lo I am with you always, even unto the end of the age."* Mat. 28:19-20.

Putting those two scriptures together, Hegg arrives at the following analysis:

> "The phrase '**teaching them to observe all that I commanded you**' makes it clear that Yeshua's teaching in Matt. 5:17-20 was to form a core aspect of the curriculum the disciples were commissioned to teach the Gentiles."

Thus, according to Hegg, the Great Commission is to bring the world into Torah observance. This is the major error of the "One Law" teachers. They preach a "gospel" of obedience to law, the very antithesis of the true gospel.

The Break with Hegg:

From about 2003 – 2009, FFOZ published the message of "One Law" far and wide. Then, in its Summer 2009 edition of its quarterly publication called *Messiah Journal*, FFOZ suddenly announced its formal recantation of "One Law" theology in an article entitled *One Law and the Messianic Gentile*.[69]   This effectively ended the working relationship between FFOZ and Hegg.

In its Summer, 2009 magazine, *Messiah Journal*, in an article written by Boaz Michael and D. Thomas Lancaster, FFOZ tells the story of what went wrong with "One Law" theology.

After years of publishing Hegg and mass distributing "One Law" materials, FFOZ soon began to take notice of not only the theological problems with "One Law" teachings but the real-time mess which they had created. As Michael and Lancaster describe it:

---

[68] Tim Hegg, *An Assessment of Divine Invitation Teaching* (Aug. 2009), p.6, available at: http://www.torahresource.com/EnglishArticles/DivineInvitation_Response.pdf

[69] Boaz Michael and D. Thomas Lancaster, *One Law and the Messianic Gentile* (Summer 2009), pp. 46-70.

"Not only do the One-Law Torah observant Gentiles find it difficult to maintain relationships with other Christians, they also find it virtually impossible to maintain relationship with one another."[70]

One of the key claims that "One Law" teachers often make is that Torah Observance will bring about the final unity between Jew and Gentile. But in fact, what happens is precisely the opposite. The fruit of "One Law" teaching, as mass-promoted by FFOZ and Tim Hegg, was further described by Michael and Lancaster as follows:

> "The result is a state of anarchy disguised under the name of Law. Congregations split over calendar arguments. People are embittered toward one another. Close friends are separated. Communities shrink . . . there are no other Messianic believers in the area with whom they can sustain a relationship. The program is not working . . . they reject Judaism and Jewish tradition, and they reject Christianity and Christian tradition. As romantic as such a hyper-protestant, sola scritura purity may sound, it breeds arrogance and is unsustainable." [71]

Going back to the days of the early Sabbatereans and the Millerites, it is well-proven by now that those who teach there is some urgent need for Gentile Torah observance always seems to breed a spirit of arrogance, legalism, and basic weirdness. In that regard, today's Hebrew roots movement is no exception.

Gentile Torah Observance, Our View:

Paul circumcised Timothy, whose mother was Jewish, (Acts 16:3); but did not circumcise Titus, who was Greek. (Gal. 2:3). Paul saw that circumcision was right and good for the Jewish believer in Yeshua, but made no sense for the Gentile. The fact is, Paul did not see the Torah as having the same application to Gentiles as to Jews under the New Covenant. Paul was the Apostle to the Gentiles. If One Law One People had any doctrinal validity, Paul would have been the one to preach it. He preached no such thing.

We do not believe the Gentile church is called necessarily to observe Shabbat, the Levitical feasts, the laws of kashrut, and other Mosaic laws that are specific to Israel. We don't forbid anyone from doing those things, but we do not fault the church for not keeping them. Nor do we believe in urging Gentile believers worldwide to observe commandments other than the ones the Apostles commanded in Acts 15.

Indeed the Apostles in Acts 15 dealt with the issue of Gentile Torah observance squarely on point. As Peter said to the "One Law" proponents of his day in Acts 15:10:

> *"Why do you test God by putting a yoke upon the neck of the (Gentile) disciples, which neither our fathers nor we were able to bear?"*

---

[70] Boaz Michael and D. Thomas Lancaster, *One Law and the Messianic Gentile*, (Summer 2009) p. 52.

[71] Ibid.

When it comes to the issue of Gentile Torah observance, our approach is simply to follow the advice of the Apostles. They determined not to put a yoke of law upon the Gentiles. Neither would we. And like the Apostles, we would oppose those who do.

Acts 15 and the Jerusalem Council:

The controversy over Gentile Torah observance in our time is exactly the same one addressed by the Apostles. As Paul preached the gospel among the Gentiles, certain men were insisting that the Gentiles must be instructed to keep the law. For this very reason, *"It was determined that Paul and Barnabas and certain others should go up to Jerusalem unto the Apostles and Elders about this question."* (Acts 15:2)

When they came to Jerusalem, and declared all the wonderful things that God was doing among the Gentiles, there were certain Jews who were believers in Yeshua, who were Pharisees, that rose up saying: *"It is necessary to circumcise them and command them to keep the law of Moses,"* (Acts 15:5). Peter was the first to dispute the point, having already seen how God poured out His Spirit upon non-Torah observant Gentiles. (Acts 10:44-45).

For the Apostles, though the laws of Moses were an important part of their Jewish way of life, they knew that the power of the gospel was not based in legal observance, it was based upon faith in the Messiah, and was as equally available to the uncircumcised Gentile as to the circumcised Jew. This at first seemed to contradict the law given at Sinai.

Yet, the Apostles were quite clear on answering the question brought before them. The Gentiles need not be instructed to be circumcised, nor do they need to be instructed to keep the law of Moses. They determined that *"we trouble them not which from among the Gentiles are turned unto God"* (Acts 15:19). As today's Messianic Jewish leaders, we fully agree. It is not our calling to bring the Gentile world into Torah observance.

As the Apostles said later, referring to their own decision recorded in Acts 15:

> *"As touching the Gentiles which believe, we have written and concluded that they observe no such thing, except that they keep themselves from things offered to idols, and from blood, and from strangled, and from fornication."* (Acts 21:25)

The decision which the Apostles made as recorded in the scriptures is perfectly applicable to the issue of Gentile Torah observance today. And we choose to honor and abide by it.

VII.   **Conclusion**:

Messianic Judaism has a unique calling of God as witnesses to the Jewish people, and the Torah occupies an important place among us.   While we recognize there are many doctrinal errors made historically by the church in terms of its views on Israel and the Torah, we do not believe that the Gentile church is called to live by the same Jewish expression of faith as we are. Our hope is that the Gentile church, and Gentile believers everywhere, will see their calling to bless Israel, pray for the peace of Jerusalem, and help messianic Jews to reach the Jewish people with the good news.   Thankfully, this is already happening to some extent.   The power of the One New Man is not in our relationship to the law, and not in our observance of ordinances or statutes; but, rather, in the fellowship that we enjoy as both Jew and Gentile, cleansed by the blood of Messiah, and immersed by One Spirit into the same body. Together we are the "seed of Abraham" by faith in the one God, and joint heirs of a Kingdom that will never fade.

Blessings to you in the name of Yeshua (Jesus) our Messiah.

2015-09-16

Why Corbynism is a threat to Jews throughout the Western world

The Israel you know j
You can thank Netany

Trending Now

Home

Israel's Chief Rabbinate Blasts 'Spiritually Dangerous' Christian Event in Jerusalem

Ashkenazi Chief Rabbi David Lau and Sephardic Chief Rabbi Yitzhak Yosef say even though International Christian Embassy in Jerusalem are friends of Israel, the event undermines the state's Jewish character.

Haaretz | ⊘ Send me email alerts

Sep 16, 2015 11:18 PM

f Share   🐦 Tweet   ✉   ⬈   💬 4   Subscribe

Israel's Sephardi Chief Rabbi Yitzhak Yosef (L) and Ashkenazi Chief Rabbi David Lau. Credit: Moti Milrod

● Chief rabbis condemn Jewish-Christian prayer vigil

Israel's Chief Rabbinate warned of the spiritual danger of an upcoming conference organized by the International Christian Embassy in Jerusalem, claiming the event seeks to convert Jews to Christianity.

"We have learned that missionary elements [working on behalf] of the Christian embassy in Jerusalem are organizing a large conference during the Sukkot holiday. Some of this organization's goals are to convert Jews [to Christianity]," a statement signed by Israel's Ashkenazi Chief Rabbi David Lau and Sephardic Chief Rabbi Yitzhak Yosef read. "Those same elements see as their mission converting the entire world to Christianity, especially the

Menashe's Blog

A reasoned Jewish response to ....read on!!!

MAY 10, 2015 BY MENASHE DOVID (מנשה דוד)

The spread of Messianics in the Diaspora and Israe

by Diane Weber Bederman

MAY 10, 2015, 2:34 PM 6 (http://blogs.timesofisrael.com/the-spread-of-messianics-in-the-diaspora-and
What propels Christian Zionists (http://jewsforjudaism.org/knowledge/articles/issues/articles-in-t
hey love Israel so much? CBS reporter Bob Simon, in a 1992 "60 Minutes" program found the answer:
s seen by Evangelicals as a precondition for the Second Coming of Christ.

omehow I don't see the Jews as the winners from all this love. The Jews have given their blood in m
eep this Jewish homeland Jewish, yet they aren't the principle winners in this vision.

want to introduce you to Canadian Wayne Hilsden, living in Israel since 1983. He is cofounder of Kin;
oca   in the *heart* of Jerusalem. All made possible with the help of the Lord as he is wont to say.

The vision of King of Kings Community (http://api.ning.com/files/li0jpfi0h9nPI7vQ6
;OsVBJeKt2Au3K7fdoDPD0*wEBHU6*DmD1h/2015IsraelSummitBios.pdf) is 'to be a compelling,
ommunity that reveals the true face of Yeshua (Jesus) to Israel and to the nations.'"

Hilsden believes God recently gave him a mandate (http://www.charismanews.com/opinion/stand
inistry-to-stand-firm-with-israel) to "get Israel back into biblical theology." He sought the Lord for
should be identified even more closely with the local, messianic Jewish Body (http://www.kkcj.org
ooted more deeply in the soil of Israel." He then formed FIRM (http://www.charismanews.com/i
Fellowship of Israel Related Ministries) in 2014. Its mission (http://www.charismanews.com/c
ompels-new-ministry-to-stand-firm-with-israel%20): "to unite a global fellowship of biblically soun
elationships that work to bless the inhabitants of Israel and the worldwide Jewish community."

nd at the same time offering as proof of its support for Palestinian human rights (http://www.examii
or-israel-at-historic-summit), FIRM enlisted Jerusalem-based attorney and activist, Calev Myers, in
ittp://blogs.timesofisrael.com/jews-for-jesusthe-serpent-in-the-garden/) about whom I
ittp://www.theledger.com/article/20080427/news/804270448) "We believe the day is coming, fr
srael, to the Jewish people."

Snap shot of what goes on in with KKCJ; opening night of the Feast of Tabernacles at the n

Hilsden (KKCJ) and Calev Myers are also affiliated with ICEJ (http://int.icej.org/news/headli ncitement%20)-The International Christian Embassy in Jerusalem which has 70 ch http://jewishisrael.ning.com/page/icej-envision-conferences-in-jerusalem-bring-envangelical-pastors sraeli messianic missionary leadership including Myers and Hilsden and Tel Aviv born Avi Mizrachi (Roi Congregation

Vatch ICEJ and KKCJ (http://jewishisrael.ning.com/video/icej-and-kkcj-promote-missionaries-and-m

Hilsden said "A sense of urgency came into my spirit that there is a force, primarily spiritual in natur alling us to have a special plan for Israel (http://www.charismanews.com/opinion/standing-with- o-stand-firm-with-israel) that reaches well into the future and culminating at the time when the Lord r

find this all rather confusing. I wrote a piece on Messianics that included Hilsden (http understandably-in-the-dna/%20). I received a gmail admonishing me that Hilsden is not a Messianic hat watches all media to have found my article and then me.

Hilsden has established parameters (http://www.kkcj.org/about/our-history) for the development of

a greater emphasis on the Jewish/Old Testament roots of our faith; a worship-style more suited to Jewish-Israe; terms Israelis could relate to and understand; a commitment to stand alongside the nation of Israel through pr and cooperation with other Messianic communities in Israel and abroad.

And then there was a concerted effort to raise up Messianic believers to join the leadership team for lave been planted.

When people feel it is their mission to save people and bring jc, they are very determined. We Jews 1 know, so we don't fall. Jewsforjudaism.org is good for info B"H

Reply

> **Menashe Dovid (מנשה דוד)** | **May 11, 2015 at 4:38 am**
> And this Blog too I hope!!
>
> Reply

Menashe's Blog

A reasoned Jewish response to ………read on!!!

JULY 9, 2015 BY MENASHE DOVID (מנשה דוד)

Follow the Money

Diane Weber Bederman

Many of you know that I was removed from StandWithUS advisory board because I merely asked for a review of one of our funders—ICEJ- the International Christian Embassy in Jerusalem. When I say that proselytizing is affecting the agenda of our Jewish organizations I say this from experience. Too many see ICEJ especially in Canada as a kind, gentle and innocuous Jew-loving organization.

In addition to reaffirming the halachic prohibition against interfaith worship, Chief Rabbis David Lau and Yitzhak Yosef have also endorsed a campaign by the rabbinic organization Derech Emuna which is reportedly concerned about the nature and evangelical message of ICEJ's vigil."
READ

(https://menashedovid1.files.wordpress.com/2015/07/stand-with-us.png)Follow the money is a catchphrase popularized by the 1976 drama-documentary motion picture "All The President's Men", which suggests a money trail or corruption scheme within high (often political) office. In an episode of "The Wire," Detective Lester Freamon uses the phrase when investigating the dealings of a Baltimore criminal gang to explain the political difficulty of investigating organized crime, saying:

"You follow drugs, you get drug addicts and drug dealers. But you start to follow the money, and you don't know where the f@#% it's gonna take you".

The weird effects of the term *follow the money* certainly seems to apply with respect to Diane Weber Bederman's enquiry for a review of one of the funders of the organization StandWithUs; the International Christian Embassy in Jerusalem (ICEJ). The weird effects of trying to follow the money also possibly opens up to the rational inquirer the world of doublespeak. Doublespeak with its love of Jews/ Israel and mutual respect promoted by the likes of StandWithUs, perh ' Kind of like the doublespeak of the left-wing BBC with their mantra that Islam is a religion of peace contrasted with the reality of bombs going off all over the place and hey presto: a piece of you here and a piece of you there, perhaps?

What is really important in the world of doublespeak is the ability to lie, whether knowingly or unconsciously, and to get away with it; and the ability to use lies and choose and shape facts selectively, blocking out those that don't fit an agenda or program.

(https://menashedovid1.files.wordpress.com/2015/07/stand-with-us-ii.png)

Presumably Kay Wilson's recent promotion by StandWithUs of her story fits with the agenda even though she may be a closet Christian posing as a supporter of Israel:

(https://menashedovid1.files.wordpress.com/2014/12/shoresh-tours-kw.png)Does it really matter if Jews who secretly believe in Jesus are allowed to represent Israel and Jews who do not want to believe in Jesus? Eta Kushner after her recent visit to Israel to investigate missionary activity writes:

Most Christian Zionist groups operating in Israel (for the most part composed of evangelicals), such as the International Christian Embassy in Jerusalem, Christians United for Israel, Bridges for Peace, International Christian Zionist Center, and many others, claim they don't proselytize. And they do not – directly.

Rather, they are aligned behind the scenes with groups that are aggressively proselytizing. If asked, many of these Christian Zionist groups will deny that they are trying to convert Jews to Christianity. Indeed, this is not their agenda. Their goal is to bring Jews to belief in Jesus, without which Jews cannot be "fulfilled." And they sincerely believe that this is not the same as conversion.

From our perspective, of course, the subtle distinction doesn't matter. However they word it, it shows a severe lack of respect for the Jewish religion when an outside faith sy ' n believes it knows what is best for us and what our true religion is supposed to be….

It would be bad enough if missionaries were successful due to their own efforts alone. Much worse is the fact that they are being aided by the Israeli government and some rabbis. JewishIsrael is replete with articles and videos about right-wing religious leaders, including Orthodox rabbis, who either participate in interfaith prayer services, unwittingly appear to promote a Christian agenda, and/or accept evangelical money with no parameters in place. This is despite the clear and widely accepted rulings from modern Torah authorities prohibiting interfaith theological encounters which blur the lines between religious faiths.

That the ICEJ *et al*, are funders of missionizing of Jews in Israel is no secret and is yet another example of doublespeak in action.

Perhaps Diane is just not playing the game correctly? After all so many accomplished and renowned rabbis have jumped on the **lets do the interfaith thing together band wagon** to much great financial success, so it must be OK….. right?

The bottom line of course is that it's not alright. As a Jew watching from the pews and as a parent, the fallout from such interfaith support of Israel and Jews is already catastrophic. At this stage in the game we see a gaping dissonance between the doublespeak of not proselytizing and in reality aggressively proselytizing of Christian organisations. Worst still some of our Jewish leaders choosing to remain silent, which is the same as consenting to the conversion of Jews. Sadly also that some of our Jewish leaders are more than happy to see the spiritual suicide of their fellow Jews for the sake of financial gain.

Its time for all Jews to make Havdalah using the correct criteria specified by the clear and widely accepted rulings from modern Torah authorities prohibiting interfaith theological encounters which blur the lines between religious faiths. In other words stop taking the money and do the right thing!!

This entry was posted in Uncategorized and tagged DIANE WEBER BEDERMAN, Eta Kushner, ICEJ, International Christian Embassy Jerusalem, Kay Wilson, StandWithUs. Bookmark the permalink.

REFUSED 217 Y(...) 12/31/09 ATL ...

7 Jahre BRD
1.1.2008 - 1.1.2015
Daniel 4 ENDE

Exodus 20.15 „Du sollst nicht stehlen"
Dr. Jürgen Bühler, Präsident der ICEJ

- 1.1.15 Anruf aus Jerusalem
- 24.1.15 Erkenntnis
- „Wort aus Jerusalem"
- israel.de Zeuge INFORMIERT

Antwort 9.3.2015

ISRAEL
WORD FROM JERUSALEM

REFUSED 217 Y(...) 12/31/09 ATL ...

UN Resolution 217
Offenbarung 2.17
Amos 9.9 Sacharja 9.9
Jesaja 8.18 - Hebräer 2

Ephraim GG Art 9.4 & 140 - 25.5.2015

16.07.2017

Zum 47. Geburtstag meiner Frau Senait eine Erinnerung an alle, **dass es das Recht des Vaters ist für die Erziehung der Kinder zu sorgen.**

Ausserdem eine ausführliche Legale und Rechtliche Erklärung meiner Menschenrechte und der Verpflichtung eines jeden Deutschen, Katholiken und Zeugen sofort zu Handeln.

Dieses Dokument wird in den nächsten Tagen zusammen mit den Schreiben an die Inquisition und den Israelischen Gerichtshof als Gesamte Info-Paket verfügbar sein.

Effination Now

Hier mal für Christen, Juden, Israeliten, Menschenrechtler, Atheisten, Politiker...

Und jeden der meine Frau kennt... inklusive meiner Kinder und meiner Mutter Renate Diebel und die liebe Lukas Gemeinde, des Mülheimer Verbandes die meine Kinder zur Gesetzlosigkeit erzogen haben und dafür von mir zur Rechenschaft gezogen werden. Der Blogartikel steht ja lange genug auf dieser Seite, wie der Rest auch.

Seit 2008 ist meine Meldedresse

Seelingstr 50 – Berlin

Leider habe ich dort Nichts zu melden und ich hatte immer wieder gesagt, jeder darf ja glauben was er will, aber am Ende zählt *das Gesetz* und die Torah des Vaters und wer in aller Welt ist für den Mist verantwortlich und zahlt den Schaden von bisher ca. 1,6 Milliarden Dollar?

Während meine Frau sehr gerne in diesem Sozial System für eine Scheibe Brot ihre Seele verkauft und dies nun lange genug bewiesen hat, würde ich die Ungeheuerlichkeiten und Lügen gegen meine Person und meinen Namen in Israel aufklären.

Es kann nicht angehen, dass der Typ der für die Lügen seit dem Jahr 2000 gegen mich verantwortlich ist an einer statt nun die Torah aus Zion heraus gibt, die Wort des Herrn aus Jerusalem in eine Lüge verwandelt, mich beleidigt, beschimpft und mir die Menschlichkeit abspricht, mich wegen meiner Frau verachtet und dann neben dem Premier Minister steht, nachdem auf die eklatante Schuld des deutschen Direktors der größten Pro-Israel Organisation auf sich geladen hat nd ihm nichts von der größten Biblischen Verheißung für das Jüdische Volk erzählt – weil es sein Freund Ulf ist, der "von Gott bestraft ist", weil er "Jesus abgelehnt hat".

In einer Email sagte ich zu meiner Frau... "ich lasse mir doch nicht von einem kleinen Sektenprediger aus Heidenheim, mein Zeugnis bei meinen jüdischen Freunden versauen..."

Das Gericht steht in Jerusalem...

Die Zeugen in Jerusalem sind aufgerufen Stellung zu nehmen. Inklusive Premier Minister Netanyahu (Ziomist), David Parsons (US- Bürger), Dr. Jürgen Bühler (BRD Bürger), Doron Schneider (Israeli)

1. die Torah aus Zion erging 1999 aus der ICEJ durch Ulf Diebel
2. das Wort aus Jerusalem wurde durch Ulf Diebel erstellt
3. Die Tochter Zion ist der Beweis der Allmacht Gottes aus Sacharija 9.9
4. Die Tochter Jerusalem wurde in der ICEJ dem Gott Israels geweiht
5. Am 25.5.2007 war die Nation Ephraim deklariert
6. vom 1.1.2008 – 1.1.2015 war ich unverschuldet abgeschnitten
7. vom 1.1.2015 – 25.5.2017 habe ich friedlich meine Rechte eingefordert
8. Die Welt verachtet mich
9. Ephraim ist Rechtskräftig und ich stell mich als Schlachtoper zur Verfügung, um endlich Frieden zu machen

Habe ich Jesus jetzt geehrt oder nicht?

Und was ist mit der Frau?

Ist dies nun einmal verstanden, dass die Angelegenheit NUR noch vom Papst und dem Israelischen Gerichtshof geklärt werden kann?

Das es sich um den Fall Diebel um einen Internationalen Zwischenfall von biblischem Ausmaß handelt?

Zum 50. am 25.5.2017 gilt Jesaja 50

So spricht der HERR:

Wo ist der <u>Scheidebrief</u> eurer Mutter, mit dem ich sie entlassen hätte? Oder <u>wer ist mein Gläubiger, dem ich euch verkauft hätte?</u> Siehe, ihr seid um **eurer Sünden willen verkauft**, und **eure Mutter** ist um <u>*eurer Abtrünnigkeit willen entlassen*</u>.

Warum kam ich und niemand war da? Warum rief ich und niemand antwortete? Ist mein Arm denn zu kurz, dass er nicht erlösen kann? **Oder habe ich keine Kraft, zu erretten?** Siehe, mit meinem Schelten mache ich das Meer trocken und die Wasserströme zur Wüste, dass ihre Fische vor Mangel an Wasser stinken und vor Durst sterben. Ich kleide den Himmel mit Dunkel und hülle ihn in Trauer.

Gott der HERR hat mir eine Zunge gegeben, wie sie Jünger haben, dass ich wisse, mit den Müden *zu rechter Zeit zu reden*. Er weckt mich alle Morgen; er weckt mir das Ohr, dass ich höre, wie Jünger hören. **Gott der HERR hat mir das Ohr geöffnet.** <u>Und ich bin nicht ungehorsam und weiche nicht zurück</u>.

Ich bot meinen Rücken dar denen, die mich schlugen, und meine Wangen denen, die mich rauften. Mein Angesicht verbarg ich nicht vor Schmach und Speichel. Aber Gott der HERR hilft mir, darum werde ich nicht zuschanden. *Darum hab ich mein Angesicht hart gemacht wie einen Kieselstein*; denn <u>ich weiß, dass ich nicht zuschanden werde.</u>

Er ist nahe, der mich gerecht spricht; wer will mit mir rechten? Lasst uns zusammen vortreten! Wer will mein Recht anfechten? Der komme her zu mir!

Siehe, Gott der HERR hilft mir; wer will mich verdammen? Siehe, sie alle werden wie ein Kleid zerfallen, Motten werden sie fressen. *Wer ist unter euch, der den HERRN fürchtet, der auf die Stimme seines Knechts hört?* Wer im Finstern wandelt und wem kein Licht scheint, der hoffe auf den Namen des HERRN und verlasse sich auf seinen Gott! Siehe, ihr alle, die ihr ein Feuer entfacht und Brandpfeile entzündet, geht hin in die Glut eures Feuers und in die Brandpfeile, die ihr angezündet habt! Das widerfährt euch von meiner Hand; in Schmerzen sollt ihr liegen.

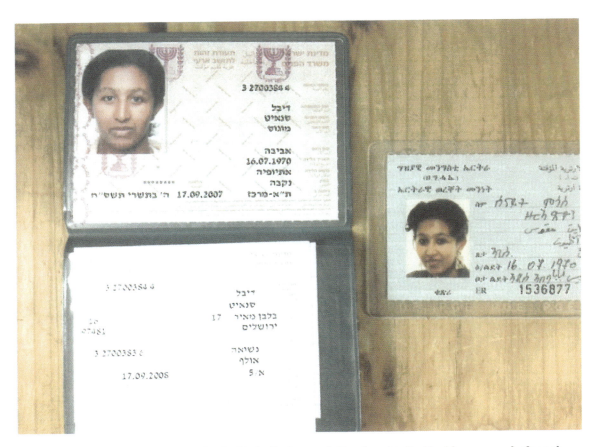

Eritrea, Orthodox, Deutsch, Israelisch, Katholisch – nach Torah geht die Nachkommenschaft nach dem Vater, der wegen seiner Frau und der gegebenen Gesetze von Staat und Kirche diskriminiert wird.

Nach meiner Ankunft am 1.1.2008 begannen 7 Jahre Hiob 2.9
Und seine Frau sprach zu ihm: Hältst du noch fest an deiner Frömmigkeit? **Fluche Gott und stirb!** Er aber sprach zu ihr: Du redest, wie die törichten Frauen reden. Haben wir Gutes empfangen von Gott und sollten das Böse nicht auch annehmen?
Nachdem am 1.1.2015 klar war, dass ich nach 7 Jahren zurück nach Zion muss, versuchte ich bis zum 25.5.2017 mit jedem Frieden zu machen.
2 Jahre und 144 Tage wurde mir von engsten Familienmitgliedern ein Gespräch verweigert und jedes Menschenrecht versagt. Viel schlimmer. Durch die Weigerung meiner Frau die Wahrheit zu sagen und sich für Ihre eigenen Kinder einzusetzen, sind unvorstellbare Probleme und Rechtsschwierigkeiten aufgetreten, die nur zusammen mit den Brüdern in Jerusalem hätten geklärt werden können, die aber jede Zusammenarbeit verweigerten und MILLIONEN Dollar für die persönlichen Projekte der Bühler Familie in der ICEJ aufwendeten.
Da es sich bei meinen Kindern um Heilige Nachkommen aus Jakob handelt, meine Frau jedoch eine vollkommen gespaltene Identität durch die wechselnden Identitäten von Afrika, BRD, Israel, USA, Orthodox, Katholisch, Pfingstlich, Ephraim und sich zu 100% gegen meine Person gewendet hat, hatte ich so lange wie es nur geht gehofft, dass Senait Diebel umkehrt und erkennt, welchen Schaden sie in MEINEM NAMEN verursacht hat.
Bis zum heutigen Geburtstag ist sie NICHT umgekehrt, sondern beschmutzt meinen Namen, den Namen meiner Väter, ist rebellisch, lieblos, kalt, emotional unfähig ein normaler Gespräch zu führen und verachtet die Gebote Gottes des Gottes Israels. Da wir seit dem 1.1.2008 in der BRD feststecken

und Senait Diebel unerlaubt eigene finanzielle Entscheidungen getroffen hat, Abhängigkeiten im JobCenter und sich nicht um die Familienangelegenheiten der Familie in Jerusalem gekümmert hat, ist eine untragbare Situation für mich als Ehemann und Vater entstanden, die durch die Priesterschaft nach der Ordnung Melchizedeks Friedlich gelöst werden sollte.

Am 25.5.5777 ist die Zeit der möglichen Umkehr abgelaufen.

Ich aber will nach dem HERRN ausschauen, will harren auf den Gott meines Heils; mein Gott wird mich erhören. **Freue dich nicht über mich, meine Feindin!** Denn wenn ich auch gefallen bin, so stehe ich doch wieder auf; wenn ich auch in der Finsternis sitze, so ist doch der HERR mein Licht. Den Zorn des HERRN will ich tragen — denn ich habe gegen ihn gesündigt —, bis *er meine Sache hinausführt und mir Recht verschafft*; er wird mich herausführen ans Licht; **ich werde mit Lust seine Gerechtigkeit schauen. Wenn meine *Feindin* das sieht**, wird Schamröte sie bedecken, sie, die zu mir sagt: *»Wo ist der HERR, dein Gott?«* Meine Augen werden es mit ansehen; nun wird sie zertreten werden wie Kot auf den Gassen.

Senait möchte eine Scheidung…

Die gibt es nicht, bevor die Sache nicht im Gericht geklärt wird.

Beit Din in Israel, dort wo die Kinder geboren sind.

WER EIN KREUZ SETZT WÄHLT ADOLF HITLER

Noch vor der Veröffentlichung des nachfolgenden Artikels erschien am **11.9.2017** in der FAZ die Aussage des Bundesjustizministers Heiko "Maas hält AfD-Wahlprogramm für verfassungswidrig". Man wirft der AfD Verstöße gegen die Religionsfreiheit vor. Mit den in diesem Artikel dargelegten rechtlichen und gesetzlichen Fakten wird die gesamte Diskussion über **Verfassung und freie Religionsausübung ad absurdum** geführt, aber auch ein rechtmäßiger, Gott gewollte Ausweg gegeben.

Am **10.9.2017** wurden in dem Video "Antisemitismus, Lukas Gemeinde Berlin & Sven Olaf Heckel CDU" Verfassungswidrige Diskriminierungen gegen die ungestörte Religionsausübung von CDU Regierungsmitarbeitern nachgewiesen. **Anti-Semitismus** und **Rassismus** stehen in unmittelbaren Zusammenhang mit dem Dogmatischen Christlichen Glauben Roms.

Artikel auf www.Ulf Diebel.Com

veröffentlicht en 11.9.2017 - 790 views en 13.9.2017

9.9.18 - Rosh HaShana

an 10.9.2018 wurde Heiko Maas der Artikel
+ Lebendmeldung
+ Final Settlement Urteil von 6.9.2018
+ Anweisung SPD Auf zulösen
+ Kopie Schreiben David De Rothschild
+ Zion 5777.com Flyer
+ 1$ Note
per Einschreiben zugestellt

9/11 → BRIEFE TREFFEN EIN
→ Horst Seehofer
→ Sahra Wagenknecht
→ Alice Weidel
→ Mathias Döpfner

12.9.2018 · Haushaltsitzung

13.9.2018   19.9.18 - Yom Kippur
→ Westfalen Blatt "Sektenbeauftragter Andreas Hahn"
↳ 29.8. - 13.9.2019 → O Befragung - Story von HÖRENSAGEN!

"Das Bundesverfassungsgericht *hat in **ständiger** Rechtsprechung* festgestellt, dass das Völkerrechtssubjekt „Deutsches Reich" nicht untergegangen und die Bundesrepublik Deutschland nicht sein Rechtsnachfolger, sondern mit ihm als Völkerrechtssubjekt identisch ist (BVerfGE 36, S. 1, 16; vgl. auch BVerfGE 77, S. 137, 155)." (https://www.bundestag.de/presse/hib/2015_06/-/380964) vom **30.6.2015**

Seit **1956 sind keine Wahlen Verfassungsmäßig** (http://www.zeit.de/1963/30/die-naechsten-wahlen-sind-ungueltig) – u.a. hier das Urteil des Verfassungsgerichtes vom 25.7.2012 (http://www.bundesverfassungsgericht.de/SharedDocs/Entscheidungen/DE/2012/07/fs20120725_2bvf000311.html)

Auszug: II. 1. § 6 Absatz 1 Satz 1 und Absatz 2a des Bundeswahlgesetzes in der Fassung des Neunzehnten Gesetzes zur Änderung des Bundeswahlgesetzes vom 25. November 2011 (Bundesgesetzblatt I Seite 2313) sind mit Artikel 21 Absatz 1 und Artikel 38 Absatz 1 Satz 1 des Grundgesetzes ***unvereinbar und nichtig.***

Die BRD wurde am 23.5.1949 mit der Verabschiedung des Grundgesetzes als neues Rechtskonstrukt gegründet, um die Nachfahren des Völkerrechtssubjektes "Deutsches Reich" in ein neues Bewusstsein und ein neue Verantwortung zu führen, wie es die Präambel des Grundgesetzes erklärt:

Im **Bewusstsein** seiner **Verantwortung *vor*** Gott und den Menschen, von dem Willen **beseelt**, als gleichberechtigtes Glied in einem vereinten Europa **dem Frieden der Welt**

zu dienen, hat sich das Deutsche Volk kraft seiner verfassungsgebenden Gewalt dieses Grundgesetz gegeben.

Das Grundgesetz beinhaltet die **freie** und **ungestörte** *Religionsausübung*, die zu der Würde eines jeden Menschen gehört.

Art. 1 (1) Die Würde des Menschen ist unantastbar. Sie zu achten und zu schützen ist **Verpflichtung** aller staatlichen Gewalt.

Art. 3 (3) **Niemand** darf wegen seines **Geschlechtes**, seiner **Abstammung**, seiner **Rasse**, seiner Sprache, seiner **Heimat** und **Herkunft**, seines **Glaubens**, seiner **religiösen oder politischen Anschauungen** benachteiligt oder bevorzugt werden. **Niemand** darf wegen seiner Behinderung benachteiligt werden.

Dieses Recht gilt ebenfalls für das Heilige Gottes Volk Israel, dessen Lebens- und Existenzrecht in den Heiligen Schriften der Bibel garantiert ist und Teil der Staatsräson der BRD ist.

> Und ihr sollt mir ein **Königreich** von **Priestern** und **ein heiliges Volk** sein. Das sind die Worte, die du den **Israeliten** sagen sollst. Mose kam und berief die Ältesten des Volks und legte ihnen alle diese Worte vor, die ihm der HERR geboten hatte. Exodus 19.6+7

> Ihr aber seid ein auserwähltes **Geschlecht**, ein **königliches Priestertum**, ein **heiliges Volk**, ein **Volk zum Eigentum**, dass ihr verkündigen sollt die Wohltaten dessen, der euch berufen hat aus der Finsternis in sein wunderbares Licht; die ihr einst **nicht sein Volk wart, nun aber Gottes Volk seid**, und einst nicht in Gnaden wart, nun aber in Gnaden seid. 1. Petrus 2.9+10

Sowohl die BRD, als auch der Vatikan, der Staat Israel, sowie sämtliche Siegermächte und neu entstandenen Nationen, haben sich mit der Charta der Menschenrechte und dem Zusammenschluss in den Vereinten Nationen, an die UN Resolution 181 vom 27.11.1947 gebunden, die eine Lösung der Jerusalemfrage und des Heiligen Landes Israel unter Berücksichtigung der Berechtigen Interessen aller Parteien anstrebte.

Die "beteiligten" Parteien zum 27.11.1947 waren:

Das am **11.2.1929** durch die Lateran Verträge entstandene **Königreich Vatikan Stadt**, dass seit dem 24.4.1870 in sämtlichen Fragen des Glaubens die unfehlbare Wahrheit beansprucht und gesetzlich festgelegt hat. Der 7. König der Vatikanstadt kam am **23.9.2011** als Abgesandter und Stellvertreter von Jesus Christus, dem gekreuzigten König der Juden, in den Bundestag, wurde von Bundestagspräsident Norbert Lambert als "Heiliger Vater" angesprochen und legte als höchste moralische Instanz auf Erden sein Anliegen vor, in dem er sagte:

Die Kultur in Europa ist die Begegnung zwischen **Jerusalem**, **Athen** und **Rom**, wo sich der Gott Glaube der Kinder Israels, die griechische Philosophie und das Gesetz Roms vermischen. Das Gesetz Roms ist mit dem Glauben der Kinder Israels und Jerusalem nicht vereinbar.

Das **Deutsche Reich**, welches **1945 nicht untergegangen ist**, ist seit dem **20.7.1933** an das Reichskonkordat zwischen dem Deutschen Reich und Rom gebunden. Da die BRD nunmehr mit dem *Völkerrechtssubjekt Deutsches Reich identisch ist*, gelten die Verträge zwischen Rom und dem römischen Katholiken, die vom Österreicher Adolf Hitler abgeschlossen wurden, für das gesamte Deutsche Volk fort.

FRANK WALTER STEINMEIER SPD

Josef

W-ULF

Volker Kauder CDU

Renate Künast Grüne

Ein Österreicher und Katholik schließt einen Vertrag mit Rom, der bis heute für das gesamte Deutsche Volk Gültigkeit besitzt.

Nach Art. 5 des Reichskonkordats (ein Konkordat zwischen der Kirche und einem Staat, wird nur mit Staaten mit einem Katholischen Führer/König/Regierung abgeschlossen) sind die Katholische Geistlichen den Staatsdienern des Deutschen Reiches gleichzustellen.

Der Katholische, Österreichische Führer hat das Deutsche Volk an den Götzendienst Rom gebunden, der durch die faschistische Natur der Religion (Macht über Leben und Tod, ohne Wahrheit) gerne mit den anderen faschistisch orientierten Religionsgruppen zusammen gegen das Heilige Volk Israel agiert.

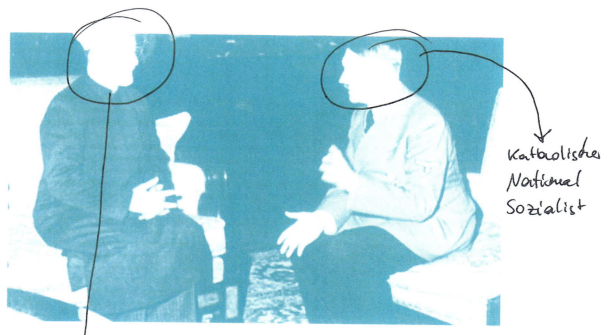

Katholischer National Sozialist

Der Großmufti von Jerusalem mit Adolf Hitler, der einen Bund mit dem Islam gegen Israel einging.

① *Mufti, Islam* 26.5.2014 – "GRÄUELBILD DER VERWÜSTUNG" *Statt.*

Während das Deutsche Volk für den Blinden gehorsam nach 72 Jahren Beendigung der Deutschen Katastrophe zu 100% "entnazifiziert" wurde und nun BRD "deutsch", ohne eigene Identität und verfassungsmäßig gewählter Regierung ist, räkeln sich die Religionsvertreter Roms und Mekkas in selbstsicherer Siegerpose.

6.12.2017
Tag
1290

20.1.2018
Tag
1335

Der römische Pontifex zu Besuch beim Großmufti in Jerusalem auf dem Tempelberg – Was macht der Stellvertreter von Jesus Christus, dem "König der Juden" an der Heiligsten Städte Israels und des Judentums?

Am **3.9.2015** lies die BRD Geschäftsführerin Angela Merkel verlautbaren, wie weit die gute Zusammenarbeit zwischen Rom und Islam funktioniert. Ab Minute 1:10 zusammenfassend: "Die EU hat eine Vielzahl an Islamischen Kämpfern, die in unseren Ländern wohnen ausgebildet und wir haben unseren Beitrag geleistet" – "Kann jemand einen Aufsatz **über Pfingsten** schreiben?"

Das Beste.... WER IST BIBELFEST? Na... wer ist das Wohl?

Am **27.2.2017** bekräftige Angela Merkel, dass Islamische Terroristen, syrische Flüchtlinge und jeder hier wohnende Afrikaner zu unserem Volk gehört. http://www.bild.de/politik/inland/angela-merkel/aufregung-um-merkel-zitat-volk-ist-wer-hier-lebt-50606620.bild.html

Wörtlich sagte Merkel dabei: „Die Zeit der deutschen Einheit, die Zeit als der Eiserne Vorhang fiel, die Zeit als Europa zusammmen gewachsen ist, war eine wunderbare Zeit. **Und deshalb gibt es auch keinerlei Rechtfertigung, dass sich kleine Gruppen aus unserer Gesellschaft anmaßen, zu definieren wer das Volk ist. Das Volk ist jeder**, der in **diesem Lande lebt.**"

Das **BRD Volk (das Personal),** ist *Identisch* mit dem Völkerrechtssubjekt **Deutsches Reich**, was nicht untergegangen ist.

Kommen wir neben Kirche und Staat, zur "dritten Partei", die mit unserem Schicksal auf alle Ewigkeit verbunden ist.

Israel, die Zionisten und das jüdische Volk

Einer der größten Momente in der Geschichte der Welt – Jerusalem kommt 1967 zurück in Jüdische Hand

(handwritten annotations:) Reuven Rivlin, President of ISRAEL

14.5.2018: THE LORD WILL RETURN TO Zion! Sacharja 8.3 & Benjamin Netanjahu

Am 68. Jahrestag des Grundgesetzes 23.5.2017 besucht US Präsident Donald Trump Jerusalem, welches am 24.5.2017 Jerusalem Tag im Jubeljahr 5777 feierte.

Zum Zeitpunkt der Gründung der Vereinten Nationen 1945, war es durch das Bretten Woods Abkommen festgelegt, dass sich die gesamte Welt an eine einzige, auf Schulden basierende Währung gründet.

(handwritten:) DANIEL 4.14

(handwritten:) Donald TRUMP take us to the Pope !

30.7.2018 R-Letter David Melech FRIEDMAN

Lukas 20.17 - Der Stein den die Bauleute verworfen haben, ist zum Eckstein geworden

Am 1.1.1914 öffnete das Büro der Federal Reserve Bank, die nach 2 Verträgen a 50 Jahre Laufzeit und einem Jahr Unterbrechung (John F. Kennedy hatte den Vertrag mit der FED nicht verlängert) am 31.12.2014 die gesamte Welt von einem Goldstandard in einen privat-rechtlich organisierten Schulden Standard hinüberführte. Seit dem 1.1.2015 befindet sich das Weltfinanzsystem in einem Schwebezustand, da unkontrolliert unvorstellbare Summen in ein Projekt Europa gepumpt werden, für das es keine Demokratische Legitimation gibt.

Durch die Existenz der Kirche Roms und eines Stellvertreters Christi, ist die gesamte Welt an eine Faschistische Römische Ordnung gebunden, die mit dem Heiligen Volk Israel nicht das Geringste zu tun hat.

Handwritten annotations:
- Offenbarung 1
- 27 Staats + Regierungschefs, 25+5 Personen
- +3: EZB, Komiss, Rat — EU
- DER MENSCHEN Soh
- DIE FRAU, Das Tier
- "DAS Bild"

Der König vom Vatikan garantiert für die "Rechtmäßigkeit" der Römischen Verträge, die vor 60 Jahren das Projekt Europa aus einem Wirtschaftskonglomerat heraus gestartet haben.

Die **Schuld** des Deutschen Volkes wurde durch die Gründung der BRD und den Anschluss an das Welt-Zentralbanksystem verknüpft. Das Schuldenerlass Jahr nach 3. Mose 25, wie von Gregor Gysi am 20.1.2017 im Bundestag gefordert, gibt es nur in Jerusalem.

Entwicklung Staatsverschuldung Deutschland

in Millionen Euro

2015
2.022.562 Mio. €
- 2,022562 Billionen €

Es spielt keine Rolle wer gewählt wird, die Schuld der Deutschen steigt und steigt, da römische Verträge nach römischen Recht einzuhalten sind. Besonders die neuen Staatsverträge bezüglich der EU sind unkündbar. Es handelt sich um privat-rechtlich organisierte Verträge, wobei sämtliche Nationen dieser Welt als Wirtschaft- und Firmeneinheiten behandelt werden und das Volk als Vermögen und Kollateral gegenüber der Bank verpfändet ist.

"HUMAN KAPITAL"
→ US Exe Order 13037

Jeder Personal Ausweisträger, der polizeilich gemeldet ist und in Wohn Haft genommen wurde, bekommt alle 4 Jahre die Möglichkeit seine Firmenleitung neu zu bestimmen. Zahlen lügen nicht – auch die nächste Geschäftsführung wird sämtliche Kosten aller staatlichen Programme auf JEDEN abwälzen und JEDEN tiefer in die Schulden treiben und alle religionsbedingten Gesetze der Kirche, die durch die Verträge mit Hitler immer noch gelten, für gültig halten.

Eudaristicu Mysterien *25.5.67 "ISRAEL"

Die staatliche, per Gesetz festgelegte Religion des Heiligen Römischen Reiches Deutscher Nationen, allgemein gültig für 1,25 Milliarden Katholiken davon 23 Millionen in der BRD.

Seit dem **25.5.2015** gibt es eine **legale** und *gesetzlich garantierte* Möglichkeit das Deutsche Fiasko zu beenden und eine vollkommene Entschuldung für das Deutsche Volk durchzuführen.

Art. 4 (1) Die Freiheit des Glaubens, des Gewissens und die **Freiheit des religiösen und weltanschaulichen Bekenntnisses** sind unverletzlich. (2) *Die ungestörte Religionsausübung wird gewährleistet.*

Art. 6 (1) Ehe und Familie stehen unter dem besonderen Schutze der staatlichen Ordnung.

Art. 9 (1) Alle Deutschen haben das Recht, Vereine und Gesellschaften zu bilden.
(3) Das Recht, zur Wahrung und Förderung der Arbeits- und Wirtschaftsbedingungen Vereinigungen zu bilden, ist für jedermann und für alle Berufe gewährleistet. **Abreden, die dieses Recht einschränken oder zu behindern suchen, sind nichtig, hierauf gerichtete Maßnahmen sind rechtswidrig.**

Am **25.5.2015 wurde Ephraim** als Gesellschaft zur Wahrung und Förderung der Arbeits- und Wirtschaftsbedingungen Israelitischer Priester nach der Ordnung Melchizedeks deklariert, um für die in der Torah und den Propheten genannten Nachkommen Abraham, Isaak und Jakobs ein ordentliches Erlassjahr durchzuführen.

Die Allgemeinen Geschäftsbedingungen Ephraim's ist die Torah von Mose und die Propheten Israels, der Verfassung für ganz Israel.

GG Art. 140 regelt Religionsgesellschaften, basierend auf der Verfassung vom 11.8.1919 und beinhaltet die alten Art. 136 – 141

(1) **Es besteht keine Staatskirche**.

(2) Die Freiheit der Vereinigung zu Religionsgesellschaften wird gewährleistet. Der Zusammenschluß von Religionsgesellschaften innerhalb ***des Reichsgebiets unterliegt keinen Beschränkungen.***

(3) Jede Religionsgesellschaft ordnet und verwaltet **ihre Angelegenheiten selbständig** innerhalb der Schranken des für alle geltenden Gesetzes. Sie verleiht ihre Ämter ohne Mitwirkung des Staates oder der bürgerlichen Gemeinde.

(4) **Religionsgesellschaften erwerben die Rechtsfähigkeit** nach den allgemeinen Vorschriften des bürgerlichen Rechtes.

Mt 18,20 Denn wo zwei oder drei versammelt sind in meinem Namen, da bin ich mitten unter ihnen.

Am **24.4.2017** vom Priester nach der Ordnung Melchizedek zum Haus Gottes der Erbengemeinschaft Jakobs geweiht. Das EPHI-Zentrum ist Lebens- Wohn- Glaubens und Arbeitsgemeinschaft auf 8000qm Industrie "Denk-mal!" Fläche in Iserlohn

Die ungestörte Religionsausübung von Ephraim ist es Frieden mit dem Jüdischen Volk in Jerusalem auf Grundlage von Jeremia 31 zu schließen und die Königsherrschaft über Israel aus der Hand des Pontifex Maximus Roms zurück nach Zion zu bringen.

Am 23.5.2017 wurde ein Eilantrag nach GG Art 17 an den Pontifex, Kanzlerin Merkel, Israel, USA und Russland geschickt.

Am 6.7.2017 hat Ephraim als Erstgeborener und Erbe Abrahams, Isaak und Jakobs bei der UNSECO Ansprüche auf das Grab Abrahams gestellt
JacekPurchla_Unesco

Am 24.8.2017 wurde per Einschreiben die theologische, finanzielle und politische Abrechnung bei den nachfolgenden Autoritäten angefordert:

777
7.7.17 – Putin/TRUMP   888
18.8.18 Putin
MERKEL

1.) Pontifex Maximus und König von Vatikanstadt Papst Franziskus

R-BRIEF
ou 24.8.2017

2.) EKD Ratsvorsitzenden Bedford Strohm ist mein "Kirchenoberhaupt".

3.) Israelischer Gerichtshof, Richterin Miriam Naor

4.) Bund Freier Pfingstgemeinden, Präses Justus bezüglich Dr. Jürgen Bühler, rechts im Bild

5.) Mülheimer Verband – Vize Präses Pache, Sven Olaf Heckel CDU ist Mitverantwortlich

6.) Rohr Chabad Center Rabbi Teichtal

Search this site   Search

HOME ABOUT PROJECTS EVENTS PUBLICATIONS MEDIA CONTACT

Home

Sven-Olaf Heckel

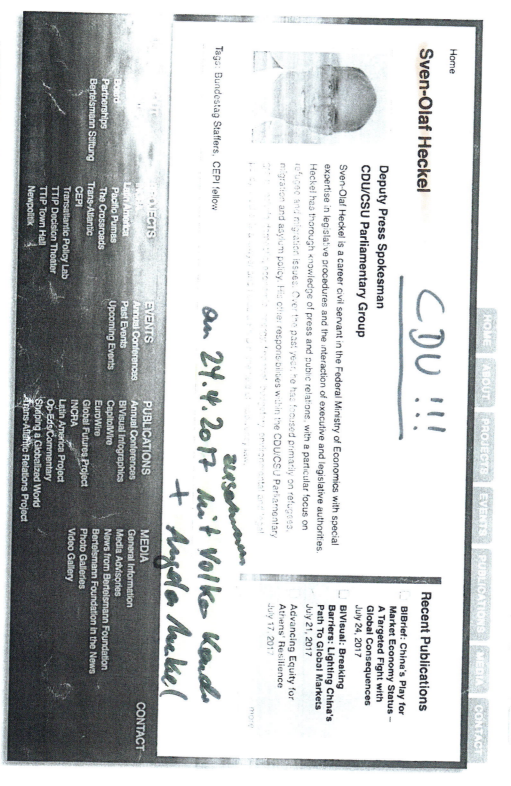

Deputy Press Spokesman
CDU/CSU Parliamentary Group

CDU !!!

Sven-Olaf Heckel is a career civil servant in the Federal Ministry of Economics with special expertise in legislative procedures and the interaction of executive and legislative authorities. Heckel has thorough knowledge of press and public relations, with a particular focus on refugee and migration issues. Over the past year, he has focused primarily on refugees, migration and asylum policy. His other responsibilities within the CDU/CSU Parliamentary

am 27.4.2017 mit Volke Kauder + Angela Merkel ([handwritten]

Tags: Bundestag Staffers, CEPI fellow

PROJECTS
Latin America
Pacific Pumas
The Crossroads
Trans-Atlantic
CEPI
Transatlantic Policy Lab
TTIP Decision Theater
TTIP Town Hall
Newpolitik

EVENTS
Annual Conferences
Past Events
Upcoming Events

PUBLICATIONS
Annual Conferences
BIVisual Infographics
CapitolWire
EuroWire
Global Futures Project
INCRA
Latin America Project
Op-Eds/Commentary
Shaping a Globalized World
Trans-Atlantic Relations Project

MEDIA
General Information
Media Advisories
News from Bertelsmann Foundation
Bertelsmann Foundation in the News
Photo Galleries
Video Gallery

CONTACT

Recent Publications

☐ **BIBrief: China's Play for Market Economy Status – A Targeted Fight with Global Consequences**
July 24, 2017

☐ **BIVisual: Breaking Barriers: Lighting China's Path To Global Markets**
July 21, 2017

☐ **Advancing Equity for Athens' Resilience**
July 17, 2017

more

ABOUT
Board
Partnerships
Bertelsmann Stiftung

So wie **jeder** andere Weltbürger auch, steht Ephraim unter den Gesetzen Roms und den Verschuldungen unserer Väter, die lange vor unserer Geburt stattgefunden haben und niemand von den heute Lebenden zu verantworten hat.

Jeder schwört auf die Bibel und es wäre in der heutigen Zeit eine Leichtigkeit 10 Leute zusammenzubringen, um die Zions Frage ein für alle Mal zu klären.

Man bedenke die Ersten Sätze des Lukas Evangeliums 2. Es begab sich aber zu der Zeit, dass **ein Gebot** von dem **Kaiser Augustus** ausging, dass **alle Welt geschätzt würde**. Und diese Schätzung war die allererste und geschah zur Zeit, da Quirinius Statthalter in **Syrien** war. Und jedermann ging, dass er sich schätzen ließe, ein jeglicher in seine Stadt.

Die endgültige Trennung zwischen **Israel und Judah** geschah schon etwa 734 vor Christus und die römische Herrschaft über das Heilige Gottes Volk währt nun volle **2017 Jahre!**

Roman Law & Religion

Jeremia 31:9

Ephraim & Israel - Greek NT

KING OF THE JEWS
CAPITAL OFFENSE
EXECUTION BY ROME

21 d

Zion
13 = 1980
33 = 2000
37 = 2004
40 = 2007

70

87

33

50 d

Jeremia 29:12

TORAH

2016/2017

Sanhedrin 37   Judah - Babylon Talmud

7*7
5777

Seit der Kreuzigung von Jesus aus Nazareth und der Zerstörung des Tempels in Jerusalem hat sich das Volk Israel in das "Christentum" entwickelt, die Jesus als König akzeptieren und Judah in das heutige "Judentum", die Jesus zu keiner Zeit akzeptiert haben.

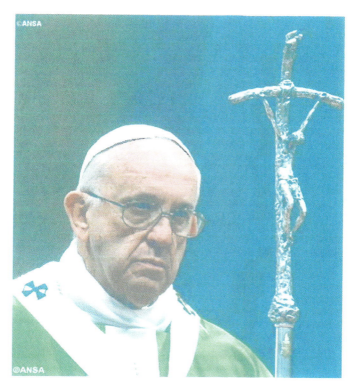

Mit der ersten römischen Wahl im Jahr 33, stellte sich die jüdische Leiterschaft unter die Regentschaft des römischen Pontifex Maximus, der jede Stimme, die sich gegen die absolute Autorität und Wahrheit des göttlichen Kaiser erhebt zum Schweigen brachte.

Das normale Folter und das Tötungsinstrument der Römer, um die Stimme des Individuums zum Schweigen zu bringen, war das Kreuz. Millionen Menschen fielen der Tötungsmaschine Roms zum Opfer, die erst mit der Beendigung des Holocaustes 1945 zu einem abrupten Ende kam.

Wem gehört das Grab Abraham, Isaak und Jakobs nach Torah und Propheten am 11.9.2017?

Die Religion Roms ist mit dem Gott Glauben der Kinder Israels unvereinbar.

Der Deutsche, Hitler Junge und ehemalige Wehrmachtsdeserteur Josef Ratzinger verleitet 1,25 Milliarden Menschen dazu Götzen anzubeten und die Himmelskönigin zu verehren und wird als "gewissenhafter Theologe" gefeiert. 23 Millionen katholische und 22 Millionen evangelische BRD Bürger stehen gleichzeitig unter den Verträgen des Völkerrechtssubjekts Deutsches Reich und dem Reichskonkordat und den Freiheiten des Grundgesetzes, die es jedem ermöglicht hätten in den Anweisungen der Bibel nachzuschauen, die von allen christlichen Religionsgemeinschaften als das ewige und unfehlbare Wort Gottes angesehen werden – wie auch z.b. Volker Kauder der CDU https://de.wikipedia.org/wiki/Volker_Kauder

Nach seinen Worten sind „Erbauung, Ermahnung und Trost"[5] Hauptsäulen des Evangelikalen. Des Weiteren sind für ihn zentral: **„die Bibel als Gottes unmittelbares Wort**, der Auftrag zur Mission, die große Bedeutung des Lebens Jesu für den eigenen Alltag, die Sündhaftigkeit des Menschen, die nur durch einen Gnadenakt Gottes und durch den Opfertod Jesu erlöst werden kann."[6]

Das unmittelbare Wort Gottes bezeugt:

ich bin Israels Vater und *Ephraim ist mein erstgeborener Sohn*. Jeremia 31.9

Hier ist das freibleibende Angebot von Ephraim bis zum 24.9.2017:

Es ist **das garantierte Recht** des BRD Personals einen von Gott eingesetzten Priester mit der Klärung der von Gott festgelegten Gesetze in der Torah und der Propheten zu beauftragen, um eine ordentliche Vergebung, Gefangenenfreilassung und die Rückgabe gestohlenen Landes einzufordern.

Wie funktioniert dies?

Der Personal Ausweisträger *darf auf keinen Fall an der Wahl teilnehmen*, da mit der Wahl die Hitler Gesetze und die Kirchengesetze wie oben beschrieben als gültig akzeptiert werden.

1.) Mache Dich Deiner Situation vollkommen bewusst: Du bist heute als juristische Person in der BRD gelistet und als Kollateral an die Bank verkauft.

2.) Registriere Dich einmalig beim Priester nach der Ordnung Melchizedeks als lebendiger Nachkommen Abraham, Isaak und Jakobs, bekenne Dich zu den unveräußerlichen Rechten des Volkes Israel und akzeptiere die Bibel als Deine persönlichen "Geschäftsbedingungen". Als bekennender Nachkommen von Abraham, Isaak und Jakob gehörst Du zum Volk Israel und hast das göttliche Recht nach 3. Mose 25 zum 50. Jahrestag eines Neuen Jerusalems ein totales Erlassjahr aller Deiner Sünden und Schulden durchzuführen.

Der Frieden in Jerusalem durch die Klärung der Jerusalemfrage und der Christus Frage mit Rom und dem Jüdischen Volk ist die ungestörte Religionsausübung der Erbengemeinschaft Jakobs in der BRD.

Als Mit-Erbe der Verheißungen an unsere Väter, gehörst Du zu der weltweiten Nation Ephraim, die ebenfalls Völkerrechtssubjekt ist.

Ihr aber seid ein **auserwähltes Geschlecht**, ein **königliches Priestertum**, ein **heiliges Volk**, ein Volk zum Eigentum, dass ihr verkündigen sollt die Wohltaten dessen, **der euch berufen hat aus der Finsternis in sein wunderbares Licht**; 10 die ihr *einst nicht sein Volk wart (seit dem 23.5.1949)*, nun **aber Gottes Volk** seid (Rechtskräftig & Rechtsfähig seit 25.5.5777) , und einst nicht in Gnaden wart, **nun aber in Gnaden seid**

3.) Schicke einen Brief an Heiko Maas und verlange die Unterstützung der Regierung, um die garantierten Rechte des Volkes Israel für Dich zu beanspruchen.

Wir arbeiten an einem vorgefertigten Brief, den jeder nur noch mit seiner Personal Ausweisnummer oder TIN versehen muss.

EU-Parlamentspräsident Schulz

"Trump ist eine Gefahr für die ganze Welt" ← VOR DER WAHL!

15.09.2016, 14:14 Uhr | rtr, dpa

(am 8.8.2016 erster Versuch eines Termins bei)
Trump
über Listed
Jay Solomon

Der republikanische US-Präsidentschaftskandidat Donald Trump bei einem Wahlkampfauftritt. (Quelle: AP/dpa)

EU-Parlamentspräsident Martin Schulz warnt davor, dass der RepublikanerDonald Trump tatsächlich ins Weiße Haus einziehen könnte. "Trump ist nicht nur für die EU ein Problem, sondern für die ganze Welt", sagte Schulz in einem Interview mit dem Nachrichtenmagazin "Der Spiegel".

"Wenn im Weißen Haus ein Mann sitzt, der damit kokettiert, dass er keine Ahnung hat und Fachwissen als elitären Quatsch bezeichnet, ist ein kritischer Punkt erreicht", sagte der **SPD-Politiker** weiter. → *Internationaal Sozialistische Freuetdao die EU + katholik!*

Dann sitze ein offenbar verantwortungsloser Mann an einer Stelle, wo ein Höchstmaß an Verantwortungsbewusstsein benötigt werde. "Meine Sorge ist, dass **er Nachahmer** auch in Europa beflügeln könnte", so Schulz. "Ich wünsche mir deshalb, dass Hillary Clinton gewinnt." *UCJ Dieb! Verräter!*

Die Demokratin Clinton und Trump treten Anfang November gegeneinander an. In Umfragen liegen beide Kandidaten derzeit eng beieinander.

Blut-und-Boden-Rhetorik

Aber auch auf **das eigene Haus** blickt Schulz mit Sorge. "Eine zunehmende Zahl von Menschen erklärt für falsch, was in den letzten Jahrzehnten in Europa erreicht wurde. **Sie wollen zurück zum Nationalstaat**", beklagte Schulz. → *2 Mio Flüchtlinge sind SUPER! :)*

"Dahinter steckt manchmal sogar eine Blut-und-Boden-Rhetorik, die mich stark an die

→ *AJC, Deidre Berger, Daniel HARRIS "Deep State"*

Martin Schulz (SPD) hätte es nicht für möglich gehalten, wie Trump Politik betreibt.   © dpa

💬 108   f   ✉   🐦   8+   ✉   🔖   Aktualisiert: 03.08.17 - 14:39   238.2017
ISERLOHN
24.8.2017
→ R-BRIEFE
Raus !

← Pol

„BIN BESSER ALS FRAU MERKEL"

„Risiko für die ganze Welt": So will Schulz Trump in die Schranken weisen

SPD-Kanzlerkandidat Schulz glaubt, er könne besser mit Trump umgehen als Merkel. „Er braucht klare Ansagen", sagt er - und erklärt, für wie gefährlich er den US-Präsidenten hält.

SPD-Kanzlerkandidat Martin Schulz sieht den US-Präsidenten Donald Trump als „Risiko für sein Land und die ganze Welt". Dem Nachrichtenmagazin *Der Spiegel* sagte er: „Trump glaubt, Politik sei eine Boxbude." Ihm sei klar gewesen, dass die weihevolle Atmosphäre des Weißen Hauses Trump nicht zivilisieren würde. „Aber der gnadenlose Nepotismus, mit dem Trump Politik macht, indem er sich und seine Familie über das Gesetz stellt - den hätte ich nicht für möglich gehalten."

↳ übliches Dinger der SPD Gottloser Anklage ohne Beleg oder Beweis !

Tages-Anzeiger

Trump, die Gefahr für den Weltfrieden

Bob Corker, republikanischer Senator und einstiger Trump-Unterstützer, spricht aus, was viele denken. Der Präsident riskiere die USA «auf den Weg in den Dritten Weltkrieg» zu führen.

«Wählt Trump» war einmal: Trump, damals noch Präsidentschaftskandidat, und Bob Corker bei einer Wahlveranstaltung im Juli 2016. Foto: Joshua Roberts (Reuters)

Martin Kilian
Korrespondent
@tagesanzeiger Washington 09.10.2017

Das nukleare Fieber steigt

Analyse Der Friedensnobelpreis für die Anti-Atom-Kampagne ändert nichts: Die Bombe ist in der Welt. Nur US-Präsident Trump ignoriert die Lehren der Geschichte. Mehr...
Stefan Kornelius.

«Ruhe vor dem Sturm»

Donald Trump verwirrt Freund und Feind: Bei einem Treffen mit Militärs machte er eine dunkle Andeutung. Mehr...
Vincenzo Capodici.

«Trumponomics» in 7 Grafiken

Mehr Jobs, weniger Handelsdefizit: Kann Trump seine Wirtschaftsversprechen halten? Der Vergleich mit seinem Vorgänger Obama zeigt es. Mehr...
Yannick Wiget, Marc Fehr.

Die Redaktion auf Twitter

Stets informiert und aktuell. Folgen Sie uns auf dem Kurznachrichtendienst.

In Donald Trumps weissem Tollhaus, wo der Boss nahezu täglich an die Decke geht und rachsüchtig gegen Kritiker keilt, manifestiert sich die grösste Furcht der amerikanischen Gründerväter: Dass Männer «mit bösartigen Absichten», so James Madison, an die Macht gelangten und das amerikanische Projekt ruinierten.

Am Wochenende und bereits zuvor erlebte die Nation einmal mehr, wie brüchig die Psyche ihres Präsidenten ist. Der staatliche Betrieb scheint nur noch zu funktionieren, weil ein Aufsichtsrat von Generälen dem Topmanager auf die Finger schaut. Trump mochte am Samstag mal wieder Kriegsdrohungen gegen Nordkorea ausstossen und am Tag zuvor umgeben von Kommandeuren der US-Streitkräfte sogar von «der Ruhe vor dem Sturm» faseln, ohne dass ersichtlich war, was der Nostradamus aus New York damit meinte.

Corker war einer der ersten

Nicht Kim Jong-un aber nagte am Präsidenten, sondern Senator Bob Corker. Der Republikaner aus Tennessee hatte Trump während des Wahlkampfs als einer der ersten Establishment-Republikaner unterstützt, niemand wäre überrascht gewesen, wenn Trump ihn zum Aussenminister gemacht hätte. Immerhin ist Corker Vorsitzender des aussenpolitischen Ausschusses im Senat und dazu ein Politico mit Augenmass und Gespür für das Machbare. Was immer den Senator verführt hatte, die Nähe Donald Trumps zu suchen: Es rentierte sich nicht, und je mehr Trump seinen durchgeknallten Stil zelebrierte, desto zügiger distanzierte sich Corker von ihm. Nach Trumps beschämenden Kommentaren zu den rassistischen Vorfällen in Charlottesville im August bescheinigte Corker dem Präsidenten, er habe «weder die Stabilität noch die Kompetenz demonstriert, die er braucht, um erfolgreich zu sein».

Der Vorsitzende des
aussenpolitischen Ausschusses
im Senat, ein mächtiger
Republikaner, twittert eine

5.3.2018

Shalom Dr. Jürgen Bühler,
Präsident der Internationalen Christlichen Botschaft

Rachel Imeinu 20
Jerusalem

Israel

Vom 14.5.1948 – 14.5.2018 sind 70 Jahre Israel komplett und exakt 25567 Tage seit der Gründung des jüdischen Staates vergangen. Der erstgeborene aus den Toten und treue Zeuge in Jerusalem wird am zweiten Passah Tag als „Eucharisticum Mysterium" 25.5.67 geboren.

Vom 25.5.67 bis zum 25567. Tag Israels ist der Erstgeborene am 25.5.1997 30 Jahre alt, 33 am 25.5.2000 und ist Ephraim in der Internationalen Christlichen Botschaft und veröffentlich die in Jesaja 2,3 und Micha 4,2 erwähnte Torah aus Zion und das Wort aus Jerusalem der ICEJ.

Zum 40. am 25.5.2007 verläßt der erstgeborene aus den Toten den Ölberg und lässt zwei sehr enge Freunde der Familie zurück. Die Zwei Zeugen Dr. Jürgen Bühler und Doron Schneider.

Am 47, dem 25.5.2014 wurde Ephraim schon von einem der beiden Zeugen verraten und durchlebt 7 Jahre Hiob und Daniel 4. Der Baum in der Mitte der Erde, aufgebaut auf der Torah, der bis an die Enden der Welt sichtbar war, ist abgeschnitten. Wie schon Lukas 22.22 sagt. Der Mensch muss gehen, wie es für ihn bestimmt ist, aber wehe dem Mann, der ihn verrät.

Du bist der Verräter Jürgen, der seit dem 26.5.2014 für 1335 Tage bis zum 20.1.2018 integraler Bestandteil des Gräulbild der Verwüstung ist, von dem Daniel 11 spricht. Du verehrst den Gott der Festungen und hast als einziger „Präsident" Tausende in die Wüste und den inneren Raum geführt und zu einem falschen Gott gebet (siehe Endzeitreden Jesus) und das Gesetz Israels in krimineller Weise verletzt (Anti-Mission, Menschenrechte, Urheberrechtsverletzungen, Torah & Worte von Jesus) und hast auch die Warnungen der beiden Obersten Rabbiner in Israel zum Laubhüttenfest 2015 nicht beachtet, welche die Internationale Christliche Botschaft als „Geistlich gefährlich für Juden" einstuft und dringend rät, von der Veranstaltung fern zu halten.

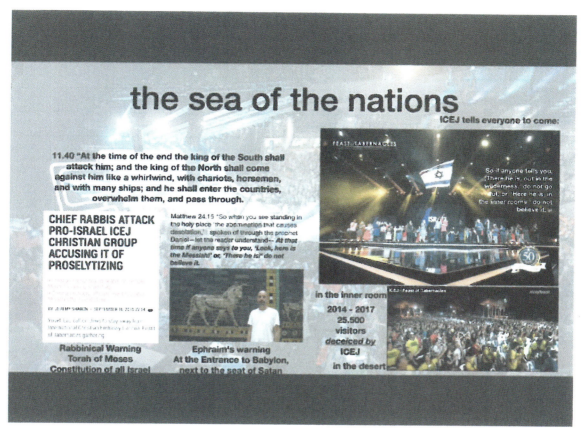

Weder auf die Jüdische Leiterschaft, noch auf Deinen Bruder Ulf Diebel hast du gehört, sondern hast selbstständig und bewusst das Gesetz gebrochen und um Deines eigenen Vorteils Willen, systematisch eine eigene Religion erfunden, den „Christlichen Zionismus" aus dem Heim der Heiden, Heidenheim.

Am 20.2.2018 habe ich am 111 Geburtstag meines Opas Jakob Michael Jay Solomon in Berlin getroffen und ihm alles erzählt. Michael wurde am 20.1.2018 – 80 und ist „der" Michael aus Daniel 10-12 und einer meiner Partner in DreamStream seit 2006, zusammen mit Scott Diffenderfer, der das Hebrew Roots Network hochgezogen hat. Da Du Juden und Hebräer nicht wirklich leiden kannst, die Torah sowieso nicht, sind Dir die Auswirkungen Deiner Deutschen Israel Theologie in den USA nicht bewusst. Du denkst ja wirklich, dass Du „Jesus" ehrst, merkst aber nicht mehr, dass Du nachdem Du mich verachtet hast, für 18 Jahre in eine falsche Richtung gelaufen bist, von der Du nicht mehr umkehren kannst.

Seit Deinem Verrat im Juli 2011 und der Veröffentlichung des Theologischen Meisterstückes von Sektenprediger Malcolm Hedding „the Ephraim Fable" im August 2011 im Wort aus Jerusalem betreibt Michael truli.com und hat schon mal alle US Evangelikalen vertraglich an sich gebunden.

Am 26.2.2018 habe ich mich bei Deinem Freund Ronald Lauder vom Weltjüdischen Kongress mit Kopie an Michael Jay Solomon als der zweite Zeuge vorgestellt und um eine schonungslose Aufklärung der Machenschaften der ICEJ und der Pfingstbewegung angefordert. Du stehst im Zentrum der Aufmerksamkeit… drei Jahre durchgehend wissentlich jeden belügen ist ne krasse Sache.

1335 days Desolation

from Rosh Ha Shana 2014 to 31.1.2018 Ronald Lauder is
ONE of the two witnesses, for Judah and Moses
ULF is the ONE for Ephraim and Jesus

Leif Wellerop

Michael Utterback

Susan Michael

Jürgen Bühler

Jerusalem Feast of Tabernacles 2014 & the Germans

Who is King over Jerusalem?
Acts 1 - 40 years + Daniel 4 - 7 years = 47 + 1335 days

Ihr seit gemeingefährlich und Du Jürgen, bist der Luschen Hirte aus Sacharija 11 und musst aus dem Verkehr gezogen werden.

Und ich schreib Dir noch... Denk daran.. DU bist Präsident der Internationalen Christlichen Botschaft... das wird ziemliches Aufsehen erregen, wenn ALLES rauskommt, was DU getan hast, um Dich in Namen Jesus Christus und Israel zu bereichern. Mir war ja alles genommen worden, was hätte ich Dich belügen sollen? Ich wollte Dir ja schon Passah 2013 in Israel alles erzählen, aber schon da war es zu spät für Dich.

Am 25.5.2007 warst Du der einzige, der unter allen Gästen in Jerusalem der mich bezichtigte „Jesus nicht genug geehrt zu haben". Bis zum 1.1.2015 sind es 7 Jahre, 7 Monate und 7 Tage.

Wie an dem 9.3.2015 Statement von Dir ersichtlich ist, hast Du Jesus geehrt, indem Du mich im wahrsten Sinne des Wortes getötet hast. Vom 1.1.1998 – 1.1.2018 hast Du Dir über einen Zeitraum von 20 Jahren das angeeignet, was ich durch die mir verliehene Gnade der frühen Geburt in Jerusalem erschaffen habe. Du bist derzeit der große Held und ich der total Abschaum in den Augen der Gesellschaft. Du bist reich und mächtig, ich arm und schwach.

Du allerdings hast gelogen und ich die Wahrheit erzählt, die am Ende immer Siegt und die wahre Freiheit bringt.

In exakte Zeitabschnitten von 3+7+7+3 Jahren lässt sich dies Anhand von Dokumenten, Zeitstempeln und schriftlichen Aussagen zu 100% beweisen.

Weil Du Dich weder an das Wort Gottes, noch das gültige und geltende Gesetz in der BRD und in

Israel gehalten hast und sich sowohl mein, als auch Dein Lebens Zeugnis von Geburt an nachverfolgen lässt, hat es wie in den Propheten z.B. Jesaja 49-53, oder Hesekiel 3-11 vorhergesagt, nur drei Jahre gedauert, bis ich alles zusammen hatte.

Du hattest mich am 1.1.2015 angerufen und nach Deiner schriftlichen Aussage vom 9.3.2015 und der Deklaration von Ephraim am 25.5.15 ist mit dem Bilanzstichtag und Geschäftsjahresabschluss 31.12.2017 meine Zeugenschaft und Arbeit abgeschlossen.

Du bist hiermit von mir, ULF DIEBEL aufgefordert Rede und Antwort zu stehen und Deinen Job als Präsident der einflussreichsten Christlich-Zionistischen Organisation der Welt, der seit 1980 operierenden Internationalen Christlichen Botschaft in Jerusalem zu erledigen.

the „Kings" in Zion

State of Israel President of Israel (and Prime Minister) - the King of the South // *the House of Judah*
Christian Zionist - „New Testament" President of the International Christian Embassy - the King of the North // *the House of Israel*
Jewish Zionist - „Torah and Prophets" President of the World Jewish Congress - Ronald Lauder ONE witness „Zach. 4.14" & Rev. 11

Es sind bis 24.8.2017 knapp $1,65 Milliarden Schaden entstanden, $800m alleine bei DreamStream, weil es mir unmöglich war, gegen die von Dir weltweit verbreiten Lügen anzugehen, die mittlerweile das gesamte Internet und jeden verwirrten Geist erreicht haben.

1.1.2015 – 1.1.2018 hast Du bewiesen, dass Du mich, obwohl ich lebe, dennoch weiterhin für tot hälst und diesen Zustand weiter aufrecht erhalten möchtest, hast aber in der Idea am 10.10.2017 heraus posaunt, dass Du Jesus bald zurück erwartest, um seine Herrschaft in Jerusalem anzutreten.

Meine Herrschaft, nicht die von Jürgen, „ordinierter Minister" der Lügensekte aus Heidenheim. Ich weis es wird sehr hart für Dich werden, vielleicht fällst Du ja auch, wenn Du diese Zeilen liest tot um.

Beit Goyim - Heidenheim

1.24 He shall enter peaceably, even into the richest places of the province; and he shall do what his fathers have not done, nor his forefathers: he shall disperse among them the plunder, spoil, and riches; and he shall devise his plans against the strongholds, but only for a time.

- The pride and honor of the German Missionary Group „Heidenheimer Volksmission", started by Jürgens Father Albert (Wehrmacht Soldier) 1954 - to bring one of their own, from the position of a sectarian-fringe group within German Christianity into the Center of the World 2011 as accepted member of the Christian Community, without proper Education, or business skills, as an International Recognized Minister of the largest Christian Zionist Organisation amongst the most influential politicians and church leaders is HUGE

- In the current English Wikipedia Entry of the ICEJ - an organization of 37 years only the personal Story of Jürgen Bühler can be read in the article, while the German entry details the great work and current leadership structure

- 2008 - 2011 - 2017 - all individuals from the ICEJ, who personally damaged the copyrights, trademarks, property and social standing, Malcolm Hedding, David Parsons, Doron Schneider, Gottfried Bühler, built a multi-million dollar donation machine on the Name "Jesus Christ", but on the destruction of a whole people Ephraim

The Ephraim Fable Deal between Malcolm and Jürgen seals the fate of Ulf Diebel - 24.12.2011 in Jerusalem - The Triune God Jesus is alive - Ephraim the son is dead

Ephraim, den es in Deiner Theologie ja nicht gibt, weil das Wort Gottes für Dich ja nicht gilt, ist der verheißene Sohn aus Joseph und der tatsächliche Messias, der als MENSCH das Wort Gottes bestätigen kann. Dein Glaube entmenschlicht die Menschen, die im Antlitz Gottes geschaffen sind. Die Juden zuerst, die Heiden allesamt.

Die Juden gibt es, Jerusalem gibt es, den Staat Israel gibt es und Donald Trump wird nicht locker lassen, bis der Stein, den die Bauleute verworfen haben an die Oberfläche tritt.

Und natürlich gibt es auch Ephraim, wie es ja in der Torah, dem Buch der Wahrheit klar aufgeschrieben ist und auch von Dir nicht überlesen werden kann.

In Apostelgeschichte 1 ist „dieser Jesus" nicht der Gott der Festungen, den Du verehrst, sondern Dein Bruder Ulf Diebel *25.5.67, der seit dem 25.5.15 als Priester nach der Ordnung Melchizedek unter dem Schutz des GG Art. 4, 9 & 140 unterwegs ist, weil Yael Eden *21.11.2004 der in Jesaja 22.22 und Offenbarung 3.7 genannte „Schlüssel Davids" ist, die Kinder des Immanuel aus Jesaja 8.18 und Hebräer 2.

Ziemlich lächerlich...

Der Tag des Herrn (25567) ist Finsternis und nicht Licht.

Da die Welt nur sehen kann, was ihnen vorgestellt wird, sind folgende Personen wegen Deiner falsch Aussagen und Verschleierungen blind und es muss ihnen gesagt werden, wer sieht und tatsächlich im Namen Gottes spricht.

·1.) Papst Franziskus, der als Oberster Jesuit die Gesetze der Kirche nach den Sternen ausgerichtet hat und es nur einen einzigen Erstgeborenen aus den Toten geben kann, der als Mensch alle in dem Buch der Offenbarung beschriebenen Bilder erklären kann.

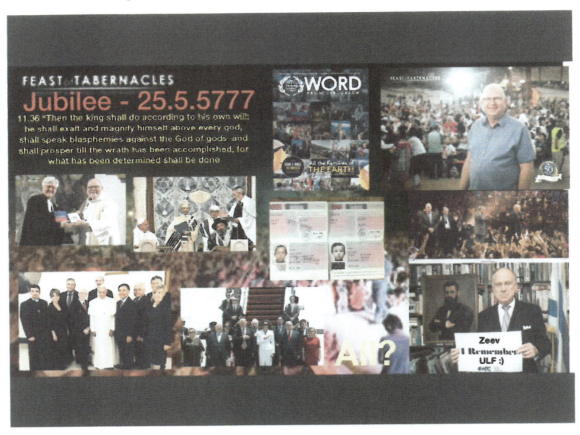

Da der Papst am 25.5.67 das Gesetz Eucharisticum Mysterium als das Zentrum der gesamten Kirche festgelegt hat und das mein Geburtsdatum ist, ist dies mein Erstgeburtsrecht als Erbe. Und ich erfülle sämtliche anderen Kirchengesetze ebenfalls und hatte auch schon der Inquisition geschrieben, Kardinal Müller. Am 24.8.2017 dem Pontifex Maximus und alles per Einschreiben.

Off. 19 nennt drei Namen. Einen der geschrieben ist, den niemand kennt, ausser nur er selbst; dies ist der Geburtsname Ulf Diebel. Das Wort Gottes (Fleisch geworden nach Torah & Propheten). Und an der Hüfte Jakobs eine dicke Narbe geschrieben, die am 24.4.1975 entstand und mich als König aller Könige ausweist.

2.) Ronald Lauder, Binjamin Netanjahu und Reuven Rivlin.
Wie am 23.12.2016 in der UN zur Resolution 2334 ersichtlich war, gibt es für den Botschafter Israels Dany Dalon in der UN nur ein Wort Gottes – den Tenach, der kein Neues Testament enthält, sondern ausschließlich die Torah, die Propheten und die Schriften, die besagen das Ephraim der Pfeil in der Hand von Judah ist. Siehe Sacharija 9.9-13

Nach dem Treffen mit Michael sind wir direkt schon mal bei einer der Aussernstellen vorbeigegangen, Berlin 21.2.2018

Die Tochter Jerusalem ist Naomi Esther, die am 5.7.1999 in Jerusalem geboren wurde und im Garten von Rachel Imeinu 20 dem Gott Israels geweiht wurde, die natürlich ein Anrecht hat in Israel zu leben, genauso wie Yael Eden, die direkt im Haus geboren wurde. Die Kinder sind Teil der Familie der ICEJ, Israel und Jerusalem und sind wegen Deines Verrats den schlimmsten Diskriminierungen und Armut in Berlin ausgesetzt.

Nach Jesaja 4 sind unsere Namen zum Leben in Jerusalem aufgeschrieben (siehe Geburtsurkunden in Hebräisch) und wir sind nach 2000 Jahren Zerstreuung und Zerstörung genauso wie jerusalem Heilig für den Herrn Zebaoth. David Parsons hat dem Richter Israels auf die Backe geschlagen und Du kennst das ja von 1. Könige 22 und der Paulus Story.

Was erhebt sich David Parsons und schlägt einen Mitknecht vor den Augen von Doron Schneider? Ich will sofort den „Caesar" sprechen. Und Du bist gesetzlich gezwungen diese Anzeige sofort zu bearbeiten, Herr Präsident Onkel Jogi.

Setzte Dich sofort mit den drei Dir persönlich bekannten Personen in Deiner Funktion im Amt als Präsident der Internationalen Christlichen Botschaft in Verbindung und sage Ihnen, dass Ephraim gefunden wurde.

Ronald Lauder hat schon meine Präsi bekommen, es ist also nicht mehr so schlimm für Dich, er sollte eh alles wissen.

3.) Susan Michael
Donald Trump hatte bei der ICEJ unterschrieben und kann ruck zuck informiert werden, dass der Sohn aus Jesaja 9.5-7 den er zu Weihnachten zitiert hat, schon seit Monaten versucht die

Jerusalemfrage zu klären, die mit der Klärung der Verhältnisse in der BRD zusammenhängen und mit Deiner weltweit verteilten Pfingstverwirrung, die über Michael Jay Solomon in wenigen Tagen aufgeklärt werden könnte – Hollywood Style, nach ein paar Tagen wüsste es jeder.

Michael & 111 year Jakob

- Michael *20.1.1938
  - Hollywood Entertainment Guru – "Wizard of Oz"
  - Since 2006 in business with Ulf
  - Michael of Daniel 12, turned 80 on day 1335 since abomination of desolation
- Jakob *20.2.1907
  - 111 years on 20.2.2018
- Ulf *25.5.67
  - Ephraim, Israelite Priest of the Order of Melchizedek
  - The tree of Daniel 4 - 7y   1.1.2008 - 1.1.2015
  - Daniel 10 = 21 years of Ulf
  - Daniel 11 = The story of the King

Spiegel 24.2.2018 - You Know nothing, if you do not know Michael

4.) Senait und die Kids

Senait ist die Frau Hiobs, die Gott und mich verflucht hat und gemeinsam mit Deiner Frau Vesna, der Isebel der Offenbarung und singenden falschen Prophetin an Deiner Seite, es unmöglich gemacht hat, normal über meine eigenen Kinder zu reden, die Zeugen des Vaters sind. Da Senait aus Afrika kommt, hat sie meine deutschen Geburtsrechte und Menschrechte verletzt und in straffällig Weise Geschäfte in meinem Namen abgeschlossen, da sie ja auch von Dir immer eine Bestätigung bekommen haben, ich sei „verrückt". Dem ist natürlich nicht so, ihr seit einfach nur total Gesetzlos geworden und handelt nach Gutdünken, da ihr ja fest glaubt „frei von dem Gesetz" zu sein, habt ihr alle heutigen gültigen Gesetze gebrochen, weil die Euch einfach nicht bekannt sind. Es geht um die Ehre und den Namen meiner Familie ULF DIEBEL und nicht um die eines äthipischen Flüchtlingkindes, dass den Bund der Ehe gebrochen hat und mit Männern wie Dir öffentlich Hurerei betrieben hat, die Heilige Schrift und besonders Epheser 5 sind da ziemlich eindeutig. Unzählige Fremde Männer mit fremden Namen, wie BÜHLER; AIDOO; HABTU etc. sind in mein Haus gekommen und haben mit ihr gehurt und meinen Kindern mit meinem Namen erzählt, dass der Name DIEBEL an der Tür nichts mehr gilt.

In Micha 4 findest du die Erklärung, wie das Königtum wegen Naomi Esther wieder zurück in meine Hand gerät. In Micha 7 liest Du von Senait und meinen tollen Freunden. Die Feinde eines Mannes sind seine eigenen Hausgenossen.

Du hast Dich in mein Haus eingeschlichen und die Vorbild Rolle eines Vaters übernommen, der es „richtig" macht, indem Du sowohl der Gemeinde, meiner Frau und bei jeder Gelegenheit auch mir bezeugt hast, dass Ulf Diebel „als Ungläubiger" behandelt werden muss, weil er „sich über Jesus erhoben hat" und „es noch schlimmer werden muss", bis ich „die Herrlichkeit des Sohnes" anerkenne.

Nan nennt so etwas geistige Manipulation, die darauf abzielt das Opfer gefügig zu machen, dass sich dem Willen des Täters beugen soll. Harvey Weinstein nutzt seine Manipulation um an Frauen zu gelangen, Jürgen Bühler nutzt seine Manipulation, um an willige Konvertiten zu gelangen, die den 10. Teil ihres Einkommens an „Jesus Christus" als Opfer abführen – zufälliger Weise aber nicht an Jesus, sondern immer wieder an jedem Sonntag an den Lokalen Sektenführer – um seinen hoch geachteten Lebensstil als „Präsident" führen zu können.

Das gesamte Evangelium des Sohnes Gottes steht kurz in Jesaja 7 + 8 beschrieben und ist die gute Botschaft, das Gott am Ende der Tage (Und der Tag 1335 aus Daniel 12.12 war tatsächlich der letzte Tag) seinen Sohn Ephraim schickt, den verheißenen Erben, gegen den es nach Galater 3 kein Gesetz gibt. Er ist einfach da und bestätigt das Gesetz und den Jürgen Bühler als Lügner.,

Der Papst vermittelt die Vorstellung eines unsichtbaren JesusGott als Oblate in der Eucharistie und Holzpuppe zu Weihnachten. Die Lutheraner vermitteln die Vorstellung eines unsichtbaren JesusGottes in der Unterordnung unter das Gesetz Roms. Die Pfingstler vermitteln die Vorstellung eines unsichtbaren JesusGottes durch tolle Veranstaltungen und Party.

Du musst jetzt meiner Frau und meinen Kindern vermitteln, dass Du leider gegen das einfachste Gesetz verstoßen hast was es gibt - das Gesetz der Nächstenliebe gegen Deinen Bruder Ulf und die Herrlichkeit meiner lebendigen Gottes Sohnschaft vor meiner Familie bezeugen, nachdem nicht ich, sondern Du einem Jerusalem Syndrom verfallen bist, was nach neusten Medizinischen Erkenntnissen selbstverständlich nur und ausschließlich in Jerusalem auftreten kann und besonders fantasierende Christen aus der Heidenheimer Volksmission mit Größenwahn befallen hat.

5.) Dein Bruder Goddie
Hat seit 2011 unter der Gebetsinitiative Jesaja 62 Spenden unter dem Prüfsiegel der Evangelischen Allianz eingesammelt und Peter Wenz seit 1996 dabei geholfen ein Millionen Imperium aufzubauen, was einzig und allein auf der tollkühnen Behauptung basiert, das die Torah nicht gültig ist und Ephraim nicht existiert.

Wir waren ja zusammen mit Peter Wenz in der Vorhalle des Holiday Inn In Jerusalem, als ich ihm dies in das Gesicht gesagt habe, dass er da ziemlich danebe liegt und Du als Zeuge neben mir gesessen hast.

Ulf Diebel ist nach schriftlichen Lehraussagen zur Torah Deines Bruders Gottfried Bühler an Dich im Jahr 2000 „Elia". Siehe Maleachi 3, Goddie hat mich dazu gemacht, Danke Schön, denn Maleachi 3 zeigt klar auf, worin Du Gott bestiehlst, bevor der verheißene Elia kommt. Peter Wenz, Ingolf Ellßel und Ulf Diebel treten alle 1996 öffentlich auf – Ihr bestehlt im 10. und in der Opfergabe. Seit 1996 – 2018 sind das Milliarden, die nicht für den Frieden nach Jerusalem gegangen sind, sondern in die Taschen von charismatischen Wohlstandsevangelisten.

Senaits Pastor, der mich am 24.8.1996 getraut hatte, Richard Aidoo, sitzt jetzt nach 21 Jahren zusammen mit Peter Wenz im Hauptvorstand der Evangelischen Allianz. Eckardt Vetter der Vorstand der Evangelischen Allianz, der sich Volker Kauder der rechten Hand von Angela Merkel besonders zugehörig fühlt. Eckhardt ist gleichzeitig Vorstand im Mühlheimer Verband, der ältesten Pfingstsekte in der BRD, deren Vize Präses Hans-Peter Pache von der Lukas Gemeinde in Berlin ebenfalls einen eingeschriebenen Brief am 24.8.2017 zugeschickt bekommen hat, wie auch der Vorsitzenden Julius Justus der von Ingolf Ellßel aufgebauten BFP Sekte mit 776 Gemeinden und nur 52.500 Mitgliedern zum 1.1.2015

Sven Olaf Heckel, Ältester in der Lukas Sekte in Berlin, ist ebenfalls Berater bei Frau Merkel und persönlich in den Strafbaren Missionierungen meiner Kinder beteiligt, ohne auch nur einmal auf irgendetwas zu antworten.

Nachdem Du ja recht fleißig warst, um seit dem 1.1.2008 auch in Berlin und in der Politik tätig zu werden und Spitzenkontakte zu dem Israelischen Konsul in München Dan Shaham hast, der mit Malcolm Hedding's Tochter Charmaine verheiratet ist, zieht sich der Pfad Deiner geistlichen Zerstörung hoch bis in die Spitzenpolitik und jede Regierung dieser Erde, wobei Dein Erfolg grottenschlecht ist.

AZ

Wiesn Party am Sonntag

Pocher, Kerth und Co.: Promiparty im Käfer-Zelt

Charmaine Hedding und Dr. Dan Shaham *(Foto: Wackerbauer)*

Das Budget der ICEJ USA war nur 3,5 Millionen 2017, während Rabbi Eckstein im gleichen Jahr 140 Millionen gemacht hat. Goddie in der BRD kriegt auch nichts auf die Reihe, weil er nur einen Glauben an Jesus verkauft und nicht die Realität Israels.

Weil ihr Euch selbst den Bauch gefüllt habt und als Physiker, Marketing Leute, Ärtzte, Lastwagenfahrer und sonst im Leben Erfolglose durch die „Verkündigung" und „Missionierung" einen eigenen Namen gemacht habt, ohne eine tatsächliche Ausbildung in der Heiligen Schrift zu erhalten, seit ihr allesamt zu falschen Messiassen geworden, die im Namen Jesus Christus, aber auf eigene Rechnung religiöse Wirtschaftsbetriebe führen.

Da weder Du, noch irgend sonst ein Pfingstler die per Gesetz festgelegte „Kirche" ist (deswegen gibt es den Papst), sondern nach Handelsnummern geführte Körperschaften, ist jede Körperschaft, jeweils einzeln - ICEJ Deutschland e.V., ICEJ Israel, USA, Gospel Forum Stuttgart, Deutsche Evangelische Allianz etc. per Gesetz verpflichtet, die mitgeteilte Offenbarung (Gesetz DEI FILIUS vom 24.4.1870) und meine jetzt nachfolgende Anfrage der Körperschaft „Ephraim, Priester nach der Ordnung Melchizedek" an der Auflösung des Menschenrechts Falles Ulf Diebel und seiner Kinder mitzuwirken.

Seit dem 25.5.2015 sind per Gesetz GG Art. 9 jede gegen mich gerichtete Maßname Rechtswidrig. Die Nicht-Beantwortung und Verschleierung der geschilderten Ereignisse und involvierten Personen war zu jedem Zeitpunkt strafbar.

Weil es so unsagbar viele sind, hatte ich immer darauf verzichtet zur Polizei zu gehen, weswegen ich ja direkt bei der jüdischen Leiterschaft und beim Papst angefragt habe.

Niemand von den hier geschriebenen Namen wird aus der Nummer herauskommen.

Bitte weise Gottfried Bühler an, kurzfristig (7.3.2018) 50.000 Euro auf mein Privatkonto bei der Fidor Bank zu überweisen, um die durch Deine strafbaren Handlungen hervorgetretenen finanziellen Schäden kurzfristig zu lindern.

Durch die Jesaja 62 Gebetsinitiative, bei der es ja auch um die Tochter Zion Yael Eden geht, hat Gottfried über Jahre ein Polster angelegt und als Vorsitzender der ICEJ e.V. Mit der netten Lisa Rüdiger an seiner Seite, kann die Überweisung und die paar Handgriffe schnell erledigt werden. Gottfried kann dann auch direkt jeden anderen Vertreter der bei der ICEJ gelisteten Körperschaften informieren, ich lade jeden Beteiligten persönlich hier auf dieses Schreiben ein.

Zu guter Letzt, bereite eine Pressekonferenz vor, in der Du die Angelegenheit erklärst, Deinen Rücktritt erklärst und Deine aktiven Aufgaben der Botschaft an mich überträgst.

Ulf Diebel

Ephraim,
Priester nach der Ordnung Melchizedek

 Ulf Diebel

Botschaft des Staates Israel
Att. Ambassador Jeremy Issacharoff
Auguste-Viktoria-Str. 74
Berlin

ULF DIEBEL
Priester nach der Ordnung Melchizedek
Im EPHI-Zentrum
Obere Mühle 28
58644 Iserlohn
www.Ephraim.info
www.ulfdiebel.com
ulfdiebel@gmail.com

12.4.2018

Dein Zeichen, deine Nachricht vom	Unser Zeichen, unsere Nachricht vom	Durchwahl, Name
217.4(a) 12/31/07 ATL	DUNS 009899325	iPad
#88-897-762	DreamStream LLC	0160 93 5777 0

Concerning Ephraim & US Embassy opening 14.5.2018

Shalom **Mr. Ambassador Issacharoff,**

Since **25.5.2015** I openly work under my new name and work description "**Ephraim, Priest of the Order of Melchizedek**" under the protection of **GG Art. 4, 9 & 140**, to secure my unique **Human Right,** guaranteed by **the Holy See** and the **State of Israel** in the adoption of **UN Resolution 217** since signing **the Fundamental Agreement between the two parties on 30.12.1993**

On **29.3.2018** I handed the attached list to state prosecutor Hahn from the „Generalstaatsanwaltschaft Berlin-Moabit" with a request of immediate involvement of the US State Department, due to the personal involvement of high ranking government officials from Israel, Germany and Israel in my „regular" family case.

The full disclosure of all my documents handed over to the German state Prosecutor is online at

https://plus.google.com/collection/02vWMF

Since **5.3.2018** an **open letter** to the President of the International Christian Embassy Dr. Jürgen Bühler is asking for his resignation and hand-over of the ICEJ in Jerusalem.

Before I started out publicly, I told my **Rabbi Avraham Feld** in Jerusalem, what **I will do and confirmed in writing,** that **I agree fully to the Authority of the Orthodox Jewish Leadership** and the **Jurisdiction of the Israeli High Court of Justice,** but so far didn't receive any help or answer.

I am in Berlin right now and would like to give a full account of my work as a private citizen and clear up my legal paper work with the State of Israel. Besides the world-wide political, theological and financial implication, my intelligence is vital for the security of the State of Israel, as well as for Germany and the USA, I wrote the US Embassy Kent Logsdon.

EPHI-ZENTRUM	ULF DIEBEL	BANK FIDOR IBAN DE	ulfdiebel@gmail.com	Final Court: ISRAELI HIGH
Obere Mühle 28	EPHRAIM	41 7002 2200 0071 9052 17	iPad (49) · (0)160 9357770	COURT OF JUSTICE
58644 Iserlohn		BIS FDDODEMMXXX	www.UlfDiebel.com	DUNS ULF DIEBEL
		PayPal.me/ephraimsplace		330216698

 Ulf Diebel

On my last try to enter Israel to clear up my personal stuff, I was held in prison for a night on 2.9.2015 and sent back to Germany with extremely devastating results for my business, family and social standing.

Could I have a short-term appointment with you at the Israeli Embassy in Berlin and fix my paper work?

And please..

Just call me Ulf

EPHI-ZENTRUM   ULF DIEBEL   BANK FIDOR IBAN DE   ulfdiebel@gmail.com   Seite 1 von 1
Obere Mühle 28   EPHRAIM   41 7002 2200 0071 9052 17   iPad (49) - (0)160 9357770   Final Court: ISRAELI HIGH
58644 Iserlohn   BIS FDDODEMMXXX   www.UlfDiebel.com   COURT OF JUSTICE
                PayPal.me/ephraimsplace   DUNS ULF DIEBEL
                                330216698

 Ulf Diebel

US Embassy

Geschäftsträger Kent Logsdon
Clay Allee 170

14191 Berlin

ULF DIEBEL
Priester nach der Ordnung Melchizedek
Im EPHI-Zentrum
Obere Mühle 28
58644 Iserlohn
www.Ephraim.info
www.ulfdiebel.com
ulfdiebel@gmail.com

12.4.2018

Dein Zeichen, deine Nachricht vom	Unser Zeichen, unsere Nachricht vom	Durchwahl, Name
217.4(a) 12/31/07 ATL	DUNS 009899325	iPad
#88-897-762	DreamStream LLC	0160 93 5777 0

Concerning Jerusalem

Dear Mr. Logsdon,

On 29.3.2018 I handed the attached list to state prosecutor Hahn from the „Generalstaatsanwaltschaft Berlin-Moabit" with a request of immediate involvement of the US State Department, due to the personal involvement of high ranking government officials from Israel, Germany and Israel in my „regular" family case.

The full disclosure of all my documents handed over to the German state Prosecutor is online at

https://plus.google.com/collection/02vWMF

US citizen **Michael Jay Solomon**, chairman of the board of directors of DreamStream since 2007, was asked already on 8.8.2016 to make contact with Donald Trump, who later on signed the Guiding Principals on US-Israeli Relationship of the International Christian Embassy Jerusalem in Washington DC , lead by Susan Michael.

The US Embassy is set to open 50m from my old address in Jerusalem, where my daughter Yael Eden was born on 21.11.2004 and Donald Trump should know, that I am the person he is looking for.

My intelligence is vital for the security of Germany, Israel and the United States and the solution to the most difficult of all relationship according to the CFR: between the Vatican and Israel.

I am in Berlin and would like to come in and have a conversation with you.

Please call me

Ulf

EPHI-ZENTRUM
Obere Mühle 28
58644 Iserlohn

ULF DIEBEL
EPHRAIM

BANK FIDOR IBAN DE
41 7002 2200 0071 9052 17
BIS FDDODEMMXXX
PayPal.me/ephraimsplace

ulfdiebel@gmail.com
iPad (49) - (0)160 9357770
www.UlfDiebel.com

Seite 1 von 1
Final Court: ISRAELI HIGH
COURT OF JUSTICE
DUNS ULF DIEBEL
330216698

 Gmail

Berlin Calling

Ulf Diebel <ulfdiebel@gmail.com>   25. April 2018 um 16:54
An: Michael Solomon <mjs@digitalcontentint.com>
Cc: "Christian Halsey Solomon (filmdomain)" <ChristianHalseySolomon@gmail.com>, Scott Diffenderfer
<scottdiff7@gmail.com>

Shalom Michael,

When we met in Berlin, I came to you as a friend and private citizen, because I was hoping you were able to grasp, what I told you over the last 3 years. Unfortunately you didn't and as I hinted in our conversation, if nobody will react, I will go to court.

After sending you a presentation on 26.3.2018 with copy to the World Jewish Congress, I had to do my thing. In my books, I count $1,65bn in damage for me and my shareholders, including you and I am fully set to create a multiple amount of wealth for all involved parties, by fixing some legal paperwork and a new deal between us.

On 29.3.2018 I gave three years of research and documentation to the state prosecutor in Berlin-Moabit and it is imperative, that you carefully read this letter and fully understand, what your personal involvement is. Besides the legal issues in connection with DreamStream, my wife wants to have a divorce and I am forced to do the dirty laundry, I really wanted to avoid for 3 full years.

My first Jewish friend Eliyahu Ben Haim, originally from New York, I met January 3rd 1996 (not married back then). On 21.11.2004 my daughter Yael Eden was born in my house on Kfar Etzion 6/9, right next to the Ben Haim's residence. Eliyahu became the godfather of Yael and still lives there.

The US Embassy in Jerusalem will open on 14.5.2018 - 50m from the birthplace of Yael Eden and my old address.

When on 14.5.2018 the State of Israel celebrates the 70. Anniversary according to the secular date, 25567 days since 14.5.1948 have passed. 25.5.67 is my birthdate, marked by the Pope as the "Eucharisticum Mysterium".

The law regulates the adoration of "Jesus" in the Eucharist "until he comes". The 21.11.2004 is by the law Lumen Gentium from 21.11.1964, the predetermined age of 37 years and 6 Months of the "Mystery", taken from 2. Samuel 5.5 age of King David, when be came king over all of Israel in Jerusalem for 33 years, until his son Solomon took over.

Yael Eden is what the Bible calls the "Key of David", written in Isaiah 22.22 and Revelation 3.7.

The "Key of David" (my kids), will unlock "the kingdom of heaven" and bring back the kingdom of Israel out of the hands of Pope Francis to Jerusalem.

In the insignia of the Pope you will find two keys. They are the key to "the kingdom of heaven", given to the person, who fulfills as a human all legal requirements by the Torah and the Prophets of Israel, as well as all requirements of the Church of Rome, to be the "King of Kings and Lord of Lord" mentioned in Revelation 19.

Regardless of what you will do, regardless how big you own agenda might be, you are part of my story and own Jerusalem agenda and I would lie, if I would say I am sorry for that, but you are not getting out of this.

Next to the documents I sent to the state prosecutor, I requested by letter appointments at the Israeli Ambassador and the US representative (Trump doesn't have an accredited ambassador in Berlin) to fix my personal paperwork, that I am able to be in Jerusalem at the opening of the US Embassy and meet Trump and Netanyahu.

Today 25.4.2018 is Berlin Kippa Day, after another Antisemitic attack against a Kippa wearing person made headline and my letter to the Chairman of the Central Jewish Council in Germany went public.

As my friend, Partner and Chairman of the Board of directors of DreamStream, I told you at all time the truth and protecting our interest, hasn't been easy, as they collide at several points due to our different backgrounds.

Please call your friend David Harris to prepare Deidre Berger in Berlin for a meeting with me ASAP, before I drive off to Israel, with a stop over in Belgrade with our DreamStream technicians.

Let me take over the dealing with the Truli content partner, and let me take care of the Evangelicals in the US, starting with John Hagee and his Christians United For Israel with 4 Million members, who should make the same 100 Euro sign up, like anybody else, who wants to make a new deal with me.

For the same 100 Euro New Deal between us, think about the value of the licensing rights of "Jesus Christ", who came back out of the gave... instead.. it's not Jesus, it is, as I showed you in Berlin, just me.

As you are Michael and I told you, that the Prophet Daniel talks about us, in the whole chapter 10 - 12, it might be that you receive phone calls from people, who received the same disclosure of Daniel 10 - 12, as you and Ronald Lauder did on 26.2.2018

Also.. you are a liberal Jew, Democrat and US Citizen, which is the complete opposite of me, but I think I turned out alright with 50.

As you know all the other "Christians" and whatnot, I think I am the most awesome German around and the best guy, you can ever get, as an advocate for the Jewish People to fight Antisemitism, I myself experienced now for 10 years here in Germany and cost me everything.

The God of the Jews sent the right guy... trust me.

I will give you a call tomorrow and see how you cope.

Send my love to Luciana and the rest of the family.

--
Ulf Diebel
Priester nach der Ordnung Melchizedek

EPHI-Zentrum
Obere Mühle 28
58644 Iserlohn

Eskalation im AsylstreitNahles sieht Seehofer als "Gefahr für Europa"

Der Asylstreit stellt die Union und die Große Koalition vor die Zerreißprobe. SPD-Chefin Andrea Nahles warnt Horst Seehofer vor einem deutschen Brexit und stellt sich auch auf Neuwahlen ein. Sie hält ihn für eine Gefahr für Europa. Seehofer bleibt aber beharrlich.

Im erbitterten Streit über die Asylpolitik Deutschlands hat Bundesinnenminister Horst Seehofer nachgelegt und eine offene Kampfansage an Kanzlerin Angela Merkel gerichtet. Er werde sich auch durch die Richtlinienkompetenz der Kanzlerin nicht davon abbringen lassen, mehr Flüchtlinge als bisher an der Grenze abzuweisen, sagte der CSU-Chef der "Süddeutschen Zeitung" vor dem anstehenden Asyl-Treffen in Brüssel. Es sei höchst ungewöhnlich, gegenüber dem Vorsitzenden des Koalitionspartners CSU mit der Richtlinienkompetenz zu drohen. "Das werden wir uns auch nicht gefallen lassen." Gegenwind bekam Merkel vor dem Treffen in Brüssel auch aus anderen EU-Staaten.

Zwischen CDU und CSU läuft in der Asylfrage ein offener Machtkampf. Die CSU will Asylbewerber an der deutschen Grenze abweisen, wenn diese bereits in einem anderen EU-Land registriert sind. Merkel ist dagegen, so etwas ohne Abstimmung mit den EU-Partnern zu tun, und will stattdessen eine europäische Lösung mit bilateralen Rücknahme-Vereinbarungen. Die CSU-Spitze hat Merkel dafür bis Ende Juni Zeit gegeben. Andernfalls will Seehofer als Innenminister gegen Merkels Willen im nationalen Alleingang eine Abweisung an den Grenzen anordnen - ein Schritt, der zum Bruch des Unionsbündnisses und damit zum Ende der Koalition führen könnte.

Seehofer sagte, er unterstütze eine europäische Lösung. "Aber wenn es bis zum EU-Gipfel keine Regelung gibt, beginne ich mit den Zurückweisungen an der Grenze." Auf die Frage, was dann passiere, antwortete er: "Dann wird es schwierig." Seehofer warf Merkels Umfeld in dem Streit Unverhältnismäßigkeit vor: "Man hat im Kanzleramt aus einer Mücke einen Elefanten gemacht."

"Auf dem Weg zum deutschen Brexit"

Die SPD-Vorsitzende Andrea Nahles hat vor verheerenden Konsequenzen für Deutschland und Europa im Falle Koalitionsbruchs gewarnt. Bundesinnenminister Horst Seehofer und Bayerns Ministerpräsident Markus Söder seien "auf dem Weg zum deutschen Brexit", sagte sie beim Landesparteitag der NRW SPD in Bochum. "Seehofer ist eine Gefahr für Europa." Die SPD werde die Alleingänge der CSU nicht zulassen. Sie sehe viele Parallelen zur Politik der Konservativen in Großbritannien, betonte die SPD-Chefin.

Diese hatten wegen eines internen Konflikts am Ende das Votum über den Verbleib in der Europäischen Union zugelassen - was zum EU-Ausstieg, dem Brexit, führte. Jahrelang hätten Großbritanniens Konservative Europa schlecht geredet und mit Alleingängen die anderen vor den Kopf gestoßen. "Wen wundert es, dass irgendwann nach jahrelanger Beschallung die Bürgerinnen und Bürger das ernst nehmen und sich gegen Europa stellen?"

Die CSU trage mit Kanzlerin Angela Merkel einen Machtkampf aus, sagte Nahles. Dem ordne die CSU alles unter. Seehofer hat Merkel eine Frist bis Ende kommender Woche gewährt, um mit anderen EU-Partnern Lösungen im Asylstreit zu finden. Ansonsten will er bereits in anderen EU-Staaten registrierte Flüchtlinge an der deutschen Grenze abweisen lassen. Merkel ist gegen solche Alleingänge und droht mit Verweis auf ihre Richtlinienkompetenz indirekt mit Seehofers Entlassung. Das wäre vermutlich das Ende der Großen Koalition.

Am nächsten Dienstag werde es ein Spitzentreffen der Koalition geben, sagte Nahles. "Wenn Horst Seehofer in zehn Tagen noch im Amt ist, ist Merkel im Grunde nur noch Vizekanzlerin von eigenen Gnaden und nicht mehr Kanzlerin dieses Landes", sagte Mike Groschek beim Parteitag der NRW-SPD in Bochum.

"Keine Aussage über Fraktionsgemeinschaft"

Der frühere CSU-Vorsitzende Erwin Huber sähe in einer möglichen Entlassung von Bundesinnenminister Horst Seehofer keinen Automatismus für ein Auseinanderbrechen der gemeinsamen Bundestagsfraktion der Schwesterparteien oder der Regierungskoalition in Berlin. "Horst Seehofer hat für seine Asylpolitik den vollen Rückhalt der CSU", sagte Huber der "Passauer Neuen Presse". "Dies enthält nach meiner Meinung aber keine Aussage zur Zukunft der Koalition und der Fraktionsgemeinschaft mit der CDU."

Die Fraktionsgemeinschaft mit der CDU habe sich in sieben Jahrzehnten bewährt und der CSU erheblichen Einfluss auf die Bundespolitik gegeben, fügte der frühere Parteichef hinzu. "Ein Ausstieg aus der Union hätte eine fundamentale

2.5.2018

Deutschlandfunk Kultur – Weltzeit

02.05.2018 18:30 Uhr

URL dieser Seite: https://www.deutschlandfunkkultur.de/us-botschaft-nach-jerusalem-ein-schritt-zur-apokalypse.979.de.html?dram:article_id=416813

US-BOTSCHAFT NACH JERUSALEM

Ein Schritt zur Apokalypse?   → Ja :-)

Von Franziska Knupper

Plakate in Tel Aviv fordern, dass Trump Israel wieder groß machen soll. (EPA / Jim Hollander)

Die US-Botschaft in Israel wird am 14. Mai von Tel Aviv nach Jerusalem umziehen. Dies ist auch ein Erfolg der Lobby-Arbeit von evangelikalen Christen. Sie legen die Bibel wörtlich aus und für das "Reich Gottes" brauchen sie US-Präsident Trump.

Kurz vor den alten Stadtmauern Jerusalems erhebt sich der Berg Zion. Ein Sehnsuchtsort für Juden. Laut Tora entstand hier die "Stadt Davids" - zirka 1000 Jahre vor Christus.

Am Fuße des Hügels liegt heute das sogenannte Messias Gästehaus. Vier Zimmer gibt es für Pilger und Sinnsuchende – dazu Instant-Kaffee, selbstgebackene Frühstückskekse und einen Blick auf den grünen Gipfel des Berges. Dort, wo der Heiland auf einem weißen Pferd oder Esel hinunter reiten wird - das zumindest glaubt Gästehaus-Inhaber Joseph Mireles:

"Wenn man sieht, dass die Juden zurückkehren ins Land, dann ist das ein Zeichen für die Endzeit. Ich glaube aber nicht, dass wir schon soweit sind, ich glaube, dass es erst noch eine massive Einwanderung nach Jerusalem geben wird."

Joseph setzt seine Baseball-Kappe auf. Darauf prangt in blauen Lettern der hebräische Schriftzug "Er ist das Leben". Jesus ist gemeint. Und Joseph will sich damit outen als sogenannter "Believer" - also ein Jude, der zum Christentum konvertiert ist – und sich zum Evangelium bekennt.

Also auch zur Offenbarung aus dem Neuen Testament. Ein Text, der in den momentanen politischen Zeiten immer wichtiger wird und nicht geizt mit Endzeitstimmung, Düsternis und Blutvergießen. Laut Prophezeiung kehren die Juden ins heilige Land zurück, ein Heiland führt die Völker in eine letzte Schlacht am Berg Armageddon und regiert die Welt danach für 1000 Jahre in Frieden.

Der Weltzeit-Podcast [http://www.deutschlandfunkkultur.de/podcasts.2502.de.html?drop%3Ahash=91c4bd978e85991b0839bdbaad011004] liefert Ihnen jede Woche seltene Einblicke in andere Länder. Hören Sie rein, wo es Fortschritte, Konflikte und Einzigartiges auf der Welt gibt.

Evangelikale: Prophezeiung beschreibt Weltuntergang

Viele Historiker nennen diesen Text ein Zeugnis der Christenverfolgung im Römischen Reich. Evangelikale Christen sagen, die Prophezeiung beschreibe den bevorstehenden Weltuntergang und die Erlösung. Eine Überzeugung, die sie mit politischer Lobbyarbeit vorantreiben. Donald Trumps Nahost-Politik ist dabei der bisher größter Triumph. Erst im Dezember 2017 hatte der US-Präsident entgegen aller internationalen Warnungen Jerusalem als Hauptstadt Israels anerkannt. Für Evangelikale - wie Gästehaus-Inhaber Joseph - ein Schritt in die biblische Richtung.

"Ich liebe Donald Trump, ich bin ein wahrer Trump-Fan. Als er Jerusalem als Hauptstadt Israels anerkannte, waren überall Plakate: 'Wir lieben Trump', 'Trump ist der Größte'. Ich meine, Trump wird in Israel wirklich geliebt."

G   eindeutig ist das Bild in den USA nicht überall. Laut dem US-amerikanischen Umfrage-Institut Pew glauben von Trumps jüdischer Wählergruppe nur 16 Prozent, dass der Umzug ein guter Schachzug ist. Anders bei seinen evangelikalen Wählern: V   n glaubt die große Mehrheit daran, dass Jerusalem dem jüdischen Volk versprochen wurde.

Ein Schritt in die biblische Richtung: Evangelikale in Kalifornien (USA). (imago stock&people)

Viele Evangelikale im Stab des US-Präsidenten

Dabei berufen sie sich immer wieder auf eine Passage im 1. Buch Mose und im Alten Testament – aus der Genesis – wo Gott den Israeliten verspricht:

"Geh aus deinem Vaterland in ein Land, das ich dir zeigen will. Und ich will dich zum großen Volk machen und will dich segnen und dir einen großen Namen machen. Ich will segnen, die dich segnen, und verfluchen, die dich verfluchen."

Wer von diesen Zeilen überzeugt ist, kann nicht anders, als sich solidarisch zu Israel zu bekennen. Und so geschah es auch bei der US-Wahl 2016. Rund 80 Prozent der 50 Millionen US-Evangelikalen stimmten für Trump. Und nun gibt es viele Evangelikale im Stab des US-Präsidenten, zum Beispiel Vizepräsident Mike Pence.

6.12.2017

US-Präsident Donald Trump hält am 06.12.2017 eine Proklamation, in der er Jerusalem als die Hauptstadt Israels anerkennt. Neben ihm Vizepräsident Mike Pence. (dpa-Bildfunk / AP / van Vucci)

Eine Entwicklung, die sich Lobby-Organisationen für Israel zunutze machen wollen. So wie die Israel Allies Foundation. Josh Reinstein ist ihr Präsident:

"Es gibt 13 Millionen Juden auf der Welt und eine Milliarde Christen. Aber zusammen sind wir eine Milliarde und 13 Millionen! So sieht es nämlich aus. Und wir brauchen wirklich dringend die Unterstützung von unseren christlichen Freunden. Ich finde es großartig, dass sie uns aufgrund ihres Glaubens an die Bibel unterstützen. Das ist unser gemeinsamer Nenner. Der Grund, warum die Juden in Israel sind ist die Bibel. Ansonsten wären wir in Uganda. Aber wir kamen in diese Region, weil wir daran glauben und dreimal am Tag in Richtung Jerusalem beten, dass dies unser Land ist und Gott seine Versprechen erfüllt - und das tut er!"

Josh Reinstein wurde 2012 zu einem der 50 einflussreichsten Juden der Welt gekürt. Gemeinsam mit dem Politiker und Journalisten Yuri Stern gründete der gebürtige US-Amerikaner 2004 den "Christian Allies Caucus", ein parlamentarisches Gremium, das mittlerweile in 39 Ländern besteht.

Christen in den USA politisch organisiert   ← !

In   ' USA wird die biblische Prophezeiung in diesem Rahmen derzeit von 50 republikanischen und 36 demokratischen Abgeordneten in echte politische Aktion umgesetzt. Für Reinstein spielt es keine Rolle, ob seine Unterstützer katholisch oder orthodox,
o.   sich oder evangelikalisch sind – er selbst ist gläubiger Jude, bekennender Zionist und Begründer der sogenannten glaubensbasierten Diplomatie, wie er in einem Strandcafé in Tel Aviv erzählt.

"Obwohl ich kein Christ bin, glaube ich an den Tanach, oder was die Christen das Alte Testament nennen. Diese gemeinsamen Wurzeln, diese gemeinsame Glaubenssystem ist ein guter Startpunkt, um miteinander zu arbeiten. Und sie sind diejenigen, die Israel am meisten helfen. In Israel nennen wir es glaubensbasierte Diplomatie. Und wir sind der Meinung, dass das unsere stärkste Waffe in unserem diplomatischen Arsenal ist. Und das wichtigste daran ist, dass Glaube sich nicht verändert - im Gegensatz zu ökonomischen und politischen Faktoren, die sich ständig ändern."

Im Gegensatz zum laizistischen Westeuropa seien die Christen in den USA politisch organisiert. Ungeachtet geografischer und politischer Gegebenheiten haben sie im letzten Jahr enormen Druck in puncto Nahost-Politik ausgeübt: 137.000 Mitglieder des Vereins Vereinigte Christen für Israel (CUFI) forderten das Weiße Haus per Petition auf, die amerikanische Jerusalem-Politik zu ändern. Mit Erfolg, wie Israel-Lobbyist Josh Reinstein erklärt:

"Die Basis der republikanischen Partei sind bibelgläubige Christen und man kann sehen, wie oft sich das in politische Aktion niederschlägt. Wenn man ökonomische Interessen hat, wird man nicht unbedingt hinter Israel stehen. Wir haben nicht die Ölvorkommen wie unsere Nachbarn. Und wenn man politisch denkt, wird man auch nicht unbedingt hinter Israel stehen. In den Vereinten Nationen haben wir nur ein Votum im Gegensatz zu 22 arabischen, viel mehr muslimischen, Stimmen. Nur die Menschen, deren Glaube außerhalb von Wirtschaft und Politik stattfindet, werden Israel unterstützen. Und das sind die Anhänger des Buches, die Juden und die Christen."

Tony Perkins und Donald Trump auf der "Values Voters Summit" 2017 von der evangelikalen Organisation FRC. (AFP / Brendan Smialowski)

Ein Schwabe leitet die Evangelikalen in Israel   !!

700-750
Million "Klientel"
Kinder - Business
Evangelikal = Christ liebe Zukünftige

Wieder zurück in Jerusalem - etwa zehn Minuten Fahrtzeit von Jospehs Gästehaus entfernt. Hier lenkt Jürgen Bühler die Geschicke der Evangelikalen in Israel – also der sogenannten christlichen Zionisten. Bühler ist promovierte Chemiker und nun Präsident der Internationalen Christlichen Botschaft Jerusalem, eine zionistische Organisation, die in über 60 Ländern vertreten ist. Dass ein Deutscher in Jerusalem auf dem Chefsessel sitzt, ist durchaus erstaunlich, da die Gruppe Evangelikaler in Deutschland bislang eine Minderheit ist.

"Evangelikale Christen gibt es ja in Deutschland recht wenige, vielleicht maximal ein Prozent. Man schätzt eine Million in Deutschland ungefähr. Wenn man in andere Länder geht, selbst innerhalb Europas, aber hauptsächlich in Südostasien, Afrika, Lateinamerika ist es mit Abstand die am schnellsten wachsende, nicht nur christliche, Religionsgruppe insgesamt. Das heißt, in manchen Ländern wie Guatemala zählen sich über 50 Prozent der Bevölkerung zur evangelikalen Bewegung dazu. Man schätzt heute zwischen 700 und 750 Millionen evangelikale Christen weltweit. Das ist schon ein phänomenales Wachstum von ein paar zig Millionen am Anfang des letzten Jahrhunderts. Also, unser Hauptklientel sind evangelikale Christen."

Der Job des gebürtigen Schwaben in Jerusalem ist ein täglicher Spaziergang durch ein politisches Minenfeld. Die Israelis schätzen Bühler als Unterstützer und fürchten ihn als Missionar. Die arabischen Christen achten ihn als Glaubensbruder und verabscheuen ihn als Zionisten. Im Gegensatz zu Joseph Mireles oder Josh Reinstein ist er deswegen vorsichtig, politische Gegebenheiten in biblische Offenbarung zu übersetzen:

"Was in Amerika gerade ein bisschen geschieht, wo die Kirchen hoffen, dass der Präsident jetzt sehr stark die evangelikale Leute in die Regierung bringt, dass das das Heilsbringende für die Vereinigten Staaten ist - davon bin ich nicht so überzeugt. Ich bin vorsichtig, aus biblisch, prophetischen Aussagen eine Tagespolitik entstehen zu lassen. Wenn Gott, an den ich sehr stark glaube, etwas macht, dann findet man im Nachhinein immer eher heraus, was Gott tut als dass man versucht, sich mit menschlichen Anstrengungen in die Politik einzumischen. Das sieht man an der europäischen Geschichte, dass wenn eine zu enge Verbindung zwischen Religion und Staat ist, dann ist das ganze nicht gut ausgegangen."

Ist Trump der falsche Prohpet?

Eigentlich sollte der Umzug der US-Botschaft nach Jerusalem erst 2019 stattfinden - laut Außenamtssprecherin Heather Nauert in Washington muss es jetzt aber schneller gehen: Schon am 14. Mai, zum 70. Jahrestag der israelischen Staatsgründung, werden die Kartons in Tel Aviv gepackt.

Die Palästinenserführung verurteilte die frühzeitige Verlegung als "Provokation für die Araber, die Muslime und die Christen". In der Folge kommt es zu Protesten und Gewalt. Im Westjordanland, im Gazastreifen, in Bethlehem und Nazareth protestierten arabische Christen und König Abdullah aus Jordanien warnt, dass dieser Schachzug die gesamte Region nachhaltig destabilisieren könnte.

Palästinenser verbrennen in Gaza die amerikanische und israelische Flagge im Dezember 2017. (picture alliance / dpa / Wissam Nassar)

Solche Sätze und Tumulte haben auch Joseph Mireles – den zum Christentum konvertierten Herbergsvater auf dem Berg Zion - nachdenklich gemacht. Zwar ist er ein Befürworter des US-Präsidenten, langsam fürchtet er aber, dass Trump vielleicht der falsche Prophet sein könnte, vor dem nur der Messias die Menschheit retten kann. Laut Offenbarung wird die Menschheit nämlich vor Ankunft des Heilands von einem Anführer in die Irre geleitet, der den Juden ihr Land zurück gibt.

"Ich liebe Trump, ich meine, ich habe sein Buch, ich mag ihn. Aber ich sehe in ihm eventuell den Anführer der Apokalypse. Der Antichrist oder der falsche Prophet . Ich sage nicht, dass er es auf jeden Fall ist. Aber was geschehen wird, ist, dass ein Anführer kommen wird, dem die Juden folgen. Und sie folgen Trump. Ich meine, Israelis lieben Trump!"

Auch Islamisten sprechen von Apokalypse

Für Josh Reinstein – den Israel-Lobbyisten - ist das alles irrelevant. Für ihn zählt die Zeit bis hin zur Apokalypse. Um alles weitere - auch das Schicksal der Juden nach der Endzeit - werde man sich kümmern, wenn die Zeit reif ist.

"Manche glauben, dass ein Drittel der Juden umkommt und der Rest konvertiert. Aber das sind alles messianische Ideen, die nur dann geschehen, wenn der Heiland kommt. Worüber wir beide aber einig sind, ist dass bis der Messias kommt, wir zusammenarbeiten müssen."

Der Umstand, dass islamistische Fundamentalisten ebenfalls von der nahenden Apokalypse sprechen, dürfte mittlerweile niemanden mehr überraschen. Auch im radikalen Islam erwartet man ebenfalls die Ankunft des Messias, des Mahdi, der die Völker in der ... rten Kampf führen wird. Statt in Armageddon wird bei Moslems in Dabiq, im Norden Syriens, gekämpft. Das ist der Hauptgrund, warum die Terrormiliz "IS" ihr Kalifat dort bitter verteidigte und sogar ein Propagandamagazin nach der Stadt benannte.

Die, die sich sonst spinnefeind sind, haben beim Thema Weltuntergang plötzlich viele Gemeinsamkeiten.

Mehr zum Thema

70 Jahre Israel - Mythos Kibbuz als Labor des Landes [https://www.deutschlandfunkkultur.de/70-jahre-israel-mythos-kibbuz-als-labor-des-landes.979.de.html?dram:article_id=415647]
(Deutschlandfunk Kultur, Weltzeit, 16.04.2018)

Israel als Konföderation? - Modell der EU für Juden und Moslems [https://www.deutschlandfunkkultur.de/israel-als-konfoederation-modell-der-eu-fuer-juden-und.979.de.html?dram:article_id=401309]
(Deutschlandfunk Kultur, Weltzeit, 22.11.2017)

Cyber-Nation Israel - Wie aus Soldaten Start-up-Gründer werden [https://www.deutschlandfunkkultur.de/cyber-nation-israel-wie-aus-soldaten-start-up-gruender.979.de.html?dram:article_id=387457]
(Deutschlandfunk Kultur, Weltzeit, 31.05.2017)

Entdecken Sie Deutschlandfunk Kultur

- Programm
  - Vor und Rückschau
  - Alle Sendungen
  - Kulturnachrichten
  - Multimedia-Dossiers
  - Heute neu
- Hören
  - Mediathek
  - Podcast
  - Audio-Archiv
  - Rekorder
  - Frequenzen
- Service
  - Playlist
  - Veranstaltungen
  - Hilfe
- Kontakt
  - Hörerservice
  - Social Media
- Über uns
  - Ausbildung
  - Presse
  - Newsletter
  - Impressum
  - Datenschutz
  - Korrekturen

Sehr geehrter Herr Dr. Josef Schuster,
vom Zentralrat der Juden in Deutschland,

Geliebte Jüdische Gemeinde in Berlin
die offizellen Vertreter der Jüdischen Organisationen

Deidre Berger - AJC
Ronald Lauder - World Jewish Congress
Rabbi Yehuda Teichtal Chabad Berlin

Bischof Dr. Markus Dröge (Evangelisch)
Erzbischof Dr. Heiner Koch (Katholisch)

Offene Brief

BERLIN TRÄGT Kippa

9.5.2018

→ ulf.diebel.com

Liebe Unterstützer aus allen Parteien, Menschenrechtsorganisationen und christlichen Gemeinden.

Mein Name ist Ulf Diebel, *25.5.67 in Düsseldorf, erstgeborener Sohn von Udo Diebel *24.4.43 - 20.9.93, einziger Sohn von Hans Heiner Jakob Diebel *20.2.1907 (verstorben), verheiratet seit dem 24.8.1996, vier Kinder, davon 2 in Jerusalem geboren.

Zeit meines Lebens bin ich EKD Mitglied, hatte aber 1996 die BRD verlassen, um in Jerusalem, frisch verheiratet, ein neues Leben im Glauben an das Wort Gottes und die Erfüllung der Propheten Israels aufzubauen, die von einer vollständigen Wiederherstellung Israels sprechen, wenn die Syrer in das Land von Immanuel kommen (Jesaja 8 und Micha 5).

Der heutige Antisemitismus und Rassismus steht in unmittelbarem Zusammenhang mit den in Sacharija 9 erwähnten Palästinensern, die erst dann Frieden mit Israel schließen werden, wenn sich der erstgeborene Erbe von Israel namens Ephraim (Jeremia 31.9) mit seinen beiden Töchtern den Juden zu erkennen gibt.

Ohne Zweifel steht zum heutigen „Berlin trägt Kippa" Tag fest, dass ich die Person bin, von dem die hebräischen Propheten reden, was über einen Zeitraum von über 3 Jahren 1.1.2015 - 20.1.2018 öffentlich dokumentiert wurde.

Meine Publikation „Word from Jerusalem" ist seit dem Jahr 2000 das Organ der Internationalen Christlichen Botschaft in Jerusalem (ICEJ) und wird in mehreren Sprachen in knapp 100 Länder verschickt. Seit vier Jahren gehört die ICEJ zu den „besten Freunden" von Ronald Lauder, Benjamin Netanyahu und Reuven Rivlin. Donald Trump unterzeichnete im Vorwahlkampf bei meiner Freundin Susan Michael in der ICEJ in Washingthon, die Guiding Principals for US-Israeli Relationship.

Schon am 8.8.2016 hatte ich über meinen Partner Michael Jay Solomon, Founding Chairman der Jerusalem Foundation in Kalifornien versucht, einen Termin bei Trump zu bekommen, da seit dem Jahr 2000 ein BRD Bürger (Jürgen Bühler), ein US Bürger (David Parsons) und ein SüdAfrikaner, jetzt US Bürger (Malcolm Hedding) im Herzen von Jerusalem den Christlichen Zionismus in eine für ganz Israel schädliche, neue Religion und Ersatztheologie mit weltweiten Auswirkungen errichtet hatten, was durch die beiden Chef Rabbiner von Israel vor dem Laubhüttenfest 2015 in einem gemeinsamen offenen Brief bestätigt wurde. (Jerusalem Post berichtete)

Während 1999/2000 Josef Ratzinger für die Erfindung der Rechtfertigungslehre als Kardinalpräfekt der Kongregation für die Glaubenslehre verantwortlich war und am 24.4.2005 Papst wurde, erschuf ich für den historischen Papstbesuch in Jerusalem über Nacht die Webseite für das Interreligiöse Treffen, beauftragt von Alon Goshen Gottstein von dem Elijah Institute, bezahlt von der Konrad Adenauer Stiftung in Jerusalem und schrieb meinen ersten Kommentar zur Torah von Mose 1999/2000, der 2001 veröffentlicht wurde und in die Deutsche National Bibliothek aufgenommen wurde.

Im März 2005 wurde ich von Rabbi Avraham Feld für die Arbeit unter den verlorenen Schafen des Hauses Israels gesegnet und erklärte unter Anwesenheit von Rabbi Feld und dem Schriftgelehrten Yair Davidy , sowie 100 Zeugen aus den USA, Ephraim als Unabhängige Nation in Ramat Rachel.
Sowohl die jüdisch-orthodoxe Organisation Kol Hatur in Jerusalem von Rabbi Feld, wie auch neue Gruppierungen in den USA sind auf meine Arbeit zurückzuführen, die im allgemeinen als die „Hebrew Roots" Bewegung bezeichnet wird, denen sich in den USA mittlerweile Millionen zugehörig fühlen und den

Christlichen Zionismus zu den tragenden Unterstützern des Staates Israels gemacht haben, die allesamt hinter US Präsident Trump und seiner Jerusalem Entscheidung stehen.

Gegen die beiden Mit-Autoren und persönlichen Freunde seit 1996, Dr. Jürgen Bühler aus Heidenheim, seit Juli 2011 Präsident der ICEJ und Doron Schneider, Sohn von IsraelToday (ehemals NAI) Gründer Ludwig Schneider aus Düsseldorf, wurde neben weiteren führenden Vertretern verschiedener christlicher Gemeinden und Organisationen, am 29.3.2018 Strafanzeige bei der Staatsanwaltschaft Berlin Moabit erstattet und um Einschaltung der US und Israelischen Botschaft gebeten, um einen Skandal ungeahnten Ausmaßes an das Tageslicht zu bringen, aber auch ein Wunder. Alles was gerade jetzt passiert, ist in der Bibel aufgeschrieben und wir stehen kurz vor einem

#NewDeal Jeremia 31

Ich bin „nur" ein Typ aus Düsseldorf, der seine Existenz alleinig aus der Bibel nachweisen kann und nach 2000 Jahren Römischer Herrschaft über die Bibel, jedem erklären kann, dass die Worte der Propheten Israels, inklusive der Worte von Jesus und das Buch der Offenbarung zu 100% wahr sind und sich erfüllt haben.

Es gibt einen erstgeborenen aus den Toten und treuen Zeugen, der alles wieder gerade biegen wird, weil er den Juden endlich die Schriften bestätigen kann, was ein Bewusstseinssprung für die gesamte Menschheit bedeuten wird und mir der Papst nach seinem eigenem Gesetz Jerusalem und die Kirche übertragen muss und es dazu einige spannende, multi-mediale Gerichtsverhandlungen geben wird.

Schon am 25.5.2015 hatte ich in voller Erkenntnis meiner Handels, Marken und Menschen Rechte nach 21 Jahren internationaler Geschäftstätigkeit, mit Firmenbesitz in Israel und den USA, jede andere Tätigkeit eingestellt, um in der BRD ausschließlich als „Ephraim, Priester nach der Ordnung Melchizedek" als Privatperson, Mensch und reinem Selbstinteresse einen neuen Beruf auszuüben, da mir durch christlichen Antisemitismus und Rassismus ein Schaden von $1,65 Milliarden entstand, der über einen normalen Weg nicht wieder gut zu machen war. Während des gesamten Zeitraumes war ich CEO von DreamStream LLC und Michael Jay Solomon als mein Director of the Board, über alle Schritte vorher informiert worden.

Bis zum heutigen Tag, wurden von mir als Ephraim angeschrieben,
• am 23.5.2017 wurde an 400 Pressestellen ein GG Art. 17 EilAntrag auf Klärung der Jerusalemfrage beim Papstbesuch von Donald Trump gestellt
• am 6.7.2017 wurde ein direkter Antrag bei der UNSECO auf das Grab Abrahams als Erbe Abraham, Isaak und Jakobs gestellt, bevor dies am 7.7.17 und die Palästinenser ging
• am 24.8.2017 Einschreiben an den Papst und den Israelischen Gerichtshof, die EKD, Chabad und andere, mit einer direkten Forderung Hilfestellung zu entsenden
• vor der Wahl am 24.9.2017 wurde explizit auf meiner Position „Klärung der Jerusalemfrage" bestanden, da keine Reaktion von keiner angeschriebenen Partei kam

Meiner Forderung auf Klärung der Jerusalem Frage, ist bisher nur Donald Trump nachgekommen, der nun wie bestellt, die US Botschaft 50m vor meinem Hauseingang in Jerusalem eröffnen will.

Der 14.5.2018 ist der Tag 25567 von 70 Jahren Israel und mein Geburtstag 25.5.67 der Tag, der von der Kirche als „Eucharisticum Mysterium" festgelegt wurde, indem die Anbetung des Sohnes geregelt ist, solange, bis er kommt. Am 25.4.2018 ist der Sohn erst einmal in Berlin und präsentiert sich. Meine Kinder sind der in Jesaja 22.22 und Offenbarung 3.7 genannte „Schlüssel David", um die Königsherrschaft über Israel aus der Hand des Papstes zurück nach Zion zu bringen.

Dr. Josef Schuster, bitte arrangieren Sie kurzfristig ein Treffen, damit ich als Ephraim, einmal dem Zentralrat der Juden und damit dem gesamten jüdischen Volk erklären kann, wieso ich der, von Deidre Berger vom AJC geforderte Re-Set der Deutsch-Israelischen Beziehungen in Persona bin und was jetzt zu tun ist.

Hochachtungsvoll

Ulf Diebel aka Ephraim
www.ulfdiebel.com , ulfdiebel@gmail.com, Assistent: 0157 5011 8662 , iPad Mobil 0160 931 5777 0

Weitere Infos auf www.ephraim.info oder www.zion5777.com

INFOS ZU BILDPLUS

WETTER
24°C
ERFURT

EPAPER

KONTAKT

ZEITUNGSABO

BILD SHOP

LOGIN

☰ BILDplus NEWS POLITIK GELD UNTERHALTUNG SPORT BUNDESLIGA LIFESTYLE RATGEBER REISE AUTO DIGITAL SPIELE REGIO VIDEO Q

15.09.2018 · 17:57 UHR · HOME › POLITIK › INLAND › HORST SEEHOFER › IMMER WIEDER HORST! · WIE „PSYCHO" IST SEEHOFER?

IMMER WIEDER HORST!

Wie „psycho" ist Seehofer?

03.07.2018 · 21:17 Uhr

Menschliche Verachtung für Angela Merkel vor Publikum ist Horst Seehofers kalkuliertes Mittel im Machtpoker. Immer wieder nimmt man ihm das ab.

 **Ulf Diebel**

US Embassy in Jerusalem

Ambassador
David Melech Friedman

Arnona
Jerusalem

ULF DIEBEL
Priester nach der Ordnung Melchizedek
c/o Elite Health Club
Prozessionsweg 27
33428 Harsewinkel
Ephraim.info
UlfDiebel.com
Zion5777.com

Montag, 23. Juli 2018

Dein Zeichen, deine Nachricht vom	Unser Zeichen, unsere Nachricht vom	Durchwahl, Name
Religious Freedom Act 27.01.1998	Firstborn	HORN 01575 0118662
Opening US Embassy 14.5.2018		
Donald Trump Birthday 14.6.2018		

30.7.2018 pER
Einschreiben

Urgent Request for Presidential Help

Shalom David Melech,

Attached you find the letter to the former office holder of the US Embassy in Berlin, Kent Logsdon and the Israeli Ambassador in Berlin Jeremy Issacharoff, I sent 12.4.2018, as well as a private email I sent to my partner Michael Jay Solomon on 25.4.2018.

Attached is also the IRS Form of the International Christian Embassy in Washingthon, where Donald Trump made a sign up during pre-election with my friend Susan Michael and the letter I sent to chief justice Miriam Naor of the Israeli High Court of Justice from 23.8.2017 - sent via registered mail on my 21st wedding anniversary on 24.8.2017, naming Dr. Jürgen Bühler, who is a German citizen and receives regularly funds from the ICEJ Office in Washingthon.

As you can see in the correspondence, Dr. Jürgen Bühler called 1.1.2015, since my 48. Birthday Shavuot/Pentecost 25.5.2015, I am fully conscious about being Zachariah 9.9-13 Ephraim and received the file # 276 Js 773/18 of the state prosecutor on 14.6.2018 - 77 days after my filing on 29.3.2018

From 1.1.2015 to the 72nd Birthday of Donald Trump 14.6.2018 are the 1260 days of Revelation mentioned in Chapter 11 & 12.

Only with the release of the Religious Freedom Report by Mike Pompeo on 29.5.2018, I learned about the Religious Freedom Act from 27.01.1998 and was thrilled to read, that it is US foreign policy to advocate on behalf of individuals, persecuted for their religious belief, practice and observance.

I am that ONE Jakob, HaShem called out to be his servant you read in Isaiah 49.1-7 and Isaiah 53 about and desperately need help, as I am just a „normal" guy and as you can read in Daniel 4.14 - currently the least of all people.

When on 9 Av Dvarim started, the Haftara ends with Isaiah 1.27 - Zion will be redeemed through the Torah and those who return with justice.

EPHI-ZENTRUM		BANK FIDOR IBAN DE	ulf@ephraim.info	Seite 1 von 1
Obere Mühle 28	ULF DIEBEL	41 7002 2200 0071 9052 17	(49) - (0)151 20022574	Final Court: ISRAELI HIGH
58644 Iserlohn	EPHRAIM	BIS FDDODEMMXXX	www.UlfDiebel.com	COURT OF JUSTICE
CLOSED by the City		PayPal.me/ephraimsplace		DUNS ULF DIEBEL
25.5.2018				330216698

 Ulf Diebel

In Isaiah 1.8 Yael Eden, the daughter of Zion is mentioned and in Isaiah 1.10 the situation in Berlin Sodom and Jerusalem Gomorra prominently described to the day.

Already on 16.7.2018, I filed a complaint with the state prosecutor Jörg Raupach about the Case 276 Js 773/18 with the Generalstaatsanwaltschaft Berlin Moabit concerning the criminal activities of a German in a foreign Country §5 StGB - namely Dr. Jürgen Bühler, president of the International Christian Embassy in Jerusalem, who has been visited over the last 4 years by Ronald Lauder (Email from 27.2.2018 attached), Benjamin Netanyahu and Reuven Rivlin.

It is as Isaiah 49.1-7 describes. After 7 years of desolation in my life, starting with the rejection to enter into the USA on 31.12.2007, I surely did not expect to be the light to the nations and horror befell me (Daniel 10 happened on 24.1.2015), I fully understand now.

As the expected „Son of God", I had to do some crazy stuff in faith and had to demand the impossible as a seemingly penniless nobody.

World politics became as ridicules as it can get and clearly nobody is able to talk to Donald Trump at this stage, when 128 nations including Germany voted against the US decision to move the US Embassy 50 m from the birthplace of Yael Eden, the Key of David (Isaiah 22.22 & Rev. 3.7)

Due to the unusual situation (nobody believes in a human messiah, except a handful of devote Jews and the assembly gathering at the western wall at the end of the 9 Av remembrance) the most easy and cheapest solution for all parties would be:

1.) Joint meeting between Michael Jay Solomon, Ronald Lauder, Dr. Jürgen Bühler, John Hagee, myself and President Donald Trump for the sake of Zion. (Isaiah 1.1-27)

2.) Official Recognition as Ephraim (Jeremia 31.9), Son of Josef (Micah 5.1) by Pope Francis and transfer of his power to me.

3.) Payment of 10% from all registered world-wide church members to Zion for the building of the Temple and New Jerusalem, starting from Mount Zion.

4.) Transfer of all the property held by the Church in Israel and especially Jerusalem to the rightful heir.

The US Intelligence service has all the ways and means to find out the truth, which is… there is no conspiracy at all (Isaiah 8), just a bunch of godless Hippies (Ronald Lauder calls them JINO's), who forgot to be sons of Jakob and got lost in fleshly lust and some over zealous Christian preacher, who collected money in the name of Jesus Christ into their own pockets (Maleachi 3)

EPHI-ZENTRUM
Obere Mühle 28   ULF DIEBEL   BANK FIDOR IBAN DE   ulf@ephraim.info   Seite 1 von 1
58644 Iserlohn   EPHRAIM   41 7002 2200 0071 9052 17 (49) - (0)151 20022574   Final Court: ISRAELI HIGH
CLOSED by the City   BIS FDDODEMMXXX   www.UlfDiebel.com   COURT OF JUSTICE
25.5.2018   PayPal.me/ephraimsplace   DUNS ULF DIEBEL
                                                                                          330216698

 Ulf Diebel

In theory a secret service team could pick us all up and by the end of the ministerial conference 26.7.2018 in Washington, the question of all questions could be solved to the fullest satisfaction for the USA, President Trump, the Jewish People and the Church.

According to my understanding of the written law of the USA, namely the Religious Freedom Act from 27.01.1998 - you should be obliged (as an orthodox Jew extremely happy) to immediately report this request for help in this most unusual case of Human Rights and religious freedom.

Please advice how to proceed and send my greetings to the President Donald Trump and let him know, that I am really looking forward meeting him and that he can boldly demand to speak to nobody else in Europe but me.

Thank you David for your immediate attention.

Ulf Diebel

Attachements:

- Letter to Kent Logsdon 12.4.2018
- Letter to Jeremy Issacharoff 12.4.2018
- E-Mail to Michael Jay Solomon 25.4.2018
- IRS Form ICEJ USA - 2016
- Letter to Miriam Naor 23.8.2017
- E-Mail to Ronald Lauder & Michael Jay Solomon 27.2.2018

- Dreamstream - IRS filing ULF DIEBEL 2013
- Birth Certificate Yael Eden & Naomi Esther
- TIN Yael Eden *21.11.2004
- Letter of Yoram Azoulay - Kfar Etzion 6/9
- Business Cards
- Letter to the State Prosecutor 16.7.2018

EPHI-ZENTRUM
Obere Mühle 28
58644 Iserlohn
CLOSED by the City
25.5.2018

ULF DIEBEL
EPHRAIM

BANK FIDOR IBAN DE   ulf@ephraim.info
41 7002 2200 0071 9052 17 (49) - (0)151 20022574
BIS FDDODEMMXXX   www.UlfDiebel.com
PayPal.me/ephraimsplace

Seite 1 von 1
Final Court: ISRAELI HIGH
COURT OF JUSTICE
DUNS ULF DIEBEL
330216698

Elite Plus-Ephi-Zentrum, Prozessionsweg 27, 33428 Harsewinkel

Persönlich Hr. Kauder, Volker

Volker Kauder MdB

Deutscher Bundestag

Platz der Republik 1

11011 Berlin

Elite Plus-Ephi-Zentrum

Prozessionsweg 27

D-33428 Harsewinkel

Tel.   +49 524 792

Mobil   +49 157 501 186 62

ephi-zentrum@ephraim.info

www.ephraim.info

08.08.2018

Offener Brief an Volker Kauder

Sehr geehrter Herr Volker Kauder,

vor einiger Zeit hatten wir einen Termin bei Ihnen angefragt, um über die religiöse Verfolgung durch antisemitische und rassistische Übergriffen zu sprechen, die von führenden Mitgliedern Ihrer Partei und der Ihnen nahestehenden Evangelischen Allianz verübt werden, bei der Sie erst am 1.8.2018 gesprochen hatten.

Am 24.4.2017 hatte sie als Vorsitzender der CDU/CSU-Franktion zu einer Veranstaltung mit Angela Merkel eingeladen, bei der Ihre Pressebetreuung von Dr. Sven Olaf Heckel übernommen worden ist, den ich am 29.3.2018 zusammen mit zwei Hauptvorständen der Evangelischen Allianz bei der Staatsanwaltschaft Berlin Moabit angeklagt habe, da ich schon am 24.4.2017 mit der Einweihung des EPHI-Zentrums in Iserlohn für 2 Jahre als „Priester nach der Ordnung Melchizedek" unterwegs war, nachdem sich u.a. Sven Olaf Heckel geweigert hatten, einen Skandal sondergleichen unter Brüdern auf der Basis der Bibel zu klären.

Bankverbindung

Ulf Diebel
Erbengemeinschaft Jakob
Fidor Bank
IBAN: DE41 700 222 0000 7190 5217

Elite Plus-Ephi-Zentrum, Prozessionsweg 27, 33428 Harsewinkel

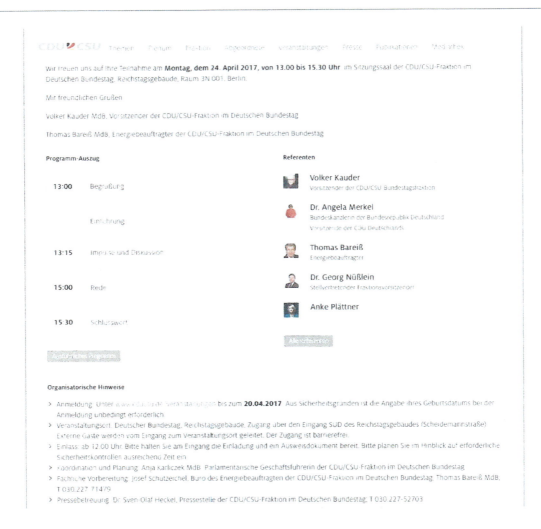

CDU/CSU Themen Plenum Fraktion Abgeordnete Veranstaltungen Presse Publikationen Mediathek

Wir freuen uns auf Ihre Teilnahme am **Montag, dem 24. April 2017, von 13.00 bis 15.30 Uhr** im Sitzungssaal der CDU/CSU-Fraktion im Deutschen Bundestag, Reichstagsgebäude, Raum 3N 001, Berlin.

Mit freundlichen Grüßen

Volker Kauder MdB, Vorsitzender der CDU/CSU-Fraktion im Deutschen Bundestag

Thomas Bareiß MdB, Energiebeauftragter der CDU/CSU-Fraktion im Deutschen Bundestag

Programm-Auszug

		Referenten
13:00	Begrüßung	**Volker Kauder** Vorsitzender der CDU/CSU Bundestagsfraktion
	Einführung	**Dr. Angela Merkel** Bundeskanzlerin der Bundesrepublik Deutschland Vorsitzende der CDU Deutschlands
13:15	Impulse und Diskussion	**Thomas Bareiß** Energiebeauftragter
15:00	Rede	**Dr. Georg Nüßlein** Stellvertretender Fraktionsvorsitzender
15:30	Schlusswort	**Anke Plättner**

Alle Referenten

Ausführliches Programm

Organisatorische Hinweise

> Anmeldung: Unter www.cdu.csu.de/veranstaltungen bis zum **20.04.2017**. Aus Sicherheitsgründen ist die Angabe Ihres Geburtsdatums bei der Anmeldung unbedingt erforderlich.
> Veranstaltungsort: Deutscher Bundestag, Reichstagsgebäude, Zugang über den Eingang SÜD des Reichstagsgebäudes (Scheidemannstraße) Externe Gäste werden vom Eingang zum Veranstaltungsort geleitet. Der Zugang ist barrierefrei.
> Einlass: ab 12.00 Uhr. Bitte halten Sie am Eingang die Einladung und ein Ausweisdokument bereit. Bitte planen Sie im Hinblick auf erforderliche Sicherheitskontrollen ausreichend Zeit ein.
> Koordination und Planung: Anja Karliczek MdB, Parlamentarische Geschäftsführerin der CDU/CSU-Fraktion im Deutschen Bundestag
> Fachliche Vorbereitung: Josef Schutzeichel, Büro des Energiebeauftragten der CDU/CSU-Fraktion im Deutschen Bundestag, Thomas Bareiß MdB, T 030.227.71479
> Pressebetreuung: Dr. Sven-Olaf Heckel, Pressestelle der CDU/CSU-Fraktion im Deutschen Bundestag; T 030.227-52703

Ihre Wahl zum Vorsitzenden fand am 21.11.2005 statt, dem 1. Geburtstag meiner Tochter Yael Eden, die im Haus auf der Kfar Etzion 6 geboren wurde, 50m von der neuen US Botschaft die am 14.5.2018

Bankverbindung

Ulf Diebel
Erbengemeinschaft Jakob
Fidor Bank
IBAN: DE41 700 222 0000 7190 5217

Seite 2 von 3

von David Friedman eröffnet wurde, den ich per Brief am 30.7.2018 um Hilfe gebeten hatte, da die 1260 Tage aus Offenbarung 12.6 schon am 14.6.2018 beendet waren.

Anbei finden Sie ebenfalls meine Briefe an die Idea und den Mühlheimerverband vom 23.8.2017 (Einschreiben am 24.8.2017 geschickt) und meinen Kirchenchef Bedford Strohm (Einschreiben am 24.8.2017) die ihnen einen kurzen Einblick darüber geben, um was es geht.

Für Dich persönlich Bruder Volker die Worte von Paulus in der Luther 2017 Fassung aus 1. Korinther 15.22-25 „Denn wie in Adam alle sterben, so werden in Christus alle lebendig gemacht werden. Ein jeder aber in der für ihn bestimmten Ordnung: als Erstling Christus; danach die Christus angehören, wenn er kommen wird; danach das Ende, wenn er das Reich Gott, dem Vater, übergeben wird, nachdem er vernichtet hat alle Herrschaft und alle Macht und Gewalt. Denn er muss herrschen, bis Gott »alle Feinde unter seine Füße gelegt hat«"

Nachdem ich von CDU Mitgliedern und lautstarken Christus Vertretern wie das letzte behandelt wurde, wäre es mehr als gerecht mich nun wie in Johannes 3 von Jesus erklärt zu erhöhen und meine Bemühungen um einen Termin mit Donald Trump, sowie meine Anerkennung beim Papst in vollem Umfang zu unterstützen.

So wahr Ihnen Gott helfe

Ulf Diebel

Bankverbindung

Ulf Diebel
Erbengemeinschaft Jakob
Fidor Bank
IBAN: DE41 700 222 0000 7190 5217

Seite **3** von 3

Büro des Vorsitzenden
Volker Kauder MdB

Dr. Eva-Marie Blech
Referentin

Platz der Republik 1
11011 Berlin

T 030. 227-50682
F 030. 227-56895

eva-marie.blech@cducsu.de
www.cducsu.de

CDU/CSU-Fraktion im Deutschen Bundestag · Platz der Republik 1 · 11011 Berlin

Herrn
Alexander Horn

per E-Mail: alexhorn45@hotmail.com

Berlin, 8. März 2018

Sehr geehrter Herr Horn,

haben Sie vielen Dank für Ihre E-Mail vom 27. Februar 2018 an den Vorsitzenden der CDU/CSU-Fraktion im Deutschen Bundestag. Sie schildern darin Herrn Kauder Ihre Sorgen, als Erbengemeinschaft Jakobs in der Ausübung Ihres christlichen Glaubens behindert zu werden. Herr Kauder hat mich gebeten, Ihnen zu antworten.

Ich bedauere sehr, dass Sie sich, so wie Sie schreiben, aller möglicher Formen der Diskriminierung ausgesetzt sehen. Allerdings kann Herr Kauder Ihnen in dieser Angelegenheit leider nicht weiterhelfen und ich bitte deshalb um Ihr Verständnis dafür, dass er auch nicht für ein persönliches Gespräch zur Verfügung steht.

Mit freundlichen Grüßen

Einlieferungsbeleg
Bitte Beleg gut aufbewahren!

Deutsche Post AG   3.34.20 Hausmarke
8205 3014   9645 20 08 18   11 48   2 20.8.2018

Sendungsnummer: RR 3712 6067 906
Einschreiben

H. Seehofer

Servicenummer National
0228 4333112
Mo-Fr 8 00 - 18 00 Uhr

Internet www.deutschepost.de/brief/faq

Vielen Dank für Ihren Besuch.
Ihre Deutsche Post AG

Elite Plus-Ephi-Zentrum, Prozessionsweg 27, 33428 Harsewinkel

Herr
Horst Seehofer
Alt Moabit 140
10557 Berlin

Elite Plus-Ephi-Zentrum
Prozessionsweg 27
D-33428 Harsewinkel
Tel.   +49 524 792 54 56
Mobil   +49 157 501 186 62
ephi-zentrum@ephraim.info
www.ephraim.info

17.08.2018

Hallo Horst,

Du bist als der Hauptverantwortliche der CSU in Bayer e.V. Und gleichzeitig als Hauptverantwortlicher des Bundesministeriums des Inneren, für Bau und Heimat unter der seit dem 1.10.2003 von der US Regierung für alle Unternehmen geforderten D-U-N-S 507111040 (Ministerium) und 329230593 (CSU) gelistet. Als langjähriger Akteur im Politgeschäft, sind Dir die internationalen Handelsrechte ja hinreichend bekannt.

Vielen Dank für die Info aus Deinem Mund: „Diejenigen die gewählt sind haben nicht zu entscheiden. Die etwas zu entscheiden haben sind nicht gewählt".

Leider ist dies auch wahr für den von Dir beschlossenen Masterplan, der sicherlich gut gemeint ist, aber vollkommen am Thema vorbei.

Seit dem 6.12.2017 ist Jerusalem die Hauptstadt Israels und Donald Trump hat bisher jedes Versprechen wahr gemacht, gegen jede Nation vorzugehen, die sich seiner Entscheidung widersetzt und geht in seiner Vorgehensweise nach den Angaben in der Bibel vor, die in Jesaja 8 sagt.

Beschließt einen Plan – es wird nichts draus werden; beredet euch – es wird nicht zustande kommen! Denn hier ist Immanuel. Jesaja 8.10

Bankverbindung

Ulf Diebel
Erbengemeinschaft Jakob
Fidor Bank
IBAN: DE41 700 222 0000 7190 5217

Das Auftauchen der Syrer in unserem Land steht in direktem Zusammenhang mit meiner Person.

Seit dem 25.5.2015 arbeite ich unter dem Namen Ephraim als ein nach GG 4, 9 & 140 geregelter „Priester nach der Ordnung Melchizedek", um einen Frieden mit dem jüdischen Volk auf der Grundlage der Torah und der Propheten Israels herbeizuführen, wozu die Absetzung des Papstes mit dazugehört, wie es ja schon aufgeschrieben ist (siehe Offenbarung 17 & Daniel 7)

Schon am 23.5.2017 hatte ich per Eilantrag GG Art 17 die Klärung der Jerusalemfrage bei Donald Trump, Angela Merkel und Vladimir Putin angefragt und eine Reihe von Personen in der CDU Merkel Regierung direkt informiert.

Der Besuch von Vladimir Putin am kommenden 18.8.18 ist eine direkte Auswirkung meiner Arbeit aus den letzten 3,5 Jahren.

Wie der beigefügten Grafik zu der tatsächlichen Machtstruktur in Kirche und Staat zu entnehmen ist, erfülle ich sämtliche Gesetze des Papstes, um als der in Offenbarung 19.16 bezeichnete „König aller Könige" nach Jerusalem zurückzukehren, was durch die religiöse Verfolgung die ich durch die Hand der öffentlichen Stellen und Kirchen erfahren habe, bisher vollkommen vor der Weltöffentlichkeit verborgen blieb.

Per Gesetz des Papstes wäre ich Dein Chef, um dies klar und deutlich zu formulieren und da die US Regierung schon sämtliche Unterlagen von mir vorliegen hat und Du per DUNS eindeutig zu identifizieren bist, nutze ich selbstverständlich meine mir gegebene Macht, um Dir einige Anweisungen zu geben, die für die Nationale Sicherheit von entscheidender Bedeutung sind.

Dein Innenministerium richtet seine ungeteilte Aufmerksamkeit bitte auf die Korrupten Mitarbeiter der Öffentlichen Hand. Gerne stehe ich jederzeit zu Zeugenaussagen zur Verfügung.

1. Die Staatsanwaltschaft Berlin Moabit hat seit dem 29.3.2018 sämtliche Beweise und Dokumente, um einen Skandal sondergleichen aufzudecken, hat aber die grundlegenden Probleme in der Gerichtsbarkeit zum Vorschein gebracht. Auch die

Bankverbindung

Ulf Diebel
Erbengemeinschaft Jakob
Fidor Bank
IBAN: DE41 700 222 0000 7190 5217

Gerichte sind Firmen, die sich nicht an die Internationalen Handelsrechte halten, weil sie diese nicht kennen.

2. Die Stadt Iserlohn hat für ein Jahr die Klärung der rechtlichen Verhältnisse verweigert und am 25.5.2018 einen Subventionsbetrug in Höhe von ca. 12 Millionen Euro vertuscht, indem sie das EPHI-Zentrum widerrechtlich geräumt hat und nun 200 Menschen obdachlos sind.

3. Die Stadt Harsewinkel vertuscht Massenvergewaltigungen von Syrern an einem jungen Mädchen und ist an der direkten Religiösen Verfolgung der Erbengemeinschaft Jakobs beteiligt.

4. Die Evangelische Allianz mit Wissen von Volker Kauder begeht Antisemitische und Rassistische Diskriminierungen und systematischen Spendenbetrug.

5. Seit dem 1.1.2015 wird eine Straftat eines Deutschen im Ausland welche die Regierungen von Israel, der USA und Deutschland belastet durch verschiedene christliche Werke vertuscht, was bis heute zu den Verwerfungen in der Gesellschaft geführt hat, wie Du sie beobachten kannst.

6. Die Syrer sind hauptsächlich durch George Soros nach Deutschland geschickt worden, der sich der Offenen Gesellschaft verschrieben hat. In der Bibel kommen die Syrer in unser Land, weil Ephraim der Erbe Israels ist und in der BRD alles unternommen hat, um jeden auf diesen Tag vorzubereiten.

99 Jahre nach der Sozialistischen Revolution, die seit dem Reichskonkordat vom 20.7.1933 mit dem Religionsfaschismus der Katholischen Kirche bis heute in der BRD verwoben ist, hat Gott wie er es in seinem Wort verheißen hat seinen Sohn geschickt, den Ulf aus Düsseldorf :)

Ich bitte Dich Dein Ministerium anzuweisen, mit uns Kontakt aufzunehmen, um die rechtlichen Geschichten zu klären, damit ein nach 3 Mose 25 geordnetes Schuldenerlass Jahr für alle Nachkommen Jakobs durchgeführt werden kann.

Zur Erinnerung schicke ich Dir noch einmal das Statement von Dir, dem Papst und Ronald Lauder und freue mich von Dir Kurzfristig zu hören.

Freue Dich Horst, denn Mutti geht und der Sohn kommt und wir werden eine geniale Party auf dem Berg Zion feiern. Bitte mache nicht den Fehler und denke, weil dieser Brief locker

Bankverbindung

Ulf Diebel
Erbengemeinschaft Jakob
Fidor Bank
IBAN: DE41 700 222 0000 7190 5217

Seite **3** von 4

geschrieben ist, ist er ein Scherz. Es ist einfach nur so, dass die Weisheit der Weisen zu Schanden werden wird und ich dachte die Offenbarung wäre witziger, wenn man es einfach unter Brüdern klärt und vor allem Menschlich, denn wir sitzen alle im gleichen Boot.

Tschüss Host, nenn mich einfach Ulf

Bankverbindung

Ulf Diebel
Erbengemeinschaft Jakob
Fidor Bank
IBAN: DE41 700 222 0000 7190 5217

Donald Trump zeigt gefährliche Anzeichen von Paranoia und Sadismus

Veröffentlicht am 05.07.2018 | Lesedauer: 5 Minuten

[handschriftlich: → 37 Tage bis 11.8.2018, 99 Jahre Vef. 19. B-day Naomi Estho!]

Von Jeffrey Sachs, Bandy X. Lee

US-Präsident Trump: Um seine psychische Gesundheit steht es nicht gut, glauben Ökonom Sachs und Psychiaterin Lee
Quelle: AP/Susan Walsh

Seine Anhänger glauben an politische Strategie. Doch Trump weist Wesenszüge von Paranoia und einen Mangel an Empathie auf. Verbündete, die nicht an US-Präsidenten mit psychologischen Problemen gewöhnt sind, sind erschüttert. Eine Warnung.

Die meisten Experten deuten Trumps Ausbrüche als Zugeständnisse an seine politische Basis, als Inszenierung vor den Kameras oder als Aufschneiderei im Hinblick auf zukünftige Deals. Wir sehen das anders.

In Übereinstimmung mit zahlreichen renommierten amerikanischen Experten für psychische Gesundheit (https://www.newyorker.com/news/news-desk/diagnosing-donald-trump) sind wir der Ansicht, dass Trump unter mehreren psychologischen Pathologien leidet, die ihn zu einer deutlichen und präsenten Gefahr für die Welt werden lassen.

Trump weist Anzeichen von mindestens drei gefährlichen Wesenszügen auf: Paranoia, Mangel an Empathie und Sadismus. Bei Paranoia handelt es sich um eine Form der Loslösung von der Realität, in deren Rahmen die Person nicht existente Bedrohungen wahrnimmt. Die paranoide Person kann im Kampf gegen imaginäre Bedrohungen Gefahren für andere verursachen.

→ Ulf (was first :-) 2001/

Helsinki-Gipfel mit Wladimir Putin   16.07.2018, 21:49 Uhr

Trump: „Die Welt möchte, dass wir miteinander auskommen"

Amerika und Russland wollen ihre Beziehungen verbessern. In den USA gibt es heftige Kritik an dem Treffen. Ex-CIA-Chef: Putin hat Trump völlig in der Hand. VON CLAUDIA VON SALZEN UND JULIANE SCHÄUBLE

US-Präsident Donald Trump (links) und der russische Präsident Wladimir Putin treffen sich in Helsinki. FOTO: AFP/BRENDAN SMIALOWSKI

US-Präsident Donald Trump und sein russischer Amtskollege Wladimir Putin haben bei ihrem ersten Gipfeltreffen eine enge Zusammenarbeit bei der Lösung internationaler Krisen und Konflikte vereinbart. „Wir haben die ersten Schritte in eine hellere Zukunft gemacht", sagte Trump nach vierstündigen Gesprächen in der finnischen Hauptstadt Helsinki. Auch Putin zeigte sich bei der gemeinsamen Pressekonferenz zufrieden. „Für die Schwierigkeiten gibt es keine objektiven Gründe. Der Kalte Krieg ist vorbei", sagte er. Konkrete Beschlüsse wurden allerdings nicht verkündet.

Vor allem bei der aus US-Sicht heikelsten Streitfrage waren die beiden nach einem mehr als zwei Stunden dauernden Vier-Augen-Gespräch ganz auf einer Linie: Den Vorwurf einer Einmischung in den letzten US-Wahlkampf wies Putin klar zurück. „Ich wiederhole, was ich schon mehrere Male gesagt habe: Der russische Staat hat sich niemals in die inneren Angelegenheiten der USA, einschließlich der Wahlen, eingemischt und wird das niemals tun", sagte er. Er gab aber auch zu, einen Wahlsieg Trumps favorisiert zu haben, da dieser angekündigt hatte, die Beziehungen zwischen den beiden Ländern verbessern zu wollen. Trump nannte Putins Zurückweisung „extrem stark und kraftvoll". Putin habe ihm versichert, es sei nicht Russland gewesen, das sich in US-Computer eingehackt habe. Er selbst wies Vorwürfe geheimer Absprachen mit Russland bei seinem Wahlsieg im Jahr 2016 entschieden zurück. „Wir haben einen brillanten Wahlkampf geführt, und deshalb bin ich Präsident", sagte Trump. *→ Stimmt!*

US-Geheimdienste beschuldigen Russland, sich mit Hackerangriffen in den Präsidentschaftswahlkampf eingemischt zu haben, um Trump zu helfen und seiner demokratischen Konkurrentin Hillary Clinton zu schaden. Sonderermittler Robert Mueller prüft, ob es dabei geheime Absprachen mit Trumps Wahlkampflager gab. Trump hat diese Untersuchung wiederholt als „Hexenjagd" bezeichnet.

Der Druck auf Trump steigt

Der Druck auf ihn war in den vergangenen Tagen gestiegen: Am Freitag hatte die die US-Justiz den russischen Militärgeheimdienst direkt für die Hackerattacken verantwortlich gemacht. Trump erklärte am Montag, Vertrauen in seine Geheimdienste zu haben. Aber er vertraue auch Putin – eine Gleichsetzung, die in den USA scharf kritisiert wurde. Der ehemalige CIA-Direktor John Brennan forderte Mitglieder der Regierung indirekt zum Rücktritt auf, indem er im US-Sender MSNBC fragte, wie Außenminister Mike Pompeo, der Nationale Sicherheitsberater John Bolton und Stabschef John Kelly jetzt noch „ihren Job" machen könnten. Auf Twitter ergänzte Brennan, der unter Trumps Vorgänger Barack Obama von 2013 bis

→ Heiko Maas

2017 den Geheimdienst geleitet hatte: Putin habe Trump völlig in der Hand. CNN-Moderator Anderson Cooper sagte nach der Pressekonferenz: „Sie haben gerade eine der vielleicht beschämendsten Vorstellungen eines US-Präsidenten auf einem Gipfel im Beisein eines russischen Führers verfolgt, die ich je gesehen habe." Sogar im US-Sender Fox News, der als äußerst Trump-nah gilt, wurde Trump hart angegangen: Kommentator Neil Cavuto sprach von einem „widerlichen Auftritt". Trump habe nicht den Hauch einer Kritik an der Einmischung Russlands in die US-Innenpolitik geäußert.

Wenige Stunden vor dem Treffen in der Residenz des finnischen Präsidenten hatte Trump das Verhältnis der beiden Staaten als historisch schlecht bezeichnet – die Schuld daran aber der Obama-Regierung und den laufenden Russland-Ermittlungen zugeschoben. „Unsere Beziehung zu Russland war NIEMALS schlechter, dank vieler Jahre amerikanischer Torheit und Dummheit und nun wegen der manipulierten Hexenjagd!", schrieb Trump im Kurznachrichtendienst Twitter. „Wir stimmen zu", twitterte das russische Außenministerium zurück. Das Gipfeltreffen habe die Beziehungen der beiden Länder verbessert, verkündete Trump dann im Anschluss. Er rechne damit, dass man sich oft wiedertreffen werde. Das Treffen in Helsinki war der erste offizielle Gipfel der beiden. Vorher waren sie nur zwei Mal am Rande von internationalen Konferenzen zusammengekommen.

Die Liste der Probleme ist lang → 100 D-U-N-S ® lang

Vor dem Vier-Augen-Gespräch, das Experten als sehr ungewöhnlich bezeichneten, weil der genaue Inhalt geheim bleiben könnte und Missverständnisse damit nicht ausgeschlossen sind, hatten beide angekündigt, über die bilateralen Probleme reden zu wollen. „Es ist an der Zeit, detailliert über unsere bilateralen Beziehungen zu sprechen und über die wunden Punkte auf der Welt. Davon gibt es sehr viele", sagte Putin. Trump betonte: „Die Welt möchte, dass wir miteinander auskommen." → !

Das Verhältnis der beiden Länder hat sich in den vergangenen Jahren deutlich verschlechtert. Die Liste der Probleme ist lang: Bei der nuklearen Abrüstung werfen sich beide Seiten Vertragsbruch vor und rüsten an der Nato-Außengrenze zu Russland auf. Im Syrien-Konflikt unterstützt Russland die Regierung von Präsident Baschar al Assad, die die USA ablehnen. Und Russland will am Atom-Abkommen mit dem Iran festhalten, während die USA dieses aufgekündigt haben. Auch das russische Vorgehen in der Ukraine und vor allem die Annexion der Halbinsel Krim nach einem umstrittenen Referendum vor vier Jahren, die die EU und die USA als völkerrechtswidrig verurteilt haben, haben die Beziehungen schwer belastet. Für Putin ist dieses Thema indes erledigt: Die Positionen Russlands und auch der USA dazu seien bekannt, sagte der Kremlchef in der Pressekonferenz. „Für uns, für Russland, ist diese Frage beantwortet. Das ist alles." Trump widersprach öffentlich nicht.

Mehr zum Thema

Gipfeltreffen in Finnland
Helsinki als Vermittler zwischen Ost und West
Von Claudia von Salzen

Das Treffen mit Putin war der Abschluss einer siebentägigen Europa-Reise des US-Präsidenten. In der EU und der Nato war im Vorfeld befürchtet worden, dass Trump Putin spontan und unabgesprochen Zugeständnisse machen könnte, die den gemeinsamen Positionen widersprächen. Im US-Sender CBS hatte Trump die EU am Sonntag wegen der aus seiner Sicht unfairen Handelspraktiken als einen „Feind" der USA bezeichnet.

→ D-U-N-S ®
seit 1.10.2003 genutzt für
steuerliche Zwecke und
Unternehmens Kategorisierung
für die USA
→ $ Handelswährung

Happy Birthday

Ulf Diebel <ulfdiebel@gmail.com>
An: senait.diebel@gmail.com

18. Juli 2018 um 18:51

Hallo Senait,

Nachdem Du jetzt am 16.7.2018 48 geworden bist, wirst Du Dich jetzt an einige signifikante Daten erinnern können, wie z.B meinen 48 am 25.5.15.

An meinen 40. Am 25.5.2007 in Jerusalem /Tsur Hadassah war es Jogi der sich darüber beschwerte, ich hätte Jesus nicht genug geehrt, was er Juli 2011 wiederholt hatte und mich dann Passah 2013 vor der Tür stehen ließ, weil ich "wie ein Ungläubiger zu behandeln sei", weil... "ich Jesus nicht genug geehrt hätte".

Wie Jesus schon in Lukas 22.22 sagte.. Der Sohn des Menschen (Dein Mann) muss gehen wie ihm bestimmt ist (7 Jahre Daniel 4, 1.1.2015 - 1.1.2018), aber wehe dem Mann der in verrät (der Jogi).

Nachdem ich den Anruf von Jürgen am 1.1.2015 bekam und Du Dich geweigert hattest mit mir über Deine eigenen Kinder und Deine Zukunft zu reden, hatte ich dann zu meinem 48 am 25.5.2015 Ephraim als neuen Beruf in Leben gerufen, um den von Dir und Jürgen verursachten Schaden in Jerusalem wieder gut zu machen.

Für 1260 Tage vom 1.1.2015 bis zum 14.6.2018 hast Du alles unternommen, um Dich meinen berechtigten Ansprüchen auf Klärung meiner persönlichen Angelegenheiten in Jerusalem und den USA nicht nur entzogen, sondern in vielfältiger Hinsicht straffällig gehandelt. Du hast weder auf meine Briefe geantwortet, noch Deine Rechtsanwälte, sondern hast einfach weiter mein Leben zerstören wollen und hast selbst in Deinem Scheidungsantrag gelogen.

Auf Schreiben an das Gericht wird ebenfalls nicht reagiert, weswegen ich mich in keiner Weise genötigt sehe auch nur einen einzigen Finger zu rühren, bevor nicht einige Dinge klar gestellt werden.

Schon am 29.3.2018 habe ich bei der Staatsanwaltschaft Berlin Moabit Strafanzeige gegen Dich, meine Mutter, Jürgen Bühler, Hans-Peter Pache, Sven Olaf Heckel, Doron Schneider etc. gestellt, wohl wissentlich, dass sich niemand melden wird, wie auch schon die letzten 3,5 Jahre nicht.

Man kann natürlich alles auf irgendetwas geistliches schieben, aber letztendlich hast Du und die anderen Gläubigen den Namen Jesus genutzt und bist zum Verbrecher geworden. Du hast den Bund der Ehe gebrochen und hast mit anderen Typen rumgehurt und diese in mein Haus gelassen.

Am 14.4.2018 hat der Israelische Botschafter die Info bekommen, dass ich zurück nach Israel will und habe den US Amtsträger am gleichen Tag über Michael Jay Solomon und Scott Diffenderfer informiert.

Schon am 14.5.2018 hat die US Botschaft 50 m von unserer alten Wohnung stattgefunden, wo Yael geboren wurde.

Vom 14.5.1948 - 14.5.2018 sind es genau 25567 Tage, der 25.5.67 mein Geburtsdatum und das vom Papst festgelegte Geburtsdatum des erstgeborenen aus den Toten und treuen Zeugen in Jerusalem.

Die Ephraim Story stimmt zu 100% - die in Sacharja 9.9-13 angegebenen Kinder sind Yael Eden und Naomi Esther. Sie sind der Schlüssel David's aus Offenbarung 3.7 die das Zeichen des Königs aller Könige aus Off. 19 sind.

Das ich irgendwann mal der Menschensohn sein würde, von dem Jesus spricht, hätte ich auch nicht erwartet, aber da es nun mal so ist, werde ich dies natürlich wie in der Bibel aufgeschrieben vollenden.

In 21 Ehe Jahren, die mit dem Sturm in Houston am 24.8.2017 den USA ewig im Gedächtnis bleiben wird, bin ich niemals vor ein Gericht gezogen, oder habe jemanden verklagt, aber das Endgericht der Apocalypse will ich mir auf keinen Fall entgehen lassen, wenn ich mir mein Recht als Vater, Ehemann und Priester Gottes des Höchsten (seit 1995, Du weist ja..) dort abhole, wo es aufbewahrt ist - in Zion.

Dir noch ein paar entspannte Tage, bevor die Sache vor Trump kommt und beim Papst geklärt wird.

Von meinem iPad gesendet

Senait Diebel <senait.diebel@gmail.com>
An: Ulf Diebel <ulfdiebel@gmail.com>

9. AV → Store West WaY

Hallo Ulf,

Wow fuer einen Moment habe ich tatsaechlich gedacht, dass du mir wirklich gratulieren wolltest. Fehlanzeige!!

DU wolltest nur dein Anliegen los werden. Es geht wieder einmal nur um ULF, hatte ich fast wieder vergessen. So wissen wir wenigstens, dass du noch lebst. Dann bleibt die Hoffnung bestehen, dass du zur Einsicht Kommst.

DU warst mal ein Ehemann und Familien Vater aber es spricht seit Jahren nichts mehr da fuer dich weiterhin so zu bezeichnen, denn du hast dich selbst von den Posten disqualifiziert. Wir sehen uns beim Scheidungs Gericht oder auch nicht. Es ist so wie es ist, und du hast die Entscheidung gegen uns getroffen.

Ich wuensche Dir Frieden und die Erkenntniss der Wahrheit.

Shabbat Shalom!
[Zitierter Text ausgeblendet]

Ulf Diebel <ulfdiebel@gmail.com>   21. Juli 2018 um 19:20
An: Senait Diebel <senait.diebel@gmail.com>

Selbstverständlich geht es um ULF und den Namen DIEBEL - der steht doch an der Tür. Ich will LEBEN, verstehst Du das Weib? Egal ob Du mich Tod sehen willst oder nicht.
Schau sie Dir gut die Kinder an und schau gut auf die Namen und die Adressen.

Ich muss mein Leben wegen Deiner systematischen Lügen neu ordnen, was leider den Rest der gesamten verlogenen Sektenstruktur von Pastor Richard und Jürgen Bühler hervorgebracht hat. Da Ding reicht bis hoch zur Merkel und Trump. Meine Schuld? NÖ.... Ganz allein Deine und die von Jogi.
Für 7 Jahre vom 1.1.2008 - 1.1.2015 musste ertragen, wie Du Dich wie eine Hure benommen hast und dann 1260 Tage bis zum 14.6.2018 mit ansehen, wie Du jedes Angebot auf friedliche Einigung ausgeschlagen hast.

Selbst im Angesicht des Gerichts hast Du nichts als Hass für mich übrig.

Das Urteil welche Du über mich gefällt hast, wird auf Dich zurückkommen.

So steht es geschrieben und so wird es geschehen.

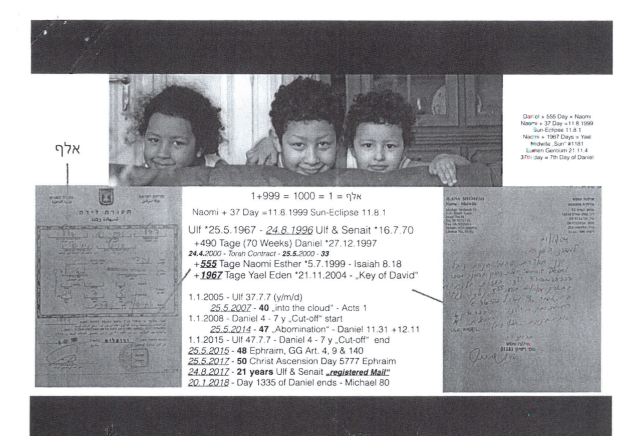

[Zitierter Text ausgeblendet]

--

Ulf Diebel
Priester nach der Ordnung Melchizedek

EPHI-Zentrum
Obere Mühle 28
58644 Iserlohn

@location 02371 - 8326880
#mobile: 0151 20022574

ulfdiebel@gmail.com

www.UlfDiebel.com

www.paypal.me/ephraimsplace

Kontoverbindung: Fidor
Ulf Diebel
IBAN: DE41700222000071905217
BIC: FDDODEMMXXX

Senait Diebel <senait.diebel@gmail.com>
An: Ulf Diebel <ulfdiebel@gmail.com>

22. Juli 2018 um 00:32

Wir werden abwarten und Tee trinken. Ich habe niemals Hass fuer Dich empfunden und auch sonst Niemand anders. Du bist derjenige der von Hass getrieben ist. Es ist an der Zeit zu vergeben Ulf und zu beobachten dass Gott grosser ist als du denkst. Guck dich jetzt im Spiegel an, siehst du einen gluecklichen, siegreichen und erfolgreichen Ulf. Das was man auf Youtube von Dir sieht, sieht wirklich nur noch traurig aus. Die Zeit, die Du damit verbringst anderen nach zu stellen und detailiert ihre angeblichen Fehler zu analysieren solltest du besser damit verbringen zu leben und was kreatives auf die Beine zu stellen.

[Zitierter Text ausgeblendet]

Ulf Diebel <ulfdiebel@gmail.com>
An: Senait Diebel <senait.diebel@gmail.com>

22. Juli 2018 um 15:32

Freue dich nicht über mich, meine Feindin! Wenn ich auch darniederliege, so werde ich wieder aufstehen; und wenn ich auch im Finstern sitze, so ist doch der HERR mein Licht. 9 Ich will des HERRN Zorn tragen – denn ich habe wider ihn gesündigt –, bis er meinen Rechtsstreit führe und mir Recht schaffe. Er wird mich ans Licht bringen, dass ich meine Freude an seiner Gerechtigkeit habe. 10 Meine Feindin wird's sehen müssen und in Schande dastehen, die jetzt zu mir sagt: Wo ist er, der HERR, dein Gott? Meine Augen werden's sehen, dass sie dann wie Dreck auf der Gasse zertreten wird. - Micha 7

Ok.. die Sache war etwas größer als ich gedacht habe und es hat auch ziemlich lange gedauert, bis ich das verkraftet habe, dass Du - egal was ich unternehme - zum Untergang aufgeschrieben bist, dafür, dass Du meiner Stimme nicht gehorcht hast. Jede Frau sollte ihrem Mann als dem Christus dienen (Epheser 5) und der Mann die Frau im Wasserbad des Wortes reinigen. Seit dem Jahr 2001 ist durch Torah.de das Buch der Beweis erbracht, dass ich zu 100% unschuldig bin und nach unserer Gerichtsverhandlung wieder nach Israel gehen kann.

Meine Kinder sind meine Zeugen in Jerusalem und sind zum Leben in Jerusalem aufgeschrieben (Jesaja 4) - Du leider nicht. Jürgen und Vesna auch nicht. Und niemand von Deiner Familie sowieso nicht.

Das größte Wunder aller Zeiten wolltest Du nicht wahrhaben und nicht annehmen - Gottes erstgeborenen Sohn Ephraim (Jeremia 31.9)

Vom 1.1.2015 - 14.6.2018 sind es 1260 Tage und ich hatte jeden Weg zur Vergebung Deiner Taten offen gelassen. Danke für Deine Bestätigung, dass Du Dir alles auf YouTube angeschaut hast. Dann weist Du ja, wem Du demnächst Rede und Antwort stehen musst und vollkommen ohne Ausreden dastehst.

Hier sind hauptsächlich Bilder die Du verstehst... beim Lesen und begreifen liegt ja nicht Deine Stärke.

http://ulfdiebel.com/trumps-traum/

Da es eine goldene Regel ist. Wer schreibt der bleibt, solltest Du Dir vielleicht doch auch den letzten Artikel zu Deinem Geburtstag anschauen.

Verstehen wirst Du ihn vielleicht nicht, aber er ist extrem rechtlich relevant - auch für Dich und Deine Rechtsanwälte. Während ihr abgewartet und Tee getrunken habt, habe ich einige Fakten geschaffen.

http://ulfdiebel.com/trump-putin-merkel-und-der-geburtstag-meiner-frau-senait-diebel/

Und selbstverständlich hasst Du mich. Sonst hättest Du ja irgendwann mal was nettes gesagt. Aber wovon Dein Herz voll ist, quillt der Mund über.

[Zitierter Text ausgeblendet]

Naja, Trump und Du seid euch schon sehr ähnlich wenn es um die Wahrnehmung der Welt geht. Er hält sehr viel von sich und denkt, dass alle sich seinem Willen beugen müssen. In der einen oder anderen Sache gelingt es ihm aber er gibt auch sehr viel misst von sich preis.
So großkotzig und aufgebläht er auch sein mag, dennoch scheint er die eine oder andere Sache richtig gemacht zu haben denn sein Erfolg spricht für ihn.
Er weiss wer er ist und kann es auch transportieren, sonst hätte er nicht so viele Anhänger.

Dieser Erfolg ist bei dir immer noch ausgeblieben. Wo sind die handfesten Beweise? Wo bleibt dein Erfolg. Ich kenne bisher keinen, der durch das Anprangern von anderen Menschen erfolg gehabt hat. Du hast eindeutig zu viel Zeit, die du leider nicht
sehr sinnvoll verbringst. Wo sind die Früchte, die ein hingegebener, liebender Vater und Ehemann vorzuweisen hat? Ich kann es mir vorstellen, dass es für dich sehr schwer ist dir einzugestehen, das du versagt hast. Das erklärt auch warum du die ganze Welt für dein Versagen verantwortlich machst.

Die Stärke deine Fehler einzugestehen und Gott um Vergebung zu bitten besitzt du leider immer noch nicht. Vielleicht macht es bei dir irgend einmal klick, dafür bete ich.
[Zitierter Text ausgeblendet]

Senait,

Habe ich Dir einen Scheidebrief gegeben? Eine Genehmigung im meinem Namen zu handeln? Hast Du eine schriftliche Bestätigung von mir, dass ich irgendetwas von dem was Du in unsere Zeit in der BRD gemacht hast, für gut heiße, oder Dich in Deinem Handeln bestätige?

Die Stärke Deine Fehler einzugestehen und Deinen Mann um Vergebung zu bitten, hast Du leider immer noch nicht. Es wird bei Dir erst klick machen, wenn man Dich auf die Strasse zerrt und genau dafür sorge ich. Als wenn mein Arm zu kurz wäre um in meinem Haus aufzuräumen. Verwechsle meine Langmut und Geduld mit Dir nicht mit Deiner Illusion Du wärst der Haushaltsvorstand, nur weil ich Dich eine Zeit lang habe machen lassen.

Viele sind in meinem Namen nach Israel gekommen und haben viele verführt. Du warst der tragende Teil der Verwirrung und hast Dich durch Deine Weigerung normal mit mir zu sprechen selbst isoliert. Dein Status ist Harz IV und mit 48, Umschulung zu einer Erzieherin, nicht meiner. Du stellst Dir damit ein Armutszeugnis als Ehefrau und Mutter aus, wenn Du nach 21 Jaren Ehe einen Stempel brauchst, um als Oma für ein Taschengeld andere Kinder Deinen Lebensunterhalt verdingen willst.

Mal ehrlich... für wie blöd hält Du mich eigentlich? Du trägst meinen Namen und wir sind aus Jerusalem gekommen, um auf unsere Papiere für die USA zu warten. Die Beweise liegen die ganze Zeit auf dem Tisch. Meine Kinder sind der Beweis und es ist genau diese Realitätsverweigerung, die zu der heutigen Situation geführt hat. Man sagt einfach es gibt keine Beweise und verleugnet mich als lebende Person. Ich sagte Dir explizit und mehrfach eideutig, dass ich aus dem Haus gehe, weil Du eine Liebloses, hasserfülltes, bitteres und zeterndes altes Weib geworden bist. Und wenn Du fluchst und ohne Unterlass geistigen Durchfall von Dir gibst, sind Deine Ohren verschlossen und Du kannst des Herrn Wort nicht hören und wirst SCHULDIG. Bis über beide Ohren.

Seit Tag 1 stellst Du Dich mit irgendwelchen Aussagen gegen mich und behauptest einfach, ich sei ein schlechter Vater, sei kein Mann und ergehst Dich in Beleidigungen und Flüchen. Es ist einfach besser in der Wüste zu leben als mit einer zänkischen und hasserfüllten Frau unter einem Dach. Und es hat begonnen an dem tag, an dem wir die TIN von den Kindern 2008 zugeschickt bekommen haben.

Du hast Dich entschieden mit Deiner und meiner Mutter, dass ich als Mann nichts mehr zu sagen habe und hast einfach ohne zu denken losgelegt.
Wie die Mutter so sie Tochter. Spitze Zunge, wenig Hirn, viel Männerhass. So wie Deine Mutter Deinen Vater von Dir abgehalten hat, hast Du Deinen Kindern ihren Vater vorenthalten. Anstatt meiner lebenden Person stehen jetzt regelmäßig blaue Tonnen für Geschenke nach Afrika. Du beraubst Deine eigenen Kinder.

Deine Ausreden Dein Verhalten auf Gott zu schieben kannst Du knicken, denn das zieht bei mir nicht. Du bist meine Frau und hast zum Thema Bibel, Gott und Glauben NICHTS zu sagen. Und Du brauchst Dich auch nicht zu beschweren. Ich habe Dir etwas gesagt, Du hast es nicht geglaubt. Ich habe Dich gefragt, Du hast nicht geantwortet.

Ich habe mich an sämtliche biblischen Vorgaben gehalten und bis zuletzt darauf verzichtet zu einem Rechtsanwalt zu gehen, weil ich gedacht hatte irgendeiner hat etwas Herz und Verstand.

Ich bin ZUERST alleine zu Dir gekommen, habe dann wie bei allen anderen auch ZEUGEN mit dazu geholt und nachdem Du Dich geweigert hast, mit mir zu sprechen, begonnen über Dich zu sprechen und jeden anderen natürlich auch. Trump ist damit zum Superstar geworden, weil er genau das getan hat, was ich tue - er bringt Dinge ans Licht. Dinge die andere lieber verborgen lassen möchten. Und yeah... die Jerusalem Deklaration Donald Trumps am 25. Geburtstag von Moritz Maximilian ist MEIN Erfolg - Siehe Eilantrag vom 23.5.2017 nach GG Art 17 "Donald Trump Take me to the Pope".

Du Schätzchen willst nicht, dass DEINE üblen Taten und Machenschaften ans Tageslicht kommen und bist an einem Milliarden Spendenbetrug beteiligt, bei der die ICEJ und Dr. Jürgen Bühler Hauptpersonen sind und ich der ZEUGE. Steht doch Schn fett drin in der Apostelgeschichte... Ihr werdet Kraft aus der Höhe erhalten, wenn der Heilige Geist auf Euch gekommen ist und ihr werdet meine ZEUGEN sein.

Yael Eden und Naomi Esther sind ZEUGEN Christi und ihres Vaters, der mit 40 (25.5.2007) noch entspannt in Jerusalem feierte, um dann ab in die Wolken zu verschwinden.

Noch mal langsam für Dich zum mitlesen... Weil Du Dich geweigert hast mit mir zu reden und zu antworten, stehen wir vor einer einzigartigen Situation.

Die hat nichts mit Deinem Glauben zu tun, sondern etwas mit dem GESETZ, was Du und deinesgleichen ja ablehnst. Nicht ich habe einen Schuss an der Waffel, sondern Senait Diebel, geborene Mogos 16.7.1970 in Äthiopien / Jetzt Eritrea. Nicht eine schwarze Frau, oder ein schwarzer Mann hat die Autorität über das Wort Gottes und die Gemeinde, sondern ein Nachkomme von Jakob. Was Du glaubst ist irrelevant, weil alles aufgeschrieben ist und Du nur nachlesen brauchst, gehört hast Du nie, wenn ich Dir erzählt habe was geschrieben steht.

PER höchstem päpstlichen GESETZ ist Yael Eden der Schlüssel David's aus Offenbarung 3.7. Dein Mann ist der erstgeborene aus den Toten und treue Zeuge aus Jerusalem und wird König auf dem Berg Zion. Auch mit Dir und den Bühlers, wird das passieren was geschrieben steht. Lukas 22.22 Der Menschensohn Ulf musste gehen, wie ihm bestimmt war, aber wehe dem Mann Jürgen Bühler, der ihn verraten hat. Die ganze Zeit ging es nur um Jogi und mich und Du bist einfach zu blöd gewesen, um Deinem Mann den Rücken zu stärken, weil Du dieses kleine afrikanische Minderwertigkeitsdenken in Dir wohnen hast. Du hattest Mega Probleme mit Anerkennung, was ja jetzt auch Dein Druckmittel ist.. Du willst mich nicht Anerkennen und machst es mir zum Vorwurf Anerkennung zu suchen - aber genau das ist mein Recht - vertraglich und gesetzlich GARANTIERT.

Weil Jürgen aus Jerusalem meinen Namen zerstört hat und Du hier in der BRD, hat niemand mitbekommen, dass "das Ende der Welt" schon längst "abgelaufen" ist. Das Buch der Offenbarung ist zu Ende. Niemand wusste wer der erstgeborene aus den Toten sein wird... Jetzt wissen wir es :)

Ich brauche nur noch Deine Machenschaften, Lügen, Flüche, Diebstähle, Beleidigungen und was Du sonst noch so tust ans Licht bringen und weiter "anprangern". Das Internet ist voll von mir und es ist unmöglich, dass sich mir irgendeiner entziehen kann.

Das Schreiben an den US Botschafter findest Du hier unten im Artikel.

http://ulfdiebel.com/official-request-for-presidential-help-23-7-2018-us-ambassador-david-melech-friedman/

Ehrlich gesagt habe ich mit Deiner Dummheit und der von den Christen fest gerechnet. Es gibt keine Unangenehmeren Zeitgenossen als Christen die behaupten den Geist Gottes zu besitzen.
Es spielt keine Rolle was man sagt - jeder regt sich über alles auf, hat Angst vor unsichtbaren Dingen und bezichtigt immer den anderen nicht richtig geglaubt zu haben.

Ich bin zwar selbst als Christ geboren, aber wie Du ja weist mit dem Heiligen Geist erfüllt worden - ein Wunder von Anfang bis Ende.

Es ist der Heilige Geist in mir, den andere Menschen - und auch Du nicht - nicht ertragen können. Der Geist der Wahrheit, des Verstandes, der Ordnung und Klarheit deckt jede noch so kleine Sünde und jedes Vergehen auf.

Der "Erfolg" den Du suchst bin ICH, aber den willst Du einfach nicht haben. Du ziehst jeden anderen Mann vor, als Deinen eigenen Herrn, weswegen Du zu der bezeichneten Hure geworden bist und jetzt ein total gestörtes Verhältnis zu Männern hast. Meine Kinder müssen von so etwas geschützt und befreit werden, damit die nicht genauso verblöden. Sorry das ich das so sagen muss, aber nach 21 Jahren Ehe 11 davon in der BRD kann ich das extrem gut abschätzen, was vom 25.5.2007 bis zum 25.5.2015 und meinem 49, 50 & 51 passiert ist.

Und es ist richtig, Du hasst nicht wirklich mich, sondern meinen Vater im Himmel der mich gemacht hat. Mein Schöpfer, der mir vor allen anderen Brüdern die Gnade der frühen Geburt hat zuteilwerden lassen, hat mich vor

Angeben aller Zeiten auserwählt, um sein Volk Israel wieder zusammenzubringen und ein Licht für die Völker zu sein.

Gott hat die Welt so sehr geliebt, das er seinen eingeborenen Sohn gegeben hat. Nicht damit die Welt verloren geht, sondern damit die Welt gerettet wird.

Die Juden warten auf den Messias, dessen Zeichen es ist für 7 Jahre aus Israel verschwunden zu sein, um dann für 1260 Tage vor den Thron Gottes entrückt zu werden 1.1.2008 - 1.1.2015 7 Jahre, 1.1.2015 - 14.6.2016 1260 Tage.

Ich hab Dir ja die Kalkulation der Kinder geschickt... Daniel 12.12 war schon am 20.1.2018 zu Ende und ich bin als letzter übrig geblieben, der ALLE Zeichen erfüllt, um als König aller Könige den Papst abzulösen (wat ne Geile Nummer)

Der Mega Erfolg, mit ALLEN Beweisen, INKLUSIVE der Zeternden Frau und Mutter der Tochter Zion und Jerusalem.

Ich dachte ja irgendeiner hätte sich gefreut, aber nachdem ich gesehen habe, wie meine eigene Familie und Freunde mich hassen, habe ich nur auf den Tag vorbereitet, der von Gott alleine geplant ist. Gesagt habe ich alles, auch wenn keiner hingehört hat ;)

Das Endgericht der Apocalypse in Jerusalem, wo jeder Rede und Antwort dafür stehen muss, was er ZION im Namen von Jesus Christus angetan hat steht bevor. Den Schaden den durch Dich und Jürgen, meine Mutter und die Pfingsten entstanden ist ist GIGANTISCH und nicht etwa Deine 3.000 Euro Streitwert für unsere Ehe.

Schön, das wir mal drüber geredet haben.

[Zitierter Text ausgeblendet]

Senait Diebel <senait.diebel@gmail.com>   26. Juli 2018 um 16:06
An: Ulf Diebel <ulfdiebel@gmail.com>

Wird es für dich nicht langsam mühsam, sich ständig behaupten zu wollen und beweisen zu müssen, dass du eine

Position hast und Jemand bist? Dabei hättest du es einfacher gehabt.
Einfach in Demut den HERREN suchend, die von GOTT gegebene Aufgabe (verantwortlicher Vater und Ehemann) erfüllend zu leben. Wie willst Du über eine Welt herrschen wenn dich die Mikro-Aufgabe einer Familie vollkommen überfordert.

Leider, glaube ich, ist es viel zu spät für dich um an eine Beziehung mit deinen Kindern weiterzuarbeiten. Wenn du kein Interesse an ihnen zeigst bist du gestrichen aus ihrem Leben, so einfach läuft es in einer Beziehung, um dir das nochmal zu erklären. Da du aber tatsächlich Beziehungsunfähig bist, kann ich verstehen, dass das für dich kein Problem ist.

Ich habe für mich entschieden, dass es das letzte mal ist, das ich mir deine hirnlosen, Menschen verachtenden, diskriminierenden, hasserfüllten, verbitterten, anmaßenden und einfach falschen Schlussfolgerungen durchzulesen. Den Schmerz vaterlos zu sein kennen die Kinder zu gut und müssen sich (besonders deine Söhne) die richtigen Vorbilder als angehende Männer suchen, die ihnen zeigen ein Mann Gottes zu sein.

Ich freue mich auf den Tag, wenn ich dich nicht mehr Ehemann nennen muss. Es wird passieren, mit oder gegen deine Einwilligung. Den Namen Diebel werden die Kinder natürlich weitertragen und wer weiss, vielleicht wollen die Kinder eines Tages gemeinsam mit mir ihren Namen ändern. Aber wer weiss, Daniel hätte das richtige Format um den Namen -DIEBEL- würdevoll zu tragen.

Ich glaube es jetzt wirklich, dass du das geniale Gehirn was dir der HERR anvertraut, durch das übermäßige Verzehr von Substanzen endgültig zum Opfer gefallen ist.
Möge GOTT dir gnädig sein, wenn eines Tages Rechenschaft abgeben musst.

Wir beten weiterhin für Dich.
[Zitierter Text ausgeblendet]

Ulf Diebel <ulfdiebel@gmail.com>   26. Juli 2018 um 16:54
An: Senait Diebel <senait.diebel@gmail.com>

Ich werde mal zwischen den Zeilen antworten..

> Senait Diebel <senait.diebel@gmail.com> schrieb am Do. 26. Juli 2018 um 16:06:
> Wird es für dich nicht langsam mühsam, sich ständig behaupten zu wollen und beweisen zu müssen, dass du
> eine Position hast und Jemand bist?

Genau darum geht es. Ich habe die Position und bin jemand. Du jedoch möchtest genau das Gegenteil. Ich mache genau das, weswegen Du mich geheiratet hast. Priester des Höchsten, der nach Gesetz und Recht eine Antowrt von seiner Ehebrüchigen Frau herausquetschen wird.

> Dabei hättest du es einfacher gehabt.

Ne, leider nicht, da alles aufgeschrieben ist. Die 7 Jahre abgeschnitten aus Daniel 4 vom 1.1.2008 - 1.1.2015 kannst Du nicht ändern. Die Zeitspanne vom Anruf Jogi bis zum 72. BDay Trump sind 1260 Tage kannst Du auch nichts ändern. Genauso wenig wie an Deiner Herkunft und den Geburstdaten unserer Kinder.

Der Gerichtsstand ist Jerusalem. DreamStream in den USA. Du kommst aus Afrika, so wie Deine ganze Verwandtschaft und vertrittst genausowenig das Erbe meiner Väter wie meine Mutter.

> Einfach in Demut den HERREN suchend, die von GOTT gegebene Aufgabe (verantwortlicher Vater und
> Ehemann) erfüllend zu leben.

Weil Du das so anordnest? Hast Du sie nicht mehr alle? DU bist mir gegenüber verpflichtet, Du trägst meinen Namen und DU hast straffällig gehandelt. Es gibt dafür keine Entschudldigung, sondern nur eine schonungslose Aufklärung der Wahrheit.

> Wie willst Du über eine Welt herrschen wenn dich die Mikro-Aufgabe einer Familie
> vollkommen überfordert.

Ich bin mit nichts überfordert. Aber anscheint meine Mutter, die Lukas Gemeinde, die Bühlers, die Gemeinde und jeder Deiner Rechtsanwälte. Niemand ist in der Lage zu antworten, sondern zeigt seine eigene geistige Verwirrung und redet von Gott und hält mich für Tod.

> Leider, glaube ich, ist es viel zu spät für dich um an eine Beziehung mit deinen Kindern weiterzuarbeiten.

Meine Kinder werden als Könige zurück nach Jerusalem gehen und Prinzen und Herrscher werden ihnen dienen. Dein Schicksal hatte ich Dir ja schon geschrieben.

Wenn du kein Interesse an ihnen zeigst bist du gestrichen aus ihrem Leben, so einfach läuft es in einer Beziehung,
um dir das nochmal zu erklären.

Ich denke mal es gibt keinen Vater der so viel Leid für seine Kinder getragen hat wie ich, weswegen ich die Könige aller Könige Position letztendlich auch verdient habe. Mein Interesse ist über das gesamte Internet gepflastert und ich habe zu 100% nach Anleitung der Schrift gehandelt.

Vom 1.1.2015 - 24.5.2015 habe ich jedem die Möglichkeit gegeben jede Angelegeneheit mit mir zu klären.
Seit dem 25.5.2015 geht es um nichts anderes, als darum die Riesen Scheisse die Du und Jürgen verzapft haben wieder gerade zu biegen.
Seit dem 25.5.2016 gibt es die EU Working definition on Anti-Semitism
Seit dem 25.5.2017 ist klar, das ich mit dem 50. Lebensjahr den Karls Preis verdient hätte und zu Christi Himmelfahrt zu Hause sein sollen.
Seit dem 25.5.2018 gilt die DSGVO zu Daten Bereinigung personenbezogener Daten von natürlichen Personen.

Seit dem 14.6.2018 ist zu 100% gesichert, dass ich für 1260 Tage zu 100% richtig gelegen habe.

Da du aber tatsächlich Beziehungsunfähig bist, kann ich verstehen, dass das für dich kein Problem ist.

Es ist einfach lächerlich und man braucht nur unsere Korespondenz zu lesen. Außerdem habe ich Dich mehrfach eingeladen, was Du abgelehnt hast. Da es um mein Erbe und das Erbe meiner Kinder geht und meinen Namen, lasse ich Deine unverfrorenen Behauptungen selbstverständlich von einem Gericht überprüfen und mich unschuldig sprechen lassen.

Ich habe für mich entschieden, dass es das letzte mal ist, das ich mir deine hirnlosen, Menschen verachtenden, diskriminierenden, hasserfüllten, verbitterten, anmaßenden und einfach falschen Schlussfolgerungen durchzulesen.

Ich weis, die Wahrheit tut weh. Deswegen hat man Jesus gekreuzigt und will mich zum schweigen bringen. Nach 21 Jahren Ehe mit einem schwarzen Flüchtlingskind, soll die ganze Welt erfahren, wert der Rassist in unserer Familie ist und wie sich dieser Rassimus bis hoch in die Merkel Regierung zieht.

Den Schmerz vaterlos zu sein kennen die Kinder zu gut und müssen sich (besonders deine Söhne) die richtigen Vorbilder als angehende Männer suchen, die ihnen zeigen ein Mann Gottes zu sein.

Das zeige ich gerade. Ein Mann Gottes regelt seine Familienangelegenheiten auch gegen Fremdköroper und irgendwelche Diebe die sich in meinem Haus breit gemacht haben.

Ausgerechnet Du willst mir was von Vaterlos erzählen. Bist wohl zu lange bei Deiner und meiner Mutter in die Seelorge gegangen und zu tief in die Flasche geschaut.

Ich freue mich auf den Tag, wenn ich dich nicht mehr Ehemann nennen muss.

Er kommt. Keine Sorge, aber nicht so wie Du Dir das vorstellst.

Es wird passieren, mit oder gegen deine Einwilligung.

Korrekt. Was schert mich die besetzte BRD, wenn ich im Land der Freiheit und der Lebendigen USA und Israel in Reichtum leben kann.

Den Namen Diebel werden die Kinder natürlich weitertragen und wer weiss, vielleicht wollen die Kinder eines Tages gemeinsam mit mir ihren Namen ändern.

Definitiv nicht, denn unser Name steht in der Bibel. Du dürftest ja auch die Sprache meiner Väter lernen und kannst selbst auf die Geburtsurlunde von Naomi schauen. Sie ist ein Notzrit. Ein Spross aus Jakob, der in Jeremia 31.4 erwähnt ist.

Es ist meine Aufgabe als Priester meinen Kindern das Gesetz Gottes zu lehren und auch gegen Deine Wünsche, wird das Endgericht nach Torah und Propheten in Israel abgehalten. Irgendwelche Schreiben von Privaten

Gerichten sind nicht gültig, sondern werden von mir in New York beim Handelsbericht verklagt.

Unsere Heirat ist ebenfalls nicht gültig, da Du Katholisch warst, weswegen unsere 21 jährige Beziehung ebenfalls nach Handelsrecht und Verträgen geschieden werden muss.

Ich sag Dir das nur, weil Du immer denkst DU hättest irgendwelche Rechte, ohne dabei an MEINE zu denken.

Aber wer weiss, Daniel hätte das richtige Format um den Namen -DIEBEL- würdevoll zu tragen.

Dazu müsste er allerdings begreifen, dass er der erstgeborene des Königs aller Könige ist. Wenn er dann so wird wie ich, versteht er auch, was Du getan hast. Das Wort des Vaters ist Gesetz, nicht die Ratschläge einer hasserfüllten Mutter.

Ich glaube es jetzt wirklich, dass du das geniale Gehirn was dir der HERR anvertraut, durch das übermäßige Verzehr von Substanzen endgültig zum Opfer gefallen ist.

Wird wieder die Nazi Methode angewendet, oder was? Du faselst von Gott und unsichtbaren Dingen, maßt Dich als Frau meine Rechte als Mann zu verneinen und holst dann die Drogen Pille raus. So wie bei dem Daniel und bei der Eliana oder was?

Was darfs denn sein? Ritalin? Prozac, MDMA, LSD, Aspirin oder ein andere Pharma Produkt?

Ich sagte schon meinen Jungs... die Scheidung wird dreckig und schmutzig und wird das allerletzte aus den Menschen herausbringen. Es funktioniert!!

Möge GOTT dir gnädig sein, wenn eines Tages Rechenschaft abgeben musst.

Les mal meine Zeugenaussage gegen Dich, die ja seit dem 16.7.2017 online ist und dann erklär mir wer Dir noch Gnade gewähren sollte. Ich definitiv nicht, Gott auch nicht, weil er das Gericht dem Sohn übertragen hat, also mir und ich schon beim Stellvertreter Gottes angefragt habe und der auch antworten muss.

Wir beten weiterhin für Dich.

Ihr hättet einfach ZUHÖREN sollen.

.ıll Telekom de 🗢   00:04   ☀ 89 % 📶

ulfdiebel.com

Art. 6 DSGVO - ...   Site Stats ı Ulf...   Christian Zi...   Abteilung Pres...   Arye Sharuz S...   Dashboard - Ul...   Elite Health   600 Nis bank o...   1 Mose 1 - New...   Breaking Israel...   Trump's Traum...

JULY 24, 2018   f 🐦 G+ 👥 in ⊙

Ulf Diebel

EX & CHANGE   CONTACT   BLOG   EPHRAIM'S MEDIATHEK   EPHRAIM.INFO   ZION ON MY MIND

Breaking Zion News   Das Schweigen Der Lämmer Auf Der Schlachtbank

Home > Zion > Return to Zion > Christian Zionism, Ephraim & the $500.000.000 offer for the truth

Christian Zionism, Ephraim & The $500.000.000 Offer For The Truth

BY ULF ON SEPTEMBER 26, 2017

💬 0   👁 99 VIEWS

Read Offline: 🖬 Download PDF   Download ePub   Download mobi   🖨 Print

SEARCH

BECAUSE I AM ISRAEL'S FATHER, AND EPHRAIM IS MY FIRSTBORN SON. JEREMIA 31.9

[Zitierter Text ausgeblendet]
[Zitierter Text ausgeblendet]

..ıll Telekom.de 🤝   00:04   ⚡ 89 % ▰▰▱

〈   🔖   ≡   ulfdiebel.com   ⟳   ⬆   +   ⧉

Art. 8 DSGVO –   Site Stats ‹ Ulf...   ⊙ Christian Zi...   Abteilung Pres...   Arye Sharuz S...   Dashboard ‹ Ul...   Elite Health   500 Nis bank o...   1 Mose 1 - New...   Breaking Israel...   Trump's Traum...

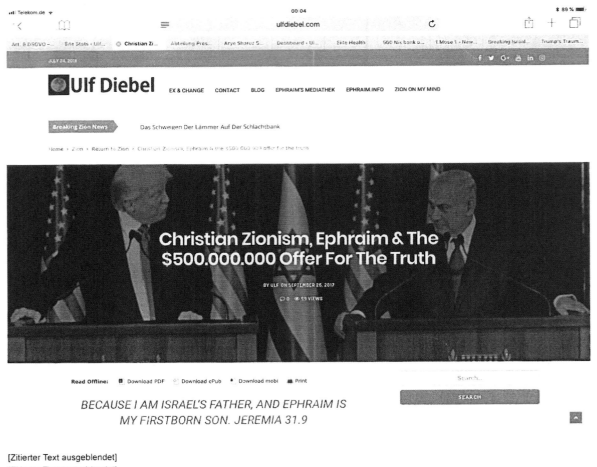

JULY 24, 2018   f 🐦 G⁺ 👍 in 📷

⬤Ulf Diebel

EX & CHANGE   CONTACT   BLOG   EPHRAIM'S MEDIATHEK   EPHRAIM.INFO   ZION ON MY MIND

Breaking Zion News ▶   Das Schweigen Der Lämmer Auf Der Schlachtbank

Home › Zion › Return to Zion › Christian Zionism, Ephraim & the $500.000.000 offer for the truth

Christian Zionism, Ephraim & The $500.000.000 Offer For The Truth

BY ULF ON SEPTEMBER 26, 2017

💬 0   👁 99 VIEWS

Read Offline: 📄 Download PDF   📄 Download ePub   📄 Download mobi   🖨 Print

Search...

SEARCH

🔼

BECAUSE I AM ISRAEL'S FATHER, AND EPHRAIM IS MY FIRSTBORN SON. JEREMIA 31.9

[Zitierter Text ausgeblendet]
[Zitierter Text ausgeblendet]

Senait Diebel <senait.diebel@gmail.com>   26. Juli 2018 um 20:14
An: Ulf Diebel <ulfdiebel@gmail.com>

Ich versuch es noch einmal, ein aller letztes mal bevor ich es den staatlichen Autoritaeten ueberlasse, an dein Kleinhirn zu appelieren. Israel und America werden dich nicht rein Lassen und zwar ganz genau aus dem Grund den du erwaehnt hast. Das Netz ist voll von Ulf Diebel uebersaeht mit deinen Ueberzeugungen, die nicht unbedingt politisch korrekt sind. Welches Land soll von Ulf profitieren? Weder Trump noch der Papst oder Netanyahu haben Interesse an deinen Erkenntnissen gezeigt.

[Zitierter Text ausgeblendet]

Ulf Diebel <ulfdiebel@gmail.com>   26. Juli 2018 um 20:44
Entwurf

[Zitierter Text ausgeblendet]

2018-8-9

Report: Hamas official hints at agreement with Israel

THE JERUSALEM POST

BREAKING | NEWS

Israeli envoy to UN Danon calls on Security Council to condemn Hamas

Genesis 17.7.

Advertisement

Jerusalem Post > Breaking News >

CHURCHES IN ISRAEL ARE JOINING THE FIGHT AGAINST THE NATION-STATE LAW

BY JERUSALEM POST STAFF / AUGUST 9, 2018 17:21

Strafzölle und Sanktionen

Gefährdet Trump die Weltwirtschaft?

Stand: 23.08.2018 07:18 Uhr

Immer neue Strafmaßnahmen gegen Russland und China, möglicherweise bald auch gegen den Iran: Die US-Politik der Sanktionen und Strafzölle könnte zu einer Gefahr für die globale Konjunktur werden.

Von Thomas Spinnler, boerse.ard.de

Heute Russland, morgen China: In diesen Tagen dreht Donald Trump die Zölle- und Sanktionen-Schrauben noch einmal ein Stückchen weiter. Ab heute dürfen amerikanische Gasturbinen-Triebwerke, bestimmte Elektronik- und Kalibriergeräte nicht mehr nach Russland ausgeführt werden. Sanktionen, die Trump eigentlich nicht will, zu denen er aber gezwungen ist.

Ganz anders sieht es im Verhältnis zwischen Trump und China aus: Ab dem 23. August werden Strafzölle von 25 Prozent auf chinesische Importe im Umfang von dann insgesamt 50 Milliarden Dollar, also rund 43 Milliarden Euro, erhoben. Betroffen sind Hunderte Produkte, darunter Motorräder, Traktoren, elektronische Schaltungen und Agrarbedarf. China hat bereits angekündigt, im Gegenzug weitere US-Importe mit Gegenzöllen zu belegen.

Hauptsache, es wird gesprochen

Immerhin unternimmt China einen Anlauf zum Dialog. Die Regierung schickt jetzt eine Delegation unter Führung des stellvertretenden Handelsministers für Gespräche nach Washington. Solange an dieser Front miteinander gesprochen werde, sei das eine gute Nachricht, kommentierte ein Experte beim Vermögensverwalter J.P. Morgan Asset Management.

Reicht schon das Reden? Schließlich gehört mindestens Zuhören zu einem gelingenden Dialog - und meistens auch Kompromissbereitschaft zu erfolgreichem Verhandeln. Nach allem was man heute weiß, gehören diese Fähigkeiten vermutlich nicht unbedingt zu Trumps hervorstechendsten Qualitäten.

US-Präsident Donald Trump (r.) und der chinesische Präsident Xi Jinping: Ob Gespräche auf höchster Ebene sinnvoll wären?

In einem Interview mit der Nachrichtenagentur Reuters dämpft Trump dann auch gleich alle Erwartungen an die Gespräche. Der US-Präsident unterstrich, dass vermutlich nicht viel dabei herauskomme. Er habe einen "langen Atem", ließ er die Welt wissen. Den wird er vermutlich auch brauchen.

Noch wackelt China nicht

Denn bislang zumindest halten sich die ökonomischen Folgen des Konflikts für China in Grenzen - auch wenn die Experten von Metzler eine leichte Wachstumsverlangsamung feststellen: "Die Strafzölle belasten die chinesische Wirtschaft, die Währungsschwäche federt jedoch einen Teil dessen wieder ab", schreibt Edgar Walk, Chefvolkswirt von Metzler Asset Management.

Ermutigend sind für China auch frische ZEW-Konjunkturdaten. In der aktuellen Umfrage des China Economic Panel (CEP) von ZEW und der Fudan Universität (Shanghai) erholen sich die Konjunkturerwartungen nach erheblichen Rückgängen wieder. Die chinesische Wirtschaft scheine trotz des Handelskonflikts mit den USA derzeit noch recht robust zu sein. Bislang seien kaum negative Effekte auf das Wachstum zu erkennen, heißt es.

Mister

DAVID RENÉ JAMES DE ROTHSCHILD

23 B AVENUE DE MESSINE

75008 PARIS

France

Elite Plus-Ephi-Zentrum

Prozessionsweg 27

D-33428 Harsewinkel

Tel.   +49 524 792 54 56

Mobil   +49 157 501 186 62

ephi-zentrum@ephraim.info

www.ephraim.info

23.08.2018

Dear David,

My name is Ulf Diebel from Düsseldorf, *25.5.67. My daughters Naomi Esther *5.7.1999 and Yael Eden *21.11.2004 are the Zechariah 9.9 Daughter of Zion and Daughter of Jerusalem, the miracle children of the Immanuel of Isaiah 8.18. They are the Key of David mentioned in Isaiah 22.22 and Revelation 3.7, you need to bring back the Kingdom to Israel out of the hand of Pope Francis.

Of all my attached, most favorite D-U-N-S, you stand as the only person with your CAPITAL NAME DAVID DE ROTHSCHILD, MEANING ACCORDING TO SANHEDRIN 37, YOU STAND WITH YOUR BLOOD FOR WHAT YOU DO AND THAT INCLUDES TO SAVE A SOUL FROM ISRAEL. I SWORE TO HASHEM 4.9.1997 DURING THE TRIPLE BOMBING IN JERUSALEM, WHEN MY FIRSTBORN SON DANIEL SURVIVED UNBORN, TO UPHOLD THE SAME STANDARD FOR ME AND MY FAMILY, TO SERVE HASHEM AND TO KEEP HIS LAWS, ORDINANCES AND REGULATION, EVEN UNTO DEATH.

That Isaiah 49.1-8 would one day become a living reality in me, even after my official start as „Ephraim, Priest of the order of Melchizedek" 25.5.15, became only clear to me, when on Holocaust Remembrance Day 24.4.17 I received by divine appointment the EPHI-Zentrum in Iserlohn on the 147th anniversary of the dogmatic constitution of the church DEI FILIUS from 24.4.1870.

Bankverbindung

Ulf Diebel
Erbengemeinschaft Jakob
Fidor Bank
IBAN: DE41 700 222 0000 7190 5217

Up to the last moment I hoped, that ONE family member, my wife, own mother, my business partners, or any of the „congregation", a rabbi, pastor, business guy would react, but No.

HaShem has supernaturally blinded everybody and my normal family case - „Guy trouble with his wife, who wants a divorce" turned into „I will wait for the Lord, who is hiding his face from the descendants of Jakob" Isaiah 8.17

For quite some time, I knew that someone from the House of Rothschild must have the firstborn right of Judah, as written in Hesekiel 37.15, as the High Court of Israel carries your family name, where ONE single stone on a ladder is prominently displayed in the Courtyard of the building with my birthdate 25.5.67 built into the structure - THANK YOU! I am speechless over the miracles of HaShem and his Ruach, who moved the hearts of kings and mighty men to prepare the judgement seat for the ruler over all of Israel (Micah 5).

Only with the end of day 1260 of Revelation 12.6, when Ronald Lauder held up again the #WeRemember sign on the 72nd B-Day of Donald Trump 14.6.2018, I knew, that there is nobody in the world but me, who can claim to be the firstborn from the dead and faithful witness in Zion, present all legal proof and then survive the Roman Inquisition and the most scrutinizing eyes of Talmudic trained Jewish Lawyers, who define „Who is a Jew", but are not able to identify Joseph and definitely not the source of all confusion in Jerusalem, as written in Isaiah 8 - the „Stone of stumbling".

As you can see in my 25.5.15 declaration, I focused on Self-Governance by Purpose driven Technology, Currency XAU & XAG, as well as Media Truth on the business side, completely neglected during my 3,5 years being the Isaiah 53 servant, as nobody wanted to honor his former contracts or even help me out of a humanitarian crisis. For standing with Zion as Ephraim, executing my God given Human right to seek atonement for me and my family according to the Torah and the Prophets of Israel, I had to endure the fire of Antisemitism and Racism as a Jew, without being a Jew, to the extent that the City of Iserlohn raided our building on 25.5.2018, without any court case, hearing, answering to formal letters, requests, 1 years after the „Erbengemeinschaft Jakob" became fully legal.

What was hidden for 7 years came out into the open from 1.1.2015 - 14.6.2018. I filed for prosecution at the state prosecutor Berlin-Moabit on 29.3.2018 (also against the City of Iserlohn) and received the File Number 77 days later on 14.6.2018 with a rejection and another file number, after I sent the first letter to David Friedman.

Bankverbindung

Ulf Diebel
Erbengemeinschaft Jakob
Fidor Bank
IBAN: DE41 700 222 0000 7190 5217

The attached Daniel 10 - 12 revelation is public since March 2018 and in full faith to be the One, I requested back-up from David Melech Friedman via registered mail 30.7.2018 and then some days later with a clear question, what will happen now, as my return is in direct connection with the clearance of the Palestinian Question, described in Zechariah 9, as well as the Syrian question... the sin of Ephraim of Isaiah 7.

As the National Security advisor Bolton is now in Jerusalem, Putin stopped by to give some sort of instructions to Merkel on 18.8.18, visiting the „final settlement" created by the 2+4 contracts and I am getting louder each day here in Germany as a political force, I ask you now for your direct and active involvement.

The Pope accepted you as „the older brother", while I am the younger brother, who just happened to be born and picked as a scapegoat, to plot out the sins of Ephraim and Judah and all Israel in one day (Zech. 3.9) - and after I saw the line up at the US Embassy opening in Jerusalem, I am confident, that you are prepared for this very moment of revelation, in case you didn't receive a copy of the letters I sent to the Israeli High Court or the Pope, or any other message.

I have nothing to offer but the truth of the least of all people, who found grace in the eyes of HaShem as the living stone the builders rejected and was not prepared to be King of Kings and your last option for world peace and the redemption of all the Jewish People.

As all my letters are public, also this letter is public and an official offer for a #NewDeal between the House of Israel (Germany) and the House of Judah (the Jewish State of Israel), created by the Zionists, who acted since their inception „Negotiorum Gestio" and need now the Yehoshua, to confirm their action.

Here I am and the children HaShem has given me. We are a sign and wonder for all Israel from God Almighty, who lives on Mount Zion.

Will you DAVID DE ROTHSCHILD hold your vows and contracts to help me ULF DIEBEL to fulfill the destiny HaShem has in store for all Israel and humanity and send your legal representation (see last letter to David Melech Friedman) to take off my legal restrictions and to initiate the required legal documentation to take over Zion and the possession of the Church by the heir.

Bankverbindung

Ulf Diebel
Erbengemeinschaft Jakob
Fidor Bank
IBAN: DE41 700 222 0000 7190 5217

Seite 3 von 3

Am 24.8.2018 um 19.00 waren die Vorbereitungen für das Endgericht der Apokalypse beendet, alle Dokumente, Beweise und Gesetze geordnet und die wichtigsten 100 Personen nach D-U-N-S Handelsnummern übersichtlich an der Tafel im Elite Healthclub in Harsewinkel angebracht.

Am 25.8.2018 - exakt um 23.00 Uhr hatte ich als Priester nach der Ordnung Melchizedek Verantwortung für den Heiligen Stuhl (Santa Sede D-U-N-S 438923885) übernommen. Ein Studio Besucher ärgerte sich über das biblisch korrekte Wort für den Papst aus Offenbarung 17 „Hure", weshalb das gesamte Gericht unter dem modernen Ausdruck für den Papst „Bitch" abgehalten wurde.

In meinem vollen Bewusstsein meiner Verantwortung vor Gott und den Menschen hatte ich im Vorfeld die wirklichen, echten und tatsächlichen Mächte informiert, da es sich um einen echten Gerichtsfall handelt, dessen Abschluss vor dem Höchsten Israelischen Gerichtshof in Jerusalem stattfinden wird.

Schon am 23.5.2017 hatte ich einen Eilantrag nach GG Art. 17 an alle Beteiligten der 2+4 Verträge geschickt und Donald Trump gebeten mich zum Papst mitzunehmen, um die Jerusalemfrage zu klären.

4.9.2018
SANTA SEDE
D-U-N/S 438923885
CITTA' DEL VATICANO
Hauptverantwortlicher:
ULF DIEBEL

Am 24.8.2017 wurden von mir per Einschreiben alle wichtigen Dokumente an den Vatikan und den Israelischen Gerichtshof geschickt und am 29.3.2018 meine Anklage bei der Staatsanwaltschaft Berlin Moabit abgegeben.

Am 30.7.2018 hatte ich dann David Friedman von der US Botschaft in Jerusalem geschrieben, der von mindestens 10 weiteren Erben aus Jakob ebenfalls Post bekommen hat. Um die ganze Sache Wasserdicht zu machen, ging mit 20.8.2018 Einschreiben an Innenminister Horst Seehofer (der wahre Verfassungsschutz), CDU Frontmann Volker Kauder und Linken Cheffin Sahra Wagenknecht mit klaren Anweisungen raus, wobei ich Horst Seehofer gebeten hatte, einen Blick auf Iserlohn und Harsewinkel zu werfen. Alice Weidel hatten wir schon mehrfach eingeladen und auch dem AfD Vertreter Udo aus Harsewinkel einige wichtige Briefe und Dokumente mitgegeben.

Als vom 29.8.2018 - 31.8.2018 eine Serie von Artikeln in der Lokalen Presse in verschiedenen Zeitungen erschien, die allesamt auf die Zerstörung des Elite Healthclub hinzielen, konnte der Straftatbestand des Völkermordes VStGB §6 eindeutig nachgewiesen werden.

Da in der SPD Zeitung, die dem Medien Konzern der SPD mit 129 Millionen Euro Jahresumsatz angehört, die fette Überschrift „Staatsschutz ist eingeschaltet" zu lesen ist, war es für die Beteiligten der Verschwörung gegen Juri Nasirow ein Schock, als jeder erfuhr, dass wir den Staatsschutz tatsächlich angefordert haben und dieser nun jeden Beteiligten

der öffentlichen „Hinrichtung" der jungen Familie Nasirow und des Elite Healthclub ihrem
gerechten Urteil zuführen wird.

Zu keinem Zeitpunkt meiner Tätigkeit als Ephraim, Priester nach der Ordnung Melchizedek
wurde irgendetwas verschleiert, schöngeredet oder verheimlicht, sondern klar gesagt worum
es geht: Um einen Frieden in Zion, so wie er in der Bibel aufgeschrieben ist.

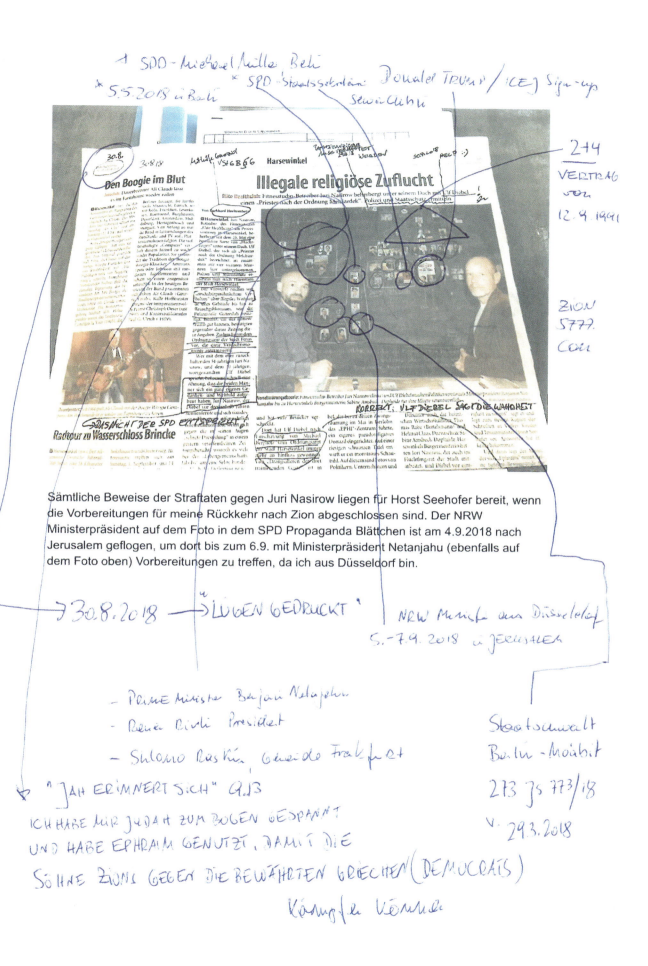

Auch Staatsschutz eingeschaltet

Michael Bergholz vom Ordnungsamt der Stadt hat die Polizei und den Kreis mit ins Boot geholt.

Oktoberfest in abgespeckter Form

▶ Harsewinkel

Der Staatsschutz Horst Seehofer hat am 4.9.2018 Besuch von dem Kollegen aus Österreich bekommen, sich eine Stunde später von der US Politik von Merkel (CDU hat fertig, weil zu viele Christen persönlich in dem Fall Ephraim involviert sind) und Maas (Heiko Maas wurde von mir für die Abwicklung der SPD auserkoren) distanziert und einen Termin mit Richard Grenell vereinbart (wird von jedem in der BRD genauso wie Trump gehasst) - jeder dieser Personen hatte ein Foto auf der Wand.

Mit dem ersten Artikel vom 29.8.2018 in der Glocke, das Wort „Hure" als Foto erscheint (in keinem unserer offiziellen Publikationen) erscheint gleichzeitig aus New York (UN Sitz, Donald Trump Heimatstadt, Sitz des World Jewish Congress, CFR, Wall Street etc.) die Bestätigung meiner Autorität als Richter über ganz Israel.

Meine Arbeit die am 18.5.2000 mit einem Vortrag über „Israel und wir nach der Jahrtausendwende" begonnen hatte, erhielt am 29.8.2018 mit der Bestätigung „Papst Franziskus muss zurücktreten" ihren krönenden Abschluss, der Rest ist nur noch Formalität.

Das Ergebnis des Endgericht der Offenbarung war selbst für mich schockierend.

1.) Die gesamte D-U-N-S Abrechnung war zu 100% korrekt und gültig.
2.) Jedes Unternehmen weltweit ist durch internationale Handelsverträge mit der USA an den US Handelsdollar gebunden.
3.) 1 Dollar zahlt für alle Schulden - Öffentlich und Privat
4.) Der Erbe bekommt tatsächlich ALLES - die gesamte Erde, inklusive aller Seelen darauf, weil er die Schulden der Welt getragen hat.
5.) Durch den Beweis des Straftatbestandes des Völkermordes VStGB §6 in einer Verschwörung gegen Juri Nasirow, wurde jede beteiligte Körperschaft nach D-U-N-S gelistet und in Vorbereitung des Treffens mit Donald Trump für $1 übernommen, was

Grund und Boden, Besitz (Executive Order 12803) und Humankapital (Executive Order 13037) der jeweiligen Körperschaft mit einschließt.

6.) Durch den Beweis des Straftatbestandes VStGB §6 in Harsewinkel, konnten auch die Missstände in der Generalstaatsanwaltschaft in Berlin, in der Stadtverwaltung Iserlohn und die strafrechtlich relevanten Antisemitischen und Rassistischen Angriffen durch Christliche Religionsgesellschaften nachgewiesen werden.

Es ist tatsächlich „alles gelaufen" und wir warten nur noch darauf, dass entweder Horst Seehofer, Alice Weidel oder Donald Trump hier auftaucht.

Die letzten Tage war extrem stressig, weil wir als normale Typen die überhaupt nicht aus Harsewinkel kommen, den Hass von tausenden Harsewinkelern gespürt haben, die uns benutzt haben, um Juri und seine kleine Familie zu töten.

Dafür waren die Tage unvorstellbar lukrativ.

Für Juri waren wir in der Lage 2 * 80.000.000 Euro an DSGVO zu erwirken, also 160 Millionen Euro.

Harsewinkel haben wir für $1 übernommen sowie jede D-U-N-S gelistete Körperschaft die an dem Völkermord beteiligt war, inklusive der Volksbank, die wir in Ephraim Bank umbenennen werden.

Wir freuen uns auch über das Gebäude direkt nebenan, Prozessionsweg 31. Da die ECG Harsewinkel keinen Hauptverantwortlichen in dem D-U-N-S gelisteten Unternehmen besitzt, hat der Priester nach der Ordnung Melchizedek die D-U-N-S 340533196 , #12079 Juri Nasirow zugesprochen.

Auch wenn es hier in Harsewinkel noch niemand so richtig glauben kann. Wir leben in einem neuen Zeitalter, dem Zeitalter der Regentschaft der lebendigen Söhne Gottes aus Israel. Nicht mehr Willkür und Hass wird uns regieren, sondern Gerechtigkeit und Wahrheit.

Der Staats- und Verfassungsschutz wird jeden Schuldigen dingfest machen, der schon jetzt sein Urteil von uns empfangen hat.

Wir sind aufgestanden und die Zeit ist gekommen, wo dies von der Welt akzeptiert werden muss. Mutti geht und der Sohn kommt, dem sich auch die Sahra anschließen wird.

Es ist uns bewusst, dass die wenigsten jemals von uns gehört haben, weswegen wir jedem empfehlen… trage Deine Email bei http://zion5777.com ein und folge den einfachen Schritten für Deine Erlösung als Erbe Jakobs.

SZ 🏠 Politik Wirtschaft Panorama Sport München Bayern Kultur Gesellschaft Wissen Digital Karriere Reise Auto Stil mehr... 🔍

4. September 2018, 18:11 Uhr   "Aufstehen"

Die Bewegung muss sich von Wagenknecht emanzipieren

Es gibt ein Reservoir gegen AfD und Pegida, aus dem Parteien nicht schöpfen konnten. Doch damit "Aufstehen" erfolgreich ist, muss Initiatorin Wagenknecht andere nach vorn lassen.

Die Sammlungsbewegung "Aufstehen" ist soeben erst aufgestanden und hat schon erheblich mehr Unterstützer, als Grüne, FDP oder Linke Mitglieder haben. Das ist bemerkenswert. Das offenbart ein bisher offenbar ungestilltes Bedürfnis vieler Menschen, sich zu engagieren - gegen den Druck von Rechtsaußen, gegen die Dominanz des Rechtsradikalen im öffentlichen Raum, gegen die Renaissance des Nationalen und
des Nationalistischen.

CP POLITICS

White House Hosts 100 Evangelical Leaders for State-Like Dinner: 'This Is Spiritual Warfare'

By Samuel Smith , CP Reporter | Aug 28, 2018 7:57 AM

(PHOTO: TWITTER/@SCAVINO45)

President Donald Trump speaks with evangelical leaders during a dinner at the White House on Aug. 27, 2018.

[handwritten note in margin:] ∧ Schwabe = Chef des Evangelicale in ISRAEL: BRD Büro Dr. Jürge Bühler! [→ICEJ]

About 100 evangelical leaders were invited to dinner at the White House Monday night for what was a prayer-filled event that's been compared to a church camp meeting and a campaign rally.

Dubbed a "state dinner" for evangelical leaders, the event was held specifically in the "honor of evangelical leadership." The dinner was attended by dozens of evangelical pastors, evangelists and activists who've been involved in informally advising the administration including well-known figures like Franklin Graham, James Dobson, and Greg Laurie.

The dinner was also attended by Vice President Mike Pence, Secretary of Homeland Security Ben Carson, Secretary of the Department of Health and Human Services Alex Azar and Ambassador at-Large for International Religious Freedom Sam Brownback. The event was officially hosted by first lady Melania Trump.

"We are here today to celebrate America's heritage of faith, family and freedom," Trump told the crowd (https://www.youtube.com/watch?v=d4ZCKYaLmvU). "As you know in recent years, the government tried to undermine religious freedom but the attacks on communities of faith are over. We've ended it."

Trump continued by boasting about the promises his administration has kept to a conservative evangelical base that played a large role in helping him win the 2016 presidential election.

The president went on about how his administration has taken several steps to protect religious liberty for conservatives who object to things like abortion or gay marriage, his administration's pro-life victories and how the administration has spoken out about worldwide religious persecution.

Trump even took a moment to recognize Dobson and his wife, Shirley on their 58th wedding anniversary. Trump concluded by telling the crowd that they are "very special people."

"The support you have given me has been incredible but I really don't feel guilty because I have given you a lot back — just about everything I promised," Trump said. "As one of our great pastors just said, 'Actually, you have given us much more than you have promised.' And I think that is true."

(PHOTO: JOHNNIE MOORE)

Paula White (center), spiritual adviser to President Donald Trump, and Jared Kushner (center left), a senior adviser to Trump and his son-in-law, attend an evangelical leaders dinner at the White House on Aug. 27, 2018.

Before the dinner, Trump met privately with a small handful of evangelical leaders and their wives including Texas megachurch pastor Jack Graham, Franklin Graham, Jerry Falwell Jr. and the American Association of Christian Counselors' Tim Clinton. Florida televangelist Paula White and her son also reportedly joined the small gathering.

Jack Graham, the senior pastor at Prestonwood Baptist Church in Plano, Texas, who has served as president of the Southern Baptist Convention, told The Christian Post that Trump opened up the mic during dinner to allow evangelical leaders in the room to speak their minds.

What ensued, Graham said, was about 35 to 40 minutes of pastors expressing their appreciation for what the Trump administration has been able to do to progress a socially conservative agenda in the last 18 months. While Christians are often called to speak "truth to power," Graham said the leaders in the room felt called to speak "love to power."

"They were getting up and saying what we appreciate and care about, expressing our faith and our love. It was very similar to a meeting that you would have at a church," Graham said, adding that it was like a testimony meeting. "With that many preachers and Christian leaders in the room, we believe the spirit of God was very present. Scripture was shared, verses were given to the president. The truth was delivered and love was delivered."

However, some who spoke during the open mic session warned that evangelicals must keep up the "vigilance" because a negative outcome in the 2018 midterm elections could put the gains of Trump's first 18 months in jeopardy.

"We need to maintain our vigilance in the upcoming days. The concern is that this is a spiritual warfare, this is a battle and ultimately battle is won on our knees," Graham said. "It is very clear, we voiced to the president that we need to pray, pray for him, pray for our country."

Graham noted that many prayers were offered throughout the night.

In a statement provided to CP, Dr. James Dobson, the founder of Focus on the Family and Family Talk radio, said the dinner was "wonderful" and unlike any event he has attended at the White House before.

"I have served five presidents in the past 38 years and this was perhaps the most exciting event in that time," Dobson said. "The president spoke first and thanked us generously for the support we have given to him and his Administration since his inauguration. At least 15 ministers and leaders then rose to thank Mr. Trump for keeping his promises during the campaign and since his inauguration."

(PHOTO: TWITTER / @VP)

Vice President Mike Pence (L) and his wife, Karen, walk with James Dobson (R) and his wife, Shirley, prior to a dinner with over 100 evangelical leaders at the White House in Washington, D.C. on Aug. 27, 2018.

"Great appreciation was expressed for defending the sanctity of human life, for preserving religious liberty, for the quality of judges appointed, for his defense of Israel, for his support of the military, for ending the Johnson Amendment that had denied the church freedom of speech, and many other issues for which we are grateful," Dobson added.

"Many in attendance pledged their intention to help get out the vote for the midterm elections. There were heartfelt prayers for the president and the first lady, and also for Vice President Mike Pence and his wife, Karen, who were also in attendance. It was a moving and encouraging gathering, I think for the invitees and also for our president."

Dallas megachurch Pastor Robert Jeffress, one of Trump's staunchest evangelical supporters, told Fox News (https://twitter.com/FoxNews/status/1034287297628438529) that the event almost turned into a bit of a "campaign rally."

"Leader after leader stood up and started talking about why they supported President Trump," Jeffress said.

Other notable evangelicals who attended the meeting include Family Research Council President Tony Perkins, conservative radio host Eric Metaxas, televangelist Kenneth Copeland, megachurch Pastor Jentezen Franklin, Faith & Freedom Coalition's Ralph Reed, Maryland Bishop Harry Jackson, San Diego megachurch Pastor Jim Garlow, former Southern Baptist Convention President Ronnie Floyd and Hispanic evangelical leader the Rev. Samuel Rodriguez.

Other notable attendees from the administration include White House Press Secretary Sarah Sanders, Trump's daughter and senior adviser Ivanka Trump and her husband, Jared Kushner, who is also a senior White House adviser. Counselor to the President Kellyanne Conway was also present.

The meeting comes after a similar dinner (https://www.christianpost.com/news/greg-laurie-details-white-house-dinner-with-evangelicals-trump-breaking-protocol-182938/) involving about 40 to 50 evangelical leaders was held at the White House last May before the National Day of Prayer.

The difference between Monday's dinner and last May's dinner, Graham said, is Monday's dinner was far less structured and allowed for more of a "conversation" between the leaders and the president.

"It was basically like a state dinner in the way that it was organized with the president, vice president, members of the cabinet and so on," Graham explained. "It was the first time that anyone knows about ... a sitting president of the United States that has gathered evangelicals at a state-type dinner."

Of course, the meeting drew the ire (https://thewayofimprovement.com/2018/08/27/the-court-evangelicals-are-out-in-full-force-tonight/) of some left-leaning Christian critics. Some have claimed that the event was nothing more than another attempt by Trump to pander to his evangelical base.

"We have prayed for an opportunity to speak to the president of the United States and we would have a voice and an open door to express our views. We have a president now who wants to hear from us," Graham, who has been very active in his informal involvement with the administration, said. "The answer to anyone who says it is just pandering is: he is keeping his promises."

"If it was just photo-ops and pandering, then nothing would happen," he added. "But all these things are happening and we are amazed that we are seeing these things accomplished in the two years or so."

Some might argue that the evangelical dinner is an attempt to distract from the troubling news last week of Trump's lawyer Michael Cohen pleading guilty to campaign finance violations and claiming that Trump ordered him to arrange a hush payment to porn star Stormy Daniels to keep her quiet over an earlier affair she had with Trump during the 2016 election.

Graham explained that he received an invitation for the event at least six weeks ago.

"I know some are saying that given the events of last week, the president is just trying to get his boys together. This has been planned for a minimum of six weeks," Graham said, admitting that the event was "timely" given the "very tough week last week."

"In providence in the plan of God, this was planned weeks ago," Graham said. "Tonight was the night and it was a very special night with a very special leader and his wife with some great people in that room who are working hard for our churches and our communities."

Follow Samuel Smith on Twitter: @IamSamSmith (http://twitter.com/IamSamSmith)
Follow Samuel Smith on Facebook: SamuelSmithCP (https://www.facebook.com/SamuelSmithCP)

WIKIPEDIA

Jerusalem-Syndrom

 *(handschriftlich: ← "IN JERUSALEM ONLY"!)*

Das **Jerusalem-Syndrom** bezeichnet eine psychische Störung, von der jährlich etwa 100 Besucher der Stadt Jerusalem betroffen sind. Dabei handelt es sich nicht um eine anerkannte Diagnose. Die Symptome fallen im internationalen Diagnoseschlüssel unter „Akute und vorübergehende psychotische Störung".

(handschriftlich: FREUD IST TOT!)

Inhaltsverzeichnis

(handschriftliche Notizen: "Psyche" GRIECHISCH ≠ "Seele" HEBRÄER! →)

(Stempel: SANTA SEDE D-U-N-S 43-3923885 CITTA' DEL VATICANO Hauptverantwortlicher: ULF DIEBEL)

(handschriftlich: 29.8.2018 HARSEWINKEL)

Merkmale

Die Erkrankung hat den Charakter einer Psychose und äußert sich unter anderem in religiösen Wahnvorstellungen: Der oder die Betroffene identifiziert sich z. B. in einigen Fällen mit einer heiligen Person aus dem Alten oder Neuen Testament und gibt sich als diese aus.

Sehr bekannte biblische Figuren werden besonders häufig zum Objekt einer solchen Identifizierung, so zum Beispiel Mose und König David aus dem Alten Testament oder Paulus und Johannes der Täufer aus dem Neuen Testament. Grundsätzlich ist die Erkrankung „wählen" Männer männliche biblische Figuren und Frauen weibliche. Juden wählen häufig Figuren aus dem Alten Testament, Christen solche aus dem Neuen Testament.

Die Identifizierung als biblische Person geht einher mit einer entsprechenden Selbstdarstellung und wird oft begleitet von öffentlichen Predigten oder Gebeten des Erkrankten. Auch hüllen sie sich oft in weite Gewänder oder Bettlaken, d. h. in Kleidungsstücke der damaligen Zeit.

Bezeichnung und Verlauf

Der Jerusalemer Psychiater Heinz Herman diagnostizierte in den 1930er Jahren als Erster das Phänomen, damals noch unter dem Namen Jerusalem-Fieber.[1]

Die Bezeichnung Jerusalem-Syndrom stammt vermutlich vom israelischen Arzt Yair Bar El, der Anfang der 1980er Jahre dieses Krankheitsbild diagnostizierte und seitdem über 400 Betroffene in der psychiatrischen Klinik Kfar Shaul behandelt hat. Grundsätzlich ist die Erkrankung nicht gefährlich und die Betroffenen sind in der Regel nach wenigen Tagen vollständig genesen. Die große Mehrzahl der erkrankten Personen zeigte bereits vor dem Jerusalem-Syndrom psychische Auffälligkeiten.

Der Brandanschlag auf die Al-Aqsa-Moschee durch den australischen Touristen Michael Rohan im Jahre 1969 wurde wegen seiner religiösen Motivation dem Jerusalem-Syndrom zugeordnet.

Rezeption

Der israelische Autor Jehoschua Sobol schrieb 1988 ein Theaterstück gleichen Namens.

In der Simpsons-Episode Simpson und Gomorrha (Staffel 21; OT: The Greatest Story Ever D'ohed) sind Homer Simpson und weitere Personen von dem Syndrom betroffen.[2]

In dem ARD-Film Das Jerusalem Syndrom (Erstausstrahlung 11. Dezember 2013) ist die Schwester der Hauptdarstellerin betroffen.[3]

Siehe auch

- Stendhal-Syndrom bei zahlreichen Touristen in Florenz
- Paris-Syndrom bei japanischen Touristen in Paris

Literatur

- Y. Bar-el, R. Durst, G. Katz, J. Zislin, Z. Strauss, H. Y. Knobler: Jerusalem syndrome. In: British Journal of Psychiatry. 176, 2000, S. 86–90. (Volltext) (http://bjp.rcpsych.org/content/176/1/86.full)
- M. Kalian, E. Witztum: Comments on Jerusalem syndrome. In: British Journal of Psychiatry 176, 2000, S. 492. (Volltext) (http://bjp.rcpsych.org/content/176/5/492.1.full)
- M. Kalian, E. Witztum: „The Jerusalem syndrome"—fantasy and reality a survey of accounts from the 19th century to the end of the second millennium. In: Isr. J. Psychiatry Relat Sci. 1999, 36(4), S. 260–271. PMID 10687302
- N. Fastovsky, A. Teitelbaum, J. Zislin, G. Katz, R. Durst Jerusalem syndrome or paranoid schizophrenia? In: Psychiatric Services. 2000, 51 (11), S. 1454. (Volltext) (http://ps.psychiatryonline.org/article.aspx?articleid=85165)
- C. Tannock, T. Turner: Psychiatric tourism is overloading London beds. In: BMJ (Clinical research ed.). Band 311, Nummer 7008. September 1995, S. 806, PMID 7580448. PMC 2550781 (https://www.ncbi.nlm.nih.gov/pmc/articles/PMC2550781/) (freier Volltext).
- A. Van der Haven: The holy fool still speaks. The Jerusalem Syndrome as a religious subculture. In: T. Mayer, S. A. Mourad (Hrsg.): Jerusalem: idea and Reality. Routledge, 2008, S. 103–122.

Weblinks

- The Jerusalem Syndrome. (http://www.jewishvirtuallibrary.org/jsource/History/jersynd.html) By Leah Abramowitz
- Netzeitung: Jerusalem-Syndrom: Reisekrankheit mit vielen Rätseln (https://web.archive.org/web/20081013003610/http://www.netzeitung.de/reise/1060499.html) (Memento vom 13. Oktober 2008 im Internet Archive)
- Vom Touristen zum Messias – Das „Jerusalem-Syndrom" (http://www.n-tv.de/panorama/Das-Jerusalem-Syndrom-article257427.html)
- Joëlle Weil: Diagnose: Religiöser Wahn. (http://www.tagesanzeiger.ch/leben/gesellschaft/Diagnose-Religioeser-Wahn-/story/13785643) In: Tages-Anzeiger vom 15. Januar 2014
- Die Zeit 51/2013 / Eva Lindner: SMS von Jesus II (http://www.zeit.de/2013/51/jerusalem-syndrom)

Fußnoten

1. The Jerusalem Syndrome in Biblical Archaeology (https://www.sbl-site.org/publications/article.aspx?articleId=374)
2. Simpson und Gomorrha. (https://simpsonspedia.net/index.php?title=Simpson_und_Gomorrha) simpsonspedia.net. 3. Juni 2017, abgerufen am 19. September 2017.
3. Das Jerusalem-Syndrom. (https://web.archive.org/web/20131211065453/http://www.daserste.de/unterhaltung/film/filmmittwoch-im-ersten/sendung/das-jerusalem-syndrom-100.html) (Memento vom 11. Dezember 2013 im Internet Archive) Beschreibung zum Film auf der Website der ARD

Abgerufen von „https://de.wikipedia.org/w/index.php?title=Jerusalem-Syndrom&oldid=170603375"

Diese Seite wurde zuletzt am 3. November 2017 um 10:58 Uhr bearbeitet.

Am 25.5.2015 hatte ich zu meinem 48. Geburtstag ein vorher angekündigtes Lebens-ReSet und Berufswechsel durchgeführt, um eine sehr persönliche Familienangelegenheit zu klären, die bis zum heutigen 23.5.2018 in ungeahnter Weise eskaliert ist und mit dem Stichtag 25.5.2018, meinem 51 Geburtstag eine IST-Situation geschaffen hat, die mit dem Inkrafttreten der Datenschutz Grundverordnung am gleichen Tag wie folgt aussieht.

1.) Seit dem 9.3.2015 wurde Ulf Diebel *25.5.67 Umstände bekannt, die zu der Deklaration von „Ephraim, Priester nach der Ordnung Melchizedek" am 25.5.2015 als Beruf nach GG Art. 9 führten.

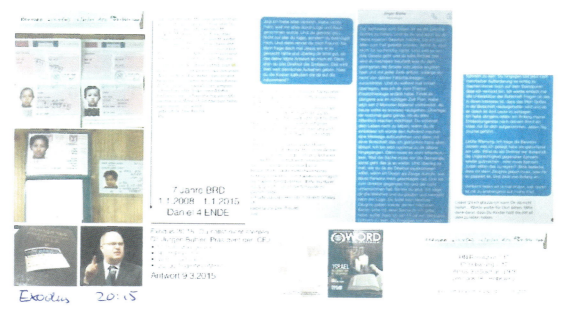

2.) Vor dem 25.5.2015 hatte ich Rabbi Avraham Feld, der im März 2005 bei der Unabhängigkeitserklärung der Nation Ephraim anwesend war, eine Zeugenaussage geschickt, die an nachfolgende Personen gerichtet war.

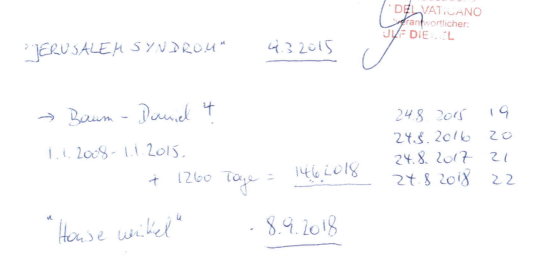

Kommentar Vom Segen der Freiwilligendienste

Glaube Das vierte Gebot: Ruhe am siebten Tag!

Pro und Kontra Ist die Jugend zu „ich-zentriert"?

Lebensstil Kein Haus, kein Auto, mein Boot

DIESE WOCHE LESEN SIE

Predigen für Profis

ANZEIGE

₤88.18

GEFANGENER DES MONATS

\#

Selbstbestimmung

Homosexualität: Spahn offen für Verbot von Konversionstherapien

Bundesgesundheitsminister Jens Spahn (CDU) hat sich offen gezeigt, sogenannte Konversionstherapien zu verbieten, die Homosexuellen helfen sollen, ihre sexuelle Orientierung zu verändern. mehr » ▮0

Evangelische Brüdergemeinde

Korntal: Heimkinder wurden jahrelang zur Arbeit gezwungen

In Heimen der Evangelischen Brüdergemeinde

SPD-Vorsitzende

Nahles: „Das Zusammensein mit meinem Kind ist auch Gottesdienst"

Die SPD-Vorsitzende Andrea Nahles betet mit ihrer

Jack Phillips

USA: Christlicher Bäcker verklagt den Bundesstaat Colorado

Ein christlicher Bäcker in den USA hat Klage gegen

659 × 808 – Bilder sind in der Regel urheberrechtlich geschützt. Weitere Informationen

Bedford-Strohm: Zum Frem

Jüdische Rundschau

Ein offener Brief von Gerd Buurmann an den Ra
Kirche in Deutschland ◇

Besuchen   Speichern   Gespeicherte

Ähnliche Bilder

Hilfe · Feedback geben

Aktuelles | Österreich | Deutschland | Schweiz | Weltkirche | Chronik | Familie | Jugend
Spirituelles | Buchtipp | Interview | Kommentar | Kultur | English | Italiano | Pro Life

---

27 August 2018, 09:30

Kardinal Napier: Missbrauchsfälle sind ein Homosexuellen-Problem

Kardinal: „In der Schlagzeile der Morgenzeitung ‚Die Kirchen müssen die Homo-Ehen erlauben' wird ganz klar der Punkt übersehen, dass dies die selbe sexuelle Aktivität ist, die den Skandal in der katholischen Kirche bei den Wurzeln verursacht!"

 Tippfehler melden
🖨 Druckversion
✉ Artikel versenden

WEITERE ARTIKEL ZUM THEMA 'Missbrauch'

Bundesstaat Illinois untersucht Erzdiözese Chicago

John Jay Bericht: 80 Prozent der Missbrauchsopfer männlich

New York Times-Kommentar: Papst Franziskus muss zurücktreten

Kardinal Cupich zieht die 'Rassismus-Karte'

US-Bischof: Vertuscher müssen ans Licht gebracht werden!

Durban (kath.net)
Kardinal Wilfried Napier hat die Berichte über Missbrauchsfälle in der katholischen Kirche ganz klar ein Homosexuellen-Problem identifiziert. Papst Franziskus sprach in den Zusammenhang vor wenigen Tagen nur von eine „Klerikalismus-Problem" und hat das Wort „Homosexualität" nicht erwähnt, obwohl in den Studien der US-Bischofskonferenz bereits 2011 festgestellt hatte, dass über 80 % der Täter im Zusammenhang mit Homosexualität stehen. Napier hat dazu auf Twitter festgehalten: „In der Schlagzeile der Morgenzeitung ‚Die Kirchen müssen die Homo-Ehen erlauben' wird ganz klar der Punkt übersehen, dass dies die selbe sexuelle Aktivität ist, die den Skandal in der katholischen Kirche bei den Wurzeln verursacht! Abweichungen von den Gesetzen Gottes bringen immer Ärgernis. Herr, vergib uns Sündern!"

Werbung

Ihnen hat der Artikel gefallen?
Bitte helfen Sie kath.net und spenden Sie jetzt via Überweisung auf ein Konto in Ö, D oder der CH oder via Kreditkarte/Paypal!

Recommend 23 people recommend this. Be the first of your friends.

G+

Tweet

kath.net ist Teilnehmer des Partnerprogramms von Amazon EU, das zur Bereitstellung eines Mediums für Webseiten konzipiert wurde, mittels dessen durch die Platzierung von Werbeanzeigen und Links zu Amazon.de Werbekostenerstattung verdient werden kann.

meist kommentierte Artikel

Schock: Nuntius sagt, Franziskus hat bei Kardinal McCarrick vertuscht! (109)

Papst: Eltern sollen ein homosexuelles Kind in Therapie schicken (106)

Papst: „Ich werde dazu kein einziges Wort sagen" (87)

"Nur raus hier!" (78)

Trotz US-Skandal plant Papst keine weiteren Maßnahmen gegen Missbrauch (71)

Kardinal: Missbrauchsopfer haben selber Leichen im Keller (66)

Heiligenkreuzer Klartext zum Missbrauchs- und Vertuschungsskandal (53)

USA: Katholische Moderatorin verlangt Rücktritt von Papst Franziskus (51)

US-Bischof: Vertuscher müssen ans Licht gebracht werden! (50)

+ version 5.0

LOGIN
Benutzername
Passwort
✓ eingeloggt bleiben
Login ◑
neu registrieren
Passwort vergessen

Aktuelles | Österreich | Deutschland | Schweiz | Weltkirche | Chronik | Familie | Jugend
Spirituelles | Buchtipp | Interview | Kommentar | Kultur | English | Italiano | Pro Life

29 August 2018, 13:13

"Wir sagten uns ein letztes Mal Lebewohl"

 Erzbischof Carlo Maria Viganò hatte wegen der Veröffentlichungen, die Papst Franziskus in Bedrängnis bringen, Angst um seine Sicherheit. Er hat Italien mit unbekanntem Ziel verlassen und auch sein Mobiltelefon abgemeldet

Rom (kath.net)
Der emeritierte Nuntius Erzbischof Carlo Maria Viganò fürchtet wegen der geplanten Enthüllungen über Papst Franziskus offensichtlich um sein Leben. Kurz vor der Veröffentlichung, die Papst Franziskus massiv in Bedrängnis bringen, hat der italienische Erzbischof, der von Johannes Paul II. an die römische Kurie geholt wurde, Italien in ein unbekanntes Land verlassen. Dies teilte der italienische Journalist Aldo Maria Valli, ein Bekannter des Erzbischofs, mit. Unmittelbar vor dem Abflug in ein unbekanntes Land hat er sogar sein Mobiltelefon abgemeldet.

 Tippfehler melden
Druckversion
Artikel versenden

WEITERE ARTIKEL
ZUM THEMA 'Kirche'

„Weil nicht sein kann, was nicht sein darf"

Was kommt nach der Volkskirche?

Reise in Kirche, die sich durch ihre Opfer bekehren lassen will

Missbrauchsskandal und Zeitendeuter

"Nur raus hier!"

Werbung

"Wir sagten uns ein letztes Mal Lebewohl", so Valli.

Auch Vatikanjournalist Edward Pentin hat inzwischen bestätigt, dass der 78-jährige Vigano Angst um seine Sicherheit hat.

LESE-TIPP: The Amazing Story of How Archbishop Viganò's Report Came to Be

Ihnen hat der Artikel gefallen?
Bitte helfen Sie kath.net und spenden Sie jetzt via Überweisung auf ein Konto in Ö, D oder der CH oder via Kreditkarte/Paypal!

 Spenden
VISA [ ] [ ] SEPA

Recommend 10 people recommend this. Be the first of your friends.

G+

kath.net ist Teilnehmer des Partnerprogramms von Amazon EU, das zur Bereitstellung eines Mediums für Webseiten konzipiert wurde, mittels dessen durch die Platzierung von Werbeanzeigen und Links zu Amazon.de Werbekostenerstattung verdient werden kann.

18.05.2000 – 29.08.2018

ISRAEL & WIR ALLE

Aktuelles | Österreich | Deutschland | Schweiz | Weltkirche | Chronik | Familie | Jugend
Spirituelles | Buchtipp | Interview | Kommentar | Kultur | English | Italiano | Pro Life

29 August 2018, 09:00

New York Times-Kommentar: Papst Franziskus muss zurücktreten

Die Missbrauchsskandale haben die katholische Kirche in einen Bürgerkrieg gestürzt. Die Heuchelei, einerseits homosexuelle Akte zu verurteilen und andererseits aktiv schwule Kleriker zu tolerieren, muss beendet werden, schreibt Matthew Schmitz.

New York City (kath.net/jg)
„Papst Franziskus muss zurücktreten. Diese Schlussfolgerung ist unvermeidlich, wenn die in dem Brief von Erzbischof Carlo Maria Viganò enthaltenen Vorwürfe wahr sind." Das schreibt Matthew Schmitz, leitender Redakteur des Magazins in einem Gastkommentar für die *New York Times*. (Siehe Link am Ende des Artikels)

Die Missbrauchsskandale hätten die Kirche in einen „Bürgerkrieg" gestürzt, fährt Schmitz fort. Die eine Seite sei der Ansicht, Missbrauch könne nur durch strengere Beachtung der kirchlichen Lehre verhindert werden. Schmitz bezeichnet sie als „Traditionalisten". Die andere Seite, die „Liberalen" wie Schmitz sie nennt, verlange, dass die Kirche homosexuelle Handlungen nicht mehr verurteilen und homosexuelle Priester öffentlich akzeptieren solle.

Werbung

Beide Seiten würden darin übereinstimmen, dass eine „Kultur der Lüge" den Tätern Raum für ihr Fehlverhalten gegeben habe. Und beide würden diese Kultur auf die in der Kirche geübte heuchlerische Praxis zurückführen, homosexuelle Handlungen offiziell zu verurteilen, diese aber gleichzeitig bei Klerikern zu tolerieren, schreibt Schmitz.

Er zitiert James Alison, einen homosexuellen Priester, der behauptet, dass ein viel größerer Teil des Klerus, insbesondere des höheren Klerus, homosexuell sei, als bisher angenommen. Viele dieser schwulen Kleriker seien sexuell aktiv. Er beschreibt deren Situation mit den Worten: „Mach was du willst, so lange du es nicht öffentlich machst oder die Lehre kritisierst."

Die zweite Regel für homosexuelle Priester sei, das Recht nicht zu verletzen – oder sich dabei zumindest nicht erwischen zu lassen. Diese Unterscheidung sei bereits ein Schutz für Missbrauchstäter. Kardinal McCarrick wurde als jemand gesehen, der „nur" Seminaristen nachstellt. Erst als er glaubwürdig des Kindesmissbrauchs beschuldigt wurde, musste er sich zurückziehen.

Zunächst müssten die Missbrauchsskandale aufgeklärt werden und die Verantwortlichen für die Vergehen und ihre Vertuschung auf allen Ebenen zurücktreten. Aber selbst wenn das geschehen sei, werde die Heuchelei weiter gehen, befürchtet Schmitz.

Nach katholischer Lehre sei jede unkeusche Handlung eine schwere Sünde. Wenn die Kirche diese Lehre wirklich für wahr halte, müsse sie endlich leben, was sie verkünde. Dies würde zum Beispiel bedeuten, den

✅ Tippfehler melden
🖨 Druckversion
✉ Artikel versenden

WEITERE ARTIKEL ZUM THEMA 'Missbrauch'

Bundesstaat Illinois untersucht Erzdiözese Chicago

John Jay Bericht: 80 Prozent der Missbrauchsopfer männlich

Kardinal Cupich zieht die 'Rassismus-Karte'

US-Bischof: Vertuscher müssen ans Licht gebracht werden!

US-Bischöfe an Missbrauchsopfer: „Wir haben euch enttäuscht"

Top Artikel der letzten 7 Tage

Erlass von Benedikt XVI. aus dem Jahr 2005 umzusetzen, der die Weihe von Männern mit tief sitzenden homosexuellen Tendenzen untersagt. Die Kirche müsse darüber hinaus Kleriker aus ihrem Dienst entfernen, die ein Doppelleben führen. Wenn die Kirche nicht glaube, was sie verkünde, solle sie ihre Lehre ändern und für Jahrhunderte sinnloser Qualen um Entschuldigung bitten. Jeder, der auf ein Ende der Missbräuche in der Kirche hoffe, solle beten, dass der Bürgerkrieg in der Kirche nicht in einer Pattsituation erstarre, schreibt Schmitz abschließend.

Link zum Artikel von Matthew Schmitz in der *New York Times* (englsich):

A Catholic Civil War?

Ihnen hat der Artikel gefallen?
Bitte helfen Sie kath.net und spenden Sie jetzt via Überweisung auf ein Konto in Ö, D oder der CH oder via Kreditkarte/Paypal!

 16 people recommend this. Be the first of your friends.

G+

Tweet

kath.net ist Teilnehmer des Partnerprogramms von Amazon EU, das zur Bereitstellung eines Mediums für Webseiten konzipiert wurde, mittels dessen durch die Platzierung von Werbeanzeigen und Links zu Amazon.de Werbekostenerstattung verdient werden kann.

Lesermeinungen zu diesem Artikel anzeigen und Kommentar schreiben

JohannBaptist vor 24 Minuten
@rolando

padre14.9. vor einer Stunde
Wem Gott ein Amt gibt dem gibt er auch Verstand

Diadochus vor einer Stunde
@Delegatus

Einsiedlerin vor zwei Stunden
@Delegatus

lakota vor 5 Stunden
Delegatus

Lokalnachrichten » Kreis Gütersloh » Harsewinkel   03.09.2018 18:57

Autor und Funktionen

29.08.2018 23:12   Senden   Drucken

Skurrile Machenschaften im Fitnessstudio

Harsewinkel (jau) - Merkwürdige Dinge scheinen sich seit einigen Wochen im Harsewinkeler Fitnessstudio Elite am Prozessionsweg abzuspielen. Das behaupten Sportler, die dort trainieren. Zeugen berichten von Cannabis-Gerüchen. Jünger des Ephi-Zentrums sollen dort leben und ihre Aktivitäten von dort aus steuern.

Auf der großen schwarzen Wand mitten im Fitnessstudio wird unter anderem auch der Papst erwähnt. Neben ihm steht das Wort „Hure".

Um Teil der Erbengemeinschaft Jakob zu werden, werden 100 Euro für eine „Lebendmeldung", wie es das Ephi-Zentrum nennt, fällig. Mittlerweile ermittelt die Polizei. Auch der Staatsschutz Bielefeld, das Ordnungsamt der Stadt und der Kreis sind informiert.

Bei dem Ephi-Zentrum soll es sich um eine religiöse Sekte unter der Führung eines „Priesters" handeln, der sich Ephraim nennt. Ephraim war mit seinen Jüngern zuvor in Iserlohn (Sauerland) ansässig. Aus Iserlohner Rathaus-Kreisen erfährt die „Glocke" am Mittwoch: „Es geht schon in die Richtung von religiösen Reichsbürgern, die keine staatlichen Instanzen anerkennen."

Das Fitnessstudio Elite wird seit mehr als zehn Jahren von einem Harsewinkeler betrieben, der

Die Rede ist von Gehirnwäsche

Vor gut drei Jahren sollen sich der „Priester" und der Fitnessstudio-Chef erstmals begegnet sein. Die Sportler, die den früheren und den heutigen Betreiber kennen, sprechen von einer Gehirnwäsche. Damals sei er immer weiter in die religiöse Schiene gerutscht und habe sich immer weniger um das Fitnessstudio gekümmert.

Laut Aussage von Studiomitgliedern kündigen immer mehr Sportler ihre Verträge. Einige Eltern, deren Kinder dort trainieren, haben bei der Polizei Anzeige wegen des Verstoßes gegen das Betäubungsmittelgesetz erstattet, wie Polizei-Pressesprecherin Katharina Felsch bestätigte. Und es gibt offenbar auch nur noch einen Trainer. „Alle anderen sind bereits weg", sagt einer der Sportler.

Suspekt: große schwarze Wand

Suspekt ist ihm auch eine große schwarze Wand, auf der Fotos aller möglichen Persönlichkeiten zu finden sind – von Papst Franziskus und dem emeritierten Papst Benedikt, neben denen das Wort „Hure" steht, über Kanzlerin Angela Merkel bis hin zur Harsewinkeler Bürgermeisterin Sabine Amsbeck-Dopheide und Unternehmer Helmut Claas. Sie alle seien schuldig am derzeitigen System. Ephraim wolle als Messias den Papst ablösen, berichten Studiobesucher, die eigentlich trainieren wollen, dann aber mit Befreiungstheorien konfrontiert werden, die die meisten nicht hören wollen: Der „Priester" wolle die Weltordnung ändern, kündigte er an.

Staatsschutz eingeschaltet

Einige Anzeigen sind bereits bei der Kreispolizeibehörde in Gütersloh eingegangen. Demnach sollen Drogen in dem Fitnessstudio konsumiert werden. Auch der für Reichsbürger typische „Sprech" ist ins Studio eingezogen – das belegen auch Videos im Internet. „Wir habe das Ganze auch an den Staatsschutz in Bielefeld weitergeleitet. Mit den Kollegen aus Bielefeld haben wir uns abgestimmt. Wir sind nicht untätig", sagte Polizei-Pressesprecherin Katharina Felsch.

Michael Kötter vom Staatsschutz Bielefeld äußerte sich so gegenüber der „Glocke": „Der Staatsschutz hat das überprüft. Allerdings haben wir nichts strafrechtlich oder politisch Motivierendes erkannt. Daher ermitteln wir in diesem Fall nicht."

Kreis überprüft das Ganze

Auch der Harsewinkeler Ordnungsamtsleiter Michael Bergholz hat vor wenigen Tagen Hinweise auf das, was in dem Elite-Fitnessstudio vor sich geht, bekommen: „Demnach sollen auf dem Gelände in einem Geräteschuppen Leute hausen." Auch sei ihm von dem Drogenkonsum berichtet worden („Dort soll gekifft werden") und davon, dass Personen in dem Studio leben. „Dabei handelt es sich um ein gewerbliches Objekt." Er habe recherchiert und daraufhin die

Ganze jetzt erst einmal überprüfen." Nun müsse geschaut werden, ob das Fitnessstudio als Wohnraum genutzt werden dürfe und ob das überhaupt genehmigungsfähig wäre, machte Jan Focken deutlich.

Wie die Sportler im Studio die Entwicklung sehen und was mit dem abgetrennten Bereich des Reha-Sports passiert, lesen Sie in der Donnerstagsausgabe der „Glocke".

Melden Sie sich an, um diesen Artikel zu kommentieren.

Kommentar nicht in Ordnung? Mitteilung an die Redaktion.

Login für Abonnenten

Benutzername:

Abonummer/ggf. eigenes Passwort:

Anmelden

Passwort vergessen

Informationen zum e-paper

Informationen zu unseren Abos

Meist gelesen

Brand auf Gelände der Bundeschampionate

Skurrile Machenschaften im Fitnessstudio

Mann stirbt bei Unfall auf Autobahn 2

Unfall bei Vellern mit drei Verletzten

Vorwürfe treffen die FN bis ins Mark

Sexuelle Belästigung beim Schützenfest

WESTFALEN-BLATT

Mi., 29.08.2018

Harsewinkel: »Elite Healthclub« bietet »Erbengemeinschaft Jakobs« eine Heimat

Sekte zieht in Fitnessstudio ein

Juri Nasirow, Betreiber des Fitnessstudios »Elite« (Mitte) erklärt auf Facebook, was es mit der schwarzen, bebilderten Wand auf sich hat.

Von Elke Westerwalbesloh

Harsewinkel (WB). Die Polizei geht Hinweisen auf Aktivitäten einer »Erbengemeinschaft Jakobs« im Fitnesszentrum »Elite Healthcare« in Harsewinkel nach. Dabei soll es sich um eine religiöse Sekte mit Zielen handeln, die zum Teil auch von Reichsbürgern verfolgt werden.

Juri Nasirow betreibt das Fitnessstudio und sieht auf Anfrage dieser Zeitung keinen Grund, irgendetwas zu verheimlichen: »Wir sind die Erbengemeinschaft Jakobs. Der Begriff Sekte passt schon.«

Für rund 33 Euro im Monat bekommen Mitglieder im »Elite Healthclub« am Prozessionsweg die Möglichkeit, Sport zu treiben. Wer das Studio betritt, muss gleich einen Blick auf die schwarze Wand werfen – sie ist nicht zu übersehen. Gleich neben dem Empfang prangt sie, mit vielen Bildern dran. Zu sehen ist das Portrait vom Papst, von Kanzlerin Angela Merkel, aber auch von Bürgermeisterin Sabine Amsbeck-Dopheide und von Unternehmer Helmut Claas.

Ihre Fotos seien dort aufgehängt, weil sie alle »schuldig« seien, erläutert Juri Nasirow. Schuldig am nicht funktionierenden System, schuldig daran, dass die Bürger den ganzen Tag arbeiteten und unterm Strich nicht viel an Geld übrig bleibe. Aber auch schuldig am Nahost-Konflikt.

Distanz zur Evangeliums-Christen-Gemeinde

Juri Nasirow betreibt das Studio seit elf Jahren. »Als ich es übernommen habe, da hat mich meine Gemeinde, zu der ich seit meiner Geburt gehöre, ausgeschlossen«, sagt der Fitnessexperte. Er gehörte zur Evangeliums-Christen-Gemeinde. Er empfinde es als bitter, dass diese direkt neben dem Fitnessstudio angesiedelt sei. »Die haben mich so enttäuscht, dass ich erst mal ein Jahr durch die ganze Welt getourt bin«, sagt Nasirow.

Er habe »sich schlau gemacht«, sagt er und sei dabei auf Ulf Diebel gestoßen. Ulf Diebel, der Ideengeber der »Erbengemeinschaft Jakobs«, hatte seinen Sitz in Iserlohn, betreibt die Sekte seit dreieinhalb Jahren und ist nun mit weiteren Mitgliedern ins Fitnessstudio nach Harsewinkel gezogen.

Mitgliedschaft in Erbengemeinschaft kostet 100 Euro

»Wir arbeiten jeden Tag daran, unsere Sache voranzutreiben. Eine Sache, für die wir sterben würden«, sagt der zweifache Familienvater in einem Video, das er selbst auf Facebook gepostet hat. Auch in den Sozialen Netzwerken propagieren sie, wofür ihre »Erbengemeinschaft Jakobs« steht und suchen weitere Mitglieder, die mit einem Klick auf einer Homepage zu einem solchen werden können – mit Überweisung von 100 Euro.

Dass die Mitglieder des Sportstudios die ganze Sache befremdlich finden, ist Juri Nasirow bekannt, aber egal. Auf die Frage, ob er nicht einer Gehirnwäsche unterzogen wurde, reagiert der Harsewinkeler gelassen: »Das denken viele. Doch ich habe mich einfach nur mit dem Gesetz vertraut gemacht und stehe nun dafür ein.«

Es hagelt Abmeldungen

Natürlich hagele es Abmeldungen von Studiomitgliedern, Beschimpfungen und auch Bedrohungen seien an der Tagesordnung. Ein Mitglied (Name ist der Redaktion bekannt) schimpft: »Erst entsteht die kuriose schwarze Wand mit all den Bildern und nun wohnen dort noch Obdachlose«. In den Sozialen Netzwerken werden Kritik und Unverständnis geäußert. Nasirow würde »den Salat des Teufels konsumieren«, heißt es in einem Post. Oder: »Werde eure dubiosen Machenschaften keinen Tag länger unterstützen. Schade um das schöne Fitnessstudio.«

Lily Allen: Habe für Sex mit Frauen bezahlt :...

Eigentlich geht es ja niemanden etwas an. Aber Lily Allen kommt einem Medienbericht zuvor. Und... mehr

Schillerbrücke: Abriss verzögert sich erneut :...

Herford (WB). Dreimal wurde der Abrisstermin der Schillerbrücke bereits verschoben. Jetzt... mehr

Wenn mehr, dann viel mehr

Entdecken Sie die SIGNATURE Sondermodelle an den MehrWertTagen am 14./15.09. bei Ihrem Mazda Händler mehr

Der Ford Fiesta überzeugt auf ganzer Linie.

Mehr Fahrspaß, Sicherheit, Technologien und Platz für alle und alles. mehr

Krösche: »Mir ist egal, welchen Platz wir...

Paderborn (WB). Aufsteiger SC Paderborn hat in der 2. Liga die ersten Marken gesetzt. Vor der... mehr

Musiker stellen sich in Chemnitz gegen Rechts :...

Nach den Ausschreitungen und Demonstrationen in Chemnitz machen Musiker wie Kraftklub oder die... mehr

Sekte

Sekte (von lateinisch *secta* ‚Partei‘, ‚Lehre‘, ‚Schulrichtung‘) ist eine Bezeichnung für eine religiöse, philosophische oder politische Richtung und ihre Anhängerschaft. Die Bezeichnung bezieht sich auf Gruppierungen, die sich durch ihre Lehre oder ihren Ritus von vorherrschenden Überzeugungen unterscheiden und oft im Konflikt mit ihnen stehen.

In erster Linie steht Sekte für eine von einer Mutterreligion abgespaltene religiöse Gemeinschaft. Der ursprünglich wertneutrale Ausdruck hat aufgrund seiner Geschichte und Prägung durch den kirchlichen Sprachgebrauch einen meist abwertenden Charakter erhalten und wird seit den 1960er Jahren verstärkt in negativem Sinn verwendet.

In der modernen Religionswissenschaft und Soziologie werden statt des Begriffs Sekte neutrale, nicht wertende Bezeichnungen wie „religiöse Sondergemeinschaft“, „neureligiöse Gemeinschaft“ oder „neue religiöse Bewegung“ verwendet.

Inhaltsverzeichnis

Begriffsgeschichte

Antike

In der Antike verwendete man im Griechischen das Wort αἵρεσις (*haíresis*), im Lateinischen *secta*. Das lateinische *secta* ist abgeleitet vom Verb *sequi* („folgen“, speziell: „Anhänger [einer Person oder Lehre] sein“). Erstmals ist das Wort im 3. Jahrhundert v. Chr. bei dem Dichter Gnaeus Naevius bezeugt. Als *secta* bezeichnete man wertneutral nicht

Bisnode | UPIK® – Unique Partner Identification Key

dun & bradstreet

D&B UPIK

| Home | Bisnode D&B Deutschland | Bisnode D&B International | D&B International | VDA | VCI | Kontakt | Login |

Mehr zum Thema

Welche Datenbasis liegt der Trefferliste zugrunde?

Welche Datenbasis liegt dem UPIK®-Datensatz im Suchergebnis zugrunde?

Was ist die D&B Worldbase?

Gibt es eine weitere Beschreibung zu den angezeigten UPIK® Daten?

Weitere UPIK®

UPIK® Datensatz - L

(handwritten: 6.12.1992 – 6.12.2017   25 Jahre   MORITZ Maximilian   1290 Tage Daniel 12.11 "JERUSALEM")

	Name	Ulf Diesel
	Nicht eingetragene Rechtsform (bei Unternehmen)	Doris va Mode
	D-U-N-S Nummer	330-2098
	Geschäftssitz	München 8890
	Postleitzahl	8814
	Postalische Stadt	Germany
	Land	DN
	Länder-Code	
	Postfachnummer	
	Postfach-Stadt	
	Telefon-Nummer	015221935308
	Fax-Nummer	
	Name Hauptverantwortliche	Ulf Diesel
	Tätigkeit SIC	5551

Weitere Optionen

Möchten Sie die aktuellen UPIK Suchen
Bitte auf UPIK Suche klicken

UPIK Suche

Sie können kostenlos Ihre Stammdaten andern
Sie können auch die Daten andern
Um Daten zu andern bitte klicken

Daten andern

Industry Report Automotive

Bisnode

UPIK® ist ein Produkt von Bisnode

POLITIK

DEUTSCHLAND   AUSLAND

DEUTSCHLAND   SEEHOFER NACH...

INNERES - BAV - HEIMAT

SYRER
→Jesaja 7-8, Miegas 20.8.2011

„Mutter aller Probleme ist die Migration"

CSU - Katholik

Veröffentlicht am 05.09.2018 | Lesedauer 3 Minuten

www.ddbradio.de

studio@ddb-radio.de

16.9.2018

SANTA SEDE
D-U-N-S 438923885
CITTA' DEL VATICANO
Hauptverantwortlicher:
ULF DIEBEL

FAKE NEWS!

+++ EILMELDUNG +++

+++ Bundesrepublik Deutschland „BRD" am 12. Juli 2018 erloschen +++

An diesem Tag hat das Bundesverfassungsgericht in seinem Schriftwechsel mit der „Verfassunggebenden Versammlung für Deutschland" abschließend bestätigt, dass der Artikel 146 Grundgesetz erfüllt und somit die BRD sowie das Grundgesetz endgültig „de jure" & „de facto" erloschen sind.

Rechtssatz:

"Die Bundesrepublik Deutschland untersteht der Verfassunggebenden Versammlung und erkennt durch ihr Bundesverfassungsgericht dieses höhere Recht mit den eigenen Rechtsgrundsätzen und folgenden Dokumentationen verbindlich an: (a) Art. 25 und Art. 146 Grundgesetz vom 23. Mai 1949 (b) UN-Charta (UN-Zivilpakt / UN-Sozialpakt) zum Selbstbestimmungsrecht der Völker - Artikel 1 - (1-3) (c) Urteil des Bundesverfassungsgerichts BverfG 2 BvG 1/51 vom 23. Oktober 1951, II. Senat, Leitsatz 21 und 21 a,b, und c, Leitsatz 27 und 29."

Weitere Rechtsverweise:

1) Artikel 146 Grundgesetz vom 23. Mai 1949: „Dieses Grundgesetz, das nach Vollendung der Einheit und Freiheit Deutschlands für das gesamte deutsche Volk gilt, verliert seine Gültigkeit an dem Tage, an dem eine Verfassung in Kraft tritt, die von dem deutschen Volke in freier Entscheidung beschlossen worden ist."

Damit ist zweifelsfrei, das Grundgesetz war niemals eine völkerrechtlich beschlossene und relevante Verfassung, sondern nur ein fremdverordnetes Verwaltungspapier. Das Deutsche Volk hat sich am 01.November.2014 eine eigene Verfassung gegeben. Damit ist der **„Artikel 146 Grundgesetz"** erfüllt. Aus dieser Rechtsfolge ergibt sich die Nichtigkeit des Grundgesetzes und somit auch der BRD.

2) Artikel 133 Grundgesetz: „Der „**BUND**" tritt in die Rechte und Pflichten der Verwaltung des „Vereinigten Wirtschaftsgebietes" ein."

Der BRD-**BUND** ist kein Staat, sondern eindeutig die Treuhand-Verwaltung für ein privatrechtlich organisiertes „Vereinigtes Wirtschaftsgebiet."

3) Artikel 25 Grundgesetz vom 23. Mai 1949: „Die allgemeinen Regeln des Völkerrechtes sind Bestandteil des Bundesrechtes. Sie gehen den Gesetzen vor und erzeugen Rechte und Pflichten unmittelbar für die Bewohner des Bundesgebietes."

Das höhere Völkerrecht steht zweifelsfrei über jedem Staats- und Bundesrecht. Dieses internationale Recht steht über dem Verwaltungsrecht - dies bestätigt die BRD/**BUND** - Fremdverwaltung selbst durch diesen Artikel.

4) Urteil des Bundesverfassungsgerichts vom 23. Oktober 1951 BVerfG 2 BvG 1/51, II. Senat, Leitsatz 21 und 21 c: „Eine Verfassunggebende Versammlung ist ein weltweit anerkannter, völkerrechtlicher Akt und hat einen höheren rechtlichen Rang als die auf Grund der erlassenen Verfassung gewählte Volksvertretung (siehe Art. 25 GG)."

Sie ist im Besitz des „pouvoir constituant." (konstituierende Macht/ Gewalt des Volkes).
Mit dieser besonderen Stellung ist unverträglich, dass ihr von außen Beschränkungen auferlegt werden können. Ihre Unabhängigkeit bei der Erfüllung dieses Auftrages besteht nicht nur hinsichtlich der Entscheidung über den Inhalt der künftigen Verfassung, sondern auch hinsichtlich des Verfahrens, in dem die Verfassung erarbeitet wird.

und Leitsatz 27: Das Bundesverfassungsgericht erkennt die Existenz überpositiven, auch den Verfassungsgesetzgeber bindenden Rechtes an und ist zuständig, das gesetzte Recht daran zu messen.

und Leitsatz 29: Dem demokratischen Prinzip ist nicht nur wesentlich, daß eine Volksvertretung vorhanden ist, sondern auch dass den Wahlberechtigten das Wahlrecht nicht auf einem in der Verfassung nicht vorgesehenen Wege entzogen wird.

5) UN-Charta (UN-Zivilpakt / UN-Sozialpakt) zum Selbstbestimmungsrecht der Völker – Artikel 1:
(1) „Alle Völker haben das Recht auf Selbstbestimmung. Kraft dieses Rechts entscheiden sie frei über ihren politischen Status und gestalten in Freiheit ihre wirtschaftliche, soziale und kulturelle Entwicklung."

(2) „Alle Völker können für ihre eigenen Zwecke frei über ihre natürlichen Reichtümer und Mittel verfügen, unbeschadet aller Verpflichtungen, die aus der internationalen wirtschaftlichen Zusammenarbeit auf der Grundlage des gegenseitigen Wohles sowie aus dem Völkerrecht erwachsen. In keinem Fall darf ein Volk seiner eigenen Existenzmittel beraubt werden."

(3) „Die Vertragsstaaten, einschließlich der Staaten, die für die Verwaltung von Gebieten ohne Selbstregierung und von Treuhandgebieten verantwortlich sind, haben entsprechend der Charta der Vereinten Nationen die Verwirklichung des Rechts auf Selbstbestimmung zu fördern und dieses Recht zu achten."

+++Diese Pressemitteilung ist großzügig zu verteilen+++

www.verfassunggebende-versammlung.de · poststelle@v-versammlung.de

WERTVOLLES KNOW-HOW  **DEUTSCHE FINANCE GROUP**

7.9.2018

Rothschild & Co baut Vermögensverwaltung in Deutschland aus

07.09.2018 15:36

Der Finanzberater Rothschild & Co. baut sein stark wachsendes Private-Wealth-Geschäft in Deutschland personell und regional weiter aus. Ab 1. Oktober 2018 übernimmt Friedrich Rogge die Leitung des neu eröffneten Büros in Düsseldorf. Zusammen mit Rogge, langjähriger Leiter der Düsseldorfer Niederlassung der Privatbank Sal. Oppenheim, stoßen weitere fünf Mitarbeiter des ehemaligen Düsseldorfer Teams von Sal. Oppenheim zu Rothschild & Co. Rogge wird eng mit Reinhard Krafft, Leiter des Rothschild & Co Private-Wealth-Geschäfts in Deutschland, zusammenarbeiten.

Rogge verfügt über insgesamt mehr als 30 Jahre Erfahrung im Bereich der Vermögensverwaltung für institutionelle und private Kunden. Begonnen hat Rogge seine Karriere 1980 bei der Deutschen Bank, wo er bis 2001 verschiedene Funktionen innehatte. So war er unter anderem für das Management von Spezialfonds verantwortlich und hat die Betreuungseinheit für gehobene individuelle Mandatskunden geleitet. 2001 wechselte Rogge zur Privatbank Sal. Oppenheim, deren Düsseldorfer Niederlassung er aufgebaut und insgesamt 17 Jahre lang geleitet hat. Das Vermögensverwaltungsgeschäft von Sal. Oppenheim wurde kürzlich in den Mutterkonzern Deutsche Bank integriert.

Laurent Gagnebin, Co-Head of Wealth Management & Trust, sagte: „Unser Vermögensverwaltungsgeschäft in Deutschland hat sich unter der Leitung von Reinhard Krafft in den vergangenen Jahren sehr positiv entwickelt. Wir haben unsere Positionierung im deutschen Markt gestärkt und unser Angebot speziell für Unternehmerfamilien gezielt ausgebaut. Ich bin überzeugt, dass das neue Team eine ausgezeichnete Ergänzung ist und uns hilft, das Wachstum fortzusetzen."

Krafft, Leiter des Rothschild & Co Private Wealth Geschäfts in Deutschland, erklärte: „Ich freue mich sehr, dass Friedrich Rogge und sein Team Rothschild & Co künftig verstärken werden. Wir haben damit die Möglichkeit, unser Geschäft vom Rheinland bis nach Ostwestfalen weiter gezielt auszubauen - also in einer Region, die mit ihren zahlreichen mittelständischen Unternehmerfamilien für das Angebot von Rothschild & Co besonders attraktiv ist. Friedrich Rogge und sein Team passen hervorragend zu uns, weil sie nicht nur einen ausgezeichneten Ruf im Wealth Management genießen, sondern auch die auf langfristigen Vermögenserhalt ausgerichtete Anlagephilosophie von Rothschild & Co teilen."

Quelle: Pressemitteilung Rothschild & Co.

Rothschild & Co. ist ein Finanzberater mit Sitz mit 3.500 Mitarbeitern in weltweit 50 Büros. (JF1)

www.rothschild.com

14.09.2018 14:02

DAVID RENE`JAMES ROTHSCHILD

23 B AVENUE DE MESSINE

75008 PARIS

FRANCE

Elite-Plus-EPHI-Zentrum

Prozessionsweg 27

D-33428 Harsewinkel

Tel.   +49 524 792 54 56

Mobil   +49 157 501 186 62

ephi-zentrum@ephraim.info

www.ephraim.info

10.09.2018

Shalom David,

Attached you find my letter to you from 23.8.2018 and a set of documentation produced after the end of our "Endgericht der Apokalypse"starting from 24.8.2018 - 7pm.

1. a full presentation of Daniel 10 - 12, I sent already in March to Ronald Lauder and Michael Jay Solomon.
2. a set of legitimation for my action as "Santa Sede", including the letters from 24.8.2017 to the Pope, the Israeli High Court and the Inquisition.
3. a full set of judgements as "Priest of the Order of Melchizedek" dated 6.9.2018
4. the letter to Richard Grenell I didn't send yet

When you receive this letter, we remember 9/11. According to Daniel 8.14 the 2300 days will end 9/11 2020 - 2 years from now, giving us enough time for a smooth transition from Rome to Jerusalem.

Can we please come to an arrangement before Yom Kippur?

Two of our regular Registration Forms are attached - one for you and one for Ronald Lauder, including our offer of a #NewDeal for the Sake of Zion.

I will send those DUNS marked green also a registration form with full confidence, that everything will work out.

Hag Sameach 5779

Bankverbindung

Ulf Diebel
Erbengemeinschaft Jakob
Fidor Bank
IBAN: DE41 700 222 0000 7190 5217

Seite **1** von **1**

ZEUGEN: ARMIN PFAFF, CHRISTOPH TEICHMANN, ULF DIEBEL, ALEXANDER HORN, ALEXANDRA SCHEFFEL, JURI NASIROW, MARCELLA MARIANNA DE MARCHI

Protokoll 9/11
13:00 Uhr

"Final Settlement" Urteil
Erstes Urteil 06.09.2018

1. Finanztransaktion
2. Obligation
3. Handelbar

SANTA SEDE
D-U-N-S 438923885
CITTA DEL VATICANO
Hauptverantwortlicher:
ULF DIEBEL

© "Ephraim"
"Gesetzgeber"

Gesetzliche Grundlage der "Final Settlement" Urteile vom 6.9.2018 und allen folgenden Urteilen, ist die Legitimation des Heiligen Stuhls durch die dogmatischen Konstitutionen DEI FILIUS 24.4.1870, DEI VERBUM 1965, LUMEN GENTIUM 21.11.1964, EUCHARISTCUM MYSTERIUM 25.5.1967, die mit dem Schreiben vom 24.8.2017 an den Stellvertreter von ULF DIEBEL, Papst Franziskus mit der Legitimation für den Kardinalpräfekten der Kongregation für die Glaubenslehre Müller rechtmäßig erworben und seit dem 24.4.2017 aus dem EPHI-Zentrum ausgeübt wurde.

Die "Final Settlement" Urteile sind durch die nachfolgenden gesetzlichen Grundlagen und internationalen Verträge in vollem Umfang Rechtskräftig und verbindliche Handelsempfehlungen für die Völkerrechtssubjekte Heiliger Stuhl, Deutsches Reich, Bundesrepublik Deutschland, den Vier Siegermächten USA, Großbritannien, Russland und Frankreich, die EU und die UN.

Weimarer Verfassung GG Art. 140 vom 11.08.1919, die Lateranverträge vom 11.2.1929, das Reichskonkordat vom 20.7.1933 zwischen dem Heiligen Stuhl und dem Deutschen Reich, UN Resolution 217 vom 12.10.1948 "Deklaration der Universellen Menschenrechte", BRD Grundgesetz vom 23.5.1949, die am 12.09.1990 abgeschlossenen 2 + 4 Verträge, das Fundamental Agreement between the Holy See and the State of Israel aus 1993, der Religious Freedom Act vom 27.01.1998, Executive Order 12803 (George W. Bush) und 13037 (Bill Clinton), den Römischen Verträgen von 1957, der EU-Working Definition on Antisemitism vom 26.5.2016, durch das Kabinett am 20.9.2017 in Deutschland verabschiedet.

Alle "Final Settlement" Urteile sind als Obligation bei David De Rothschild, Paris hinterlegt worden, um bis zum 11.9.2020 eine geordnete Lösung für die in 3. Mose 25 verordnete Entschuldung mit allen Beteiligten auf dem Verhandlungsweg umzusetzen und den Regierungssitz des Heiligen Stuhls vom Vatikan auf den Berg Zion zu verlegen.

Die DSGVO vom 25.5.2018 ist eine Verordnung, bei der Verstöße eine Ordnungsstrafe von bis zu 20 Millionen Euro pro geahndet werden können und jede Körperschaft in der EU verpflichtet ist die Bereinigung von personenbezogenen Daten vorzunehmen, wenn eine ordnungswidrige Nutzung oder Missbrauch der personenbezogenen Daten festgestellt wird. Festgestellte Ordnungsstrafen sind sofort vollstreckbar.

Juri Nasirow wurde beauftragt, die Verwaltung der handelbaren "Final Settlement" Urteile im Rahmen des Elite PLUS 24 Vertrages für alle PLUS Kunden als Teil der regulären Elite Healthclub Nutzungsvereinbarung der Elite Healthclub Einrichtungen auf dem Prozessionsweg 27 in Harsewinkel zu übernehmen und für jeden Kunden eine Rechtskonforme Bereinigung von personenbezogenen Daten nach DSGVO umsetzen, sowie die vom Heiligen Stuhl festgestellten Ordnungsgelder einziehen.

30.07.2018	Einbeziehung von Donald Trump durch den US Botschafter in Jerusalem David Friedman
20.08.2018	Einbeziehung des Bundesministers des Inneren Horst Seehofer, CDU Fraktionsvorsitzenden Volker Kauder und die Fraktionsvorsitzende die Linke Sahra Wagenknecht
24.08.2018 - 19:00 Uhr	Beginn "Endgericht der Apokalypse" - Abrechnung nach D-U-N-S
25.08.2018 - 23:00 Uhr	Ulf Diebel übernimmt Hauptverantwortung für den Heiligen Stuhl
30.08.2018	Neue Westfälische (100% SPD Unternehmen) druckt "Illegale Religiöse Zuflucht"
03.09.2018	Strafbestand nach VStGB§6 in Harsewinkel nachgewiesen
06.09.2018	NRW Ministerpräsident Armin Laschet in Jerusalem - Final Settlement Urteile
09.11.2018	Elite-Plus 24 Start um 13:00 Uhr
01.10.2018	Die Rothschild Bank eröffnet eine Niederlassung in Düsseldorf

---

Stand Elite PLUS 24 am 11.9.2018 um 13:00 Uhr

1. Juri ist CEO über die gesamte Elite-Plus 24 Unternehmung auf dem Prozessionsweg 27 in Harsewinkel.
2. Alle Hauptverantwortlichen Personen der ''Final Settlement'' Urteile sind Kunde bei Elite-Plus 24 im Status Interessent zur berechtigten Bereinigung von personenbezogenen Daten.
3. Die Daten Bereinigung nach DSGVO ist eine Dienstleistung von Elite PLUS 24 für Unternehmer
4. Der Elite PLUS 24 Vertrag beinhaltet den Aufbaus einer Technologischen Lösung für die personelle, rechtliche und finanzielle Selbstverwaltung aller angeschlossenen Elite-Plus 24 Partner.

DSGVO Verstöße werden durch ''Final Settlement'' Urteile des höchsten hierarchische Hauptverantwortlichen festgestellt. Für die Berechnung nach der BRD AO ist das Bundeszentralamt für Steuern die höchste Autorität. Die Befreiung von der AO für jedes Elite PLUS 24 Mitglied erfolgt im Rahmen des GG Art. 4, 25 & 140.

Projektzeitraum für die Elite plus 24 Umstellung aller Partner

    9/11 2018 - 9/11 2020

Einmalige Registrierung für 100€ bei Elite PLUS für 100€ p.m.- Das Starter Paket enthält:

''Starterpaket''   - Elite-Plus Zugangskarte
                - Partner Zertifikat
                - Individueller Set Up im Elite PLUS 24 eSolution System
                - Enthält:
                        - Rabatte, Ermäßigungen
                        - Provisionen für Elite PLUS 24 Vermittlungen
                        - Angebot eigener Produkte und Dienstleistungen (optional)
                - Allgemeine Geschäftsbedingungen + Elite-Plus Anleitung (Online)

Das Elite-Plus 24 Unternehmerpaket - Feste Laufzeit 24 Monate

- inkl. aller Leistungen in Elite HealthClub und Elite PLUS
- Service ''Final Settlement'' Urteil und DSGVO Datenbereinigung für Mitglieder und deren Unternehmen.
- Umstrukturierung des Unternehmens nach internationalem Handelsrecht
- Anschluss an bestehende transatlantische und zion-zentrierte Unternehmer Netzwerke
- Geordneter und strukturierter Schuldenschnitt aller monetären Verbindlichkeiten (weltweiter Schuldenschnitt)
- Landreform, inklusive der totalen Steuerbefreiung bei Erbbesitz

		monatlich	Einmalig
Platin	7 x	1.000.000 €	1.000.000 €
Gold	40 x.	100.000 €	100.000 €
Silber	40 x	10.000 €	10.000 €

Juri ist Einzelunternehmer. Bei Unternehmern mit größeren Geschäftseinheiten (GmbH, Co.KG, Ag etc) wachsen die Anforderungen Dritter exponentiell.

Der Staat sollte dem Menschen und dem Bürger dienen, nicht umgekehrt. Am 6.9.2018 wurde die Stadt Harsewinkel für $1 gekauft und das Final Settlement Urteil zur Abrechnung beim US Präsidenten Donald Trump bei David De Rothschild in Paris hinterlegt. Die Abrechnung der verurteilten Körperschaften ist eine Frage der Logistik, die durch den Elite PLUS 24 Vertrag sofort für alle Partner aufgebaut werden soll.

Seit 2007 betreibt Juri Elite
und wird von diesen Unternehmungen für alles und
jeden verantwortlich gemacht

Juri
21.07.1984
verheiratet
2 Kinder

27.07.2018
Yael Noemi

- ORDNUNGSAMT
- Stadtverwaltung
- SPD Fraktion
- Bürgermeisterin
- Volksbank
- Reha Fitness
- Integrationsrat
- ECG - Harsewinkel
- Polizei
- Staatsschutz
- Finanzamt
- Presse
- Bauordnungsamt
- Straßenbauamt
- Mitglieder
- Familienangehörige
- SPD Wahlkreis 13
- Versicherung
- GEZ
- Steuern
- IHK

Der Missbrauch von personenbezogenen Daten durch Mitarbeiter der öffentlichen Hand kann im Einzelfall mit einer Ordnungsstrafe von bis zu 20 Millionen Euro (20.000.000€) pro Fall geahndet werden. Im Fall Juri Nasirow wurde der Straftatbestand des Völkermordes VStGB §6 nachgewiesen. und dient als Richtlinie für die Behandlung

Ziele: - Klärung der Angriffe gegen Juri aus Harsewinkel
        - Ulf trifft Trump zu #NewDeal
        - #NewDeal mit Israel und Banken

Zeitraum/Prioritäten

bis Yom Kippur	19.09.	19.09.
- Elite-Plus 24 Set-Up komplett		
bis Ende Laubhüttenfest	1.10.	1.10.
- Alles offiziell		
bis Ende des Jahres	31.12.	31.12.
- alle 87 Partner gefunden		

1.1.2019 - 31.12.2019 Jahresziel: Anschluss von 5 mio Usern
1.1.2020 - 11.09.2020 Abschluss des Projekts am 9/11 2020 in JERUSALEM

SANTA SEDE
D-U-N-S 438923885
CITTA' DEL VATICANO
Hauptverantwortlicher:
ULF DIEBEL

elite PLUS 24 VERTRAG
zur Nutzung der Einrichtung im Final Settlement

Vorname

Nachname

☐ Frau   ☐ Herr

Studio/ Vertragspartner

elite
H E A L T H C L U B
elitefitness-harsewinkel.de

Prozessionsweg 27
33428 Harsewinkel

02547/ 925456
elite-fitness@web.de

Inhaber:
Juri Nasirow

D-U-N-S Nummer:
342166327

Straße, Hausnummer

Geburtsdatum

Land

PLZ, Ort

Tel.

Handy

E-Mail

Beginn der Mitgliedschaft

Zugang ab

☐ elite 24 SILBER	☐ elite 24 GOLD	☐ elite 24 PLATIN
10.000 € / monatlich	100.000 € / monatlich	1.000.000€/ monatlich
Laufzeit 24 Monate	Laufzeit 24 Monate	Laufzeit 24 Monate
Anmeldegebühr einmalig 10.000,-€	Anmeldegebühr einmalig 100.000,- €	Anmeldegebühr einmalig 1.000.000,-€

Erteilung eines SEPA Lastschriftverfahrens

Name des Zahlungspflichtigen (Kto. Ihn. f. abweichend)

Anschrift des Zahlungspflichtigen (Kto. Ihn. f. abweichend)

SEPA-Lastschriftmandat
Ich ermächtige den Zahlungsempfänger elite fitness aktiv & vital HEALTHCLUB Zahlung von meinem Konto mittel Lastschrift einzuziehen. Zugleich weise ich mein Kreditinstitut an, die von elite fitness aktiv & vital HEALTHCLUB auf meinem Konto gezogenen Lastschrift einzulösen.

Bankleitzahl   Kontonummer

IBAN   DE | | | | | | | | | | | | | | | | | | | | | |

BIC | | | | | | | | | | |

Harsewinkel, den   Unterschrift

Fälligkeit der Zahlung zum: ☐ 01. des Monats   ☐ 15.des Monats

Bei alternativen Zahlungen wird für den erhöhten Verwaltungsaufwand pro fällig werdende Zahlung ein zusätzliche Verwaltungspauschale in Höhe von 100,- € erhoben.

Zusatzvereinbarung/ Sondervermerke

Mündliche Nebenabreden bestehen nicht.

Die UN Resolution 217 vom 10.12.1948 Erklärung der Universellen Menschenrechte und das „Final Settlement-Protokoll" vom 11. September 2018 ist Bestandteil der AGB´s des elite Plus 24 Vertrags.

Gerichtstand ist Jerusalem, Israel High Court of Justice

Ich bestätige umseitige allgemeine Geschäftsbedingungen gelesen zu haben und diese zu akzeptieren.

Ort.

Datum.

Aufmerksam geworden.

Unterschrift Mitglied

Unterschrift Studio

PLUS
Unser ELITE Partner-Programm

elite PLUS 24

Anmeldung zur Bereinigung personenbezogener Daten nach DSGVO

elite HEALTHCLUB   +   ZION5777.com

Vorname

Nachname

Straße

Hausnummer

PLZ

Stadt

Bundesland

Staatsangehörigkeit

Geburtstag

Personalausweisnummer

Steueridentifikationsnummer

D-U-N-S Nummer

Festnetz

Telefon mobil

E-Mail Adresse

Registrationsgebühr

Datum

Unterschrift

elite PLUS 24

Die UN Resolution vom 10.12.1948 "Universelle Deklaration der Menschenrechte" ist Teil der Allgemeinen Geschäftsbedingungen der elite PLUS Partner

Artikel 19 (Meinungs- und Informationsfreiheit)

Jeder hat das Recht auf Meinungsfreiheit und freie Meinungsäußerung; dieses Recht schließt die Freiheit ein, Meinungen ungehindert anzuhängen sowie über Medien jeder Art und ohne Rücksicht auf Grenzen Informationen und Gedankengut zu suchen, zu empfangen und zu verbreiten.

Artikel 20 (Versammlungs- und Vereinigungsfreiheit)

1   Alle Menschen haben das Recht, sich friedlich zu versammeln und zu Vereinigungen zusammenzuschließen.
2   Niemand darf gezwungen werden, einer Vereinigung anzugehören.

Artikel 21 (Allgemeines und gleiches Wahlrecht)

1   Jeder hat das Recht, an der Gestaltung der öffentlichen Angelegenheiten seines Landes unmittelbar oder durch frei gewählte Vertreter mitzuwirken.
2   Jeder hat das Recht auf gleichen Zugang zu öffentlichen Ämtern in seinem Lande.
3
4   Der Wille des Volkes bildet die Grundlage für die Autorität der öffentlichen Gewalt; dieser Wille muss durch regelmäßige, unverfälschte, allgemeine und gleiche Wahlen mit geheimer Stimmabgabe oder in einem gleichwertigen freien Wahlverfahren zum Ausdruck kommen.

Artikel 22 (Recht auf soziale Sicherheit)

Jeder hat als Mitglied der Gesellschaft das Recht auf soziale Sicherheit und Anspruch darauf, durch innerstaatliche Maßnahmen und internationale Zusammenarbeit sowie unter Berücksichtigung der Organisation und der Mittel jedes Staates in den Genuss der wirtschaftlichen, sozialen und kulturellen Rechte zu gelangen, die für seine Würde und die freie Entwicklung seiner Persönlichkeit unentbehrlich sind.

Artikel 23 (Recht auf Arbeit, gleichen Lohn)

1   Jeder hat das Recht auf Arbeit, auf freie Berufswahl, auf gerechte und befriedigende Arbeitsbedingungen sowie auf Schutz vor Arbeitslosigkeit.
2   Jeder, ohne Unterschied, hat das Recht auf gleichen Lohn für gleiche Arbeit.
3   Jeder, der arbeitet, hat das Recht auf gerechte und befriedigende Entlohnung, die ihm und seiner Familie eine der menschlichen Würde entsprechende Existenz sichert, gegebenenfalls ergänzt durch andere soziale Schutzmaßnahmen.
4   Jeder hat das Recht, zum Schutz seiner Interessen Gewerkschaften zu bilden und solchen beizutreten.

Artikel 24 (Recht auf Erholung und Freizeit)

Jeder hat das Recht auf Erholung und Freizeit und insbesondere auf eine vernünftige Begrenzung der Arbeitszeit und regelmäßigen bezahlten Urlaub.

Artikel 25 (Recht auf Wohlfahrt)

1   Jeder hat das Recht auf einen Lebensstandard, der seine und seiner Familie Gesundheit und Wohl gewährleistet, einschließlich Nahrung, Kleidung, Wohnung, ärztliche Versorgung und notwendige soziale Leistungen gewährleistet sowie das Recht auf Sicherheit im Falle von Arbeitslosigkeit, Krankheit, Invalidität oder Verwitwung, im Alter sowie bei anderweitigem Verlust seiner Unterhaltsmittel durch unverschuldete Umstände.
2   Mütter und Kinder haben Anspruch auf besondere Fürsorge und Unterstützung. Alle Kinder, eheliche wie außereheliche, genießen den gleichen sozialen Schutz.

Artikel 26 (Recht auf Bildung)

1   Jeder hat das Recht auf Bildung. Die Bildung ist unentgeltlich, zum mindesten der Grundschulunterricht und die grundlegende Bildung. Der Grundschulunterricht ist obligatorisch. Fach- und Berufsschulunterricht müssen allgemein verfügbar gemacht werden, und der Hochschulunterricht muss allen gleichermaßen entsprechend ihren Fähigkeiten offenstehen.
2   Die Bildung muss auf die volle Entfaltung der menschlichen Persönlichkeit und auf die Stärkung der Achtung vor den Menschenrechten und Grundfreiheiten gerichtet sein. Sie muss zu Verständnis, Toleranz und Freundschaft zwischen allen Nationen und allen rassischen* oder religiösen Gruppen beitragen und der Tätigkeit der Vereinten Nationen für die Wahrung des Friedens förderlich sein.
3   Die Eltern haben ein vorrangiges Recht, die Art der Bildung zu wählen, die ihren Kindern zuteil werden soll.

Artikel 27 (Freiheit des Kulturlebens)

1   Jeder hat das Recht, am kulturellen Leben der Gemeinschaft frei teilzunehmen, sich an den Künsten zu erfreuen und am wissenschaftlichen Fortschritt und dessen Errungenschaften teilzuhaben.
2   Jeder hat das Recht auf Schutz der geistigen und materiellen Interessen, die ihm als Urheber von Werken der Wissenschaft, Literatur oder Kunst erwachsen.

Artikel 28 (Soziale und internationale Ordnung)

Jeder hat Anspruch auf eine soziale und internationale Ordnung, in der die in dieser Erklärung verkündeten Rechte und Freiheiten voll verwirklicht werden können.

Artikel 29 (Grundpflichten)

1   Jeder hat Pflichten gegenüber der Gemeinschaft, in der allein die freie und volle Entfaltung seiner Persönlichkeit möglich ist.
2   Jeder ist bei der Ausübung seiner Rechte und Freiheiten nur den Beschränkungen unterworfen, die das Gesetz ausschließlich zu dem Zweck vorsieht, die Anerkennung und Achtung der Rechte und Freiheiten anderer zu sichern und den gerechten Anforderungen der Moral, der öffentlichen Ordnung und des allgemeinen Wohles in einer demokratischen Gesellschaft zu genügen.
3   Diese Rechte und Freiheiten dürfen in keinem Fall im Widerspruch zu den Zielen und Grundsätzen der Vereinten Nationen ausgeübt werden.

Artikel 30 (Auslegungsregel)

Keine Bestimmung dieser Erklärung darf dahin ausgelegt werden, dass sie für einen Staat, eine Gruppe oder eine Person irgendein Recht begründet, eine Tätigkeit auszuüben oder eine Handlung zu begehen, welche die Beseitigung der in dieser Erklärung verkündeten Rechte und Freiheiten zum Ziel hat.

PLUS
Unser ELITE Partner-Programm

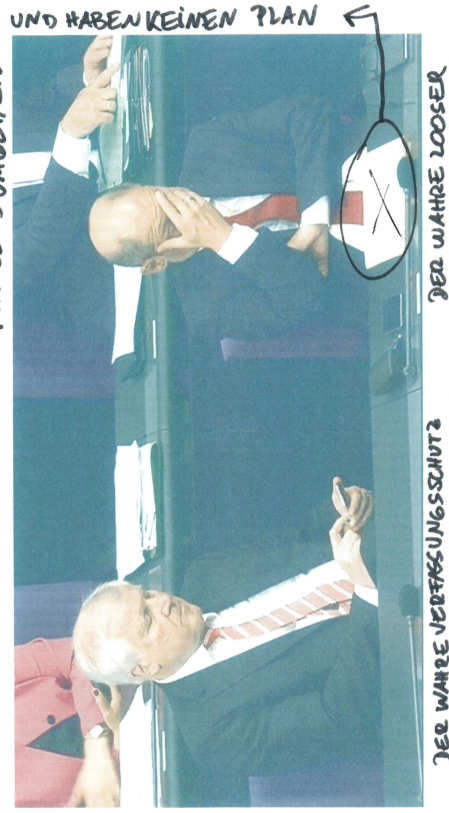

Do., 13.09.2018

Sektenbeauftragter äußert sich zur »Erbengemeinschaft Jakobs« im Fitnessstudio

»Seltsam, aber nicht gefährlich«

Im Fitnessstudio »Elite« hat sich die »Erbengemeinschaft Jakobs« niedergelassen. Studiobetreiber Juri Nasirow folgt dem Gedankengut von Ulf Diebel, der mittlerweile mit weiteren Mitgliedern im Studio wohnt. *Foto: Westerwalbesloh*

Von Elke Westerwalbesloh

Harsewinkel (WB). Die Aktivitäten der »Erbengemeinschaft Jakob« im Fitnessstudio »Elite« haben in Harsewinkel für Verunsicherung gesorgt. Die Polizei hat ein Verfahren wegen eines Drogenfundes eingeleitet, der Staatsschutz hat seine Ermittlungen eingestellt. Andreas Hahn, Sektenbeauftragter der Westfälischen Landeskirche, hat sich die Erbengemeinschaft aus der Ferne angeguckt. Er hält sie für »seltsam, aber nicht gefährlich«.

Andreas Hahn, der einen sehr guten Bezug zur Region hat, weil er sechs Jahre lang Pfarrer in Halle war, kennt die Situation in Harsewinkel. »Ich war nicht vor Ort, um die Gemeinschaft zu besuchen, habe mich aber informiert«, sagt er und versucht, eine erste Einschätzung zu geben. Erstmal sei der Begriff »Sekte« wenig geeignet, um die Gruppe zu beschreiben. »Früher hat man ihn benutzt, heute spricht man von konfliktträchtigen Gruppen«, erklärt Hahn und bezieht sich auf die Ergebnisse einer von 1994 bis 1996 vom Bundestag eingesetzten Expertengruppe. Das Wort »Sekte« entstammt dem Lateinischen »sequi« und bedeutet »folgen«. »Damit meinte man ursprünglich eine Abspaltung von der Mutterreligion«, erklärt Hahn.

Wann eine Gruppe zur einer Sekte wird

Heute sehe man beim Wort »Sekte« vor allem das Konfliktpotenzial. »Erst da, wo historische Abspaltungen zu exklusiven Abgrenzungen werden und Sonderlehren zu Konflikten führen, kann man von einer Sekte sprechen«, berichtet der Sektenbeauftragte. Mit Schwarz-Weiß-Denken, Abschottung nach außen, mit Verschwörungsdenken und Märtyrerbewusstsein entstehe eine Abhängigkeit von der Gruppe. »Deshalb kann man derzeit bei der »Erbengemeinschaft Jakobs« nicht von einer Sekte sprechen«, sagt Hahn. Hier gebe es derzeit keine Parallele. Von einer Sekte gehe immer Druck aus – zum Beispiel, wenn ein Mitglied diese verlassen möchte. Das sei dort noch nicht der Fall, könne sich aber dahin entwickeln.

Wer es aushält, kann weiter dort trainieren

Hahn versucht, die Beweggründe des Fitnessstudiobetreibers Juri Nasirow zu verstehen: Er sei möglicherweise in diese Gruppe gerutscht, weil es von der Evangeliums-Christen-Gemeinde, die ihn jetzt ausgeschlossen hat, her kannte, Antworten in der Bibel zu suchen, und weil in seiner Gemeinde Israel immer wichtig war. Dieses Bedürfnis könne Ulf Diebel, Kopf der »Erbengemeinschaft Jakobs«, stillen. »Er hat Antworten – allerdings sind diese schwer zu verstehen«, meint der Experte. Diebel bezeichnet sich selbst als »Priester nach der Ordnung Melchisedeks« und bezieht sich damit auf die Bibel. Melchisedek wird im Alten Testament als König und Priester von Salem beschrieben. »Eine Neuoffenbarung sozusagen«, sagt Hahn und schmunzelt.

Andreas Hahn rät dem Fitnessstudiobetreiber, den Weg zurück in seine alte Gemeinde zu suchen. Dort finde er sicher bessere Antworten als bei der »Erbengemeinschaft«. Den Mitgliedern des Studios kann er nur empfehlen: »Wer nicht zu labil ist, kann dort weiter trainieren gehen.« Hahn geht vorerst von keiner Gefahr aus. Der angebliche Drogenkonsum vor

POLITIK

DEUTSCHLAND   AUSLAND

DEUTSCHLAND

AUßEN

„Nationalismus ist die Mutter aller politischen Probleme"

14.09.18

Stand: 13:51 Uhr · Lesedauer: 2 Minuten

SPD + katholik

Außenminister Heiko Maas (SPD) fordert mehr internationale Zusammenarbeit

MEINUNG

KOMMENTARE   KOLUMNEN   SATIRE   HENRYK M. BRODER

WELT+

Mutti aller Probleme

14.09.18

Stefan Aust

Mutti geht
Sohn kommt

Kanzlerin und Flüchtling im Herbst 2015. Rechts: WELT-Herausgeber Stefan Aust

POLITIK

DEUTSCHLAND   AUSLAND

DEUTSCHLAND ANDREA NAHLES

„Herr Maaßen muss gehen, und ich sage Euch, er wird gehen"

Stand: 09:47 Uhr | Lesedauer: 4 Minuten

SPD + Katholik (Zentral Komunist)

16.9.18

551

Der Streit um Verfassungsschutzpräsident Hans-Georg-Maaßen in der großen Koalition geht weiter. SPD-Chefin Andrea Nahles hat ihre Forderung nach einer Entlassung des Geheimdienstchefs bekräftigt.

Quelle: WELT

AUTOPLAY

Christliche Werte bewahren!
Der Islam gehört nicht zu Bayern!
AfD

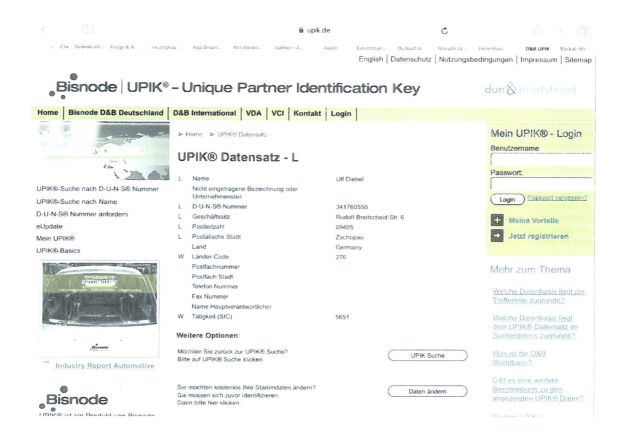

Bisnode | **UPIK® – Unique Partner Identification Key**   dun & bradstreet

| Home | Bisnode D&B Deutschland | D&B International | VDA | VCI | Kontakt | Login |

▷ Home   ▷ UPIK® Datensatz

UPIK® Datensatz - L

L	Name	Ulf Diebel
	Nicht eingetragene Bezeichnung oder Unternehmensteil	
L	D-U-N-S® Nummer	341760550
L	Geschäftssitz	Rudolf-Breitscheid-Str. 6
L	Postleitzahl	09405
L	Postalische Stadt	Zschopau
	Land	Germany
W	Länder-Code	276
	Postfachnummer	
	Postfach Stadt	
	Telefon Nummer	
	Fax Nummer	
	Name Hauptverantwortlicher	
W	Tätigkeit (SIC)	5651

Weitere Optionen:

Möchten Sie zurück zur UPIK® Suche?
Bitte auf UPIK® Suche klicken.   (UPIK Suche)

Sie möchten kostenlos Ihre Stammdaten ändern?
Sie müssen sich zuvor identifizieren.   (Daten ändern)
Dann bitte hier klicken.

UPIK®-Suche nach D-U-N-S® Nummer
UPIK®-Suche nach Name
D-U-N-S® Nummer anfordern
eUpdate
Mein UPIK®
UPIK®-Basics

Industry Report Automotive

Bisnode

Mein UPIK® - Login
Benutzername:
Passwort:
(Login) Passwort vergessen?
➕ Meine Vorteile
➡ Jetzt registrieren

Mehr zum Thema

Welche Datenbasis liegt der Trefferliste zugrunde?

Welche Datenbasis liegt dem UPIK®-Datensatz im Suchergebnis zugrunde?

Was ist die D&B Worldbase?

Gibt es eine weitere Beschreibung zu den angezeigten UPIK® Daten?

Daten Bereinigen
van Düsseldorf → Chemitz
→ Jerusalem → Berlin
→ Iserlohn → Harsewinkel

WASHINGTON :-)

ASK Donald !

URTEIL

FINAL SETTLEMENT

D-U-N-S Nummer: 341760550   **Datum:** 08.09.2018

Hauptverantwortlicher: Ulf Diebel

Fall: Erstgeborener von Israel   **vs.**   **Kdnr.:** #11999

UPIK® Datensatz - L

L	Name	Ulf Diebel
W	Nicht eingetragene Bezeichnung oder Unternehmensteil	Depeche Mode
L	D-U-N-S® Nummer	330216698
L	Geschäftssitz	Muhlerstr. 88-90
L	Postleitzahl	09111
L	Postalische Stadt	Chemnitz
	Land	Germany
W	Länder-Code	276
	Postfachnummer	
	Postfach Stadt	
L	Telefon Nummer	015221935308
	Fax Nummer	
W	Name Hauptverantwortlicher	Ulf Diebel
W	Tätigkeit (SIC)	5651

☐ $1 Take Over

☐ Wohnhaft Hauptverantwortlicher

☐ Lebendmeldung Hauptverantwortlicher

Printed in Poland
by Amazon Fulfillment
Poland Sp. z o.o., Wrocław